Free Will

As an advanced introduction to the challenging topic of free will, this book is designed for upper-level undergraduates interested in a comprehensive first stop into the field's issues and debates. It is written by two of the leading participants in those debates—a compatibilist on the issue of free will and determinism (Michael McKenna) and an incompatibilist (Derk Pereboom). These two authors achieve an admirable objectivity and clarity while still illuminating the field's complexity and key advances. Each chapter is structured to work as one week's primary reading in a course on free will, while more advanced courses can dip into the annotated further readings, suggested at the end of each chapter. A comprehensive bibliography and a detailed author index are included at the back of the book.

Michael McKenna is the Keith Lehrer Chair and Professor of Philosophy in the Department of Philosophy and the Center for the Philosophy of Freedom at the University of Arizona. He is the author of *Conversation and Responsibility* (2012) and numerous articles on the topics of free will and moral responsibility.

Derk Pereboom is Stanford H. Taylor '50 Chair and Susan Linn Sage Professor in the Philosophy Department at Cornell University. He is the author of *Living without Free Will* (2001), *Consciousness and the Prospects of Physicalism* (2011), *Free Will, Agency, and Meaning in Life* (2014), and articles on free will and moral responsibility, philosophy of mind, and the history of modern philosophy.

Routledge Contemporary Introductions to Philosophy
Series editor: Paul K Moser, Loyola University of Chicago

This innovative, well-structured series is for students who have already done an introductory course in philosophy. Each book introduces a core general subject in contemporary philosophy and offers students an accessible but substantial transition from introductory to higher-level college work in that subject. The series is accessible to non-specialists and each book clearly motivates and expounds the problems and positions introduced. An orientating chapter briefly introduces its topic and reminds readers of any crucial material they need to have retained from a typical introductory course. Considerable attention is given to explaining the central philosophical problems of a subject and the main competing solutions and arguments for those solutions. The primary aim is to educate students in the main problems, positions, and arguments of contemporary philosophy rather than to convince students of a single position.

Epistemology
3rd Edition
Robert Audi

Ethics
2nd Edition
Harry J. Gensler

Metaethics
Mark van Roojen

Metaphysics
3rd Edition
Michael J. Loux

Philosophy of Mind
3rd Edition
John Heil

Philosophy of Science
3rd Edition
Alex Rosenberg

Forthcoming:

Bioethics
Jason Scott Robert

Feminist Philosophy
Heidi Grasswick

Metaphysics
4th Edition
Michael J. Loux and Thomas M. Crisp

Philosophy of Film
Aaron Smuts

Philosophy of Literature
John Gibson

Social and Political Philosophy
2nd Edition
John Christman

Free Will

A Contemporary Introduction

Michael McKenna and Derk Pereboom

Routledge
Taylor & Francis Group

NEW YORK AND LONDON

First published 2016
by Routledge
711 Third Avenue, New York, NY 10017

and by Routledge
2 Park Square, Milton Park, Abingdon, Oxon OX14 4RN

Routledge is an imprint of the Taylor & Francis Group, an informa business

Library of Congress Cataloging-in-Publication Data
Names: McKenna, Michael, 1963– author. | Pereboom, Derk, 1957– author.
Title: Free will: a contemporary introduction/Michael McKenna and Derk Pereboom.
Description: New York, NY: Routledge, 2016. | Series: Routledge contemporary introductions to philosophy | Includes bibliographical references.
Identifiers: LCCN 2015044024| ISBN 9780415996860 (hbk) | ISBN 9780415996877 (pbk) | ISBN 9781315621548 (ebk)
Subjects: LCSH: Free will and determinism.
Classification: LCC BJ1461.M3885 2016 | DDC 123/.5–dc23
LC record available at http://lccn.loc.gov/2015044024

ISBN: 978-0-415-99686-0 (hbk)
ISBN: 978-0-415-99687-7 (pbk)
ISBN: 978-1-315-62154-8 (ebk)

Typeset in Times New Roman and Gill Sans
by Wearset Ltd, Boldon, Tyne and Wear

We dedicate this book to our most memorable undergraduate professors.
John R. Phillips II
Alvin Plantinga
Nicholas Wolterstorff

Contents

Preface

This book, *Free Will: A Contemporary Introduction*, is intended as an advanced introduction to the philosophical topic of free will. Our primary aim is to teach, and to do so at a fairly demanding level. While our target audience will be advanced undergraduates taking courses at the highest level suitable for undergraduate work, we also mean for the book to remain accessible to those less familiar with issues in philosophy. To do so, we shall at points take extra care to explain terms, arguments, and other background assumptions with which more advanced readers are already familiar. In any event, our goal is to bring readers to a point where they are able to arrive at, minimally, a graduate level understanding of this topic. We mean to invite the newcomer to philosophy to come along. But we will not purchase clarity with simplicity. The philosophical topic of free will is a challenging topic, and we mean for this book to be a challenging one as well. We want our readers to learn, and we want them to do so at an advanced level. For these reasons, we also intend for this book to be of use to graduate students in philosophy and related areas, and professional philosophers not steeped in the free will literature who are looking for a comprehensive overview of the field. Thus one will find other subsections or appendices which we will note are more suitable for a very advanced audience. In essence, we shall present the free will issue in a way that is as inclusive as possible in the hope that we can serve many audiences. But the targeted "sweet spot" for this book is the capable, advanced undergraduate seeking a treatment of the free will topic that, upon completion, would prepare that student to take with confidence classes on free will at the graduate level.

Because of our efforts to be as inclusive as possible, we invite the reader to use our book in ways that best suit her. Some readers will be especially aided by endnotes, appendices, or side bars explaining somewhat technical matters (such as what a "modal operator" is). Others quite familiar with various advanced philosophical concepts will have no need of such details and should just pass over them. Yet a different group of readers—for example, those seeking only an initial, simple introduction to free will—are also advised to pass over some of these more complex details. If we succeed in doing what we mean to do, this book should repay upon multiple readings of it.

We will do our best in the pages to follow not to advance our own views but instead try to be as fair and even-handed as possible, seeking as objective and dispassionate an assessment of various disputes as we can. Of course, this is an ideal, one that is probably not really ever fully attainable. Still, we will try. As it happens, we are philosophical opponents in the free will dispute. One of us, Michael McKenna, is a compatibilist about the relationship between free will and determinism. The other, Derk Pereboom, is an incompatibilist about this relationship. We thus disagree about many different issues, although there are numerous others where we are united. We hope that our collaborative effort in these pages will help foster a balanced, clear, and fair assessment of the field. But we remain aware that we might very well at points fall shy of this. Every experienced teacher of philosophy, and teachers of many other areas of study as well, are all too familiar with learning after years of teaching that her efforts to remain fair and unbiased in teaching her students were not completely success-ful. She discovers hidden assumptions that blinded her to the force of other posi-tions and ideas that would best serve her students. No doubt, some will probably find places where they believe we have fallen prey to this blindness. But impar-tiality is an ideal toward which we at least mean to aim. In our effort to do so, at various points, readers will find us noting how and where other philosophers would disagree with us. And, for the most part, rather than argue with them, we mark their good reasons for their difference of opinion, note our own, and leave it as an open question for the reader to settle for herself.

We have no interest in writing a book that offers the final word or the defini-tive assessment of the range of topics related to free will. We rather mean for it to be a place to begin, or instead, for those already familiar with the free will topic, a place to consider one perspective on the lay of the land. We hope this book inspires the reading of many more books and articles on free will. Its goal is not to foreclose the need for more inquiry but instead to instigate more inquiry—and so for readers at various levels of experience and ability.

For instructors interested in using this book in their classes, we have struc-tured the chapters so that each can handily be treated as the topic of a single week's seminar session. More advanced seminars can be supplemented each week with more advanced readings. Less advanced seminars can be adjusted likewise. We have included a comprehensive bibliography at the end of the book. But we shall close each chapter with suggestions for further readings, offering brief annotated remarks about them. If an instructor is interested, she can draw from these suggestions to build her syllabus.

Michael McKenna
Derk Pereboom

Acknowledgments

This book, originally a single-author project, began many years ago as a draft built from teaching notes from my time at Ithaca College. It later evolved and was used for both undergraduates and graduates at Florida State University. Once I arrived at the University of Arizona, I used it in an earlier form to teach an undergraduate class. I would like to thank my many colleagues and students at Ithaca College, Florida State University, and the University of Arizona for their helpful comments and suggestions. Of special note are my colleagues from Ithaca College, Stephen Schwartz, Craig Duncan, Carol Kates, Robert Klee, Rick Kaufman, and Richard Creel; my colleagues from FSU, Al Mele, Randy Clarke, Joshua Gert, Stephen Kearns, and Seth Shabo; and my colleagues from U of A, Carolina Sartorio, Terry Horgan, Jenann Ismael, Keith Lehrer, Shaun Nichols, Stew Cohen, and David Schmidtz. I owe special thanks to four philosophers who taught me how to understand the free will debate, John Fischer, Carl Ginet, Paul Russell, and, most notably, George Thomas, my graduate professor and dissertation supervisor from the University of Virginia. I have also profited over the years from a wonderful group of friends who work on free will and related topics, especially Nomy Arpaly, Mark Balaguer, Bernie Berofsky, Gunnar Björnsson, Joe Campbell, Ish Haji, Bob Kane, Eddie Nahmias, Dana Nelkin, Tim O'Connor, Derk Pereboom, George Sher, David Shoemaker, Angie Smith, Tamler Sommers, Patrick Todd, Manuel Vargas, Gary Watson, and Michael Zimmerman. Finally, I would like to thank my co-author for agreeing to come on board in 2013. With a considerable amount of revising and the addition of several new chapters, Derk helped make this book far more balanced and thorough. He also made completing it an especially good time and a great learning experience.

I am grateful to Peter Ohlin and Oxford University Press for permission to reprint sections of "Contemporary Compatibilism: Mesh Theories and Reasons-Responsive Theories," in R. Kane, ed., 2011, *Oxford Handbook of Free Will*, 2nd ed. (New York: Oxford University Press): 175–98. This material is used in Chapter 9. I am also indebted to the John Templeton Foundation for financial support used to travel to Cornell University to work with Derk Pereboom in July of 2015.

Michael McKenna

I would like to thank my many colleagues and students at the University of Vermont, Yale University, Cornell University, and the Central European University in Budapest for their valuable contributions. Of special note are my colleagues from the University of Vermont, David Christensen, Arthur Kuflik, George Sher, Louis deRosset, Bill Mann, Seth Shabo, and Don Loeb, and my colleague at Cornell, Carl Ginet. I would also like to thank all of the members of the free will community for discussion and interaction over the years—and let me note, specifically, John Fischer, Dana Nelkin, Lynne Baker, Michael McKenna, Randy Clarke, Al Mele, David Widerker, Bob Kane, Gunnar Björnsson, Tim O'Connor, Carolina Sartorio, Ish Haji, Joe Campbell, Manuel Vargas, Shaun Nichols, Josh Knobe, Mario De Caro, Tamler Sommers, Eddie Nahmias, Justin Coates, Patrick Todd, and my graduate students at Cornell, in particular Jona Vance, Sean Stapleton, Patrick Mayer, and Austin Duggan. Finally, I would like to thank my co-author for inviting me to come on board in 2013. Working on this book with Michael was very pleasant and a great learning experience.

Derk Pereboom

Introduction

To get us under way, consider this case, much discussed by philosophers who write on the topic of free will and the related topic of moral responsibility:

Robert Alton Harris was executed in San Quentin Prison in 1992 for the 1978 murder of two teenage boys, John Mayeski and Michael Baker. Harris and his brother Daniel came upon Mayeski and Baker while the two 16-year-old boys were eating their lunch in a parking lot of a fast-food restaurant. The Harris brothers were looking to steal a car for use in a bank robbery. When they saw the boys in their car, the brothers forced them at gunpoint to drive to a remote area. There Robert Harris convinced the two boys he would return their car and share some of the money from the robbery. The boys agreed. As they were walking away, Harris shot them from behind, something that was completely unexpected by his brother Daniel. Here is *LA Times* Miles Corwin's 1982 report of the event, at times quoting Daniel Harris:

> As the two boys walked away, [Robert Alton] Harris slowly raised the Luger and shot Mayeski in the back, Daniel said. Mayeski yelled, "Oh God," and slumped to the ground. Harris chased Baker down a hill into a little valley and shot him four times.
>
> Mayeski was still alive when Harris climbed back up the hill, Daniel said. Harris walked over to the boy, knelt down, put the Luger to his head, and fired.
>
> "God, everything started to spin," Daniel said. "It was like slow motion. I saw the gun, and then his head explode like a balloon,... I just started running and running ... But I heard Robert and turned around."
>
> "He was swinging the rifle and pistol in the air and laughing. God, that laugh made blood and bone freeze in me."
>
> Harris drove [the] car to a friend's house, carrying weapons and the bag [containing] the remainder of the slain youths' lunch. Then, about 15 minutes after he had killed the two 16-year-old boys, Harris took the food out of the bag ... began eating a hamburger. He offered his brother an apple turnover, and Daniel became nauseated and ran to the bathroom.
>
> "Robert laughed at me," Daniel said. "He said I was weak; he called me a sissy and said I didn't have the stomach for it."

> Harris was in an almost lighthearted mood. He smiled and told Daniel that it would be amusing if the two were to pose as police officers and inform the parents that their sons were killed. Then, for the first time, he became serious. He thought that somebody might have heard the shots and that the police could be searching for the bodies. He told Daniel that they should begin cruising the street near the bodies, and possibly kill some police in the area.
>
> [Later, as they prepared to rob the bank,] Harris pulled out the Luger, noticed the blood stains and remnants of flesh in the barrel as a result of the point-blank shooting, and said, "I really blew that guy's brains out." And then, again, he started to laugh.[1]

In the *LA Times* article, Corwin comments upon how even the inmates at San Quentin prison were planning to celebrate Harris's execution. Harris, it seems, was regarded as a terror of a man, even among the most hardened of criminals. And Corwin details a prior life of crime, which began with torturing animals at a young age, car theft, and beating a neighbor to death in a dispute, for which Harris was convicted of manslaughter.

What are we to make of Robert Harris? And what are we to make of our *reactions* to him, of our judgments about what he deserves, our feelings of anger, and (for some of us) our desire that he is made to suffer by being punished? It is natural in these cases, at least as many people see it, to think of Harris as more than an insane monster or a wild animal. Our indignation toward him and our judgments about what we presume he deserves are bound up with our thinking that somehow it was *up to him* how he acted. He was in the driver's seat of his own actions, of his life. He was not forced by his nature or anything else to murder those boys. He *could have done otherwise* than to murder, or for that matter, to make the choices he made earlier in life that led him to that place where doing these terrible things would count for him as a source of amusement, even delight. He, not someone or something else, was *in control* in the murdering, or, earlier on, in control of the torturing of those animals, and so on. And to the extent that he found himself in a place where it seemed only a joy to so act, we also want to think—or at least many of us are so inclined—that he made himself to be that way. He *shaped himself* to be this brutal man by his own free choices. To many, this helps to justify our sense of justice in a legal system that holds people to account. And even if one thinks the death penalty is never deserved, it remains very compelling to think that men like Robert Alton Harris deserve to be punished harshly for their crimes in some way because they freely so acted, freely so chose, freely came to be as they are.

These presuppositions embedded in the way so many of us think about a case like Harris's reveal an important feature of the conceptual framework many people are committed to in their thinking: Persons are in some important way free in acting as they do. This is a philosophical thesis, and it is not just some esoteric one. It is embedded in so much of our way of understanding the world that it is at least preliminarily hard to imagine how we would be able to think of ourselves or others without relying upon this assumption.

But along with the above presuppositions, there are other presuppositions also embedded in our everyday thinking that are in tension with those having to do with human freedom. These have to do with the facts of our lives, with the causes impinging upon them. To explain, consider again Corwin's *LA Times* article. Corwin does not fix only upon Robert Alton Harris's terrible deeds. He also explores his terrible history. As Corwin recounts it, Harris was born prematurely when his mother was kicked in the stomach by her jealous husband, who accused her of infidelity, claiming Harris was not his child. The father twice sexually molested the sisters and beat all of his children, often causing serious injury. Harris's mother became an alcoholic, and was arrested several times. Harris had a learning disability and speech problems, none of which were addressed, and he lived through school feeling stupid. He was frequently teased by his classmates. According to his sister, Barbara Harris, even as a young child his mother would not permit him to touch her. And she recalls one occasion when his mother bloodied his nose for trying to get close to her. His sister remembers him crying as a young child when Bambi was shot. He loved animals. By the age of 14 he was sentenced to a federal youth detention center for car theft. There he was raped several times and slashed his wrists in attempted suicide. Released from federal prison at 19, the boy who once cried at Bambi's death tortured and killed dogs and cats with mop handles, darts, and pellet guns. Once, he stabbed a prize pig more than 1,000 times.

Ask yourself now, reader, what you feel about Harris *the criminal*, now that you are aware of Harris the child and of his youth leading up to his adult years. What do you think Harris deserves for his crimes now that you are aware of his history? If you are like many, you are not sure what to think; you have become ambivalent (Watson, 1987), toggling between sympathy on the one hand and antipathy on the other. It is not implausible to explain your ambivalence, if indeed you are ambivalent, in terms of the thought that the causes shaping Harris's life made him into who he was, and that in some way they impaired or strongly shaped his character and his understanding of the world. His ugly history *determined him* to be this man and do these things. This thought, it seems, is at odds with our thinking that it was after all up to him whether he murdered those boys. It appears to be at odds with thinking he could have done other than murder; rather, there is the worry that the ugly history shaping him and moving through him settled what he would do then so that he really could not have done any differently. And likewise, it seems that his life was not his own making. It was made out of hatred and violence, of ridicule, self-loathing, and rape.

These competing assumptions about human freedom on the one hand and on the other about the causes shaping our lives are not just at play when we think of extreme cases like the Harris story. They apply in all sorts of situations and in all sorts of contexts. They might just as well apply when it comes to our thinking about our own lives, or about the lives of moral heroes, like Martin Luther King, rather than treacherous characters like Robert Alton Harris. Cases like those of the alcoholic or drug addict struggling to resist their plight can be viewed either in terms of what a person is free to overcome or instead in terms of the underlying physiology driving an addict's or alcoholic's cravings and decision-making.

As is illustrated by reflecting upon the case of Harris, the philosophical controversy regarding the freedom of the will is about the prospects for a distinctive sort of agency. Put simply, are persons like Harris able to control their own conduct? Likewise, was Dr. King, or the alcoholic, or any of us for that matter? Do they possess and act from a sufficiently rich freedom enabling them to shape themselves and their futures as they prefer and as they judge best? Can they, as an upshot of this sort of freedom, be morally responsible for their conduct, and so be justifiably held to account for how they treat themselves and others? And what must the natural order be like for it to be true that persons do have free will and thereby act freely? Must they be able to "free" themselves from the influences of their past to then act freely, or can their freedom still arise from within, or instead, due to their histories? Or is the presumption of the freedom we suppose people have really just mistaken and undermined by a more enlightened understanding of the underlying hidden causes of the human condition?

There are at least four distinct philosophical questions regarding free will: *First*, what is free will? What is its nature? *Second*, why is free will important? What value, if any, does it bring to human life? *Third*, is free will compatible with certain assumptions about the natural world? For instance, is it compatible with determinism? Is it compatible with indeterminism? Whether determined or undetermined, is it compatible with our being purely physical beings, part of a natural order on a continuum with the rest of the animal kingdom? *Fourth*, do we possess free will and, sometimes, act freely? As we shall see, these questions are usually not compartmentalized but are answered together as part of an overall theory. Nevertheless, it is probably correct to say that contemporary philosophical discussions of free will have focused primarily on the third question, which might be called the compatibility question. This book will be no exception to that general trend. We will structure it around different approaches to answering that question. It is in light of this question—*Is free will compatible with determinism?*—that this topic is often characterized as one of the classical problems of philosophy, the problem of free will.

Our book is set out as follows:

Chapter 1 is devoted to getting clear on the main concepts in the debate, in particular the concepts of free will, moral responsibility, and determinism. In Chapter 2, we turn to explaining the free will problem and to showing that the debate actually features a range of related problems, not just one. In Chapter 3, we present the classical free will debate as we find it in the twentieth century during the heyday of analytic philosophy.

In Chapters 4 through 6 we focus on three developments, all of which occurred in the 1960s, that resulted in major changes to the way the free will problem is approached. The first, which is the subject of Chapter 4, concerns the Consequence Argument for incompatibilism, which is designed to show that the freedom to do otherwise is incompatible with determinism. The second major development, treated in Chapter 5, features Harry Frankfurt's argument for the thesis that the freedom to do otherwise is not the sort of freedom that is required for persons to be morally responsible for what they do. It is, rather, a different sort of freedom, one that concerns the source of a person's agency. The third development, set out in Chapter 6, concerns P.F. Strawson's efforts to reconfigure the free will problem by reference to our moral emotions and how our interpersonal lives reveal our own understanding of human freedom and the conditions for moral responsibility.

Chapter 7 is dedicated to three arguments for the conclusion that freedom and responsibility are incompatible with determinism. All three are significant as influences on the contemporary debate because each aims to establish incompatibilism by way of resources that do not concern the freedom to do otherwise. Attention is rather paid to the sources of human agency in light of the prospect that determinism affects those sources in a way that precludes freedom and responsibility.

With Chapters 1 through 7 in place, we turn to an assessment of the major contemporary positions on free will and moral responsibility. Chapters 8 and 9 address the various proposals for defending *compatibilism*, which is the view that free will and moral responsibility are compatible with determinism. Chapters 10 and 11 focus on the different varieties of *incompatibilism*, which denies the truth of compatibilism. Chapter 10 is devoted to forms of incompatibilism that affirm the reality of free will and moral responsibility, known as *libertarianism*, and Chapter 11 addresses forms of incompatibilism that affirm skepticism about free will and moral responsibility, including *hard determinism* and *hard incompatibilism*.

Chapter 12 addresses Manuel Vargas's original proposal, *revisionism*, which recommends that we revise our concepts of free will and moral responsibility so as to remove their incompatibilist implications and that we preserve our practice of holding responsible. This chapter also concludes the book by addressing a range of topics we did not cover in detail: responsibility for omissions, the challenge to rational deliberation from the belief in determinism, experimental philosophy on folk concepts and presuppositions animating the free will debate, and the theological roots and implications of this debate.

Note

1   This passage is from Miles Corwin, "Icy Killer's Life Steeped in Violence," *Los Angeles Times*, May 16, 1982. Quoted from Gary Watson's highly influential article, "Responsibility and the Limits of Evil" (1987: 269–70).

1 Free Will, Moral Responsibility, and Determinism

In this first chapter, we will examine the key notions in the free will debate. We will begin by providing characterizations of free will, moral responsibility, and determinism. We will as well consider a range of related matters, such as what the will is, and we will introduce the notions of indeterminism, mechanism, and naturalism.

1.1. Free Will

As it turns out, settling upon how to use the term "free will" is a controversial matter. We propose to define the term as follows:

> *Free will* is the unique ability of persons to exercise the strongest sense of control over their actions necessary for moral responsibility.

A *free act*, as we use the expression, is an act that issues from an exercise of that ability. This definition, or something like it, while not universally accepted, is widely shared (e.g., Haji, 2009: 18; McKenna, 2008d: 187; Mele, 2006b: 17; Pereboom, 2001: xxii; Timpe, 2008: 11). True, it is just a starting point for theorizing. It leaves unsettled what the relevant sense of control is, and it leaves unspecified the nature of the moral responsibility at issue. These are topics we will address in this book. But let's begin with a few clarifications.

First, why is it common to characterize free will as a kind of control, specifically in relation to moral responsibility? Plausibly, one of at least two substantive necessary conditions of an agent's being morally responsible for something is that it was under her control. If, for instance, you accidentally hit the gear shift and wrecked the car because you had an unexpected seizure, you are not morally responsible and blameworthy for hitting the gear shift or for the damage. The reason is that you were not in control of your body. Moral responsibility very plausibly requires control over whatever it is that an agent is responsible for.

Second, as Alfred Mele explains (2006b: 27, n18), it is crucial that the control at issue is the *strongest* that is necessary for moral responsibility. There are weaker senses of control that are necessary for moral responsibility. For instance, it might well be a necessary condition of moral responsibility for what an agent does that she is able to move her body in accord with her decisions. Imagine, for instance, that a demon was manipulating your mind, causing the decisions that result in your bodily motions. You might satisfy one necessary condition for being morally responsible for what you do, that is, you are able to move your body in accord with your decisions. But you would not satisfy a stronger condition for being morally responsible because you would not be in control of the decisions you make. Free will, as we understand it, is the strongest control condition necessary for moral responsibility.

Third, on our proposed definition, exercises of free will are not limited to morally significant action for which a person is morally responsible. It is just that the ability identified by free will is the one required when a person is morally responsible for what she does. But she can exercise this ability in non-moral contexts as well. Indeed, it is possible for there to exist beings that are not morally responsible for anything—perhaps wholly amoral beings—who exercise the kind of control that is necessary for moral responsibility.[1] So on our preferred way of defining free will it is an ability whose exercise need not issue in something for which the agent is morally responsible.

At the same time, how the term "free will" is defined is itself a matter of some controversy. While numerous writers understand free will and free action in essentially the way we have defined it, others do not. It will be instructive to indicate how others use the term and register points of disagreement. Here we restrict our attention to two further ways to define the term "free will."

A number of participants in the debate define free will as having access to alternative options for action, or, as it's often put, the ability to do otherwise from what one actually does (e.g., Clarke, 2003: 3; Ginet, 1990: 90; van Inwagen, 1983: 8; Vihvelin, 2013). For instance, Carl Ginet writes:

> By freedom of will is meant freedom of action. I have freedom of action at a time if more than one alternative is then open to me. (1990: 90)

Unlike our preferred definition, this way of defining free will is not pinned to moral responsibility. Peter van Inwagen, who also defines free will in terms of the ability to do otherwise, explicitly counsels against defining free will in terms of "whatever sort of freedom is required for moral responsibility" (2008: 329, n2). On the ability-to-do-otherwise proposal, one can attend to free will just as well by ignoring moral contexts and reflecting upon whether we are able to pick up a pencil or refrain from doing so, or choose grapes rather than bananas for a morning snack.

What are we to make of this terminological difference? One might first note that it is consistent with our proposal that free will, as the strongest sense of control required for moral responsibility, will turn out to be the ability to do otherwise. The difference, however, between Ginet/van Inwagen and us would be that on our preferred strategy the proposal that free will is, or at least requires, the ability to do otherwise would amount to a substantive thesis, not a claim that is true just by how we define the term "free will." Furthermore, suppose, as many argue, that the ability to do otherwise is not required for moral responsibility but that moral responsibility still requires some sort of control condition. On our proposal, we call that sort of control "free will." Ginet, van Inwagen, and others favoring their terminological approach would need a distinct term.

In our estimation, little rides on this. People can use the term "free will" differently, so long as they specify at the outset what they mean by this term. We believe it best to theorize about free will in terms of a control condition on moral responsibility. But we grant that reasonable minds can differ. In any event, regardless of this difference in how we use the term "free will," philosophers can still have a substantive—and not merely a terminological—discussion about what sort of control moral responsibility demands, and about whether it requires the ability to do otherwise, and whether that ability is compatible or incompatible with determinism, and so on.

Next consider Robert Kane's (1996) way of defining free will. His idea is that when we act, we are guided by our ends or purposes. As Kane defines it:

> Free will is the power to be the ultimate creator and sustainer of one's own ends and purposes. (1996: 4)

Interestingly, in contrast with Ginet's and van Inwagen's proposal, Kane rejects the thesis that we should understand free will simply in terms of the ability to do otherwise, or the ability to will otherwise. Nevertheless, on his developed view, being an ultimate creator or sustainer of one's own ends entails that one is able to do otherwise. So, for Kane, free will does involve the ability to do otherwise, but it amounts to a substantive and not merely a definitional matter that free will requires this ability.

In our opinion, what it is for an agent to be a creator or sustainer of her ends and purposes—even an ultimate creator or sustainer—can be understood in stronger and weaker terms. At one end of the spectrum, it might come to mean no more than what is meant when it is remarked that, once the ball was snapped, it was ultimately up to the quarterback to make the pass. That sense is consistent with very modest demands on agency. The other end of the spectrum features a reading of being an ultimate creator that is so demanding that there may be no metaphysically possible way for such a condition to be satisfied. The virtue of defining free will in terms of a condition on moral responsibility is that it is then possible to gain some independent purchase for measuring how strong or weak the control or freedom must be. Hence, it might very well be, as Pereboom argues (2001), that free will does require being an ultimate initiator of one's free acts. But this will flow as a substantive thesis from examining the conditions on moral responsibility.

One way to handle these terminological disputes is just to avoid use of the term "free will" altogether. Better, it might be thought, to adopt more theoretically innocent terminology. This is how John Martin Fischer and Mark Ravizza (1998) proceed. Rather than offering a definition of free will, they write instead in terms of control over action. In setting out their view, they distinguish between different sorts of control over action, one involving the ability to do otherwise, and another that does not. Once these different notions of control are specified, they then proceed to ask which sort is required for moral responsibility. We do not object to this manner of proceeding. Note that our proposed definition of free will is relatively friendly to Fischer and Ravizza's strategy, since we define free will in terms of one sort of control—the strongest kind required for moral responsibility. As a general word of caution, when reading the works of those involved in the debate about free will, it will be helpful to keep in mind that these authors define free will differently, or instead avoid use of the term altogether, but that they nevertheless can be understood as involved in a substantive and not merely a verbal debate.[2]

1.2.   The Will in Free Will

A further issue concerns the notion of a will. One would think, just given the expression "free will" itself, that those who use it assume that there is such a power or faculty as the will, and when considering whether we have free will, they are asking whether that power can be regarded as free. But, perhaps surprisingly, many contemporary philosophers working on this topic reject the notion of a will as something that exists in its own right. Many philosophers who disagree about how to define "free will" agree that there is no reason to think that there is more to claims about free will than merely what is involved in attending to free action. Recall Ginet's remark above that by freedom of will is meant freedom of action (Ginet, 1990: 90). This is a sentiment shared by numerous writers (e.g., Haji, 2009: 18; McKenna, 2008d; Mele, 2006b: 17; van Inwagen, 1983: 8). Why?

Some writers report that they do not know what is meant by those who do take the term "will" to refer (e.g., Mele, 2006b: 17). Others take its meaning to be clear but wish to deny commitment to what the term "will" initially appears to pick out, namely a distinctive mental causal power involved in generating action (e.g., van Inwagen, 1983: 8). Their worry is that taking the notion of a will commits one to mental causal powers, which are recruited to account for various abilities that minds have. If the will were understood as a mental causal power, it would be a feature of persons that plays the special role of voluntarily generating actions. We could then ask whether it is free or not, or, to be more cautious, whether a person is free with respect to how that power is exercised.

David Hume (1748) famously hoped to dispense with the notion of a causal power, or more precisely a causal power that does not reduce to regularities or counterfactual dependencies, and many philosophers, particularly in the analytic tradition in the first half of the twentieth century, adopted this view. Since then, the notion of an irreducible causal power has been resurrected, and now many philosophers currently accept mental causal powers of this sort (Boyd, 1980; Fodor, 1987). Fortunately, this division does not undermine the possibility of a substantive debate about the main issues at stake in the controversy about free will and moral responsibility, since those issues need not be formulated in terms of the will as a causal power. Instead, they can be cast in terms of notions such as intention, choice, decision, desire, and reason, which are common to both sides of the divide.

Philosophers in the Humean tradition often opt to understand free will just in terms of acting freely (Ayer, 1954; Schlick, 1939). Others (e.g., Frankfurt, 1971; Kane, 1996) hold that important distinctions are lost if the discussion is restricted to freedom of action, and that a distinct notion of free will needs to be invoked. The general thesis, shared by those who wish to distinguish free will from free action, is that free action is merely a matter of being unhindered in doing what one wants, in, for example, moving one's body as one prefers. Free will, by contrast, is a matter of being in control of or free with respect to the intentions, choices, decisions, reasons, or desires that are the causal antecedents of how one acts and moves one's body.

Some philosophers are happy to agree that there is such a thing as the will, but they nevertheless tend to reduce this notion to mental states such as desires. Harry Frankfurt (1971), for instance, identifies the will with the desire that is (or would be if left unhindered) effective in leading an agent to action. To be free with respect to one's will, then, is to be free with respect to the desires that lead to one's actions. Kane (1996) proposes a more complex account of the will, which we will not set out in detail here. But the ingredients constituting it are, for the most part, those involved in one's forming and sustaining intentions. To be free with respect to one's will, in Kane's view, is essentially to be free with respect to the intentions, choices, and decisions that issue in one's actions. For both Frankfurt and Kane, then, it's important to invoke the notion of free will in addition to free action, but free will is then accounted for solely in terms of familiar sorts of mental states, without reference to an irreducible mental causal power to voluntarily produce action.

For the most part, the side one takes on the existence of mental causal powers makes no difference to the core issues in the debate about free will and moral responsibility. One exception is the issue of agent causation, which, according to most of its advocates, does require the notion of a causal power. But Kane, for instance, sets out the case of a businesswoman late for an important professional meeting who, uncertain about what to do, must decide between stopping to help a person who has just been assaulted, or instead proceeding on to her meeting (Kane, 1996: 126). We can raise the important questions about the businesswoman's freedom without ruling on the issue of the existence of the will as a causal power. For we can ask about whether in choosing as she does, she satisfies the strongest control condition necessary for being morally responsible for her decision. We can also ask about whether she was able to decide otherwise. And we can ask about whether she was ultimately settling her ends or purposes in deciding to render aid instead of heading off to her meeting. Finally, it seems that, for those who want to preserve talk of the will, as Kane himself does, we can describe this case as one in which the agent exercises her will in deciding as she does. But we can also just as easily describe the case as one in which the agent acts freely by performing the mental act of deciding in one way rather than the other.

Unless otherwise indicated, we will write in terms of free action and of acting freely when discussing free will. To address Frankfurt's and Kane's concern that indeed there is something lost in failing to distinguish between free action and free will, we offer two considerations. First, Frankfurt and Kane are correct that there is a familiar notion of free action that applies to some non-human animals and amounts to no more than being able to move one's body as one wishes, the way a dog runs free once let off a leash. But since we mean to account for free will in terms of the strongest sense of control required for moral responsibility, we can claim that this sort of freedom is not strong enough to do justice to the sort of free action that we are interested in capturing. Second, when examining the details of the will as, for instance, Kane (1996) understands it, a key ingredient—indeed, on his view *the* key ingredient—is the ability to decide in conditions of uncertainty when one is not sure what to do, or which values should be endorsed. But on a sufficiently permissive view of what actions are, decisions *are* actions—they are mental actions. Then it seems that the difference between a view like Kane's and one that denies the existence of the will becomes very small, especially if we treat freedom of decision as the especially important cases of free action, those that capture what is most distinctive in exercises of free will.

As a general point, nearly all philosophers involved in the free will debate take decisions, especially in morally loaded contexts, to be the most salient and interesting cases to fix upon when offering a theory of freedom. And the cases most emphasized involve decisions preceded by conscious deliberation. This is so regardless of how the philosopher defines the term "free will," and regardless of whether she is committed to the existence of the will.[3]

1.3. Moral Responsibility

We turn next to the topic of moral responsibility. Getting clear on moral responsibility's nature is important to all those working on the topic of free will, not just those who favor the definition of free will we endorse. It is an important question whether and how free will is related to moral responsibility, independently of one's terminological commitments. For example, suppose, as van Inwagen or Ginet would see it, and contrary to our own prescription, free will should be defined in terms of the ability to do otherwise and without any mention of the conditions on moral responsibility. It remains an important philosophical question for them if and how free will is related to moral responsibility. It is for this reason that they too discuss their views about free will in contexts where what is at issue is whether someone is morally responsible for how she acts.

So, how are we to understand moral responsibility? To begin, judgments of moral responsibility should be distinguished from the wider class of ethical or moral judgments. Morality, broadly construed, encompasses judgments of moral obligation, moral permission, and moral prohibition; judgments of right and wrong, of virtue and vice, and of good and bad. Moral responsibility concerns a person's responsibility for actions in these categories. It is one thing to settle what, for instance, a person's moral obligations are. It is another to judge that she is morally responsible for whether or not she lived up to or failed to comply with them.[4]

One of the main controversies in the free will debate concerns the skeptical thesis that no one has free will and as a result no one is morally responsible—at least in one key sense (e.g., Pereboom, 2001, 2014). Even if such a skeptical thesis were established as true, this would not by itself be grounds for a thoroughgoing skepticism about morality—a skepticism according to which no one performs acts that are morally right or wrong, good or bad, virtuous or vicious. Barring further assumptions, such moral evaluations would not be impugned just by virtue of establishing that no one is ever morally responsible for anything. It should, however, be noted that there are further moral theses that, if true, would yield this result. For instance, suppose morality is a system of categorical imperatives expressing agents' moral duties and demarcating the domain of moral right and wrong. Assume in addition that a necessary condition of any such imperative applying to an agent is that she is free to comply with it or instead act in opposition to what it demands. If it were established that no one is free in that sense, then morality would apply to no one. It is in this way that free will, moral responsibility, and morality itself *could be* tightly linked. But this is a special and complex proposal, and in general it should not be assumed that morality itself stands or falls with the prospects for free will and moral responsibility.

But what is it to be morally responsible for something? It is commonplace in these discussions to note that moral responsibility is only one sort of responsibility. There are other varieties as well, including merely causal responsibility, and more complex and evaluatively loaded notions, such as legal responsibility. Perhaps we can also speak of aesthetic responsibility, prudential responsibility, or even athletic responsibility. Mere causal responsibility, which is not evaluatively loaded, is just a matter of being the cause of something—a matter of brute fact, so to speak. A lightning bolt can be causally responsible for something, like a house fire. And a person can be merely causally responsible— but not morally, legally, or otherwise responsible—for something too, as when a person innocently flips a light switch causing a short-circuit and then a house fire. But as far as these other dimensions of responsibility go—moral, legal, aesthetic, athletic—what they all share is the potential for evaluation *of an agent* in light of an evaluation *of her action*. For instance, it is because of Matilda's doing morally wrong by violating her obligation (an evaluation of her action) that we can raise a further evaluative question about *her* in light of her wrongdoing. Was she *responsible* for her so acting?

What distinguishes moral responsibility from legal responsibility or any other variety of responsibility is a matter of the evaluative dimension of an agent's actions (moral, rather than legal, aesthetic, prudential, and so on), and then an assessment of her exercising her agency along that dimension. As far as the responsibility assessments themselves are concerned, the two fundamental types of assessment are praiseworthiness and blameworthiness. Naturally, when the issue is moral responsibility, then the assessments will involve moral praiseworthiness and moral blameworthiness. As the terms suggest, what an agent's being morally praiseworthy or morally blameworthy for something makes apt or fitting, in standard or paradigm cases, is a response of moral praise or moral blame.[5]

Even once we have zeroed in on moral responsibility, distinguishing it from other sorts of responsibility, there is more work to do. Although controversial, many philosophers have become convinced that there are different species or senses of moral responsibility (e.g., Pereboom, 2001, 2014; Scanlon, 1998, 2008; Shoemaker, 2011, 2015; Watson, 1996). These different senses involve distinct types of judgments of praiseworthiness and blameworthiness, and so make apt or fitting distinct types of praising or blaming responses. Gary Watson (1996), for instance, has distinguished between moral responsibility in the *attributability* sense and moral responsibility in the *accountability* sense. To be morally responsible for an action in the attributability sense is for that action to reveal or express one's nature or self, what one stands for or who one is. In this way, acts that are courageous or cowardly, magnanimous or petty, grand or shoddy, are acts that allow us to attribute to the agent something about her—and these attributions are in various ways means of judging her attributability-praiseworthy or attributability-blameworthy. In light of these sorts of evaluations, we are often given reasons to adjust our behavior and tailor our expectations toward those so judged. Those inclined toward shoddy conduct, for instance, are better avoided, and are best not trusted with the church's donation box. Despite these qualifications, a person's being merely responsible in the attributability sense does not entail that she is liable to expressions of indignation toward her because of what she did, or to demands that she rectify her bad conduct, or to being required to apologize to those she wronged. These are all manifestations of moral responsibility in the accountability sense, the core of which is the legitimacy of holding someone to account for her actions.[6]

Some have argued that there are yet further species of moral responsibility (e.g., Pereboom, 2014; Shoemaker, 2011, 2015). We do not need to enter that debate at this point (we will do so in our discussion of free will skepticism in Chapter 11). Given the task at hand of surveying the various positions in the free will debate, we are specifically interested at this stage in the sense that Watson identified as accountability. A key feature of moral responsibility in this sense is its connection with how others in a moral community are thought to be morally permitted or entitled to *treat* others in certain, say, blaming way, ways that involve taking up a blameworthy person's moral transgressions and demanding apology, acknowledgment of wrong done, a commitment to rectify the wrong, compensation or punishment. There appears to be in these forms of treatment the presumption of a morally justified mode of sanctioning.

A natural, albeit not universally shared, assumption about the means of moral praising and blaming responses is that they involve manifestations of what are known as the *morally reactive attitudes* (Strawson, 1962). These attitudes are moral emotions that are responses to a morally responsible agent in light of her actions. Moral anger, in the forms of moral resentment and indignation, is revealed in a blamer's treatment of a blameworthy agent, and manifesting such moral anger can function as a way of holding an agent to account. Likewise for a positive moral emotion like gratitude—it can be a way of holding the agent accountable by praising her.

Now consider the contention that when a person is morally responsible and blameworthy, others are warranted or entitled to blame them. One might also claim that it is appropriate or fitting to blame them. What is the normative basis for these claims of warrant, entitlement, appropriateness, or fittingness? Some have argued that the justification for blaming those who are blameworthy, a justification that would account for the sanctioning element in blaming, should be based on consequentialist or utilitarian considerations. There are benefits of various sorts for blaming those who are blameworthy, and these benefits can be invoked to justify a blaming and punishing practice (e.g., Dennett, 1984; Smart, 1963). Others have considered different normative bases for blaming. One option is to appeal to considerations of fairness (e.g., Wallace, 1994). The idea is that those who freely and knowingly do wrong and are thereby blameworthy cannot claim that blaming responses are unfair.

There are yet further options. But the most widely shared view is that the grounds for claims of warrant, entitlement, appropriateness, or fittingness are exhausted in the notion of fundamental or basic desert. A person who is blameworthy deserves blame on this view *just because* she has acted wrongly (e.g., Feinberg, 1970; Pereboom, 2001, 2014). And the desert at issue is basic because it is not justified by considerations of utility or any other further norm at all (even arguably fairness). It is simply good or right, because deserved, to blame and perhaps in some cases punish one who is blameworthy for her wrongdoing.

We note one more refinement in our account of moral responsibility. These claims of warrant, etc., no matter how developed, whether in terms of utility, fairness, or basic desert, are best understood as offering justifications for a *pro tanto*, that is, a defeasible, reason to blame a person. For example, a blameworthy person might deserve to be blamed for some wrongdoing, but one cannot conclude just from this that it is all-things-considered the morally right thing to do to blame her. Maybe other moral considerations are overriding. For example, imagine a person who wronged you by lying to you about a small matter. She might deserve your blame. But suppose that as chance would have it, after lying to you, her child is killed in a car accident. Mercy might provide an overriding reason here not to blame, even if the blame is deserved.

With the preceding discussion of moral responsibility available, we can now chart the important connections between moral responsibility in the sense we are interested in and considerations of free will. Because being morally responsible makes one liable to justified hard treatment when one is blameworthy, there is something at stake in a person's being morally responsible in this way.[7] This makes clear why there is a control or a free will requirement on being morally responsible in the accountability sense. It seems manifestly unfair, or unjust, or undeserving for someone to be subject, on the basis of what she did, to hard treatment and the angry demands of others blaming her if, in acting as she did, her action was not in her control, and in this way she was not free in acting as she did.

Another requirement on being morally accountable is an epistemic one. A person who is blameworthy must understand or at least be able to understand that what she is doing is morally wrong (or bad or vicious). Likewise, our excusing practices bear this out. We excuse people who, through no fault of their own, did not know that the poison was placed in the ketchup jar, or that turning the light switch on would alert a burglar, and so on.

Now consider the distinction between *morally responsible agency* and *being morally responsible for* something. Morally responsible agency in the accountability sense is a matter of status—a matter of being a person of a certain sort, one who is sufficiently developed or capable that she can be held to account for her conduct. Young children, the insane, and the severely mentally disabled, while being persons, are not morally responsible agents in the accountability sense. They are not candidates for being held to moral account for their conduct. Free will, as we shall understand it, is an ability that is a requirement for being a morally responsible agent in the accountability sense.[8] Acting freely, insofar as it is an exercise of the free will ability, is a requirement for being morally responsible in this sense for what one does.

While naturally we will be interested in various cases in which there is some dispute as to whether a person acted freely, the larger question informing the free will debate is not just about whether this act or that act was a free one but about whether and how there might be agents who act with free will. On a skeptical view about the existence of agents with free will, assuming free will is a necessary condition for moral accountability, no one is a morally responsible agent in the accountability sense.

Two points are worth noting here. First, it should be clear that if no one had free will and no one was a morally responsible agent in the accountability sense, one could not conclude from this alone that there were no persons. Our conception of what persons are would be revised insofar as we presume that most persons are or will develop into morally responsible agents in this sense. But free will skepticism would not amount to a wholesale rejection of the thesis that there are persons. Second, we can now come to see a less commonly registered manner in which the free will debate is a distinctly metaphysical issue. The commonly registered assumption is that this debate concerns a metaphysical issue because it attends to the question of how there might be agents who act with free will given various constraints about how the natural world is ordered. (This is a topic we will soon consider in detail.) However, a different way to see the free will debate as a metaphysical issue is in terms of the metaphysics of personhood. Persons are regarded as distinct sorts of beings within the domain of conscious, minded creatures; and one especially interesting issue concerns what distinguishes persons from these other creatures with minds. Questions of free will and moral responsibility are then themselves questions about, at best, a narrower class of beings—persons who satisfy both epistemic and control conditions of a sort that constitutes their being morally responsible agents in the accountability sense. This would mark out a distinctive class of persons. The free will debate has independent metaphysical importance insofar as it asks whether and how we can understand such beings.

1.4.   Determinism

In its simplest form, *determinism* is just the thesis that at any time only one future is physically possible (Mele, 2006b: 3; van Inwagen, 1983: 3).[9] *Indeterminism* is then the denial of this thesis—it is the claim that at some time more than one future is physically possible. Determinism is an entirely general thesis. It applies to any aspect of the natural order whatsoever. If tomorrow a few grains of sand on a riverbed are moved by the river's current exactly three inches downstream, on the assumption that determinism is true this is the only physically possible trajectory for those grains. Similar remarks apply to any region of space over any stretch of time for any object occupying that region. This includes the length of each hair on your head, the amount of moisture currently in your eyes as you read this sentence, and it also includes each action you perform, and each state your body is in at any moment. If determinism is true, then in one important sense, each action you perform is the only action that it is physically possible to perform.

There is hidden complexity in the preceding formulation. The key to this complexity lies both in the notion of physical possibility and in the ground for only one future's being physically possible. We'll turn to these matters shortly, but we'll start here with a transparent detail of the formulation we have before us. As set out, causal determinism is a thesis about any time—and so ranges over all times. A different way to define causal determinism is to begin not with a claim about all times, but with a statement about what is involved in an event's being determined.[10] So, consider this: An event is causally determined just in case it is not physically possible that it not occur. And one event determines another just in case, given the occurrence of the first, it is not physically possible that the other not occur. Here, we do not have a definition of the thesis of determinism; instead, we have definitions of what is involved in an event being determined, and what is involved in one event determining another. Determinism, building on this definition, can then be defined as the thesis that every event is determined by a prior event.[11]

The second characterization illuminates a feature of causal determinism that is important for the free will debate. Consider the following model of a deterministic world, Wd, followed by a model of an indeterministic world, Wi. Let "e" represent an event. Let "—" represent a causally deterministic (d) relation between events. And let "..." represent an indeterministic (i) relation between events. Now consider each world:

(Wd): e1—e2—e3—e4—e5—e6—e7—e8, and so on with only d relations

(Wi): e1—e2 ... e3—e4—e5—e6—e7—e8, and so on with only d relations

Notice that in Wi there is only one pair of events, e2 to e3, that are indeterministically related; the rest are deterministically related, just as they are in Wd. Yet Wi is a world in which determinism is false. Now for the reason this is important: Suppose that at Wi, the only events in it that are actions and that are candidates for being free occur after e3, and suppose in this respect, Wi is just like Wd. The world Wi would be a world in which determinism is not true but all human actions are causally determined. As we shall see, one of the major controversies regarding the freedom of the will concerns the prospects for free action if determinism is true. For those who contend that free action is not possible if determinism is true, it would be equally problematic if indeterminism were true but that nevertheless all human actions were causally determined, as is the case in Wi. One lesson to learn here is that for those who believe determinism undermines free will, it is not enough that indeterminism is true. It must be that the *way* indeterminism is true leaves indeterministic breaks in the relation between events in just the right places—in particular, just where free actions occur. A further lesson is that the real worry is not about whether determinism per se is true, but whether all candidates for free actions are determined, and in particular, are causally determined by factors beyond the agent's control (Pereboom, 1995, 2001) or beyond her causal reach (Sartorio, 2013).

Now let's consider that hidden complexity, starting with the grounds for its being true (if it is) that only one future is physically possible. As we have defined it, determinism is a very general thesis. Different versions of it are a function of *what* would render it true that only one future is physically possible. One version of determinism is *theological determinism*. On this view, God causally determines everything that happens by willing it to happen. God's causal determination of anything that happens at any time renders it physically impossible that anything happens other than what does in fact happen. Why? God's will is unimpedable, and necessarily so. This is one of the divine perfections. So, necessarily, if God wills what I will eat for breakfast tomorrow, then that is what I will eat, and it is not possible, given what God wills, that I eat anything else.

A version of determinism more commonly discussed in the contemporary free will debate is the thesis of *physical causal determinism*. Consider this formulation of it: Every event has a physical cause, and it is physically impossible that the physical cause occur and the event does not. This way of understanding causal determinism is no longer accepted. When it was, it was assumed that causation was essentially a necessitating or determining relation, one that absolutely ensures its effect. This conception of causation was prevalent into the early twentieth century, but also retained its influence in analytic philosophy into the 1960s. The problem with the thesis is that, especially since the development of quantum mechanics, philosophers and scientists have been open to fundamentally indeterministic causal relations, those that increase the probability that an effect will occur but do not ensure it. That is, they are open to the idea that some cause c brings about an effect e, but, given the occurrence of c and the very same conditions in which c occurred, e might not have been brought about. To address this concern for defining physical causal determinism, what is needed is the following reformulation: *Every event is causally necessitated by a physical cause.*[12]

While some philosophers work with such a formulation of determinism, others worry about building the notion of causation into a definition of determinism (e.g., van Inwagen, 1983: 65). This is in part because since Hume a number of philosophers have regarded the concept of causation as controversial, and some have doubted that there really are causal relations in the world. As a result, some philosophers have opted to work with the thesis of *metaphysical entailment determinism*, which is formulated in a way that makes no reference to causation at all. So, consider this formulation, which is a variation on one offered by van Inwagen (1983):

> *metaphysical entailment determinism*: If p and q are propositions that express the entire state of the world at some instants, then the conjunction of p with a proposition expressing the entirety of the laws of nature entails q.[13]

What is doing the work of ensuring that only one future is physically possible is the logical relation of entailment, along with propositions about both the laws of nature and the state of the world at a time.

On metaphysical determinism, it's metaphysically impossible, given the facts about the world at a time and its laws that the world at any other times be different (that is, different from what is expressed in the entailment). Another way of expressing this is that it is a metaphysical truth about the nature of that world that its physical facts are fixed in this strong way—for these facts to be otherwise, while the history of the world and the laws of nature remaining as they actually are, would involve a violation of metaphysical necessity.

Several ingredients in the preceding definition can be clarified. A first is the notion of the entire state of the world at an instant. The sense of "the world" here is all of physically extended reality at an instant. Second, the facts that the definition should be understood to specify by "the state" are all and only the *temporally non-relational facts*. That is, they are facts that, at that instant, are not logically dependent on facts about other times—and they are, or entail, *all* of those facts.[14] Another ingredient is the notion of a law of nature. Paradigmatic examples are the inverse square laws that govern gravitation and electromagnetism. We will not attempt to offer anything like a definition of what a law of nature is. As it turns out, it is hard to do this. But we can say that they are non-accidental, factual regularities that seemingly involve necessities, limits, constraints, or requirements on how the natural world unfolds.[15] However we are to understand laws of nature, they are such that, if an event contravenes what seems to be a law of nature, then what seemed to be a law of nature was no law of nature after all (e.g., van Inwagen, 1983: 61–2). If, for instance, it is claimed that it is a law of nature that nothing can travel faster than the speed of light, and if an alien space ship does in fact travel faster than the speed of light, then the claim was mistaken and it is no law of nature that nothing can travel faster than the speed of light. We would have discovered that something we thought to be a law of nature was not one.[16]

The preceding definition of determinism, while adequate, is not intuitive as a means to addressing various issues in the free will debate. This is because it does not temporally privilege the direction of past to future; it is neutral on this point.

As defined, if determinism is true, a state in the future or instead the present in conjunction with the laws of nature entails every fact about the past, as well as the future. Although there is nothing strictly speaking wrong with this way of defining determinism, for the purposes of the free will debate it is more useful to foreground determining relations that are temporally directed from past to future. This is because it is plausible to assume that a person in the present is not free to act in ways that involves making her past different than it is.[17] Rather, it seems that if a person has free will, her freedom is a function of how, in the present, she is able to control her future actions and the consequences of her actions. Hence, in the pages to follow, we will work instead primarily with this rather informal definition of determinism:

> (D): Facts about the remote past in conjunction with the laws of nature entail that there is only one unique future.

And we will take it to be implicit that the facts picked out are temporally non-relational facts that can be restricted to specific instants in time, such as just three minutes after the big bang. This is adequate to capture the simple thought that, if determinism is true, "given the past and the laws, there is only one possible future" (van Inwagen, 1983: 65).[18]

1.5. Metaphysical, Physical, and Nomic Impossibility

Above, after first introducing the formulation of determinism as the thesis that at any time only one future is physically possible, we noted two hidden complexities that needed to be addressed. One had to do with the grounds for only one future's being physically possible at any time. We have settled on D as a way of unpacking that, and D is consistent with how most contemporary philosophers writing on free will think of the thesis of determinism. The other complexity had to do with the notions of physical possibility and impossibility. We now turn to a discussion of that issue.

We have already begun to elucidate the notions of physical possibility and physical impossibility by explaining how the thesis of determinism can be taken as a metaphysically necessary conditional truth: for a proposition "P" that describes the entire state of the universe at some instant in the actual past, and a proposition "L" that details the entirety of the laws of nature, and a proposition "Q" that describes the universe at some instant in the actual future, necessarily, $P \& L$ imply Q. Given that P and L are true in the actual world, in the actual world the non-occurrence of Q would then be physically impossible, which is just to say that the non-occurrence of Q is inconsistent with the past and the laws being what they actually are. But note that the metaphysically necessary truth of the conditional "$P \& L$ imply Q" is compatible with the metaphysical possibility of the falsity of determinism. Even if in all possible worlds $P \& L$ imply Q, there will yet be worlds with a past instant of the entire universe described by P*, with the entirety of the laws, some of which are indeterministic, described by L*, and a future instant of the entire universe by Q*, where P* & L* do not imply Q*. So even if determinism is true and this can be expressed as metaphysically necessary conditional truth, determinism itself won't be metaphysically necessary.

Physical possibility is thus more restrictive than metaphysical possibility: the set of all physically possible worlds is a proper subset of the set of all metaphysically possible worlds. Some worlds that are not physically possible are metaphysically possible. For instance, while it is not physically possible for something to travel faster than the speed of light, it is (arguably) metaphysically possible. Even if a space ship traveling faster than the speed of light is metaphysically possible, it is not physically possible because it is inconsistent with the actual laws of nature. And even if Napoleon's winning the Battle of Waterloo is metaphysically possible, it is not (now, in 2015) physically possible because it is inconsistent with the actual past.

We are now in a good position to make another relevant distinction. Note, first, that traveling faster than the speed of light is metaphysically impossible holding fixed just the laws of nature, irrespective of holding fixed the past. We might therefore say that this state of affairs is also *nomically impossible*—that is, impossible with respect to the laws alone. However, some states of affairs will be physically impossible but nomically possible. Imagine that currently Juan is in Tucson, Arizona, and we ask whether it is nomically possible that he currently be in Buenos Aires instead. It is. The laws of nature, irrespective of the past, are compatible with his being in Buenos Aires right now. Nevertheless, it is physically impossible that Juan be in Buenos Aires right now. That is, it's metaphysically impossible holding fixed the laws of nature and the facts of Juan's recent past that he currently be in Buenos Aires instead.[19] The lesson to learn here is that physical possibility is a function of what the laws of nature permit given certain fixed details about how physical reality has been arranged. And we can see that while in one sense it is not possible that three seconds from now Juan will be in Buenos Aires, there is another sense in which it is. It is nomically possible. Consistent with the laws of nature, he could have arrived there three seconds from now had he bought his ticket on time.

Consider now the following issue, which often arises in the discussion of determinism as it relates to action. Suppose that Dana earlier this morning drove her children to school, and assume that our world is deterministic. On our characterization of determinism, it would then be metaphysically necessary that holding fixed the past and the laws of nature that Dana drove her children to school at this time. Are we now also forced to say that it is metaphysically necessary that she did so? That it was not even metaphysically possible that her husband Sam took the kids to school? How could this be a consequence of determinism? We are not forced to say these things, and getting clear on why will help clarify the relevant sense of physical impossibility at issue.

At this point it's important to understand how certain *modal inferences* work. Modality concerns different sorts of necessity, possibility, and impossibility, and so we have in this section and the preceding one been discussing a set of modal issues. Here we will be interested primarily in a mistake in reasoning about modality, a kind of modal fallacy. We will only explain this informally, since this will be enough to serve our purposes. Consider this non-modal pattern of inference:

> Jasmine is a pediatrician.
> If someone is a pediatrician, then she is a physician.
> Therefore, Jasmine is a physician.

Now consider a modal correlate of this pattern:

> Jasmine is a pediatrician.
> Necessarily, if someone is a pediatrician, then she is a physician.
> Therefore, necessarily, Jasmine is a physician.

This modal inference is fallacious. It is true, we're supposing, that Jasmine is a pediatrician. But from this we cannot conclude that it's necessary that she's a pediatrician; we can assume only that it's a contingent truth. But there is a necessary conditional relation between being a pediatrician and being a physician: it's impossible to be a pediatrician without being a physician. But it's clearly not necessary that Jasmine is a physician. So the premises of the argument, on our supposition, are true, but the conclusion is false, and so the argument is unsound. The diagnosis is that it is a modal fallacy to transfer the necessity of the conditional in the second premise to the consequent of that conditional unless the antecedent is also necessarily true. We can infer from the premises that Jasmine is a physician, but not the claim that, necessarily, she is physician.

Return now to the claim that it follows from the truth of determinism that it is metaphysically necessary that Dana took her kids to school. Inferring this is fallacious in just the sense identified above. Again, treat "P" as a proposition expressing the entire state of the universe at some instant in the past, and treat "L" as a proposition expressing the entirety of the laws of nature. Now, if determinism is true, then, necessarily, it is a consequence of the facts of the past, P, and the laws of nature, L, that every truth obtained about the entire state of the universe during the duration of time it took for Dana to drive her kids to school this morning. So, the truth of Dana's driving her kids to school this morning is entailed by the conjunction of P and L. Here now is the fallacious reasoning that led to the illicit conclusion:

> P and L.
> Necessarily, if P and L, then Dana drove her kids to school this morning.
> Therefore, necessarily, Dana drove her kids to school this morning.

All that we can infer from the two premises is that Dana drove her kids to school this morning; we cannot infer that it was necessary that she did so. We can claim that under the assumption that determinism is true, necessarily, Dana drove her kids to school this morning *given the entirety of the facts of the past and all of the laws of nature.* But this conditional necessity is not at all the same as an unconditional claim that it is necessary that Dana drive her kids to school this morning.

One reason that people commit the preceding fallacy is because they are implicitly assuming something that, if true, *would* validly yield the conclusion that, necessarily, Dana drove her kids to school this morning. They are assuming that it is metaphysically necessary that the past is what it is and that the laws of nature are metaphysically necessary as well. But this is not part of or a consequence of the thesis of determinism. It is fully consistent with the truth of determinism that the past is only contingently as it is. It could have been different. It just wasn't. The same applies to the laws of nature. The laws of nature might not be alterable by human beings, but it is consistent with there being laws of nature that it is a metaphysically contingent fact about this universe that the laws of nature are what they are. It is metaphysically possible, on this view, that the laws of nature might have been different from what they are. The speed of light, for instance, might have been a little faster or instead slower than what it actually is. The fact that the laws of nature are general and nonaccidental, exceptionless truths about this universe is not sufficient to conclude that it is not metaphysically possible that this universe have instead featured some different set of general and nonaccidental exceptionless truths.

Furthermore, while it is physically impossible in one sense for the future to be other than as it is (or will be) under the assumption of determinism, it might very well be possible, say nomically possible, that some feature of the present or future be other than as it was. Dana, for instance, might not have driven her kids to school this morning if her past had been slightly different from what it was, holding the laws fixed. Suppose, for instance, that Sam happened to note early in the morning that he had to pass by the school today for some other reason. Had that been a part of Dana's past, she might not have taken her kids to school even if the laws were the same as they actually are. This scenario is therefore nomically possible. Determinism only renders it metaphysically necessary that she took her kids to school this morning *given* the entirety of the actual past and the totality of the actual laws of nature. It does not impugn the metaphysical or nomic possibility of her not taking the kids to school instead.

Without distinguishing unconditional from conditional metaphysical necessity and possibility, metaphysical from physical necessity and possibility, and physical from nomic necessity and possibility, it's hard to keep track of these claims, and also of some of the more sophisticated theses that will arise in chapters to follow. For instance, some compatibilist theses contending that the ability to do otherwise is compatible with determinism are difficult to understand without tending to these modal issues. We wish to emphasize here that notions of necessity and possibility are intricately layered, and keeping this in mind is important for understanding some of the key moves in the free will debate.

1.6.   Indeterminism, Mechanism, and Naturalism

We close this chapter with a brief set of comments about a collection of related issues. As we explained above (Section 1.4), *indeterminism* is just the denial of determinism. On one characterization, indeterminism is true just in case, at some time, there is more than one future that is physically possible. As we explained, for those who contend that indeterminism is required for free will, it is not enough that determinism is false. The indeterministic breaks must be suitably located in the unfolding history of the world in a way that corresponds with potential moments for free action. Recall that the world Wi wasn't a deterministic world but did not have indeterministic relations between events at points that would matter for free action. Moreover, not only must actions have indeterministic causes suitably located, the indeterminism must be of a certain sort. This point is often expressed in connection with claims about the indeterminism that some think may occur at the quantum level. On this suggestion, our universe is not deterministic but, at the most fundamental level, indeterministic, and the laws governing the natural order at this level are probabilistic or statistical laws. Nevertheless, so the worry goes, the indeterminacy does not allow for macro-level variation of the sort that would involve, say, a person standing up rather than remaining seated, as might be involved in the free act of standing rather than sitting. For the most part, the thought is, the micro-indeterminacies "cancel each other out," and we get macro-level determinism. Hence, what physics may suggest is something like "near-determinism" or "almost-determinism." But for indeterminism to make a difference for free will, it would need to be sufficiently substantial at the macro-level for it to matter to exercises of free will.

Another issue has to do with a shift in focus away from determinism to a wider thesis, *mechanism*. Suppose it turns out that quantum mechanics disconfirms the strict thesis of determinism as narrowly characterized above. Some philosophers maintain that mechanism would appear to pose the same threat to free will as has been traditionally posed by determinism. According to these philosophers, the apparent tension between determinism and free will, and the various theoretical positions one can take on resolving that tension, are entirely preserved when mechanism is at issue and not the more precise (and less plausible) theory of determinism. Consider Hilary Bok's expression of the view, wherein she quotes Daniel Dennett:

> Mechanism is the view that human actions can be explained as the result of natural processes alone; that the "mechanistic style of explanation, which works so well for electrons, motors, and galaxies," also works well for us. If mechanism is true, then just as our explanations of the motions of the planets no longer requires the existence of prime movers to supplement natural processes, so our actions could in principle be explained by a complex neurophysiological theory, without reference to a nonnatural self that causes them. (Bok, 1998: 3, quoting Dennett, 1981: 233)

Bok and Dennett both express the view in terms of explanation, and so there is an epistemological orientation to their formulation, but one could express it in terms of the way human agency is, not about how it could in principle be explained or understood. On this metaphysical rendering of the thesis, mechanism is the view that human agency is causally rooted in, and in other ways supervenes on, complex neurophysiological states, events, and processes, as well as the causal antecedents of these. These states, events, and processes behave in mechanistic ways, are governed by mechanistic laws, and there exists no feature of human agency that is not in this way rooted in these mechanistic ingredients. This thesis is true regardless of whether the physical states realizing the mechanistic goings-on are deterministic or instead indeterministic.

The sort of indeterminism discussed above, almost-determinism, and mechanism, as well as determinism itself, might all be captured under the very general umbrella of *naturalism*. It is difficult to state clearly what naturalism is, and it seems that in philosophy it is embraced pervasively but with little consensus to its meaning (Baker, 2013: 3–27; De Caro and Macarthur, 2010; De Caro and Voltolini, 2010). Nevertheless, there is a fairly simple sense of naturalism which bears on the free will debate and in which, if determinism is true, or instead almost-determinism is true, or mechanism is true, then this form of naturalism is also true. The simple sense is just that there is no feature of reality as it bears on human activity that does not have its causal roots in the kinds of states that are widely featured in nature and are governed by natural laws that do involve the intentions of conscious agents. If naturalism is true in this sense, then all human action is causally rooted either deterministically or indeterministically in states of this sort.

Suggestions for Further Reading

Useful and extended discussions of the three basic concepts discussed in this chapter, free will, determinism, and moral responsibility, can be found in the *Stanford Encyclopedia of Philosophy*:

Eshleman, Andrew. 2014. "Moral Responsibility." *Stanford Encyclopedia of Philosophy*. http://plato.stanford.edu/entries/moral-responsibility/.
Hoefer, Carl. 2010. "Causal Determinism." *Stanford Encyclopedia of Philosophy*. http:// plato.stanford.edu/entries/determinism-causal/.
O'Connor, Timothy. 2010. "Free Will." *The Stanford Encyclopedia of Philosophy* (Spring 2002 Edition), Edward N. Zalta, ed. http://plato.stanford.edu/archives/spr2002/entries/ freewill/.

Numerous writers begin their books by offering initial definitions of free will and determinism (not so much for moral responsibility). Here are a few that are especially informative, even if their proposals differ from ours, see:

Fischer, John Martin. 1994. *The Metaphysics of Free Will*. Oxford: Blackwell Publishers.
Kane, Robert. 1996. *The Significance of Free Will*. Oxford: Oxford University Press.

van Inwagen, Peter. 1983. *An Essay on Free Will*. Oxford: Clarendon Press.
Vihvelin, Kadri. 2013. *Causes, Laws, & Free Will: Why Determinism Doesn't Matter*. New York: Oxford University Press.

As for the topic of moral responsibility, there are very few discussions in work on free will that take any time at the outset to define and explain what moral responsibility is in any detail. For a couple that do, see:

Fischer, John Martin, and Mark Ravizza. 1998. *Responsibility and Control: An Essay on Moral Responsibility*. Cambridge: Cambridge University Press.
Pereboom, Derk. 2014. *Free Will, Agency, and Meaning in Life*. New York: Oxford University Press.

For an extended discussion of moral responsibility, and especially the accountability sense that we contend is at the heart of the free will debate, see:

McKenna, Michael. 2012. *Conversation and Responsibility*. New York: Oxford University Press.
Nelkin, Dana. 2011. *Making Sense of Freedom and Responsibility*. Oxford: Oxford University Press.
Shoemaker, David. 2015. *Responsibility from the Margins*. Oxford: Oxford University Press.

And, as well, see several essays in this recent collection:

Clarke, Randolph, Michael McKenna, and Angela M. Smith, eds., 2015. *The Nature of Moral Responsibility*. New York: Oxford University Press.

Notes

1 See Mele (1995: 3) for a similar point. Mele uses an example from Aristotle's *Nicomachean Ethics* (X.7) of amoral beings who are nevertheless self-governed (free) beings.

2 *A warning to the introductory student*: Some newcomers to this philosophical topic find it nearly irresistible to take the meaning of the term *free will* to be or to include as one of its ingredients "the opposite of determinism." This thought should be strongly resisted. What "free will" *means*, on our formulation, has to do with a particular kind of ability to control one's actions; there is no mention of determinism at all in our definition. Notice that the other competitor views we considered were also formulated in ways that made no mention of determinism. Perhaps after careful reflection, one should conclude for *substantive* reasons that free will rules out determinism. But this should not be settled just by appeal to the meaning of the term.

3 One might ask why decisions have this focus in the free will debate. As an aide in thinking about these issues further, we offer the following consideration:

First, there is a familiar way of using the notion of decision that suggests that at the root of every intentional action is a decision. How so? For each intentional act a person performs, it can seem natural to ask the person, "Why did you decide to do that?" or "Why did you choose to do that?"

Second, on a more restricted way of understanding decisions, they involve intentionally settling uncertainty about what to do—say whether to buy a car or which car to buy. On this understanding, it is not true that every intentional action has a decision as one of its causal antecedents or component parts. Why? Because not every intentional action involves a circumstance in which its agent is uncertain about what to do. Indeed, most agents most of the time do most of what they do intentionally with no (conscious) uncertainty about what to do.

Third, on the familiar, less restricted way of thinking about decisions, it seems implausible to regard them as actions in their own right, since it would commit one to multiplying the number of actions an agent performs when thinking about the full extension of intentional actions. Every intentional action, such as the hitting of a baseball, would also include the act of deciding to hit the baseball. On the more restricted way of thinking about decisions, it is more plausible to regard them as acts—mental acts—that then give rise to intentions to perform further acts: for example, Joan decides to buy the car and then drives back to the dealership to buy it. Her deciding generated an intention to buy, and this latter intention then played the role of cause in her driving to the dealership (the driving itself being a distinct act from the act of deciding).

Fourth, it is commonplace to use the words "choice" and "decision" interchangeably, and there seems to be little harm in doing so. But we note that there does appear to be a subtle difference between their ordinary meanings. Choices seem to be between options. One chooses the red car over the green one. Decisions seem not to have to be between options. One decides to buy a car. This suggests that choices are a special class of decisions, and that not every decision is a choice but that every choice is a decision.

Fifth, on either the permissive or the restrictive model of choices and decisions, they occur at the initial moments of free actions, and if they have causal antecedents, those antecedents involve items that are themselves *not* part of what would constitute or be free action. They would instead be generators of it. This is likely the key to why they occupy special attention in work on free will.

4   There is a familiar way of using the expression "moral responsibility" that is apt to mislead the introductory student. One sense of "moral responsibility," different from the one we shall focus upon here, functions as synonymous with "moral obligation," as when it is said that Fred has a moral responsibility to tend to Francine, meaning that he has an obligation to tend to her. To see that this is not the relevant sense of moral responsibility, imagine that Fred *is* blameworthy for failing in his obligation to tend to Francine. If he did so freely and knowingly, then in another sense, the sense we are interested in, he would be morally responsible (and blameworthy) for failing in his obligations (responsibility in the other sense). The general lesson here is not to be tricked into associating claims about what a person is morally responsible for (in the sense we are interested in here) with claims about what a person's moral obligations are. It is worth bearing in mind that a person might be morally responsible in our intended sense *because* of complying with or failing to comply with what her moral obligations are (responsibilities in the other sense). So there might be an important connection between the two. Still, they are different.

5   Typically, writers drop the modifier "moral" from discussions of praiseworthiness and blameworthiness, and praise and blame when context makes clear that the subject concerns moral responsibility rather than some other variety, such as legal responsibility.

6 This sense appears to be structurally similar to legal responsibility where those who violate the law and are legally competent, sane adults, are held to account for doing so by others licensed or warranted with the right to so hold them.

7 Something similar is true for being praiseworthy, but set that aside here.

8 Such agents must also have abilities to understand morality properly and understand how they do and are supposed to act.

9 Qualifications have to be made for a first time or first event. We can set that aside here.

10 This is how Kane proceeds (e.g., 1996: 8; 2005: 5–6).

11 Again, qualifications have to be made for a first event. We can set that aside here.

12 Sometimes, mostly in non-philosophical discourse, determinism is restricted to a certain *type* of causal necessitation. For instance, *genetic* determinism might be understood as the thesis that any organism's features and conduct are causally necessitated solely by its genetic constitution. Or *environmental* determinism might be taken as the thesis that all behavior of an animal is causally necessitated solely by previous environmental conditioning combined with present environmental setting. These two examples of deterministic theories are highly implausible, and determinism in disciplines outside of philosophy is often *appropriately* taken to be far-fetched since it is often associated with such outlandish views. The mistake is to assume that determinism itself is implausible just because some thesis resembling determinism is.

13 We opt here for this somewhat inelegant name, metaphysical entailment determinism, so as not to suggest that causal determinism is not a metaphysical thesis. It certainly is, especially when cast in terms of causal powers. We will, however, drop the middle term in subsequent discussion.

14 To illustrate the difference between temporally relational and temporally non-relational facts, consider this: "On December 24, 1968, in New York, NY, at precisely 12:00 midnight it was 30 degrees Fahrenheit." If it is a fact, is a non-relational fact. Its truth does not depend on what happens at any time other than the moment of time specified in the statement. In contrast, "On December 24, 1968, in New York, NY, at precisely midnight, many young children were soon to be given gifts," if it is a fact, is a temporally relational fact. Its truth depends upon what happens at times other than the time specified.

15 We say "seemingly" since there is considerable controversy, originally inspired by Hume, as to whether we should understand the laws as involving any necessity at all rather than being merely stable regularities that play a certain role in explaining events. This is a very large issue that we cannot take up here. But we note its importance, and as we shall see, it crops up in some of the major disputes regarding the relation between a (putatively) free agent and the laws of nature in deterministic contexts.

16 But note the following complication. Steven Horst (2011) argues that physics, at least as we presently find it, features no departure-free laws when they are construed as describing actual motions. The inverse square law of gravity, for example, will only result in exactly accurate predictions of motions if there are no other forces, such as electromagnetism, at play. The better view, according to Horst, is to interpret the laws as governing causal powers, which in the case of fundamental physics, are plausibly forces. On this conception, laws do not primarily describe motion, but rather characterize causal powers. We'll return to this point and its significance in Chapter 10.

17 For our purposes, we can safely set aside issues regarding the possibility of time travel.

18 Here is a note for advanced students familiar with some related topics in the metaphysics of modality: Some philosophers worry that defining determinism as a relation between propositions is misleading. Propositions are abstract entities. But determinism is about the world; *it is about concrete reality*. It would be better to have a definition that expresses determinism about the world's possibilities. Consider, then, this definition, that is a rough paraphrase of the one David Lewis proposed (Lewis, 1973):

> W1 is a deterministic world just in case there exists no other world, W2, that shares with W1 at a moment in time, t, W1's entire history and the laws of nature so that until t, W2 is a duplicate of W1, and yet W2 diverges from W1 at some later time, t + n, such that W1 and W2 are no longer duplicates.

Many will protest that talk of possible worlds is no better than talk of propositions. Indeed. But Lewis's proposed modal semantics can be exploited to articulate our familiar modal judgments without buying into the existence of possible worlds. It can be used as a useful heuristic that simply translates, for a deterministic world, d, as this:

> It is not metaphysically possible for this world, d, to have more than one future, given its actual past and its actual laws of nature.

We will work with the informal formulation, D, offered in the text above. But we have no allegiance to it, and although this Lewis-inspired formulation is not often used, nearly every controversy we shall discuss that involves determinism could be recast in terms of this definition.

19 A warning here: Sometimes, to capture this later sense of physical impossibility, philosophers will, contrary to what we write here, say that it is nomologically impossible in a case like this for Juan to be in Buenos Aires in three seconds. But what they mean is that it is nomologically impossible, given Juan's present location and recent history. And so their full meaning is not just about what the laws of nature do and do not permit but what the laws of nature do and do not permit *given other facts about the arrangement of physical reality*. To keep these matters clear, we advise a more cautious and regimented way of talking about these issues.

2 The Free Will Problem

It is often remarked that the free will question is one of the classic problems of philosophy. The basic insight giving rise to the problem is easy to state. It appears that free will is in tension with determinism, that one cannot consistently believe that persons have free will and that determinism is true. Yet we have reason to believe both. It looks as if something has to go, and so we face a problem. Here, then, is a first pass at formulating the problem:

1. Determinism is true.
2. At least some persons have free will.
3. Free will is incompatible with determinism.

What makes the problem of free will a classic problem of philosophy is that it can be framed as a set of mutually inconsistent propositions, each of which there is independently good reason to accept. The philosopher's task in the face of this inconsistency is to resolve it. What must be given up, if anything must (some problems, after all, are merely apparent), is to be settled by what is true and what is false. And this is achieved by examining the best arguments for and against the various propositions comprising the problem set.

This chapter is devoted first to motivating and then formulating the free will problem. In doing so, we will identify several forms and dimensions of the problem. As the discussion unfolds, what will become apparent is that different issues emerge insofar as there are different ways of thinking about free will. Yet a further variable is the way determinism as well as indeterminism figure into the elements that generate the problem.

We'll begin with a section explaining compatibilism and incompatibilism, and the free-will-accepting and the free-will-denying versions of incompatibilism. Then, before turning our attention to developing the free will problem, we will motivate it by considering first the appeal of free will and then the appeal of determinism. It is one thing to recognize a conceptual puzzle or problem, but it is another to see the motivation for why it is important to solve it. Our intention is to convey that what is in dispute engages dimensions of our self-understanding and our conception of the natural world in a way that matters. Something considerable is at stake. Once we have shown this, we will then turn to the free will problem, explaining its various forms and dimensions. We'll conclude the chapter with a section devoted to situating the various positions one might take on the free will problem within the broader currents of philosophy, currents that can be appreciated by considering the general strategies philosophers might adopt when attempting to understand our place as human beings within the natural order.

2.1.   Compatibilism and Incompatibilism

A fundamental divide among positions on the free will problem is marked by the distinction between compatibilism and incompatibilism. Compatibilism is the thesis that free will is compatible with determinism. More exactly:

> *Compatibilism* is the thesis that it is metaphysically possible that determinism is true and some person has free will.

Incompatibilism is the thesis that free will is incompatible with determinism. More precisely:

> *Incompatibilism* is the thesis that it is not metaphysically possible that determinism is true and some person has free will.

Further refinements are required to distinguish between different types of compatibilism and incompatibilism, but this is the most fundamental starting point.

Because of the intimate connection between free will and moral responsibility, and because many participants in the free will debate are motivated primarily by concerns about moral responsibility, one often finds versions of compatibilism and incompatibilism expressed in terms of moral responsibility. On these versions, compatibilism is the thesis that moral responsibility is compatible with determinism, and incompatibilism is the thesis that moral responsibility is not compatible with determinism. Various other definitions we offer in the remainder of this section could also be modified in this way. We will tend just to definitions expressed in terms of free will. But we note that formulations in terms of moral responsibility are also prevalent.[1]

Several qualifications about the preceding definitions are needed. To begin, the definition of compatibilism does not commit to the truth of determinism. It tells us that *if* determinism were true, its truth would not entail that no person ever acts freely. This definition does not entail that any actual person has free will. It allows that while determinism is actually true, some other feature of all agents rules out their having free will. It also allows that because indeterminism of a certain sort is true, no actual agents have free will (Hobart, 1934; Hume, 1748). Nevertheless, for every philosopher we are aware of who has defended compatibilism, free will is not just an abstract metaphysical possibility. It also involves the further thesis that actual normally functioning human beings do have free will and indeed do act freely. That is, beyond the strictly metaphysical compatibility thesis about what is possible—a world that is determined and in which some persons act freely—they are *realists* about free will.

The definition of incompatibilism specifies only that free will is incompatible with determinism. Incompatibilists might or might not in addition hold that free will is incompatible with indeterminism as well. Many incompatibilists maintain that some type of indeterminism is true and makes room for free will. Others contend that even if indeterminism is true, this will not help the case for free will. These differences will be captured by further distinctions we set out below. In addition, an incompatibilist who believes that free will is compatible with indeterminism might nevertheless remain *agnostic* about whether anyone has free will insofar as he does not know whether indeterminism is true, and whether indeterminism of the free-will-friendly sort is true (e.g., Ginet, 1990).

Now consider the most basic distinction between different types of incompatibilism, the distinction between libertarianism and hard determinism. Libertarianism is the incompatibilist thesis that determinism is false and persons have free will. More carefully:

> *Libertarianism* is the thesis that incompatibilism is true, that determinism is false, and at least one person has free will.

Hard determinism is the incompatibilist thesis that because determinism is true, no one has free will. More carefully:

> *Hard determinism* is the thesis that incompatibilism is true, that determinism is true, and therefore no person has free will.

The "hard" in "hard determinism" connotes the tough-minded position one should take about the metaphysical consequences of determinism's truth. Accepting that determinism is true, according to the hard determinist, requires that we face up to the hard truth that no one has free will, and as a result, no one is morally responsible for what they do (because free will is required for moral responsibility).

There are several other useful terms that are worth setting out here. One often finds philosophers, especially in twentieth-century analytic philosophy, using the expression "soft determinism" rather than "compatibilism" (e.g., Edwards, 1958; Hobart, 1934; Schlick, 1939; Smart, 1963). While the two are closely related, there is a difference:

> *Soft determinism* is the thesis that free will is compatible with determinism, and determinism is true.[2]

One reason that the two different expressions were in earlier times often used interchangeably is because it is only in more recent times that those with compatibilist leanings have become open to conceptions of causation that are indeterministic. Indeed, many compatibilists today are not absolutely convinced that determinism is true.[3] But most are committed to the thesis that even if it is, this would have no bearing on whether persons have free will. One can endorse this compatibilist position even while strongly believing, perhaps in light of respectable scientific evidence, that determinism is false. The "soft" in the expression "soft determinism" is meant to be descriptive of an accommodating position about what is consistent with determinism's truth—that it does not preclude free will and moral responsibility.[4]

Hard determinism is in a certain respect a dated thesis that does not usefully apply to the current debates. This is because many who are inclined to the main insight of the hard determinist position allow that determinism may be false, but even if it is, that the sort of indeterminism that remains, say in the form of almost-determinism, mechanism, or naturalism, is no more compatible with free will than determinism is. These philosophers, hard incompatibilists, have taken up the hard determinists' cause and refined it to address a contemporary way of approaching the debate:

> *Hard incompatibilism* is the thesis that free will is incompatible with determinism (incompatibilism is true), that either determinism is true or a form of indeterminism is true which is also incompatible with free will, and so no one has free will regardless of whether determinism is true or false.

Hard incompatibilism as defined here is consistent with the metaphysical possibility that some persons have free will. Because hard incompatibilism includes incompatibilism, it is committed to the thesis that it is metaphysically impossible for persons to have free will in any world in which determinism is true. But it permits the metaphysical possibility that indeterminism is true in a way that is consistent with persons having free will. It is only committed to the empirical thesis that the form of indeterminism that we have reason to believe is true (perhaps in the form of mechanism or naturalism) is not enough to permit the existence of free will. So as an empirical fact about the world we inhabit, no one has free will, and hence, no one is morally responsible (Pereboom, 2001, 2014).

Hard incompatibilism, so defined, like its predecessor hard determinism, is a kind of skepticism about free will. It involves a particular way of advancing this form of skepticism. But there is a more general view to be identified here:

> *Free will skepticism* is the thesis that no one has free will, or at the very least, that we have insufficient reason to believe that any one does have free will.

While hard incompatibilism as we have defined it is a form of free will skepticism, it is not as modally strong as other versions are. It leaves open that some person in some possible world (not ours) has free will. Stronger forms of skepticism would deny this. Here, then, is a more stringent form of free will skepticism:

Impossibilism about free will is the thesis that it is not metaphysically possible for anyone to have free will. (G. Strawson, 1986, 1994)

One way to argue for impossibilism is by building on the view of hard incompatibilism and arguing that it is not metaphysically possible that if indeterminism (in any form) is true any person has free will. But a quite different way to argue for impossibilism is to argue that the concept of free will (or instead the concept of moral responsibility) is at some deep level incoherent. On this view, it is not possible for any persons to have free will, and this is so for reasons that have nothing to do with determinism or indeterminism. It is instead a matter of the structure of the concept of free will.

There are a number of other terms identifying a further range of positions with respect to the free will problem. But the ones we have canvassed here are adequate for current purposes.

2.2.   Motivating the Problem: The Appeal of Free Will and Determinism

We shall now consider free will's appeal, highlighting the reasons which make it credible that we have it and attractive to believe that we do. We'll then do likewise with the thesis of determinism.

Free will's plausibility and appeal arise from several sources. One is connected with moral responsibility. In our ordinary practices, we distinguish between persons who are morally responsible agents and persons who are not. We distinguish between, for example, young children, or the severely mentally handicapped, on the one hand, and, on the other, fully functioning adults capable of normal interpersonal relations of a sort that includes our expectations that they can be held to account for how they treat us and others. It is therefore at least plausible to assume that *there are morally responsible agents*. Given that free will is taken to be a necessary condition of morally responsible agency, it is plausible to assume that some persons have free will. An open-minded philosophical attitude should permit consideration of the skeptical possibility that perhaps no one has free will, and hence that there are no morally responsible agents. This is how free will skeptics, such as hard incompatibilists, see things. To this end, these skeptics marshal forceful arguments designed to undermine the credibility of these concepts. But in the absence of such powerful reasoning, there is *prima facie* reason to believe that there are morally responsible agents, agents who sometimes exercise their free will.

There are, however, other sources of the apparent plausibility of our having free will. Consider the first-personal point of view. From my own perspective, I have a sense, especially when deliberating about what to do in a context of choice or decision, that it is up to me what I will do, and in doing it, I will be the one who will settle if and how I will act. I experience my own agency as if I am free to settle upon whether, how, and when to act. This arguably involves a sense of ourselves as free—a way that makes the thought that we have free will appear to be plausible. Even in simple cases of a trivial sort, such as choosing between kinds of pasta in the grocery store, we have the sense that we are free to choose among options and that however we choose, we are the source of that course of action; our so acting was, on the occasion, up to us.

Now consider a different source of the apparent plausibility of free will. Most of us are familiar with circumstances in which we struggle with temptation. Sometimes we fail. Cheesecake is after all mighty tasty, and that third (or fourth) martini in the company of an old friend can seem like such good fun. But sometimes we succeed. On these occasions, one has the sense that when the pressures of one's desires or cravings are bearing down, one is still free to resist them, perhaps in light of what one judges is really best. Indeed, we describe such occasions in terms of exercising will power or self-control. Furthermore, our thinking about these cases is not limited to first-personal experience. When assessing the admirable or instead lamentable conduct of others, we assume that they too are free either to give in to their cravings or resist them. The friend struggling to quit smoking or stop binge eating, we often think, has the ability to control how she behaves, and so is free to exercise strength or instead weakness of will.

In addition, we generally assume in our interpersonal lives that our close friends, intimate others, acquaintances, co-workers, and so on, are in control of their lives. The thought here is not (or at least need not be) connected with assumptions about moral responsibility. Instead it regards simple interpersonal expectations about who cares for us and who does not, and how and why they elect to act the way they do in how they treat us and others. While love might not be subject to a person's free will, there is a common assumption that those who love us, and as well those who hate us, freely treat us as they do. And our responses to them belie our presumption that they are, in some way, in control of their manner of dealing with us and those we care about. Hence, we are prone to feel resentment or instead gratitude for the slight or instead the kindness of a friend or a co-worker.

Moreover, these assumptions about freedom are also often implicit in our assessment of the choices people make enabling them to live meaningful or meaningless lives. Our assessment of intimate others, of ourselves, and, for that matter, near strangers, is often built upon the presupposition that the value or meaning of their lives and ours is in part a function of the fact that it was or is the product of exercising free will. We might say of someone whose history included some great misfortune that she picked herself up by her own bootstraps and made something of her life, thereby expressing our admiration. And we think of those with promise and opportunity who squandered their lives on frivolities, drink, or shallow fleeting interests, that they threw their lives away. Here, this talk of picking oneself up or of throwing away one's life seems implicitly to involve the presumption that these people acted freely—they were in control of building themselves up or instead wrecking themselves. Thus there is a pervasive picture of free agency that is naturally associated with these thoughts about the meaningfulness and the meaninglessness of life.

If we were to have to give up as rationally justified our belief that most persons have free will, it seems that we would have to revise significantly our picture of ordinary interpersonal life. We would have to see most persons very differently than we do. The value that we attach to free will and moral responsibility would appear to be a value that accords to persons a kind of dignity and place of worth in the order of things. Most people wish to preserve the view that certain efforts are to a person's credit because it was within the scope of her control. Most people also wish to retain the rational basis for holding some accountable for their misdeeds, and as warranting blame and punishment.

According to a widespread conception, free will, moral responsibility, strength and weakness of will, interpersonal concern, and the meaningfulness of life, their plausibility and value, are essential features of a broader picture of human life, a picture that incorporates many elements beyond those specifically concerned with the topic of free will. These elements include the very idea of value, including moral, aesthetic, epistemological, or any other kind. They include the possibility of creativity, the possibility of rational conduct, the presumption that persons have beliefs and desires, and the presumption that persons mark a distinct and significant ontological category. This broader picture is a key part of what Wilfred Sellars has called the *manifest image* of the human condition.[5] The manifest image concerns the human worldview in which persons have worth and their lives can be imbued with meaning. It includes the point of view of persons as practical agents. It acknowledges the legitimacy of common sense, and of "folk psychological" explanations involving the reasons, goals, values, principles, wishes, and desires of persons engaged in ordinary interpersonal life.

But is determinism in fact true, and are we forced to accept compatibilism to preserve all of this? Suppose first that our best physics is deterministic. Even then, whether determinism is generally true would depend on whether everything that exists is wholly made up of what is in the purview of physics. That is controversial—many hold that conscious minds cannot be wholly physical in this sense. But even on the supposition that everything is wholly physical, note that some have argued that our best theory of the microphysical, quantum mechanics, has a correct indeterministic account. The Copenhagen interpretation of quantum mechanics supports this view. At the same time, it is very controversial, and on the contemporary scene it is typically rejected by theoretical physicists and philosophers of physics. An influential interpretation advanced in the 1950s and 1960s by David Bohm is consistent with determinism's being true, and it enjoys widespread popularity. However, one might reasonably believe that current physics is still quite far from the truth, as Carl Hoefer argues:

> Figuring out whether well-established theories are deterministic or not (or to what extent, if they fall only a bit short) does not do much to help us know whether our world is *really* governed by deterministic laws; all our current best theories, including General Relativity and the Standard Model of particle physics, are too flawed and ill-understood to be mistaken for anything close to a Final Theory. (Hoefer, 2010)

It seems reasonable to think that the verdict is still out, that consistent with what we now know about the arrangement of the natural world whether determinism is true or false remains to be established.

Let us approach the question of the truth of determinism from another angle. One way to begin to appreciate determinism's appeal is to consider the Principle of Sufficient Reason, a principle that has its roots in philosophers like Leibniz. The principle is often expressed in different ways, but in its simplest form it is the thesis that there is a sufficient reason for everything to be as it is and not otherwise (Hoefer, 2010). Determinism would have it that for each state of the world at any time, there are causal processes involving the past and the laws that guarantee that it is that way. There would then be facts about the past and the laws that explain why it is that way and no other way. And by contrast, indeterminism would have it that there are states of the world at a time for which there are no causal processes involving the past and the laws that guarantee that they are that way, and no corresponding explanations. Some philosophers and physicists find this puzzling.

These considerations alone still do not show that determinism is itself highly likely to be true, but if we are willing to expand the thesis to include almost-determinism, in terms of either mechanism or naturalism (as defined in the previous chapter), then something very much like determinism does start to seem quite credible. For instance, in the form of mechanism, the physical states of human beings, combined with the laws of nature, might roughly determine only one significant course of action for any normally functioning human person, even if, at the microphysical level, the various states of an agent's body, and in particular her brain, allow for minor variations in how those significant courses of action are realized. Perhaps philosophers continue to make use of the strict definition of determinism (requiring only one unique future) because it allows them to formulate the philosophical problems, arguments, and theories more rigorously. For the most part, the formulations could be captured when determinism is expressed more loosely. It is just that it would be more cumbersome.

So it seems that determinism, when meant to include the looser notions of almost-determinism, mechanism, or naturalism, is plausible. It is plausible because it resonates with a scientific conception of the natural order, a conception in which all aspects of nature can (at least in theory) be accounted for in terms of physical states, processes, and events behaving according to natural laws. This conception of the natural order is invited by an ever-expanding body of scientific knowledge capable of explaining a vast and diverse range of phenomena, including the state and behavior of human beings. Naturally, the fact that much of human conduct can be explained by appeal to resources that fit within larger scientific theories does not amount to the claim that all human behavior is determined, but it does make plausible the thesis that it might be, at least to the extent that the theories of explanation are (again, put loosely) deterministic.

But is there value in attempting to preserve determinism against threats to it? According to the incompatibilist thesis, free will threatens determinism just as much as determinism threatens free will. In particular, if one had good reason to endorse the reality of free will, and if one assumed that free will was incompatible with determinism, then the reality of free will would threaten the truth of determinism.[6] Restricted just to considerations of human behavior, the reality of free will would commit one to the claim that some aspects of human conduct could not be fully explained solely in terms of physical, mechanistic states and events.[7] Would this be a lamentable result? Maybe determinism, while a plausible thesis, has a significant downside, and in light of the value and importance attached to free will (and attendant concepts such as moral responsibility, creativity, etc.), proving determinism false, by proving true both incompatibilism and the reality of free will, would be all to the good.

But there is also value in preserving the open-minded attitude that perhaps determinism (in some form) is true. It is a theoretical value that embraces unification and breadth in explanatory scope. To the extent that our best scientific theories of the natural world are capable of bringing as much of nature as possible within the umbrella of a single explanatory framework, it is perhaps better that some aspect of human conduct not be partitioned off from that framework. There is a respected tradition in some philosophical quarters of acting as a conceptual aid to the sciences, clearing the way for science to incorporate within its sphere as much of human nature as possible. Philosophy's role here can be understood as aiding in the development of the *scientific image* of the human condition. Valuing the tenability of determinism as applied to human conduct is consistent with the cultivation of this image.

2.3.   Free Will Problems

We can now begin to attend with some care to an examination of the free will problem. Return to our initial formulation of it, which, we noted, was too simple and so masked too much:

1.   Determinism is true.
2.   At least some persons have free will.
3.   Free will is incompatible with determinism.

Call this formulation F1. We'll now begin to expand on F1 in various ways. To begin, a more contemporary formulation might also include almost-determinism, mechanism, and naturalism as we have characterized them. If, as regards human action, these theses have largely the same influence on action as determinism proper does, then it would be helpful to incorporate them into the mix. One way to do this is to amend "determinism" to encapsulate these broader theories of the natural order. So, treat "determinism*" as the thesis that determinism is true, or that instead almost-determinism, mechanism, or naturalism is true. We can then further expand the free will problem with F2 as follows:[8]

1.   Determinism* is true.
2.   At least some persons have free will.
3.   Free will is incompatible with determinism*.

Although we regard F2 as an improvement over F1, we will return to formulating further problems just in terms of determinism rather than determinism*. One reason for this is because other philosophers tend to think about the free will issue by working with puzzles formulated in terms of determinism strictly defined. But another reason, as will become clear shortly, is that certain ways of developing the problem involve careful expression of what possibilities are consistent with an agent's acting other than as she does. It is easier to think clearly about these issues when we have a precise way of thinking about what physical possibilities determinism leaves open, given the past and the laws. More permissive theories of what is physically possible, as would be the case with almost-determinism, mechanism, or naturalism, would not allow us to easily model these physical possibilities. So, while F2 is an improvement over F1, we will stick with F1 in order to simplify further issues. But readers should bear in mind that a more accurate way of thinking about these issues ought to make room for the apparent threat posed to free will not just by determinism but also by determinism*.

Now consider free will itself. What presumed features of acting freely appear to be under threat by the contention that determinism is true? There are at least two different ways to think about free will and about the free acts that are exercises of it. Perhaps the most familiar and pervasive way to think of such freedom is in terms of control over alternative pathways into the future, initiated by alternative acts (broadly construed to include omissions). On this model, the future can be pictured as a garden of forking paths. An agent's relation to the future, by way of her free will is a function of the leeway she has to act in ways that involve taking different paths. True, a free agent's future possibilities are not unconstrained; the past and the laws of nature structure the potential range of possibilities. But for a free agent, on this model, there is more than one, and the agent has a kind of control over which ways, within these constraints, she might act. Consider, then, Figure 2.1, representing the *Garden of Forking Paths* Model and what we shall call *leeway freedom*.[9]

The single, straight arrow to the left of the asterisk represents a free agent's past, moving from left (earlier) to right (later). Treat the dot itself as an "action

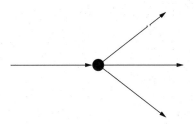

Past   Future

Figure 2.1

node" that identifies a potential locus of free will, a point at which an agent is just then able to exercise her free will ability and act freely within the leeway remaining open by the various paths. Her relation to her future, on this model, is one of an agent navigating her life, shaping her path into the future, and deciding for herself how she will live and indeed how she will be.

Using the Garden of Forking Paths Model to help represent leeway freedom, we can now set out one important problem for free will. Here is an expanded version of F1, namely F3:

1. Determinism is true.
2. At least some persons have free will.
3. Free will requires the ability to do otherwise.
4. The ability to do otherwise is incompatible with determinism.

This formulation, F3, allows us to fix on this problem: Is determinism incompatible with the ability to do otherwise?

Now consider a different way to think about free will. First, start with a typical exercise of agency by a person, setting aside the issue of freedom for a moment. An agent's action, as an event with which she is intimately connected, differs from all sorts of other events that might be part of her life. The warm sun shining on her face and the beating of her heart are events over which in a clear sense she has no control. But now consider her actions. It is an interesting question in its own right what distinguishes actions as events from other sorts of events. But however that is settled, it is also the case that in certain sorts of situations, an agent's actions are also not events over which she has control. A visceral reaction to a spider, for instance, can be an act over which an agent has no control. But on other occasions, events issue from agency in a way that involves an agent's control over those events. Recall again Kane's businesswoman and her being torn about what to do. On the Garden of Forking Paths Model we'd fix on her choosing among a number of options, and in doing so we might highlight considerations of leeway freedom. However, instead we might fix on another dimension of her freedom. In her making a choice, say to stay and help the victim of the assault, she is the source of her so acting. She brings it about and thereby settles her indecision about what to do. If in this way it was up to her, she then acted freely as the source—the initiating source—of her action. So, consider Figure 2.2 representing the *Source Model* of freedom and what we shall call *source freedom*.

The arrow to the left of the dot represents a free agent's past. The "x" just above the asterisk is an event that is not an action that simply happens to the agent, like the event of the sun warming her face. The "+" that is embedded in the agent's past prior to the dot is a compulsive act that the agent was not able to control and so did not freely initiate. Suppose maybe she is a compulsive hand washer and "+" picks out an event in which she unfreely washed her hand. The point at which the dot is placed, just after the arrow's point, as in the previous model, represents an action node that is an occasion for a free act. Now treat the

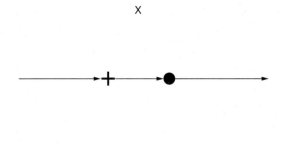

Past   Future

Figure 2.2

dot itself as representing the agent's initiation of her being the source of that act, and in this way, acting freely. Then the line to the right of the dot is the agent's future that unfolds, in part, as a product of her so acting.

Using the Source Model to help represent source freedom, we can now develop a free will problem that allows us to focus more directly on one interesting aspect of freedom. Here, now, is an expanded version of F1, namely, F4:

1. Determinism is true.
2. At least some persons have free will.
3. Free will requires that an agent is able to be the initiating source of her actions.
4. The ability to be the initiating source of actions is incompatible with determinism.

This formulation, F4, allows us to fix upon another problem: Is determinism incompatible with the agent's being the appropriate source of her actions?

Each of these models and each way of thinking about free will gives rise to distinct philosophical problems. In each case it appears that determinism is incompatible with the sort of freedom highlighted. On the first, if according to determinism the past and the laws render only one future physically possible, then it seems that it is settled at the moment of an agent's putatively free act which branch she will take into the future. If so, the previous diagram, adjusted to assume that determinism is true, seems misleading. Other than the path the agent takes, the other paths should somehow be represented as closed down or not really connected to the agent's past and present. We could do this with a break in the lines representing the paths not taken. See Figure 2.3.

On the second, if according to determinism the past and laws render only one future physically possible, then it seems that it is settled in the past what an agent does at any time, and she is not the source of her acts. Sufficient initiating conditions were set in motion long before she was born. If so, the previous diagram, adjusted to assume that determinism is true, is misleading. The act that is the agent's allegedly free act should be represented instead as another "+" rather

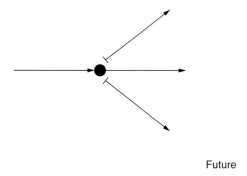

Past   Future

Figure 2.3

than as a dot, since it cannot represent a moment at which a free agent is the initiating source of her free act. The model would look as shown in Figure 2.4.

Each of these ways of theorizing about freedom can be superimposed so that
the freedom that matters for free will is understood as requiring both the leeway
facet and the source facet of freedom. But it is useful to distinguish the two, and
at least to remain open to the possibility that the solutions might turn out to be
slightly different. Perhaps, for instance, it might be established that determinism
is incompatible with leeway freedom but is not incompatible with source
freedom. The salient point here is that a solution to one problem should not be
assumed to align with the solution to another.

The preceding formulations F3 and F4 can actually be expanded yet further,
and for a useful purpose. Thus, we might further revise F3 with F5 as follows:

1. Determinism is true.
2. At least some persons are morally responsible for what they do.
3. Moral responsibility requires free will.
4. Free will requires the ability to do otherwise.
5. The ability to do otherwise is incompatible with determinism.

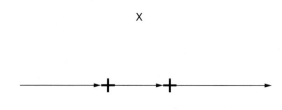

Past   Future

Figure 2.4

And we might further revise F4 with F6:

1. Determinism is true.
2. At least some persons are morally responsible for what they do.
3. Moral responsibility requires free will.
4. Free will requires that an agent is able to be the initiating source of her actions.
5. The ability to be the initiating source of actions is incompatible with determinism.

So thus far, we have formulated two problems concerning free will, resulting in F5 and F6 by attending to different facets of freedom and then considering the relation between them and determinism. But there is a less frequently recognized set of free will problems that arise, not from the concern that determinism is true, but from the worry that indeterminism is true. We turn to a brief examination of this topic.

Suppose, as would satisfy the demands of libertarians, that indeterminism is true and that the way that it is true involves suitably located indeterministic breaks just where free acts might arise, and that they occur at the macro-level, high enough to be significant for choosing and acting. Such a position faces the following challenge. If an agent's actions are not determined by events, states, and processes just prior to her acting as she does, then it seems that when she acts as she does, it "just happened" that she acted that way, and that the very same antecedent conditions prior to her acting are consistent with her acting some other way instead. Consider an agent just prior to her free act, with all of her preferences and reasons as factors bearing upon her future action. Imagine her deliberating about what to decide or choose. All of this, just prior to her free act of choosing could be just as it was, not a single thing about her would be different, including the content of her deliberations, and if she were not determined to act "freely" when she acted, then there is nothing we can say about any feature of her at all that settles that she acted as she did rather than some other way. It was, after all, not determined by any of those conditions (along with the rest of the state of the world and the laws of nature). Suppose, for instance, that the person we are imagining is from Kane's example of a businesswoman (introduced in Section 1.2) considering whether to help a person being mugged or instead rush off to an important business meeting. If there is nothing about her that settles how she decides, then it is just luck how she winds up choosing— mere chance. And now the worry presents itself: mere luck, mere chance does not enhance freedom or control—it undermines it. Indeterminism, the worry goes, is *incompatible* with free will.

Consider the leeway view of freedom. It might be thought that with determinism out of the way and future options for a free agent open in the sense that more than one is physically possible given the past and the laws, this would make having leeway freedom a breeze. But that now seems too fast. Allowing that other physical possibilities are not ruled out by the past and the laws does not establish that an agent has an ability to settle which of those options is realized. The worry here is that there are options that are physically open or possible, but that nothing about the agent would allow her to settle which option is realized. Dumb luck would be in the driver's seat, and not the agent. Here, then, is a formulation of a structurally similar problem to F5, namely, F7:

1. Indeterminism is true.
2. At least some persons are morally responsible for what they do.
3. Moral responsibility requires free will.
4. Free will requires the ability to do otherwise.
5. The ability to do otherwise is incompatible with indeterminism.

A similar case can be made for thinking about source freedom. An agent's being an initiating source of her action cannot be something that just happens to her. Here, then, is a formulation of a structurally similar problem to F6, F8:

1. Indeterminism is true.
2. At least some persons are morally responsible for what they do.
3. Moral responsibility requires free will.
4. Free will requires that an agent is able to be the initiating source of her actions.
5. The ability to be the initiating source of actions is incompatible with indeterminism.

Our goal in this section has been to make clear that the free will problem is better understood as a set of problems. Some will dispute how we have developed some of these formulations. For instance, we think it reasonable to join questions of free will to the topic of moral responsibility, and so we built F5 and F6 from F3 and F4. But those who disagree with us about the significance of moral responsibility will insist that the latter iterations F5 and F6 (as well as F7 and F8) are unnecessary and misleading. Others will also contend that we can get all of the features of action that matter for free will just out of the leeway feature of action. On this view, free will is the ability to do otherwise, and so a formulation like F3 is where discussion of formulating the free will problem should stop. But here we think it most fruitful to frame the range of free will problems that have been formulated in the literature, and we commend F5 through F8 as a useful way to understand some important contemporary work on this topic.[10]

2.4. Situating Compatibilism and Incompatibilism

We close this chapter with some broad brush strokes intended to situate the range of views we have covered. One way to understand the dispute between compatibilists and incompatibilists, as facing problems such as those identified in F5 through F8, is in the broader context of how best to negotiate two seemingly conflicting images of the human condition, the scientific and the manifest images. One longstanding philosophical enterprise attempts to sustain and preserve as much of the manifest image of the human condition as possible in the face of ever stronger challenges from the scientific image as it increases its explanatory scope and power. It is, in effect, a *reconciling* enterprise, an enterprise of reconciling the scientific and manifest images of the human condition. This enterprise can be contrasted with two other currents in philosophy, currents moving in one of two different directions. One favors the scientific image and boldly invites rejection of assumptions nested within the manifest image when conflict arises. Another current regards with suspicion the explanatory scope of the scientific image. It suggests that aspects of the manifest image are insulated from the scientific image. We might call these the *supplanting* and the *insulating* enterprises, respectively.

The reconciling, supplanting, and insulating enterprises in relation to the manifest and scientific images of the human condition are reflected in other areas of philosophy outside of the free will debate. For instance, in moral philosophy, there are those who seek to reconcile the moral property of goodness with a naturalized (i.e., scientific) understanding of it (Boyd, 1988; Sturgeon, 1982). There are, as well, those who maintain that goodness can be supplanted by appealing to only non-moral properties, that is, properties suited for the scientific image (Stevenson, 1944). There are still others who maintain that the moral property of goodness can be insulated from accounts that are in any way naturalized (Moore, 1903).

Or consider instead the debate in the philosophy of mind about mental states such as beliefs and desires. Some philosophers of mind embrace the reconciling project of preserving the legitimacy of beliefs and desires while showing them to be consistent with neurobiological explanations of human behavior (Fodor, 1974; Putnam, 1967). Other philosophers argue that appeal to beliefs and desires should be supplanted by appeal to the neurobiological explanations found in our best theories (Churchland, 1981). Yet other philosophers maintain that explanations in terms of beliefs and desires are insulated from any naturalizing account (Swinburne, 2014).

Consider now the various participants in the free will debate in light of the reconciling, supplanting, and insulating strategies. Although speaking in these terms involves generalities subject to qualification and counterexample, the various participants in the debate might be characterized as follows: Compatibilists favor the reconciling enterprise in philosophy. Incompatibilists invite either the supplanting or the insulating strategy. The form of hard determinism or instead hard incompatibilism favors the supplanting of the concepts of free will and moral responsibility in favor of a scientifically oriented image of the human condition.[11] The form of libertarianism favors insulating free will from any naturalizing threat, thereby protecting an important dimension of the manifest image from a complete scientific explanation of human conduct.[12]

We wish to emphasize that the remarks in the preceding paragraphs were meant only as generalities designed to aid in situating compatibilism and incompatibilism within broader philosophical currents. To correct any misimpressions, it should be noted that some of the best work done by recent libertarians and hard incompatibilists conflicts with the preceding remarks. For instance, many recent libertarian writers are careful to offer accounts of free will that are designed to fit with some form of probabilistic (event) causation, a form of explanation which, they reasonably maintain, is consistent with the best natural science has to offer (for instance, see Balaguer, 2010; Kane, 1996). These libertarians will argue that they in no way seek to partition off free will from the framework of the rest of scientific theory. Similarly, some hard incompatibilist writers have been very conservative in their supplanting approach, making sure to be highly selective of how much of the manifest image needs supplanting (Pereboom, 2001, 2014). Where, previously, hard determinists seemed to suggest that a great deal of the manifest image should go (for instance, all concepts of human dignity and worth, meaning in life, moral truth, and more), recently, hard incompatibilists have argued that only very little needs to be excised (the concepts of free will and moral responsibility on just one understanding and some justifications of punishment).

But despite these qualifications, these recent incompatibilists, both the libertarians and the hard incompatibilists, are committed to the view that the explanatory basis of free will and free action cannot be deterministic or near-deterministic. Granted, many contemporary libertarians are cautious in accounting for free will in ways consistent with the scientific image. And many contemporary hard incompatibilists reject the sort of free will required for accountability while preserving as much of the manifest image as possible. All the same, both of these camps are committed to the view that one plausible way in which human behavior might be brought about—deterministically—is incompatible with the sort of free will at issue in the debate. Compatibilists, then, are the most liberal in their efforts to advance the reconciling enterprise as regards the relation between the scientific and manifest images of the human condition.

Suggestions for Further Reading

For clarification about what compatibilism and incompatibilism are, see the entries on these topics in the *Stanford Encyclopedia of Philosophy*:

Clarke, Randolph, and Justin Capes. 2013. "Incompatibilist (Nondeterministic) Theories of Free Will." *Stanford Encyclopedia of Philosophy*. http://plato.stanford.edu/entries/incompatibilism-theories/.
McKenna, Michael, and D. Justin Coates. 2015. "Compatibilism." *Stanford Encyclopedia of Philosophy*. http://plato.stanford.edu/entries/compatibilism/.

For other helpful introductions to the free will problem, some as book-length treatments and others as chapters, see, for instance:

Haji, Ishtiyaque. 2009. *Incompatibilism's Allure*. Peterborough, Ontario: Broadview Press.

Kane, Robert. 2005. *A Contemporary Introduction to Free Will*. New York: Oxford University Press.

Strawson, P.F. 1992. "Freedom and Necessity," Chapter 10, *Analysis and Metaphysics: An Introduction to Philosophy*. Oxford: Oxford University Press.

Timpe, Kevin. 2008. *Free Will: Sourcehood and Its Alternatives*. New York: Continuum Press.

van Inwagen, Peter. 1993. "The Powers of Rational Beings: Free Will," Chapter 11, *Metaphysics*. Boulder, CO: Westview Press.

For a spirited essay criticizing our preferred way of framing the free will problem, see:

van Inwagen, Peter. 2008. "How to Think About the Problem of Free Will." *Journal of Ethics* 12 (3–4): 327–41.

For an excellent book-length treatment that builds on van Inwagen's way of framing the free will problem, see:

Vihvelin, Kadri. 2013. *Causes, Laws, & Free Will: Why Determinism Doesn't Matter*. New York: Oxford University Press.

Notes

1 Some philosophers pry apart the conditions for free will and the conditions for moral responsibility in a way that would make possible incompatibilism about free will and compatibilism about moral responsibility. They make a considerable deal about there being different compatibility questions. (Of course, philosophers who argue this way would not do so by treating free will in terms of being a necessary condition for moral responsibility.)

2 An even stronger version of soft determinism includes the thesis that free will *requires* determinism (Hobart, 1934; Hume, 1748). The truth of indeterminism would, on this view, undermine free will.

3 For example, see David Lewis, who explicitly distinguishes compatibilism from soft determinism, and claims that while he is a compatibilist, he is not a soft determinist (Lewis, 1981).

4 It is easy to be misled by the language of hard and soft determinism into thinking that the words "hard" and "soft" modify determinism, so that, if determinism is true, on the hard approach, that means that events are determined in an especially strict or strong or tough way; whereas, if determinism is true on the soft approach, that means that events that are determined are determined in a gentler way, perhaps by there being some permissible range of outcomes but not that many. This is a misunderstanding to be avoided. On either soft determinism or hard determinism, there is no variation in what it is for something to be determined; it's that it is the only thing that was physically possible, given the past and the laws. The variation on these competitor views—hard or soft—is only about what conclusions we should draw, given the assumption of determinism regarding freedom and responsibility, not about how "hard" or "soft" the thesis of determinism is.

5 See Wilfred Sellars (1966: 145).

6 This is how Peter van Inwagen reasons (1983: 206–8). He concludes, on the basis of these reflections, that he has reason to believe that determinism is false since he has reason to believe that there is free will, and that incompatibilism is true.

7 Some cautious libertarians do their best to avoid this implication. For an exemplar effort, see Kane (1996).

8 This is similar to how Mark Balaguer formulates the free will problem (2010: 1–15). We find Balaguer's formulation especially instructive in this regard and commend it to others interested in thinking further about how to formulate the free will problem.

9 For a similar diagram, see van Inwagen (1993: 184).

10 There are further puzzles about free agency that the preceding treatment was not able to capture, and this suggests that there are yet other ways to formulate free will problems. For example, one way to theorize about a person's freedom is in terms of her ability to do what she judges best to do under the pressure of her desires and the forces of her internal psychology when these seem incongruent with these judgments. Is a person free to act contrary to, for example, her strongest desires? Can she act contrary to the way her own psychological structure orients her in how she acts? Maybe there is a way to press these questions into the models and formulations of problems set out above. But it seems strained. Here, we have slightly different questions that might need to be approached by thinking in terms of slightly different problems. We'll not pursue this further in the pages to follow, but we do wish to note it as a further possibility.

11 For example, see B.F. Skinner (1971) and Paul Edwards (1958). A word of caution: In some fields outside of philosophy, mostly in the social sciences, it is typically assumed that free will resists *any* scientific approach to human conduct. That is, it is assumed that the only way to treat free will is by way of the supplanting or the insulating strategies. Naturally, wishing to advance their discipline, they tend toward the supplanting strategy. These scholars therefore tend to see free will only in incompatibilist terms, and do not consider the compatibilist's reconciling stance toward free will, a stance that embraces an explanation of free will and free action that is nested within a scientific framework making use of causal explanation. Psychology textbooks, for instance, typically express a view like this. Here is one representative passage:

> If human beings have some degree of freedom of choice, then a psychological system based on strict determinism cannot do justice to its subject matter. On the other hand, if causality is to be found in all natural processes, including human behavior, then belief in freedom of choice is unwarranted and may even work against our progress in understanding human experience and behavior. (Viney, 1993: 27)

The author continues:

> The doctrine of free will is the philosophical position that assumes that human beings make choices that are, to some degree, independent of antecedent conditions. The doctrine assumes that there is some sense in which the integrated personality can rise above genetic, chemical, physical, and social influences. (Ibid.)

As illustrated in these passages, the central conceptual mistake these scholars seem to make is that free will *means* that an agent's conduct is not caused or determined, and hence, that freely willed conduct cannot be nested within any explanatory framework that attempts to explain the causes of it.

12 For instance, the classic libertarian Roderick Chisholm writes:

> If we are responsible [and have free will] … then we have a prerogative which some would attribute only to God: each of us, when we act, is a prime mover unmoved. In doing what we do, we cause certain events to happen, and nothing—no one—causes us to cause those things to happen. (1964, cited from Watson, 1982: 32; our brackets)

3 Classical Compatibilism and Classical Incompatibilism

We devote this chapter to the classical free will debate. The classical debate is characterized by a collection of assumptions and arguments that in more recent times have been either rejected or substantially attenuated. Rather than attempt to state here at the outset what these assumptions and arguments are, we shall instead set out and critically assess the main contours of the classical compatibilist and the classical incompatibilist positions. In the course of doing so, the relevant assumptions and arguments distinctive of the classical debate will become clear. We'll then close the chapter with some reflections on these matters.

The classical debate persisted until the late 1960s, when three major influences radically altered the philosophical discussion of free will and moral responsibility. We'll take up each of these three influences in Chapters 4 through 6. In this chapter, we set out the classical debate by reference to various historical figures reaching back to the early modern era, but mostly in terms of how the free will debate came to have the shape it did arising out of the heyday of analytic philosophy in the first half of the twentieth century. This will set the stage for our discussion of contemporary work in subsequent chapters.

Both compatibilism and incompatibilism have been richly represented in the history of philosophy. As for compatibilism, the Stoics, Augustine, Hobbes, Leibniz, Hume, and Mill all endorsed it, as did the early American philosopher Jonathan Edwards. Historically, classical compatibilism was most thoroughly defended in the writings of Hobbes and Hume. It was later adopted by early twentieth-century analytic philosophers such as G.E. Moore, R.E. Hobart, Moritz Schlick, C.L. Stevenson, P.H. Nowell-Smith, and A.J. Ayer. Historically, classical incompatibilism was most thoroughly defended by Scotus, Ockham, Suarez, Spinoza, and Reid, while Lucretius, Berkeley, Holbach, (arguably) Kant, Schopenhauer, Nietzsche, and James also endorsed it. Sartre was an incompatibilist, and while incompatibilism was the minority position in mainstream analytic philosophy prior to the late 1960s, it had a number of able defenders, including C.A. Campbell, C.D. Broad, Paul Edwards, Richard Taylor, and Roderick Chisholm.[1]

We begin with examining the case for classical compatibilism.

3.1. The Case for Classical Compatibilism

Classical compatibilism is associated with at least four theses. One proposes a lean account of freedom. A second declares that the free will problem is illusory since it rests entirely on a set of conceptual confusions or on the misappropriation of several terms. A third claims that indeterminism would in fact undermine free will and moral responsibility. A fourth involves an attempt to explain how an agent could be free to do otherwise even if she were determined to do what she did. In this section, we'll discuss the first three. In Section 3.2 we'll discuss the fourth.

3.1.1. Classical Compatibilists' Account of Freedom

According to the classical compatibilist, the free will at issue in the debate is an agent's ability to act and to refrain from acting unencumbered, that is, free from impediments that would stand in her way. The core idea is that free will consists in the absence of impediments both to making a choice and to refraining from doing so.

A major component of this conception of free will is the notion of doing what one wants to do without impediment (a further component, the notion of doing otherwise without impediment, will be discussed below).[2] Hobbes wrote that a person's freedom consists in his finding "no stop, in doing what he has the will, desire, or inclination to doe."[3] This notion involves two aspects, a positive and a negative one. The positive aspect is doing what one wills, desires, or inclines to. The negative aspect—finding "no stop"—consists in acting unencumbered or unimpeded. The classical compatibilists' benchmark of impeded or encumbered action is compelled action. Compelled action paradigmatically arises when one is forced by some external source to act contrary to one's will.

Classical compatibilism is associated with the thesis that the only freedom worthy of attention is *freedom of action*, and with the idea of *freedom of will* being incoherent.[4] Consider, for example, Locke's remark about the question of freedom of will:

> I leave it to be considered whether it may not help to put an end to that long agitated, and I think unreasonable, because unintelligible, question, *viz. whether a man's will be free, or no.* For if I am not mistaken ... the question is itself altogether improper; and it is insignificant to ask, whether a man's *will* be free, as to ask, whether his sleep be swift, or his virtue square: *liberty* being as little applicable to will, as swiftness of motion is to sleep, or squareness to virtue.... *Liberty*, which is but a power, belongs only to agents, and cannot be an attribute or modification of the *will*, which is also but a power.[5]

Locke wanted to jettison talk of freedom of will, speaking instead only of the freedom of agents. Contrary to Locke, however, other classical compatibilists explicitly endorsed an account that retains the term "free will," even though they shared Locke's concern that attributing freedom to the will itself was problematic. For instance, Hobbes writes:

> From the use of the word *Free-will*, no liberty can be inferred of the will, desire, or inclination, but the Liberty of the man; which consisteth in this, that he finds no stop in doing what he has the will, desire, or inclination to doe.[6]

Hobbes's claim is that free will is in fact a condition of action, and not a condition of will.[7] Regardless of whether classical compatibilism is better described as forsaking the notion of free will (as Locke advises), or instead as offering a deflationary account of it (as Hobbes suggests), the classical compatibilists were in agreement that the freedom at issue did not modify a condition of willing. Whatever control is relevant for freedom, it is taken to be mistaken to think in terms of a person's freedom or control over her will; the right way to think of it is as freedom of action.

To avoid confusion generated by the use of differing formulations, let us, with Hobbes, characterize the freedom pertinent to classical compatibilism as free will, keeping in mind that this notion is meant to be a deflationary one that attributes nothing special to the will itself. We'll define the first major component of it as follows: *the unencumbered ability of an agent to do what she wants.*[8] It is plausible to assume that this component of free will, so understood, is compatible with determinism since the truth of determinism allows for agents to do what they want to do unencumbered. It's consistent with determinism, for example, that an agent who wants to leave the room faces no impediments in doing so—that there are, for example, no chains holding him back.

The classical compatibilist account of free will is often characterized as specifying only *negative freedom*, as opposed to *positive freedom*. This might seem puzzling since this account does feature both a positive aspect (doing what one wants) and a negative aspect (being unencumbered). But according to this other characterization, a positive account would analyze the requisite freedom by attributing a power to the will itself, or to the agent who acts a power over and above what is involved in the power to do what one wants. The classical compatibilists would reject any such proposal. On their view, given an agent's ability to act according to her desires, no other positive power needs to be added to it.

In advancing their account of free will, the classical compatibilists sometimes distinguished between the *liberty of spontaneity* and the *liberty of indifference*. The liberty of spontaneity just is the freedom to act as one wants without an impediment. The liberty of indifference requires the ability to act without the causal determination of a motivational state such as a desire. (We'll discuss this in more detail below.) Liberty of spontaneity, on the other hand, is compatible with causal determination, since determination does not imply that no person ever acts unencumbered. As might be expected, the classical compatibilists, while embracing liberty of spontaneity, rejected outright liberty of indifference.

How convincing is the classical compatibilist account of free will as free action? As it stands, it demands refinement. To cite one concern, an agent might have certain compulsive desires, and when she acts on those desires, she intuitively acts as she wants, and she might do so unencumbered. Yet it would seem that in such cases the agent does not act of her own free will. For example, imagine a person suffering from a powerful neurosis acts in ways that, upon subsequent calm reflection, she herself finds alien. Other examples might involve cases of drug addiction or action under enormous duress, such as in a time of war. Careful qualification, it might be thought, could rule out these deviant cases while retaining the modest sort of account of free will the classical compatibilist favors.[9]

3.1.2.   The Free Will Problem as a Pseudo-Problem

One striking feature of the classical compatibilists was their bold presumption that their account bears virtually no burden of proof. Common sense, ordinary language, and careful thought, they believed, all spoke only on behalf of the compatibilist position. On their view, the only considerations favoring incompatibilism arose from conceptual confusions or the misappropriation of terms. Once these missteps were laid bare and the terms clearly articulated, any apparent "free will problem" would vanish, exposed as the pseudo-problem that clearheaded compatibilist thinking takes it to be. This attitude is found in the opening remarks of Moritz Schlick's (1939) essay, "When is a Man Responsible?" Schlick titled the opening section, "The Pseudo-Problem of Freedom of the Will," and began as follows:

> With hesitation and reluctance I prepare to add this chapter to the discussion of ethical problems. For in it I must speak of a matter which, even at present, is thought to be a fundamental ethical question, but which got into ethics and has become a much discussed problem only because of a misunderstanding. (54)

Schlick went on to credit Hume with having put the free will problem to rest years ago, and complains that its survival well past Hume's time was a scandal.

What were these alleged misunderstandings? The classical compatibilists accused their incompatibilist rivals of several, but the most common involved running together the distinction between *causation* on the one hand and notions such as *compulsion*, *constraint*, and *coercion* on the other. When one is compelled to act in a certain way, for instance, one is forced to act contrary to what one wishes and may well not be free. To be compelled is one way of being caused. Incompatibilists, so the diagnosis went, were guilty of making a false generalization from a certain kind of cause—a compelling, constraining, or coercing cause—which does stand to undermine free will, to any kind of causation undermining free will. The classical compatibilist response is that it is only a certain kind of causation, and not causation per se, that is incompatible with freedom. For example, A.J. Ayer (1954) writes:

[I]t is not … causality that freedom is to be contrasted with, but constraint. And while it is true that being constrained to do an action entails being caused to do it, I shall try to show that the converse does not hold. (In Watson, 1982: 19)

Ayer continues:

If I suffered from a compulsion neurosis, so that I got up and walked across the room, whether I wanted to or not, or if I did so because somebody else compelled me, then I should not be acting freely. But if I did it now, I shall be acting freely, just because these conditions do not obtain: and the fact that my actions have a cause is, from this point of view, irrelevant. For it is not when it has any cause at all, but only a special sort of cause, that it is reckoned not to be free. (In Watson, 1982: 21)

Hume diagnosed another (alleged) incompatibilist mistake as arising from an improper understanding of causation itself:

But being once convinced that we know nothing farther of causation of any kind than constant conjunction of objects, and the consequent inference of the mind from one to another, and finding that these two circumstances are universally allowed to have place in voluntary actions; we may be more easily led to own the same necessity common to all causes.[10]

According to Hume, it is wrong to attribute a necessary connection between a cause and effect, or a causal power inhering in a cause and transmitted to its effect. If causes were like that, Hume thought, it would be reasonable to assume that they would undermine freedom since they would be like compelling forces. But once it is understood that causation involves no more than constant conjunction or regularity among events, and a natural propensity of the mind to infer accordingly, then it becomes clear that an agent's actions can be both free and caused, that is, arising from her desires with regularity.

Further confusions were claimed to arise when insufficient care is taken to understand the nature of the causal laws. For instance, Schlick held that causal laws are descriptions of regularities found in nature. But the laws of a legal system are prescriptive and carry with them a threat if not obeyed. By confusing the natural and legal laws, the classical compatibilists contended, incompatibilists wrongly assumed that actions necessitated by causal laws would amount to threats or forces imposed upon agents against their wills (Schlick, 1939: 65–7).

Yet another classical compatibilist diagnosis of incompatibilist confusion concerns the nature of the self. Some incompatibilists, it was suggested, assumed that a person's self is distinct from a person's causally influenced character. But, it was argued, this was simply a failure to appreciate that a person's self is not distinct from her causally influenced character (Hobart, 1934, in Berofsky, 1966: 66–72). Or instead, it was suggested by some incompatibilists that, by way of a person's self, a person could act "out of character," thereby resisting her natural (that is, causally influenced) inclinations. But, in similar fashion, compatibilists attempted to explain the phenomena of acting out of character by showing that, even in such a case, some aspect of an agent's character figured in the cause of the agent's action.

A final alleged confusion involves a failure to distinguish different kinds of freedom. Hume wrote:

> Few are capable of distinguishing betwixt the liberty of *spontaneity* and the liberty of *indifference*; betwixt that which is oppos'd to violence, and that which means the negation of necessity and causes. The first is even the most common sense of the word; and as 'tis only that species of liberty, which it concerns us to preserve, our thoughts have been principally turn'd towards it, and have almost universally confounded it with the other.[11]

It's clear that we are often free from "violence"—compulsion, constraint, or coercion—and this sort of freedom does not require indeterminism. Some classical compatibilists claim that it's only when we fail to distinguish this kind of freedom from a sort that requires indeterminism that the temptation to incompatibilism arises.

From the contemporary vantage point, the classical compatibilists' contention that incompatibilism rests only on confusions seems somewhat obtuse. It's one thing to claim that a philosophical thesis is false, or is not supported by the best reasons, but it is quite another to suggest that no good reasons speak for it at all, that it is, really, a philosophical non-starter. Does incompatibilism rest entirely on confusion, on for instance, a conflation between causation and compulsion? Reflect upon the considerations speaking on behalf of incompatibilism as set out above (in Section 2.3). There, two different intuitive sources for incompatibilism were explored. One had to do with understanding free will in terms of leeway freedom modeled on a garden of forking paths into the future. Another had to do with understanding free will in terms of source freedom. From each intuitive source, and working with the proposition that determinism is true, different formulations of a free will problem were constructed (formulations F5 and F6). Now, perhaps careful thought might reveal that each of these problems can be resolved in favor of a compatibilist conclusion, but it is hard to understand how either of these plausible intuitive sources of incompatibilist concern could be explained away in terms of assuming that all causes compel, or by way of any of the other conceptual confusions that classical compatibilists attributed to incompatibilist thinking. The classical compatibilist charge that incompatibilism is all illusion—a mere pseudo-problem—looks to be mostly unsubstantiated polemics, mere bluster that ignores the serious reflections that would give a reasonable and fair-minded inquirer grounds to question whether a determined agent could act with freedom of will.

3.1.3.   Indeterminism's Threat to Free Will and Moral Responsibility

One provocative classical compatibilist objection to incompatibilism, related to their compatibilist protest against liberty of indifference, is that indeterminism does not enhance control. Instead, it would undermine control because it would preclude a sufficiently stable relation between an agent and an action. Hume writes:

> not only 'tis impossible, without the necessary connexion of cause and effect in human actions, that punishments cou'd be inflicted compatible with justice and moral equity; but also that it cou'd ever enter into the thoughts of any reasonable being to inflict them. The constant and universal object of hatred and anger is a person or creature endow'd with thoughts and consciousness; and when any criminal or injurious actions excite that passion, 'tis only by their relation to the person or connexion with him. But according to the doctrine of liberty or chance, this connexion is reduc'd to nothing, nor are men more accountable for those actions, which are designed or premeditated, than for the most casual and accidental. Actions are by their very nature temporary and perishing; and where proceed not from some cause in the characters and dispositions of the persons, who perform'd them, they infix not themselves upon him, and can neither redound to his honour, if good, nor infamy, if evil. The action itself may be blameable; it may be contrary to all rules of morality and religion: But the person is not responsible for it; and as it proceeds from nothing in him, that is durable and constant, and leaves nothing of that nature behind, 'tis impossible he can, upon its account, become the object of punishment and vengeance.[12]

The idea is that if the relation between agent and action were indeterministic, the action would be just a random or chance happening, something that cannot warrant attribution of any moral quality in the agent, let alone blaming or punishing the agent. Moral responsibility for an action instead requires that a deterministic causal relation hold between the agent's durable and constant character on the one hand, and her action on the other. If the action were not causally determined by the agent's durable and constant character, then there would be nothing in the agent to which blame and punishment could appropriately be directed.

This argument assumes that there is no relation between an agent and her action sufficient for moral responsibility other than a causally deterministic one, and that the absence of causal determination entails that the action is merely random or a matter of chance.[13] One way that incompatibilists have resisted this argument is by arguing that there can be probabilistic causal relations between events such that causal antecedents need not determine their consequences in order to cause them (Kane, 1996). Another incompatibilist response is to maintain that agents do cause their actions but that agents are not in turn causally determined by anything to cause their actions (Chisholm, 1964; Clarke, 1993;

Griffiths, 2010; O'Connor, 2000; Taylor, 1966, 1974). Yet a third incompatibilist response specifies a non-causal relation between agent and action that at the same time is not merely chance or random (Bergson, 1889; Ginet, 1990; Goetz, 2008; McCann, 1998). In subsequent chapters, we will explore these options in detail.

Suppose, just for argument's sake, that this classical compatibilist argument is sound; indeterminism does rule out free will because the relation between agent and action will then be chance or random and thus preclude the agent's moral responsibility. Would this prove compatibilism true? No. It would only show that no sense is to be made of libertarian (incompatibilist) free will. It is worth keeping in mind that incompatibilism is minimally the thesis that determinism is incompatible with free will. A more substantive incompatibilist thesis would make the further claim that indeterminism *is* compatible with free will. But an incompatibilist need not commit to this latter thesis. One viable option, open to a moral responsibility skeptic or a hard incompatibilist, is to accept the minimal incompatibilist thesis that determinism is incompatible with free will, and to accept as well the compatibilist argument considered here that indeterminism is also incompatible with free will. According to this strategy, free will is incompatible with both determinism *and* indeterminism (e.g., Nagel, 1986; Pereboom, 1995, 2001; Strawson, 1986). In summary, this classical compatibilist argument, while provocative for placing the incompatibilist—and especially the libertarian—on the defensive, does not prove that free will and determinism are compatible. Demonstrating its soundness would not allow the compatibilist to rest her case.

3.2.   The Dispute over the Analyses of "Could Have Done Otherwise"

Consider the following classical incompatibilist objection to the classical compatibilist account of free will set out above, the unencumbered ability of an agent to do as she wants:

> If causal determinism is true, agents are causally determined to act as they do. But then, even if an agent does do what she wants to do, and she acts unencumbered, she still cannot do otherwise – because she is causally determined to act as she does. However, free will requires the freedom to do otherwise. Hence, the classical compatibilist account of free will is inadequate – causal determinism is incompatible with free will because causal determinism is incompatible with the ability to do otherwise.

Is this correct? Is the classical compatibilist account of free will incomplete? Notice that this incompatibilists' objection does not reject the classical compatibilist conditions on free will in terms of acting as one wants unencumbered—conditions cast in terms of *source* freedom. The incompatibilists' concern is a matter of *leeway* freedom. So, as this objection goes, even if acting from one's own uncompelled desires and acting unencumbered are necessary for free will, they will not capture what is required for free will independently of a condition that rules out causal determination. If this is right, the incompatibilist can build off the classical compatibilist account by tacking on a condition that the classical compatibilist cannot accept. Here is what she might specify as an adequate account of a free action:

> An agent acts freely if and only if, (1) she does what she wants; (2) she acts unencumbered; and (3) she could have done otherwise.

Can the classical compatibilist answer this classical incompatibilist objection by showing that, contrary to what the incompatibilist might think, a determined agent can satisfy all three conditions?

Some compatibilists did not take up this incompatibilist challenge. They opted for a *one-way* freedom—source freedom—requiring only that what a person did do, she did unencumbered as an upshot of her own agency. Thus, the one-way compatibilists settled for satisfaction of the conditions 1 and 2 above, while not attempting to account for condition 3. But mainline classical compatibilists took the challenge seriously and argued for *two-way* freedom—that is, leeway freedom. Mainline classical compatibilists defended a Garden of Forking Paths model of control. They responded by accounting for an agent's ability to do otherwise in hypothetical or conditional terms. Here, for example, is how Hume meant to capture the ability to do otherwise:

> By liberty, then, we can only mean a power of acting or not acting, according to the determinations of the will; that is, if we choose to remain at rest, we remain at rest; if we chose to move, we also may. Now this hypothetical liberty is allowed to belong to everyone who is not a prisoner and in chains. Here, then, there is no subject of dispute.[14]

Notice that in this brief passage Hume mentions all three conditions, doing what one wants (in Hume's terms, acting as one chooses); doing so unencumbered (not being a prisoner in chains); and being able to do otherwise, captured hypothetically: if we choose to remain at rest we do, if we choose to move we do. Consider how similar Hume's remarks are in comparison with A.J. Ayer's:

> to say that I could have done otherwise is to say, first, that I should have done otherwise if I had chosen otherwise; secondly, that my action was voluntary ... and thirdly, that nobody compelled me to choose as I did.... When [these three conditions] are fulfilled, I may be said to have acted freely. (Ayer, 1954, in Watson, 1982: 22)

In the early twentieth-century work of various analytic philosophers, beginning with G.E. Moore, and including Ayer, this approach was refined and came to be known as the *conditional analysis of "could have done otherwise."*[15]

The conditional analysis of "could have done otherwise" attempted to analyze any assertion that an agent could have done otherwise as a conditional assertion reporting what an agent would have done under certain counterfactual conditions (conditions different from the specific ones that actually led to her acting as she did). The counterfactual conditions involved variations on what a free agent wanted (or chose, willed, decided) to do at the time of her free action. Suppose that an agent freely performed act X. According to the classical compatibilist analysis, to say that, at the time of acting, she could have performed distinct action Y rather than X is just to say that, *had* she wanted (chosen, willed, or decided) to do Y at that time, *then* she would have done Y. Her ability to have done otherwise than X at the time at which she acted is captured by such a counterfactual truth.

Notice that against this formulation the incompatibilist can press essentially the same objection mentioned above. Given that a determined agent is determined at the time of action to have the wants that she does have, how is it helpful to state what she would have done had she had different wants than the wants that she did have? For one thing, given the truth of determinism, at the time at which she acted, she could have had no other wants than the wants that her causal history determined her to have. How is this counterfactual ability more than a hollow freedom? How is this analysis supposed to answer the incompatibilist's objection?

Before considering the compatibilist answer to this incompatibilist challenge, it is worth pointing out that, *if* the relevant "could have done otherwise" statements are rightly interpreted as counterfactual conditionals, then it is clear that they *do not* conflict with the truth of determinism. This is so for two reasons. First, determinism is a thesis about what future will unfold *given a specific past*, for example, given specific past wants. Determinism does not deny that, with a different past, a different future would unfold. Hence, it does not deny that, along with other conditions of the state of the world at a time, different wants would causally determine an agent to act other than the way she acted in the actual world.

Second, causal determinism is a thesis that invokes natural laws, laws that specify general causal patterns, regularities, or structures confirmed by the history of the natural world. These patterns include more in their scope than merely truths about what does happen. They also include truths about what is causally possible, which involve truths about what would happen under varying conditions. Consider a simple causal law specifying that salt dissolves in water under certain conditions. Note that a natural law that specifies a regularity in the interaction of salt and water is just as applicable to salt that is not currently placed in water as it is to salt that is so placed. The salt in one's salt shaker, for instance, is such that *if it were placed in water, then it would dissolve*. That truth is in turn indicative of the salt's *disposition* to respond in certain ways to certain causal factors. Similarly, to the extent that a statement of an agent's ability to do otherwise can be analyzed as a counterfactual conditional about what an agent would have done under different conditions, it is indicative of dispositions of agents. Our having such dispositions does not clearly conflict with the truth of determinism, since it's open that the laws that govern them are deterministic.

For the reasons just adumbrated, the classical compatibilists made much hang on the success of their conditional analysis. But the question remains, could it speak to the incompatibilist objection presented above? If an agent is determined to have the wants she has, and if these wants determine her to act as she does act, how does it aid her free will for it to be true that, with a different causal history giving rise to different wants, she would have acted differently?

The compatibilist will reply that such counterfactuals effectively locate the action-generating capacities of free agents. To illustrate, suppose that Jasmine, a free agent, lives in a deterministic world, and in that world at a certain time, say April 20, 1984 at precisely 4:20 p.m., she does exactly as she wants in purchasing the Bob Marley album, *Exodus*. Imagine that, just prior to this, say between 4:10 and 4:19 p.m., she deliberated over whether to purchase the Marley album or instead one of three other albums she had recently heard, the Rolling Stones album *Exile on Main Street*, the John Coltrane album *Blue Train*, or the Muddy Waters album *King Bee*. She could only purchase one since she did not have enough money to purchase more than one. Grant that when she purchases the Marley album she does so unencumbered. She is not constrained, coerced, or compelled by an overwhelming desire to spend all of her cash. She just does what normally functioning agents do. She acts. But she lives at a deterministic world. Hence, the facts of the past, facts made true long before her birth, combined with laws of nature, laws that she cannot alter, entail that at that moment in time, Jasmine will buy that Marley album. It seems that given that exact past and those very laws, she has no alternative to buying that album.

So how will the conditional analysis of ability help the compatibilist to claim in a convincing way that Jasmine could have done otherwise? One of the facts of the past relevant to the time of Jasmine's purchase is that, just prior to that time, at 4:19 and 30 seconds, she wanted to purchase that Marley album more than she wanted to purchase the other albums that she was considering. That is one of the facts figuring into the deterministic causal history giving rise to Jasmine's act. But imagine that she instead did not want most to purchase that Marley album and that she instead preferred to purchase the Rolling Stones album. One might also imagine that she preferred the Muddy Waters album, or the Coltrane album, or that she wanted not to make any purchase after all, wishing instead to save her money. Let's also suppose that unbeknownst to her the store she was shopping in had in stock only two of these other albums, the Stones and the Coltrane album, but were out of the Muddy Waters album. Even though it is true that Jasmine was determined to purchase that Marley album just when she did, and this fact is entailed by the facts of the past and the laws of nature, here are several other counterfactual claims involving Jasmine that are also true at 4:20 on April 20, 1984:

1. If she had wanted to purchase the Stones album, she would have purchased it.

2. If she had wanted to purchase the Coltrane album, she would have purchased it.
3. If she had wanted to purchase no album at all, saving her money instead, she would have refrained from making any purchase.

Here now are several false claims regarding what it was within Jasmine's capability to do at 4:20 on April 20, 1984:

1. If she had wanted to purchase the Muddy Waters album, she would have purchased it.
2. If she had wanted to purchase more than one album, she would have purchased more than one album.
3. If she had wanted to purchase the Moby album, *Play*, released in 2000, then she would have purchased it.
4. If she had wanted to fly like a bird to Tangier, she would have flown like a bird to Tangier.

These true and the false counterfactuals track the actions that were within, and were not within, Jasmine's ability to act at the time of her purchase—or so says the classical compatibilist. According to the classical compatibilist, this is adequate to show what Jasmine was freely able to do from what she was not freely able to do at the time she made her purchase: She was free to buy the Coltrane album, the Stones album, or no album at all. At the time she purchased the Marley album, she could have done otherwise in any of these ways. But she was not free to purchase the Muddy Waters album at that time since the store did not have it available. She was not free to purchase more than one album, because at the time of her purchase she did not have enough money for more than one album. She was not free to buy the Moby album since, in 1984, the 2000 released Moby album did not exist. She was also not free to fly like a bird to Tangier, because she did not have wings, etc.

Notice that any one of the false counterfactuals listed above could be amended to be made true. For instance, if the first were revised to read "If she had wanted to purchase the Muddy Waters album, *and if the store did have the album in stock*, she would have purchased it," it would come out true and not false. But to make it true, the counterfactual conditions require that the description of the actual world in which Jasmine purchased the Marley album be amended in ways having nothing to do with Jasmine's wants at the time of her acting. According to the classical compatibilist, for it to be true that she could have acted of her own free will in some manner other than the way in which she did act, the only thing that can explain why she did not act that way is that she did not want to. There was nothing other than her preferences that prevented that alternative outcome from having been the actual outcome.

How might the classical compatibilist reply to the classical incompatibilist challenge that the conditional analysis offers only a hollow freedom? She can maintain that, in assessing an agent's action, the analysis accurately distinguishes between those actions she would have performed if she wanted, and those actions she would not have performed even if she wanted. This, the classical compatibilist will maintain, effectively distinguishes between those alternative courses of action that were within the genuine scope of the agent's abilities at the time of action, from those courses of action that were not within the scope of the agent's abilities at the time of action. And this just is the distinction between what an agent was free to do at the time of action and what she was not free to do at the time of action. This is not at all a hollow freedom; it demarcates what persons have within their control from what falls outside that purview.

Despite the classical compatibilists' ingenuity, their analysis of *could have done otherwise* is generally regarded as unsuccessful (see Lehrer, 1968, 1976, 1980). The classical compatibilists wanted to show their incompatibilist interlocutors that when one asserted that a free agent had alternatives available to her—that is, when it was asserted that she could have done otherwise—that assertion could be analyzed as a conditional statement, a statement that is perspicuously compatible with determinism. But as it turned out, the analysis was refuted when it was shown that the conditional statements sometimes yielded the improper verdict that a person was able to do otherwise despite that at the time the person acted, she had no such alternative and therefore was not able to do otherwise (Chisholm, 1964, in Watson, 1982: 26–7; van Inwagen, 1983: 114–19; Lehrer, 1968). Here is such an example:

> Suppose that Danielle is psychologically incapable of wanting to touch a blond-haired dog. Imagine that, on her sixteenth birthday, unaware of her condition, her father brings to her two puppies to choose between, one being a blond labrador, the other a black labrador. He tells Danielle just to pick up whichever of the two she pleases and that he will return the other puppy to the pet store. Danielle happily, and unencumbered, does what she wants and picks up the black lab.

When Danielle picked up the black lab, was she able to pick up the blond lab by choosing to do so? It seems not. Choosing to pick up the blond lab was an alternative that was not available to her. In this respect, *she could not have done otherwise*. Given her psychological condition, she cannot even form a want to touch a blond lab, hence she could not choose to pick one up. But notice that, *if* she wanted to choose to pick up the blond lab (more than she wanted to pick up the black one), *then she would have done so*. Of course, if she wanted to pick up the blond lab, then she would not suffer from the very psychological disorder that resulted in her being unable even to want to pick up blond-haired dogs. So the classical compatibilist analysis of "could have done otherwise" fails: the analysis delivers the verdict that when Danielle picked up the black lab she *was* able to pick up the blonde lab, even though, due to her psychological condition, she *was not* able to do so in the relevant respect.[16]

So it appears that the classical compatibilist attempt to answer the incompatibilist objection fails. Since, as the objection goes, free will requires access to alternative possibilities, the classical compatibilist hasn't yet provided a success-ful determinism-friendly account of free will.

3.3.   The Case for Classical Incompatibilism

The case for classical incompatibilism can now be set out rather economically. Much of its content builds upon the various considerations figuring against the case for classical compatibilism, considerations we have just canvassed. Con-sider, for instance, the compatibilist thesis that the core notion of acting freely is doing what one wants unencumbered. The weakness in such a thesis, as noted above (Section 3.1), is that one's wants might be a source of one's unfreedom insofar as they too might compel a person to act as she does, such as in a case of extreme addiction. The classical incompatibilist can build on the worry arising from compulsive desires, arguing that, under the assumption of determinism, they share something with the altogether ordinary desires involved in any action at all. In particular, they arise from conditions over which an agent has no control. So, for example, in giving voice to a hypothetical hard determinist arguing against a classical compatibilist, Paul Edwards wrote:

> "You are right," he [the hard determinist] would say [to the compatibilist], "in maintaining that some of our actions are caused by our desires and choices. But you do not pursue the subject far enough. You arbitrarily stop at the desires and volitions. We must not stop there. We must go on to ask where *they* come from; and if determinism is true there can be no doubt about the answer to this question. Ultimately our desires and our whole character are derived from our inherited equipment and the environmental influences to which we are subject at the beginning of our lives. It is clear that we had no hand in shaping these." (Edwards, 1957, in Hook, 1958: 121; our brackets)

Note that this classical incompatibilist worry is a matter of source freedom. The root causes of our actions are freedom-defeating under the assumption of determinism.

Now consider the classical incompatibilist worry with respect to leeway freedom. Granting that a person's acting unencumbered from her desires is necessary for her acting freely, it is insufficient, so the classical incompatibilist will argue, if she cannot do other than act on those desires. Here is how Roderick Chisholm expressed the point (he was discussing the case of a murderer who was determined to act as he did):

> For if what we say he did was really something that was brought about by his own beliefs and desires, if these beliefs and desires in the particular situ-ation in which he happened to have found himself caused him to do just what it was that we say he did do, then, since *they* caused it, *he* was unable to do anything other than just what it was that he did do. (Chisholm, 1964, in Watson, 1982: 25)[17]

This classical incompatibilist objection is meant to force upon the compatibilist the burden of accounting for the ability to do otherwise in a deterministic context. But, as we have just explained the debate, it appears that the classical compatibilist case for the compatibility of the ability to do otherwise and determinism decisively failed, and one cannot reductively analyze claims about what an agent can do in terms of claims about what she would do if she were to choose (or want) differently.

Another classical incompatibilist thesis can be cast as a counterpoint to the classical compatibilist thesis that the free will problem is a mere pseudo-problem grounded on nothing more than misunderstanding and a misappropriation of terms. Our assessment of this compatibilist charge was that it amounted to little more than bluster. There are, contrary to what the classical compatibilists claimed, clearly identifiable puzzles about the relation between free will and determinism. A natural classical incompatibilist counterpoint to the pseudoproblem charge is that the classical compatibilists' efforts to establish their thesis by showing how terms like "cause" and "compelled" really function, along with their attempt to analyze "can" as "would ... if ..." amount to no more than a "wretched subterfuge" achieved by "petty word jugglery" (Kant, 1788)—a "quagmire of evasion" (James, 1897). Histrionics aside, the classical incompatibilist charge is that the attempts by compatibilists to locate freedom by advancing complex accounts of the notion of a law, of what a cause is, or how compulsion or coercion are ways of defeating freedom were all beside the rather simple point that transparent features of freedom appear on their face to conflict with the plain contention that if determinism is true only one future is physically possible.

Indeed, there are two very simple arguments that have appeared in slightly different guises in the long history of incompatibilism. Together, they are probably the best way to represent the core theses of classical incompatibilism. Perhaps it will come as no surprise that one features a concern with leeway freedom and the other features a concern with source freedom.[18] So, consider first the Basic Leeway Argument for Incompatibilism (BLI):

1. If a person acts of her own free will, then she could have done otherwise than she actually does.
2. If determinism is true, no one can do otherwise than one actually does.
3. Therefore, if determinism is true, no one acts of her own free will.

And now consider the Basic Source Argument for Incompatibilism (BSI):

1. A person acts of her own free will only if she is its ultimate source.
2. If determinism is true, no one is the ultimate source of her actions.
3. Therefore, if determinism is true, no one acts of her own free will.

However we assess these arguments, there is no reason to complain that their intuitive sources are rooted in mere confusions or conceptual trickery.[19] Both BLI and BSI, or some variations on them, remain to this day as clear ways of capturing core incompatibilist positions. (Perhaps they are better classified as statements of core incompatibilist positions rather than as arguments; as we will see, these statements as they stand do not have much force against compatibilism, nor, arguably, do incompatibilists intend them to.) Indeed, throughout the remainder of this book, we will from time to time make use of these two simple statements as touchstones in the course of assessing more complex controversies between compatibilists and incompatibilists.

3.4.   Classical Incompatibilism and Agent Causation

In the previous section, we canvassed three of the four classical compatibilist theses discussed in this chapter. In each case we used objections to them to unpack the classical incompatibilist position. There is one further classical compatibilist thesis that we have yet to consider. This is the thesis that *indeterminism* is incompatible with free will (and with moral responsibility). While the free will debate is mostly associated with the disputed question of the compatibility of free will and determinism, as the classical compatibilists made clear, there is also a real puzzle about accounting for free will under the assumption that determinism is false. This remains true of the contemporary debate; the puzzle abides.

How did the classical incompatibilist respond to this challenge? That depends on whether the classical incompatibilist was out to defend the reality of free will. Those who were free will and moral responsibility skeptics (e.g., Spinoza or Nietzsche) defended some variation on a hard determinist thesis or instead an impossibilist position, and so were not under pressure to solve this problem. But classical incompatibilists who were also libertarians were forced to take up the challenge.[20] While in the history of the classical debate there was no single general solution to this problem, the view of free will most commonly considered, and the one that to this day remains highly influential, is one that appeals to the notion of *agent causation*. Here, we'll consider the classical incompatibilist appeal to agent causation as a way to counter the charge that free will is incompatible with indeterminism.[21]

To appreciate the proposed solution, it's best to have in mind at least three background suppositions widely shared by those engaged in the classical debate. First, it was assumed that the causal relation involved a kind of necessity or determination: if A causes B, then A causally necessitates or determines B. Second, it was also assumed that if an event did occur without a cause it could not count as the product of an agent's control. Third, the only credible candidate explanation for the occurrence of an event—keeping in mind that actions are events—is that something causes the event. Now, with these three assumptions in mind, consider this passage by Roderick Chisholm, in which he deductively infers that agents must be causes of their (free) acts:

> Perhaps there is less need to argue that the ascription of responsibility also conflicts with an indeterministic view of action—with the view that the act, or some event that is essential to the act, is not caused at all. If the act—the firing

of the shot—was not caused at all, if it was fortuitous or capricious, happening so to speak out of the blue, then, presumably, no one—and nothing—was responsible for the act. Our conception of action, therefore, should be neither deterministic nor indeterministic. Is there any other possibility?...

We must not say that every event involved in the act is caused by some other event; and we must not say that the act is something that is not caused at all. The possibility that remains, therefore, is this: We should say that at least one of the events that are involved in the act is caused, not by any other events, but by something else instead. And this something else can only be the agent—the man. If there is an event that is caused, not by other events, but by the man, then there are some events involved in the act that are not caused by other events. But if the event in questions is caused by the man then it *is* caused and we are not committed to saying that there is something involved in the act that is not caused at all. (Chisholm, 1964, in Watson, 1982: 27–8)

As one can plainly see, given Chisholm's last sentence, with agent causation, the classical incompatibilist has an answer to the compatibilists' challenge. An act not determined in the relevant sense that it is the product of a prior event in an unfolding deterministic history need not be an act that is merely random. Such an act can be free, and the product of the free will ability, if it is caused by an agent, a person, with the power to initiate actions that are not the products of prior event causes.

Agent causation, as a solution to the charge that mere indeterminism is incompatible with free will, involves a range of controversial metaphysical commitments. One is that it requires that persons with free will be substances of a sort distinct from the sorts of entities whose existence, history, and behavior can be accounted for in terms of event causes. Free agents must instead be the kinds of things whose existence cannot be accounted for or reduced to events. And they must possess powers to cause events—in particular, actions—by resources that do not involve their being caused to cause those events. This would make free agents unique entities in the order of things, as special entities in the natural world. As Chisholm himself puts it:

If we are responsible, and if what I have been trying to say is true, then we have a prerogative which some would attribute only to God: each of us, when we act, is a prime mover unmoved. In doing what we do, we cause certain events to happen, and nothing—or no one—causes us to cause those events to happen. (32)

While the rest of the natural order could be explained by reference to event-causal histories, free agents are beings in the world whose special powers and whose ontological status cannot be neatly fit into the natural order that would account for the rest of spatiotemporal reality. Chisholm states the point starkly:

This means that, in one very strict sense, there can be no science of man. If we think of science as a matter of finding out what laws happen to hold, and if the statement of the laws tell us what kinds of events are caused by other kinds of events, then there will be human actions which we cannot explain by subsuming them under any laws. (33)

In the previous chapter (Section 2.4), one of the philosophical strategies we discussed was that of the insulator, who attempts to insulate important features of the manifest image of the human condition and thereby protect it from any challenge from the framework of the scientific image. Here, in Chisholm's remarks we have an especially vivid illustration of this strategy in an attempt to preserve free will.

The classical incompatibilists' appeal to agent causation offered an elegant way to solve the problem of accounting for free will under the assumption of indeterminism. It did, however, bring with it its own particularly heavy burdens. One was that it presupposed claims about the human condition that at least some take to be unlikely to be true. But there are further problems, internal to the structure of the concept of agent causation. For example, if agents are not events or are not constituted by events, then when they act, why do they act *when* they do? Why not a little earlier or a little later? It would seem that we cannot in principle identify any time antecedent to the free act in which there was some state or condition that agent was in that accounts for her acting that way just when she did, since such features could be accounted for in terms of prior event causes. This problem and others have been taken to count against agent causation. We shall return to this issue in Chapter 10 when examining contemporary variants of agent causation.

3.5. Reflections on the Classical Debate

We shall close this chapter by reflecting on a range of considerations that help to characterize the classical debate, considerations that in one manner or other have changed considerably.

First, focus on the classical compatibilists account of free action in terms of acting on unencumbered desires, wants, or inclinations. This simple picture of action and of agency makes use of very few ingredients. Indeed, it seems that the picture is a *very* simple one: action is produced by desire, perhaps in conjunction with belief. And while there is often mention of choice or decision, there is no detailed explanation of what these action-theoretic ingredients are. Contemporary developments make use of further ingredients, including intentions and reasons. There is currently more attention paid to the internal structure of the psychology of a free agent, concerning how her preferences can be directed toward her own internal states.

Second, the notion of causation was limited to one in which causes determine or necessitate their effects. In more recent times, it has been recognized as an open possibility that a cause might produce or generate its effect without necessitating or determining it. While in an actual situation it did produce its effect, it might not have given the exact same initial conditions. Admittedly, there is room here for critical scrutiny. But the point is that it was taken as a given (perhaps as merely analytic or definitional) that a cause necessitates or determines its effect. (We considered this point briefly in Section 1.4). At least some formulations of the disputed incompatibility of free will and indeterminism also depend on this interpretation. As we will make clear, a more open-minded approach to what causation might be like makes room for libertarians that a more restricted understanding does not.

Third, charges on both sides of the classical debate did tend toward the excessively polemical. The classical compatibilists accused the incompatibilists of simple conceptual confusions, and the classical incompatibilists accused compatibilists of subterfuge—indeed, wretched subterfuge. More recent work by both compatibilists and incompatibilists has helped to make clear to both parties that the more outlandish theses often attributed to their opponents are mostly misattributions. The competitor views are respectable theses, and no one is in a position to claim with great confidence that their opposition is simply out to lunch.

Fourth, perhaps the most contested issue in the classical debate, at least as it reached its zenith in the middle of the twentieth century, seemed to fall demonstrably in favor of classical incompatibilism. In particular, the widely shared classical compatibilists' strategy of explaining the freedom to do otherwise was discredited. Participants in the debate were generally convinced that one cannot analyze the ability to do otherwise in terms of simple counterfactual conditionals according to which an agent would do otherwise contingent on some feature of her (a want or choice) being other than it was.

Fifth, for the most part both classical compatibilists and classical incompatibilists presumed that source and leeway freedom always converged, perhaps as a matter of metaphysical necessity, perhaps just as a matter of fact. But in contemporary work, as we shall make clear, a considerable divergence among theorists has emerged about whether we should account for free will and moral responsibility in terms of just source freedom or instead by emphasizing leeway freedom.

While all of the five points above canvass ways that the philosophical landscape has changed, there are three especially significant influences that are so important that each deserves careful attention. We shall devote the next three chapters to considering each. The first examines the Consequence Argument, an especially forceful argument for the conclusion that determinism is incompatible with leeway freedom, that is, with the freedom to do otherwise. The second concerns Harry Frankfurt's thesis that the free will that matters for moral responsibility is not leeway freedom but instead source freedom. The third has to do with P.F. Strawson's reassessment of the nature of moral responsibility and our practices of holding morally responsible. Reflecting on this will help us to consider what the theoretical options would really involve—if, for instance, we were to conclude that no one is morally responsible, would our human nature really be suited for such a conclusion?

Suggestions for Further Reading

Those interested in the historical figures from the modern era should see the texts we cited above by Hume, Hobbes, Locke, Reid, Kant, and others. As for the literature from the earlier half of twentieth-century analytic philosophy, the following papers are regarded as true classics:

Ayer, A.J. 1954. "Freedom and Necessity." In *Philosophical Essays*. New York: St. Martin's Press: 3–20.

Campbell, C.A. 1951. "Is Free Will a Pseudo-Problem?" *Mind* 60: 446–65.

Chisholm, Roderick. 1964. "Human Freedom and the Self." *The Lindley Lectures*. Copyright by the Department of Philosophy, University of Kansas. Reprinted in Watson, Gary, ed., 1982. *Free Will*. New York: Oxford University Press.

Edwards, Paul. 1958. "Hard and Soft Determinism." In Hook, Sidney, ed., *Determinism and Freedom in the Age of Modern Science*. London: Collier Books: 117–25.

Hobart, R.E. 1934. "Free Will as Involving Indeterminism and Inconceivable Without It." *Mind* 43: 1–27.

Schlick, Moritz. 1939. "When is a Man Responsible?" In Schlick, M., *Problems of Ethics*. Upper Saddle River, NJ: Prentice-Hall: 143–56.

Smart, J.J.C. 1963. "Free Will, Praise, and Blame." *Mind* 70: 291–306.

There are also several collections that offer excellent and extensive essays on the free will debate from the classical period. These include:

Berofsky, Bernard, ed., 1966. *Free Will and Determinism.* New York: Harper & Row.

Honderich, Ted, ed., 1973. *Essays on Freedom and Action*. London: Routledge and Kegan Paul.

Hook, Sidney, ed., 1958. *Determinism and Freedom in the Age of Modern Science*. London: Collier Books.

Lehrer, Keith, ed., 1966. *Freedom and Determinism*. New York: Random House.

A number of philosophers have offered thoughtful book-length treatments of historical figures in relation to the contemporary free will debate. For instance, on Descartes, see:

Ragland, C.P. 2016. *The Will to Reason Theodicy and Freedom in Descartes*. New York: Oxford University Press.

On Hume, see:

Russell, Paul. 1995. *Freedom and Moral Sentiment*. New York: Oxford University Press.

On Locke, see:

Yaffe, Gideon. 2000. *Liberty Worth the Name: Locke on Free Agency*. Princeton, NJ: Princeton University Press.

On Reid, see:

Rowe, William. 1991. *Thomas Reid on Freedom and Morality*. Ithaca, NY: Cornell University Press.
Yaffe, Gideon. 2004. *Manifest Activity: Thomas Reid's Theory of Action*. Oxford: Oxford University Press.

On the free will debate in Great Britain in the eighteenth century, see:

Harris, James A. 2008. *Of Liberty and Necessity: The Free Will Debate in Eighteenth-Century British Philosophy*. Oxford: Oxford University Press.

Notes

1 The preceding grouping of incompatibilists is not altogether satisfying since there is a sharp divide between those incompatibilists who defended a libertarian theory of free will and those who instead embraced a hard determinist thesis. Lucretius, Scotus, Descartes, Berkeley, Reid, Kant, and James were all libertarians, and so were Sartre, C.A. Campbell, C.D. Broad, Richard Taylor, and Roderick Chisholm. Spinoza, Holbach, Schopenhauer, and Nietzsche were hard determinists, as was Paul Edwards. Some classify Kant as a compatibilist (e.g., Wood, 1984) because he held that free will is compatible with empirical determinism.

2 The notion of "doing as one wants" has to be understood so that this classical compatibilist characterization of freedom can be taken as even plausible. To explain, suppose that what Alfredo now really most wants to do is walk on the beach in Monte Carlo, although he currently finds himself in upstate New York. If, for instance, a genie gave him a chance to do anything at this moment, he'd say, "Genie, make it the case that I am now walking on the beach in Monte Carlo!" But Alfredo is not even near Monte Carlo. Instead he finds himself in upstate New York, happily strolling along a quiet wooded trail. Surely he can still be acting freely in strolling, even if, in a certain respect, he is not doing what he would *most* want. Does this mean that the classical compatibilist account is a complete non-starter? No. Surely, there is a sense of doing what one wants according to which Alfredo is now doing what he wants in strolling down a trail, even though, in some other sense, he'd rather be walking in the sand in Monte Carlo.

3 Thomas Hobbes, *Leviathan*, Part II, Chap. 21: 108.

4 Readers will recall our earlier discussion of the disagreement among contemporary philosophers as regards the relevance of free will as distinct from free action (see Section 1.2).

5 John Locke, *An Essay Concerning Human Understanding*, Chapter, xxi, section 14.

6 Hobbes, *Leviathan*, Part II, Chap. 21: 108.

7 This tension between forsaking the concept of free will altogether, and preserving it but restricting the relevant freedom to a modification of action, is mirrored in later advocates of classical compatibilism. A.J. Ayer (1954), for instance, in a seminal defense of classical compatibilism, adopts Hobbes's approach, embracing the expression "freedom of will" and simply characterizing the relevant freedom as a modification of action. Moritz Schlick (1939), on the other hand, appears to be in agreement with Locke. Schlick maintains that the very notion of free will should be abandoned altogether.

8 Some might object to the expression, "doing what one wants," thinking it better instead to speak in terms of doing what one chooses, decides, tries, or wills. But most classical compatibilists seemed to share a principle of motivation according to which an agent always chooses, decides, tries, wills, or does what she has the strongest desire to do (when informed by beliefs about what desires can be satisfied). Hence, on the classical compatibilist approach, doing what one chooses, decides, tries, or wills, translates into doing what one wants. Furthermore, the formulation "doing what one wants" also has expository advantages when discussing Harry Frankfurt's successor to the classical compatibilist account, a successor put explicitly in terms of wants (or desires), and clearly intended as an improvement building upon the old classical compatibilist account of moral freedom. (We'll attend to Frankfurt's views in Chapter 9.)

9 Harry Frankfurt's (1971) hierarchical compatibilist theory (to be discussed in a later chapter), while not a classical compatibilist theory, can be used to address this problem while preserving the basic classical compatibilist idea that the freedom of will is deeply connected with an agent's doing what she wants.

10 David Hume, 1748, *An Enquiry Concerning Human Understanding*, Section VIII: 71.

11 Hume, *A Treatise of Human Nature*, Book II, Part III, Section II.

12 Hume, *A Treatise of Human Nature*, Book II, Part III, Section II.

13 Recall that in Section 2.3 we considered formulations of free will problems, F7 and F8, arising from the worry that indeterminism undermines free will. Here one can see how the classical compatibilists exploit the worry to advance a positive compatibilist thesis that freedom *requires* determination.

14 David Hume, *An Enquiry Concerning Human Understanding*, Section VIII, Part I: 73.

15 What is meant by an *analysis*? This is a subject of great subtlety and controversy. For classical compatibilists, such as Ayer or Hobart, what they had in mind is best understood in terms of meaning. As they understood it, an analysis of an expression x gives a set of conditions y that exhaustively specifies the meaning of x. Let us say that y is a correct analysis of x if and only if the following is true:

> To say that x just is to say that y.
>
> To illustrate, if the term "bachelor" is correctly analyzed as "an unmarried adult male," then to say "Casper is a bachelor" just is to say "Casper is an unmarried adult male."
>
> While characterizing analysis in terms of sameness of meaning probably best describes how the majority of classical compatibilists understood analysis, it is too restrictive for how many philosophers prefer to think about it. Many philosophers prefer instead to think in terms of logical equivalence; an analysis of x in terms of y is successful just so long as the ingredients in y nontrivially provide conditions that are logically equivalent to x. (This is consistent with y not actually fully capturing the meaning of x.)

16 For a recent insightful defense of the classical compatibilist analysis in response to this criticism, see Vihvelin (2013: 196–208).

17 In using the notion of causation in this passage, Chisholm is assuming that the causation is necessitating or deterministic.

18 Readers will note the close similarity between these two formulations and the two ways we considered for formulating free will problems in Section 2.3, in particular, formulations F3 and F4.

19 See, for instance, C.A. Campbell's direct reply to Schlick, arguing that Schlick's distinctions between causal laws and civil compelling laws in no way corrupts the simple thought that unbroken causal continuity entails that no one could have done otherwise. It is this plain worry, Campbell protests against Schlick's charge of a pseudo-problem, that makes it "really inevitable that the Free Will problem should be formulated in the way to which Schlick takes exception" (Campbell, 1951, in Berofsky, 1966: 113).

20 Readers who are interested in studying the literature on libertarian freedom from the classical period will find the sort of freedom in dispute, libertarian freedom, referred to as "contra-causal" freedom. The expression itself is odd, since it suggests something that is certainly not intended, which is a freedom that is in opposition to what (otherwise?) would be caused. The meaning of the term, however, is just to be understood in terms of free action or free will that is not causally determined by prior events. We note that it has fallen out of fashion, as it should have, given how misleading it is.

21 Notably, we'll not discuss Kant's proposed solution. For a discussion of his view, see Watkins (2005) and Pereboom (2006a).

4 The Debate over the Consequence Argument

We turn in this chapter to one of the three most significant influences on contemporary debates about free will, the Consequence Argument for incompatibilism. The Consequence Argument was first introduced by Carl Ginet (1966, cf. 1990), and then developed in different ways by David Wiggins (1973) and Peter van Inwagen (1975, 1983).[1] Since its first appearance, the Consequence Argument has been the single most influential consideration in favor of the thesis that free will understood in terms of leeway freedom is incompatible with determinism. Here is Peter van Inwagen's frequently quoted pithy statement of the argument:

> If determinism is true, then our acts are the consequences of the laws of nature and events of the remote past. But it is not up to us what went on before we were born, and neither is it up to us what the laws of nature are. Therefore, the consequences of these things (including our present acts) are not up to us. (1983: 16)

This elegantly cast expression of the argument masks much interesting complexity, complexity which proponents of the argument have addressed in admirable detail. We will turn to that complexity later in the chapter. But before doing so, it will be helpful first to reflect in some detail upon the dialectical status, antecedent to the introduction of the Consequence Argument, of the controversy between classical compatibilists and classical incompatibilists regarding the relation between determinism and leeway freedom.

This chapter will proceed as follows. In Section 4.1, we'll begin by assessing the dispute between classical compatibilists and classical incompatibilists regarding the ability to do otherwise as it stood in the early 1960s, prior to the introduction of the Consequence Argument. Then in Section 4.2 we will give a first pass at setting out a relatively accessible formulation of (a version of) the Consequence Argument. We'll follow that in Section 4.3 by canvassing the main strategies compatibilists have used to resist it. Then, in Section 4.4, we shall set out the Consequence Argument at an advanced level. In Section 4.5 we will critically examine the rule of inference at work in (one version of) the argument. And in Section 4.6 we'll consider some of the most interesting recent disputes regarding its soundness.

4.1.   Reflecting on the Classical Controversy over the Ability to Do Otherwise

The classical compatibilists' proposed analysis of the ability to do otherwise can be stated roughly as follows:

> An agent is able to do otherwise just in case, if she wanted to do otherwise, she would do otherwise.

As we explained in the previous chapter (Section 3.2), compatibilists offered this proposal as a way of reductively analyzing abilities in terms of counterfactual conditionals. Since the truth of these counterfactuals in general is not threatened by the truth of determinism, this compatibilist analysis was meant to offer an explicit demonstration that the ability to do otherwise is in principle consistent with the truth of determinism. It was thus a major blow to the classical compatibilists' program that their proposed analysis was so decisively refuted.[2]

Reflecting upon this history, it is tempting to overestimate the dialectical position the classical incompatibilists came to hold. In particular, it is tempting to think that, in the wake of the refutation of the classical compatibilists' proposed analysis (an analysis with its roots dating back at least to Hobbes and Hume), the default presumption was that the preponderance of reason strongly suggested that the ability to do otherwise, and so leeway freedom, was incompatible with determinism. But we think this would be a mistake. How so? To begin, it is worth noting that a refutation, even a decisive refutation, of one argument for the compatibility of determinism and the ability to do otherwise does not itself establish that the ability to do otherwise is *incompatible* with determinism. Discrediting the classical compatibilists' analysis fell far short of showing that they were wrong to contend that the ability to do otherwise is compatible with determinism. Their argument for that thesis might have failed, but this was not proof that their compatibilist thesis itself was false.

At this point, however, an impartial spectator might point out that in the absence of some plausible *positive* account of the compatibility of the ability to do otherwise and determinism, compatibilists were at a transparent disadvantage. Why? Because, on its face, intuition strongly suggests that if an agent's actions are determined, then she cannot do otherwise. If the past and the laws causally ensure what an agent does at a time, then this gives *prima facie* reason to think that at that time the agent is not able to do otherwise. If compatibilists had no special way of accounting for the ability to do otherwise (such as by way of their conditional analysis) to counter the apparent tension between determinism and the ability to do otherwise, then it would seem that the scales were after all tipped rather heavily in favor of the incompatibilists.

The preceding assessment of the dialectic overlooks other credible claims about determinism to which compatibilists were able to point, claims that would help make plausible the thesis that determinism is after all consistent with an agent's possession of the ability (and so the freedom) to do otherwise.

To understand the resources available to the compatibilist, consider what the thesis of determinism would come to as a comprehensive thesis about the natural world. Consider, for instance, a simple instance of a dispositional property, such as the solubility of a piece of solid, dry salt sitting undisturbed in a salt shaker. That substance, salt, is understood in part not just in terms of its chemical composition, and not just in terms of how it is when it remains undissolved. It is also understood in terms of how it *would* behave were it placed in water. In this sense, the salt's solubility is a *modal* property. It is a property about the potentiality or possibility of the item in question under certain conditions. Or consider, for instance, the behavior of a plant, such as a sunflower at night. We understand its nature, even while at rest in the dark, in part in terms of how we would expect it to behave in response to sunlight: it is disposed to follow the sun's arch through the sky.

Turning to the behavior of sophisticated animals, lions, for example, it is part of our understanding of them that they have active powers or dispositions of various sorts—to seek food, to eat, to protect their young, and to evade predators. What the compatibilist can have us note at this point is that these creatures are, in an uncontroversial sense, able to act in ways that at a certain time they might in fact not be acting. If determinism is compatible with a natural world in which ordinary objects have dispositions to behave in various ways under alternative conditions, and more complex items, including various animals, have powers of this general sort, it makes sense to suppose that determinism is compatible with an ability distinctive of persons, the ability to do things that one isn't currently doing (Moore, 1912). Suppose that you have the ability to speak both English and French. You're in a café in Paris, but you order your coffee and croissant in English. Suppose your friend says to you: "You could have ordered in French instead!". In this context it seems that your companion was correct to say what she did no matter what the truth about determinism turns out to be.

Compatibilists might concede at this point that they have no positive thesis about *how* this ability, the free will ability, is to be explained in a way that makes it clear that it is after all compatible with determinism. But their inability to account for this fact about our nature, by way of an analysis of this unique ability, does not provide decisive reason to think that the ability in question is in principle incompatible with the natural world being arranged in such a way that determinism is true. Unless the incompatibilists wished to argue that determinism is incompatible with the wide range of dispositions, powers, and abilities similar to those featured in the rest of the natural world, compatibilists had credible grounds for remaining committed to the thesis that the free will ability, understood as the ability to do otherwise, is also compatible with determinism.

Given the above remarks, it may be best to see the dispute over leeway freedom between compatibilists and incompatibilists as at a relatively evenly balanced impasse. Both sides were able to offer reasonable considerations for their opposing theses. And it seemed that there was little one was able to offer an impartial inquirer to help her adjudicate matters so as to show that one side rather than the other had claim to a greater preponderance of reason on their side. So consider, in this evenly weighted dispute, the Basic Leeway Argument for Incompatibilism (BLI):

1. If a person acts of her own free will, then she could have done otherwise.
2. If determinism is true, no one can do otherwise than one actually does.
3. Therefore, if determinism is true, no one acts of her own free will.

We set out BLI in Section 3.3 as one of the two arguments capturing different core incompatibilist theses. Given the controversy currently under discussion, the dispute between compatibilists and incompatibilists amounts to a dispute over the second premise of BLI. And it seems that there was little available to move the debate along.

It is now easy for us to explain why the Consequence Argument for incompatibilism had such a powerful influence on the free will debate. Prior to its emergence in the dialectic, incompatibilists had little by way of argument for premise 2 of BLI. What the incompatibilists had to appeal to was a *prima facie*, intuitive judgment that determinism is incompatible with the ability to do otherwise. And while that is after all an initially compelling basis for favoring incompatibilism, even after the fall of the compatibilists' conditional analysis, compatibilists had available to them a plausible conception of natural abilities that underwrites the ability to do otherwise even in a deterministic context. But, as shall soon become clear, the Consequence Argument is in essence an argument—a compelling argument—for the second premise of BLI. As such, it provided a substantial source of support for incompatibilism. To this day it remains one of the most important influences on the free will debate. Many who are incompatibilists today base their commitment to it on the claim that some version of it is after all sound. We turn now to a first pass at setting out the Consequence Argument in a way that moves beyond van Inwagen's formulation of it as we quoted it at the beginning of this chapter.

4.2. A Formulation of the Consequence Argument

The version of the Consequence Argument we'll now consider, a modal version, invokes a compelling pattern of inference applied to modal propositions about what is *power necessary*.[3] Power necessity can be understood in terms of what it is not within a person's power to alter. As applied to true propositions, power necessity concerns a person's powerlessness to affect their truth. To say that a person does not have power over a true proposition is to say that she cannot act in such a way that it would be false rather than true. To illustrate, no person has power over the truths of mathematics. That is, no person can act in such a way that the true propositions of mathematics would be false instead.[4] Hence, the truths of mathematics are, for any person, power necessary. Intuitively, a valid pattern of inference, drawing upon propositions about what is power necessary, unfolds as follows:

If a person has no power over whether a certain fact obtains, and if she also has no power over whether this fact has some other fact as a consequence, then she also has no power over the consequent fact.

Powerlessness, it seems, transfers from one fact to consequences of it. Here is an example:

If poker-playing Diamond Jim, who is holding only two pairs, has no power over the fact that Calamity Sam draws a straight flush, and if a straight flush beats two pairs and we grant Jim also has no power over this, it follows that Jim has no power over the fact that Sam's straight flush beats Jim's two pairs.

This general pattern of inference is applied to the thesis of determinism to yield a powerful argument for incompatibilism. The argument requires the assumption that determinism is true, and that the facts of the past and the laws of nature are fixed. Given these assumptions, here is a rough and simplified sketch of the argument:

1. No one has power over the facts of the remote past and the laws of nature.
2. No one has power over the fact that the remote past in conjunction with the laws of nature implies that there is only one unique future (that is, no one has power over the fact that determinism is true).
3. Therefore, no one has power over the facts of the future.

According to the Consequence Argument, if determinism is true, no person at any time has any power to alter how her own future will unfold. Assuming free will requires the ability to do otherwise (leeway freedom), then, in light of the Consequence Argument, free will is incompatible with determinism.

We'll now present a more precise version of the argument. Our explanation of the argument involves three steps: first, a presentation of the logical form of the propositions figuring in the argument; second, a demonstration of the inference principle the argument uses; and third, the application of the inference principle to a specific argument for incompatibilism.

First, consider the logical form of the propositions figuring in the argument. The logical form "$N_{s,t}(p)$" expresses a proposition of the form: "It is power necessary for a person, S, at a time, t, that the proposition p is true," and we will treat this form of expression as synonymous with "p is true, and S is not free at t to act in such a way that, if S were to so act, p would not be true."

Second, the version of the Consequence Argument we'll consider exploits an inference principle (or rule) that is a modalized version of the simple argument form *modus ponens*:

1. p
2. $p \rightarrow q$
3. Therefore, q

Just as *modus ponens* allows us to infer q from the two propositions, p, and p materially implies q (p→q), so the modalized version allows us to infer that q is power necessary for a person at a time from the two propositions that p is power necessary for a person at a time, and that it is power necessary for a person at a time that q is a consequence of p. The argument form can be represented as follows:

1. $N_{S,t}$ (p)
2. $N_{S,t}$(p→q)
3.   Therefore, $N_{S,t}$(q)

Another common form of notation to represent the preceding expression of this inference rule is as follows:

$$N_{S,t}\ (p),\ N_{S,t}\,(p\to q) \vdash N_{S,t}\ (q)$$

In ordinary English, the pattern of inference reads:

1.   p obtains, and S is not free at t to act in such a way that, if S were to so act, p would not obtain.
2.   p implies q, and S is not free at t to act in such a way that, if S were to so act, p implies q would not obtain.
3.   Therefore, q obtains, and S is not free at t to act in such a way that, if S were to so act, q would not obtain.

This modal inference rule is known as *Transfer of Powerlessness*, or just *Transfer*. Transfer is supported by applications of it that demonstrate its logical force. For instance, as applied to the example presented above, if, in the midst of his poker game, and holding only two pairs, it is power necessary for Diamond Jim that Calamity Sam draws a straight flush, and if it is power necessary for Diamond Jim that a straight flush beats two pairs, then it is also power necessary for Diamond Jim that Calamity Sam's straight flush beats Jim's two pairs.

Third, we can now apply the Transfer inference principle in the service of incompatibilism. To construct the incompatibilists' Consequence Argument, three premises are needed. One premise involves the principle of the *Fixity of the Past*. It states that no person can change facts of the past relative to her present situation. A second premise involves the principle of the *Fixity of the Laws*. It specifies that no person can alter a law of nature. The third premise invites one to assume that determinism is true—it states that the facts of the past and the laws of nature entail one unique future.

Here, then, is how the Consequence Argument unfolds. Take (p&l) to stand for the conjunction of two propositions: (p) the facts of the past obtain, and (l) the laws of nature obtain. Given the principles of the Fixity of the Past and the Fixity of the Laws, one can say of their conjunction (p&l) that they are power necessary for any person. That is, for any person, S, S is not free at any time, t, to act in such a way that, if S were to so act, the propositions describing the past relative to t, or those expressing the laws of nature, would be false ($N_{S,t}$(p&l)).[5] This is the first premise of the argument.

Next, ((p&l)→f), is an expression of the thesis of determinism, that the propositions describing the past and the laws of nature (p&l) materially imply that there is only one unique future (f). Like the Fixity of the Laws and the Past, the thesis of determinism, supposing it to be true, would also be power necessary for any person at any time.[6] Hence, the second premise of the Consequence Argument is that for any person, S, S is not free at any time, t, to act in such a way that, if S were to so act, the thesis of determinism would not be true [$N_{S,t}$((p&l)→f)].

From these two premises and Transfer, it follows that for any person, S, S is not free at any time, t, to act in such a way that, if S were to so act, the actual future, f, would not obtain ($N_{S,t}$(f)). Set out formally, the argument can be represented as follows:

1. $N_{S,t}$(p&l)
2. $N_{S,t}$((p&l)→f)
3. Therefore, $N_{S,t}$(f)

We introduced the modality of power necessity just above by explaining that it is best understood as indexed to persons and times. Strictly speaking, this is correct. But since in the Consequence Argument the claims are meant to apply to any (finite) being, the indexing can safely be dropped as an unproblematic way of simplifying the argument. Hence, we offer this simplification:

1. N(p&l)
2. N((p&l)→f)
3. Therefore, N(f)

According to the Consequence Argument, given that no person can alter the past or the laws of nature, and assuming that determinism is true, and thus that each person's acts are consequences of the past and the laws, no person can alter the future from the one that is a consequence of the past and the laws given determinism's truth. No one is then able to act other than as she does—no one has leeway freedom.

The Consequence Argument's force is perhaps best captured as expressing a claim about what would have to be true if, at a determined world, a person *is* able to do otherwise. For that to be true—that is, for the conclusion to the Consequence Argument to be false, a person would have to be able to render false facts about the past or about laws of nature. But, the incompatibilist contends, it is incredible to think that whatever powers of agency a person has, they involve such abilities. Hence, according to the Consequence Argument, if determinism is true no one is free to act other than as she does.

4.3. Strategies for Resisting the Consequence Argument

The soundness of the Consequence Argument has been contested in various ways; here we focus on the three most influential challenges. A first calls into question the claim that a person is unable to act in such a way that the past would be different than it is. The second calls into question the supposition that a person is unable to act in such a way that the laws would be different than they are. The third objection contends that the inference principle on which the argument relies—the Transfer principle in the version we just set out—is invalid, and thus one cannot draw the desired incompatibilist-friendly conclusion even if the Consequence Argument's premises are all true. Each of these three compatibilist efforts has given rise to some of the most sophisticated contemporary work on the free will problem.[7]

4.3.1. Challenging the Fixity of the Past

As we set it out in the previous section, the Consequence Argument's first premise, N(p&l), relies on two principles, the Principle of the Fixity of the Past and the Principle of the Fixity of the Laws. Consider first the Principle of the Fixity of the Past, which states that a person cannot alter the past. How could a compatibilist plausibly deny this? It does seem incredible that we might be able to act in the present in such a way that the past would be different. But consider the difference between an agent who has the ability to act in such a way that *she alters the past*, as opposed to an agent who has the ability to act in such a way such that, *if she did so act, the past would have been different*—David Lewis (1981) makes this distinction. The former ability might well be thought outlandish. But the latter ability might be easier to accept.

Let us distinguish in general (and not just as applied to the topic of the Fixity of the Past) between two such notions of ability. The first is a stronger notion of ability, the second weaker. Call them *causal* (CA) and *broad* ability (BA).[8] Causal ability holds that:

> CA: A person has an ability to bring something about, p, just in case there is a course of action such that the person is able to perform such an action, and, if she were to perform it, then she would cause it to be the case that p obtains.

Broad ability holds that:

> BA: A person has an ability to bring something about, p, just in case, there is a course of action such that the person is able to perform such an action, and, if she were to perform it, then p would obtain.

These two notions of ability, CA and BA, can be employed to understand how a compatibilist could resist either the Principle of the Fixity of the Past or instead the Principle of the Fixity of the Laws. The compatibilist position currently under consideration presupposes the notion of BA as it bears on a free agent's relation to the past. When the Principle of the Fixity of the Past is interpreted so that what is at issue is BA, the compatibilist might argue that the principle is false and the ability at issue is not incredible but unproblematic.

To illustrate the difference between CA and BA, consider first what would be required for an agent to act differently (here the claim is not about an agent's *ability* to act differently from how she acted). For example, consider: *If McKenna were dancing on the French Riviera right now, he'd be a lot richer than he is.* Certainly this claim does not mean (at least not given McKenna's dancing skills) that if he goes to the French Riviera to dance, he will *thereby* be made richer. (No one in her right mind would pay to see McKenna dance!) It only means that were he to have gone there to tango, he'd have had to have had a lot more cash *beforehand* in order to finance his escapade.

Now consider an example that *is* about a claim of ability, one due to John Fischer (1994: 80–2): Each morning at 9:00 the salty old sea dog checks the weather forecast to learn what the weather will be that day. If the weather will be fair at noon, he sets sail. If not, he stays on land. Now one day, at noon, the seadog learned earlier that day, at 9:00, that the weather would be horrible. So he stayed on dry land. But, one might think (setting aside reflections on the free will debate altogether), he is *able* to sail at noon. Why wouldn't he be? There is nothing wrong with him. He is healthy, of sound mind, not hypnotized or deceived. He has what it takes, just then, to go sailing. The fact that he *does not* go sailing, Fischer observes, is not evidence that he *cannot* go sailing—that it is not within his power to do so. But what, we might safely reason, if he were, just then, to exercise his ability to sail and actually sail just then, at noon? Well, a reasonable answer is that, were he to sail just then, we can infer that the forecast at 9:00 a.m. would have been for fair weather.

With Fischer's example in mind, let us carry this over to the Consequence Argument, and consider what resources a compatibilist has in light of these ordinary patterns of inference about actions and exercises of ability in relation to the past. The compatibilist wants to resist the Consequence Argument and to say that at the moment when a free agent acted, even if she was causally determined to act as she did, she just then retained the ability to act differently. The fact that she did not exercise that ability is not itself sufficient reason to conclude that she is unable to exercise it (just like the salty sea dog was able to sail even when he didn't). Had she exercised it, and done otherwise as a result, some feature of the past prior to her so acting would also have been different. Perhaps she would have, just antecedent to her acting, wanted something other than what she actually wanted, or come to believe something different from what she actually believed. But when she acts as she actually does, she nevertheless retains that ability to act differently.

According to this first objection, the compatibilist need not say that for a causally determined agent to act otherwise, *by* her acting otherwise she would *cause* the past of her actual world to be different—which involves ability in the

CA sense. All that the compatibilist needs to invoke is BA, the weaker notion of ability—and thus that if she were to act otherwise, the past would have been different.

4.3.2.   Resisting the Fixity of the Laws

Now turn to the Principle of the Fixity of the Laws, which states that an agent cannot alter the laws of nature. The second challenge aims to resist this principle, and to argue that there is a sense in which we have the ability to act so that a law of nature is falsified. Maintaining that an agent could falsify a law of nature seems as counterintuitive as claiming that a person can alter the facts of the past. But by again invoking the distinction between broad and causal ability, compatibilists have aimed to make this challenge plausible.

One way to pursue this strategy is by way of advancing a specific account of the laws of nature. For instance, the compatibilist might argue for a Humean account that holds that a law of nature reduces to regularities among events.[9] In worlds in which determinism is true, laws that reflect such regularities will be of a sort that they, along with the facts of the past, entail every truth about all later times. Notice that, on such a view, if the history of a world were different from how it is, then different regularities in nature might emerge. Then different laws of nature would be "the" laws of nature. The compatibilist might first point out that no human being has the causal ability to make false an otherwise true law of nature. She cannot *initiate* a variation in the laws of nature by performing an action so that at the time she acts and afterwards, by her so acting, the laws and thus the regularities they reflect would be different from what they are. But an agent might still have the broad ability to act differently from how she does act, so if she were to act in this alternative way, the laws of nature that do in fact obtain would not. Some other regularities would unfold in that alternative causal history. *But she would not be the cause of this change*; her so acting would be an *upshot* of the antecedent fact that the laws were ever so slightly different.

Suppose Captain Ahab chooses in this actual world to eat fish for dinner, but just before choosing to eat the fish, he deliberated about whether to eat steak instead. (Imagine that both were offered to him and he was permitted to choose only one.) Suppose also that he was causally determined to choose to eat fish and not steak. In the actual world, as things unfold, there are regularities involving events that occur prior to his deliberating and his choosing to eat fish. On the Humean account, these regularities will count as laws. However, were Captain Ahab to have chosen to eat steak, the regularities and thus the laws would have been different. In particular, there would be different regularities and thus laws involving events occurring just prior to his deliberating and his choosing to eat steak. Now, in the actual world, as things really did unfold, Captain Ahab does not have the ability to *cause* an actually obtaining law of nature not to obtain. But he does have the broad ability to choose to eat steak and not fish (he's done it in the past!), and, were he to have chosen to eat steak, the laws of nature that do obtain in the actual world would not obtain. In particular, a different law would have governed what happened just prior to his choosing to eat steak. Hence, since he has the ability to choose to eat steak as well in the world in which he does in fact choose to eat fish, Captain Ahab thereby has the broad ability to act in such a way that a law of nature that obtains in the actual world would not obtain.

This type of compatibilist response to the Consequence Argument, first advanced by David Lewis, has come to be known as *local miracle compatibilism* (Lewis, 1981, 1979). Local miracle compatibilism (LMC) does not claim that a free agent at a deterministic world, W1, has the causal ability to break a law of nature, that is, to *cause* a miracle. Local miracle compatibilism only claims that at W1 she has the broad ability to act in a manner such that an actual law of nature would not be a law of nature. If in some other possible world, W2, she acts differently, then *relative to the laws in W1*, a local miracle would occur at W2. That is, a free agent at a deterministic world has the ability to act differently than she does act, because, if she were to act differently, then the laws of nature, just prior to her acting, would be slightly different from the way they are. It's important to emphasize that the alternative course of action in the world W2 would require a miracle *only relative to the laws in the actual world (W1)*. Were she to act on the alternative in W2, some other set of laws would hold in W2. *These she would not violate.*[10] LMC is provocative, but not clearly implausible, and has rightly earned the respect of many serious-minded philosophers.[11]

4.3.3.   Challenging the Transfer Principle

The preceding attempts to prove the Consequence Argument unsound concern different ways to demonstrate the falsity of the first premise of the argument (i.e., no one has any power to alter the past and the laws of nature). A third approach is to set aside debates about the Fixity of the Past and the Laws and instead attempt to prove that the conclusion does not validly follow from the premises. That is, this approach seeks to undermine the inference principle which allows us to infer an inability to act otherwise from an inability to alter the past and the laws.

Michael Slote (1982) proposes a challenge of this kind. His strategy is to show that the Transfer principle

$$N_{S,t}\ (p),\ N_{S,t}\ (p \rightarrow q) \vdash N_{S,t}\ (q)$$

fails because power necessity is *selective* in the inferences that it licenses. A modality is selective if the inferences it licenses are restricted to certain cases or domains and cannot be generalized as required by valid inference principles that are used to drive valid argument forms.

Consider, by analogy, the case of knowledge. Suppose that René knows that Gassendi is a bachelor, and he knows that, if Gassendi is a bachelor, then Gassendi is unmarried. Given a pattern of inference similar to Transfer, it seems right to conclude that René knows that Gassendi is unmarried. A principle that might be extrapolated from cases like René's knowledge of Gassendi has been called the Principle of the Closure of Knowledge under Known Implication ("Closure" for short). In a manner structurally similar to Transfer, Closure might be represented as follows:

1. Kp
2. $K(p \rightarrow q)$
3. Therefore, Kq

But as plausible as the inference regarding René's knowledge may seem, some philosophers, and Slote is one of them, have contended that inferences of this form are not generally permissible, and thus that Closure is invalid. In particular, they have argued that the following sort of instance is not valid:

1. René knows that he is sitting in a chair.
2. René knows that if he is sitting in a chair, then he is not having a massive hallucination.
3. Therefore, René knows that he is not having a massive hallucination.

Epistemological skeptics invoke a version (the *modus tollens* version) of this pattern of inference (that is, $\sim Kq, K(p \rightarrow q) \vdash \sim Kp$), to reason as follows:

1. René does not know that he is not having a massive hallucination.
2. René knows that if he is sitting in his chair, then he is not having a massive hallucination.
3. Therefore, René does not know that he is sitting in his chair.

But, if this inference is invalid, then it would not follow from René's failure to know that he is not having a massive hallucination that he does not know that he is sitting in his chair. Consequently, while he would not know that he is not having a massive hallucination, this lack of knowledge would not impugn the epistemic status of his external-world belief about his sitting in a chair. The trick, however, is to provide a convincing account of why it is that the sort of inference featured in the skeptic's argument is invalid. (This is not something that we will pursue here.)

In like fashion, applied to Transfer, while sometimes powerlessness over one fact as well as its implications result in powerlessness over an implicated fact, must it always? Or is Transfer selective in the way that Slote thinks Closure is?[12] His key point is that notions like *unavoidability*, or, as we have been discussing, *power necessity*, are sensitive to contexts in a way that only selectively permits the sort of inference we find in the Consequence Argument. Let us work with the idea of unavoidability, since that is the notion Slote considers. On his proposal, when we say that something is unavoidable for a person, we have in mind selective contexts in which the facts pertaining to the unavoidability are independent of or bypass that person's agency (Slote, 1982: 19). It is unavoidable for

Barack Obama, for instance, that Caesar crossed the Rubicon. Nothing about his agency—about what he can do—can alter such facts. But when discussing the range of acts Obama is able to perform but does not perform, when he is of sound mind, healthy, uncoerced, and not deceived, these are, for him, in a plain way within his power and so are avoidable. The suggestion is that Transfer-style inferences do not work when they concern aspects of a person's own agency, or at least whenever there is not some special defect or impairment of agency that is in question, such as when an agent is under the grip of an addictive desire.

Notice that in the inference invoked in the Consequence Argument unavoidability or power necessity is specified as transferring from a context in which the notion is, as Slote would have it, appropriately applied, and one in which, in his view, it is not. To illustrate his contention, suppose it is asserted that when Obama freely elects to remain at his desk and keep working, he is free just then to do otherwise and instead take a stroll in the White House gardens with his daughters (and assume that determinism is true). Then, as Slote might see it, while the following propositions are indeed true:

1. It is unavoidable for Barack Obama that the facts of the past and laws of nature (p&l) are thus and so; and
2. It is unavoidable for Barack Obama that p&l implies that he now remain at his desk and work rather than stroll with his daughters,

the following proposition is false:

3. It is unavoidable for Barack Obama that he remains at his desk and works rather than take a stroll with his daughters.

In the Consequence Argument, the first premise cites considerations that have nothing to do with a person's agency—facts prior to his birth, and the laws of nature, and the second premise cites a fact about what the past and the laws imply, namely, that they imply that he perform the action at issue. It is claimed that these facts are unavoidable for the agent, but from this a conclusion is drawn, relying upon a Transfer-like principle, that the action at issue is unavoidable for him. This, Slote and other compatibilists (such as Dennett, 1984; Mele, 1995, 2006b) have suggested, is to draw illicitly incompatibilist conclusions about unavoidability from reasonable claims regarding unavoidability.

4.3.4. A Final Challenge

The standard formulation of the core concern exploited by the Consequence Argument as a conflict between an action's being freely willed and the truth of causal determinism has in recent years been challenged by Joseph Campbell (2007, 2008, 2010). Campbell's objection is that this argument relies on the contingent assumption that the agent has a remote past—a past before she existed—and hence does not show that free action is incompatible with determinism per se. The argument tells us nothing about deterministic worlds in which an agent has no remote past.

We want to note two responses to this objection. Alicia Finch (2013) defends the Consequence Argument against Campbell by arguing that the dynamic of the argument can be restricted to a time within an agent's lifespan, thereby precluding the need for a remote past. Key to her defense is plausibility of *the trans-temporality thesis*, according to which an agent's performing a free action requires that at an earlier time it was up to the agent to perform the action at the later time. Finch's strategy is to argue that in the target cases, the laws and the state of the world at the earlier time are not up to the agent, and if causal determinism is true, this quality of not being up to the agent transfers to the action at the later time.

Carolina Sartorio (2015) responds to Campbell by defending the view that the true incompatibilist concern is not the incompatibility of free will and causal determinism per se, but rather free will and actions being causally determined by factors beyond the agent's control, and Campbell's objection does not address this thesis. We think that Sartorio is right about this. Campbell's objection and these two responses, we believe, are important and insightful.

4.4.   The Consequence Argument: A More Precise Formulation

We turn now to a more advanced formulation of the Consequence Argument, the modal version developed by van Inwagen (1983: 93–5).[13] Our goal in this section is to explain this more precise formulation and comment on details that will prove useful for understanding some of the technical debates about it. In Section 4.5 we will consider one major challenge to the argument so formulated. Introductory students might wish to pass over this section and the next. We include them since some interested in pursuing these topics might profit from a more thorough, technical presentation. But in our view, the most significant objections to the Consequence Argument have already been discussed: they are the challenges to the principles of the Fixity of the Past and the Fixity of the Laws. In Section 4.6 we offer our final assessments of these challenges.

As van Inwagen sets it out, the argument invokes two inference rules (94). The first rule he labels Rule Alpha, α. It specifies that from the fact that p is necessary one can validly infer that no one has, or ever had, a choice about whether p is true—that is, that p is power necessary:[14]

$\alpha: \Box p \vdash Np$

The second rule is similar to the one we introduced above, which we called Transfer. Van Inwagen labels it Rule Beta, β, and it can be represented as follows:

$\beta: Np, N(p \rightarrow q) \vdash Nq$

That is, from the fact that that no one has, or ever had, a choice about whether p is true, and that no one has, or ever had, a choice about whether p implies q, one can validly infer that no one has, or ever had, a choice about whether q is true. Next, van Inwagen (94) introduces names for two key propositions. One, P_o, names a proposition that expresses a complete state of the actual world at some time in the remote past. Another, L, names a proposition detailing the actual laws of nature. Finally, P is used to name a proposition about some actual state of affairs at some later time. Van Inwagen selects the proposition that Richard Nixon was pardoned for any crimes he committed while he was President of the United States (94–5), and we'll follow him in treating this as P.

Now, it follows from determinism being true that it is metaphysically necessary that P is implied by the conjunction of P_o and L, and this entailment can be formulated as follows (94–5):

$$\Box((P_o \& L) \rightarrow P)$$

Two further assumptions, the Principle of the Fixity of the Past and the Principle of the Fixity of the Laws, as applied to P_o and L, yield premises that figure in the argument. Each is expressed by making use of the power necessity operator "N":

NP$_o$ (No one has, or ever had, a choice about whether P_o is true.)

NL (No one has, or ever had, a choice about whether L is true.)

Van Inwagen introduces these two power necessities separately, and not as a single premise N(P_o&L), by contrast with how we presented it above (in Section 4.2).

Readers might have noticed that in our earlier formulation, we simply left it as intuitive that if the metaphysical thesis of determinism is true, it is power necessary for a person.[15] That is, in Section 4.2, we began with this assumption:

$$N((p\&l) \rightarrow f)$$

In doing so, we did not offer any argument for it. But with van Inwagen's Rule α, applying it to the above proposition about pardoning Nixon, the relevant proposition can be derived as follows:

1. $\Box((P_o\&L) \rightarrow P)$
2. Therefore, N($(P_o\&L) \rightarrow P$) from Rule α

As we explained earlier (Section 1.4), determinism is a thesis that involves metaphysical necessity: If determinism is true, then it is metaphysically necessary that $((P_o\&L) \rightarrow P)$, i.e., that the past and laws entail all other facts about what happens at that world. Rule α licenses inferring the power necessity of $((P_o\&L) \rightarrow P)$ from its metaphysical necessity.[16]

It bears mentioning that the propositions NP$_o$ and NL differ from the proposition N($(P_o\&L) \rightarrow P$) in that they are not derived, by way of Rule α, from a proposition involving metaphysical necessity. That is, the Consequence Argument does not proceed under the supposition that the facts of the past or the laws of nature are metaphysically necessary truths. And this is as it should be, since—barring further special metaphysical assumptions not needed for specifying the thesis of determinism—they are best thought of as contingent and not necessary truths.[17] Hence, the argument proceeds under the assumption that, although these truths, P_0 and L in particular, are merely contingent and not necessary, they are nevertheless power necessary for a person, or, as van Inwagen would put it, they are such that no one has, or ever had, any choice about them.

Consider now van Inwagen's formulation of the entire argument. In doing so, note again that we are treating P to be the proposition that Richard Nixon was pardoned for any crimes he committed while he was President of the United States, and recall that it was his successor as President, Gerald Ford, who pardoned him.

1.	$\Box((P_0\&L)\rightarrow P)$	assume determinism is true and that P
2.	$\Box(P_0\rightarrow(L\rightarrow P))$	apply logic to step 1
3.	$N(P_0\rightarrow(L\rightarrow P))$	apply Rule α to step 2
4.	NP_0	introduce premise, Principle of Fixity of Past
5.	$N(L\rightarrow P)$	apply Rule β to steps 3 and 4
6.	NL	introduce premise, Principle of Fixity of the Laws
7.	Therefore, NP	apply Rule β to steps 5 and 6

If the above modal formulation of the Consequence Argument is sound, and if determinism is true, no one, including Gerald Ford, had any choice about whether Nixon was pardoned for his crimes in office. And for any action performed by any person, the same applies. In short, if this argument is sound, then if determinism is true, no one is able to do otherwise, and, hence, no one has leeway freedom.

With one minor exception, our preceding discussion should have made every step in the above argument transparent. That exception is the step from 1 to 2. The reason the step is a valid one is because it follows from basic logic. Steps 1 and 2 are logically equivalent, and logically equivalent substitutions in an argument are permissible.[18] But what is important to understand is *why* the substitution from the formulation of 1 to the formulation to 2 is made prior to applying Rule α. The reason is that it permits the introduction of NP_0 at step 4 as a separate premise, as well as the introduction of NL at step 6 as a separate premise, rather than as a single premise of the form $N(P_0\&L)$. Otherwise, if Rule α were to have been applied to step 1 (rather than step 2), the argument would instead most naturally have to be set out as follows:

1.	$\Box((P_0\&L)\rightarrow P)$	assume determinism is true and that P
2.	$N((P_0\&L)\rightarrow P)$	apply Rule α to step 1
3.	$N(P_0\&L)$	introduce premises, Principle of Fixity of Past and Laws
4.	Therefore, NP	apply Rule β to steps 2 and 3

The problem with proceeding this way is that the reasons for thinking that the past is fixed for a person might vary from the reasons for thinking that the laws are fixed for a person. Or at any rate, it should not be assumed that the reasons are the same and that they can thus be lumped into a single claim about power necessity.[19] True, one might try to argue from NP_0 and NL *to* $N(P_0 \& L)$ by way of further steps. But van Inwagen's elegant formulation allows one to avoid these complications. (Maybe. Or maybe it illicitly masks them. This is something we'll consider in the next section.)

4.5.   Questioning Rule β and Seeking an Improved Version

Having set out van Inwagen's version of the Consequence Argument, we'll now focus on the role of Rule β in the argument. Notice that Rule β does not appear as a step in the argument (steps 1 through 7). Rather, it is an inference rule that is intended to justify or make rationally permissible transitions between steps—in this case, step 5 from steps 3 and 4, and step 7 from steps 5 and 6.

Reflect back on the formulation van Inwagen gave of the Consequence Argument in terms of it not being up to us what the laws of nature and the past are, and how from these considerations, if determinism is true, it is not up to us what we do now. We began the chapter by quoting this formulation. The insight that binds these judgments—that makes compelling the transition from powerlessness with respect to the past and laws to powerlessness with respect to our actions—is codified in Rule β. In this respect, Rule β is meant to offer a source of support for an incompatibilist conclusion. It is supposed to be an intuitively plausible principle that aids in adjudicating the dispute between compatibilists and incompatibilists. More specifically, it is meant to show, without being antecedently biased toward one philosophical position or another, that there are reasons to move one in the direction of an incompatibilist conclusion. The pattern of inference, then, must in some way have an independent standing as a valid way of reasoning. (Above we offered an illustration of this with reasoning about Calamity Sam's hand of poker in his dealings with Diamond Jim.)

Now, if it turned out that Rule β, and relevant variants, such as Transfer, were after all not valid patterns of reasoning quite generally—that is, if some instances of the application of the rule yielded invalid results—this would raise the worry that an application of Rule β itself when used in the Consequence Argument is not innocent of theoretical bias in the debate between compatibilists and incompatibilists. The trouble is, as various philosophers have pointed out, Rule β appears not to be valid, since there are instances of it that yield intuitively incorrect results.

A first concern is this. With the aid of a few innocent assumptions, a logical truth, and a few simple logical steps, one can show that Rule β is committed to agglomerativity with respect to "no one has a choice about," or what others call "power necessity" (McKay and Johnson, 1996). That is, Rule β makes permissible inferring from Np and Nq, that N(p&q). The problem is that there are clear counterexamples to this. There are cases in which it is true that Np, and true that Nq, but it would be mistaken to infer N(p&q), because, as it happens, a person who does not have a choice about p or about q *does* have a choice about (p&q), and so N(p&q) is false.[20]

We'll now explain each of these two key points: first, that Rule β strictly implies agglomerativity, and, second, that there are counterexamples to it. So first, consider the following complex proposition:

$$[p \rightarrow (q \rightarrow (p\&q))]$$

Treat "p" and "q" as any random propositions. Notice the following about the complex proposition: Whatever combination of values true and false is assigned to p and q, the complex proposition comes out as true. There is no interpretation of the truth values for p and q that will yield any result other than truth for the entire proposition.[21] Now, when a complex proposition in the language of first-order logic is true on any interpretation of the truth values of all of its constituents, it is a necessary truth. Hence:

$$\Box[p \rightarrow (q \rightarrow (p\&q))]$$

Apply Rule α, and we get:

$$N[p \rightarrow (q \rightarrow (p\&q))]$$

Setting this inference aside for the moment, consider any two propositions such that no one has a choice about them, Np and Nq. Grant them for argument's sake. Given the preceding presentation, here, in compressed form, is Thomas McKay and David Johnson's proof that Rule β, along with a few simple logical ingredients, strictly implies agglomerativity (1996: 115):

1.	Np	premise granted
2.	Nq	premise granted
3.	$\Box[p \rightarrow (q \rightarrow (p\&q))]$	necessity of a logical truth
4.	$N[p \rightarrow (q \rightarrow (p\&q))]$	apply Rule α to step 3
5.	$N(q \rightarrow (p\&q))$	apply Rule β to steps 1 and 4
6.	Therefore, N(p&q)	apply Rule β to steps 2 and 5

This proof is sound and decisive. From Np and Nq, with an application of some simple logical truths, Rule α (which seems innocent here), and Rule β, we get N(p&q).

Here, now, is McKay and Johnson's counterexample to agglomerativity for "no one has a choice about." Suppose that Jones does not toss a coin but could have. He kept it in his pocket, untossed. Set aside all assumptions about determinism or the free will debate. Now consider these three propositions, and note that, as it happens, all three are true, given that Jones kept the coin in his pocket:

p = The coin does not fall heads.

q = The coin does not fall tails.

p&q = The coin does not fall heads, and the coin does not fall tails.

As applied to Jones, granting that he has no special powers to control coins when tossed into the air, and granting that the coins are not "trick" coins, Jones has no choice about whether the coin falls heads, Np. For the same reason, Jones has no choice about whether the coin lands tails, Nq. But Jones does have a choice about whether p&q is true. He *does* have a choice about the truth of this conjunction:

p&q: The coin does not fall heads and the coin does not fall tails.

All he has to do is toss it, and it will come up one or the other. As such, it is false, for Jones, that N(p&q). And this is a counterexample to agglomerativity for "has no choice about." As a result, we have a proof that Rule β is not a valid inference principle; it strictly implies agglomerativity for "has no choice about," and agglomerativity for "has no choice about" is invalid.

In response to these sorts of assaults on Rule β, various incompatibilists wishing to defend the Consequence Argument have introduced principles that can do Rule β's work in the Consequence Argument, but are not subject to these problems. For instance, a number of philosophers, such as David Widerker (1987), Kadri Vihvelin (1988), and Alicia Finch and Ted Warfield (1998) have advocated a principle of a stronger sort instead:

β-box: Np, $\Box(p \rightarrow q) \vdash Nq$

As it turns out, this principle is not vulnerable to McKay and Johnson's criticism of Rule β. In particular, β-box cannot be used to justify the final step of the proof of agglomerativity. (This is a detail we will not explain here.)

4.6.   Assessments

As we stated earlier, we think the main concerns for the Consequence Argument are the selectivity problem that Slote sets out, and the challenges to the principles of the Fixity of the Past and the Fixity of the Laws that we have discussed. Recall the example that we used earlier to bolster the compatibilist's case. Suppose that you have the ability to speak both English and French. You're in a café in Paris, but you order your coffee in English. Your friend says to you: "You could have ordered in French instead!" It would seem that your companion was correct to say what she did no matter what the truth about determinism turns out to be. So it appears that any reasonable person should accept that there are determinism-friendly senses of "could have done otherwise." Perhaps Lewis's

LMC provides a credible semantics for such ability claims, or maybe there is a plausible semantics for this sort of ability that instead denies the Fixity of the Past.

But at the same time, such ability claims may reflect only general sorts of abilities. And as Randolph Clarke (2009) has argued, the issue between the compatibilist and the incompatibilist may be whether determinism is compatible with an agent's exercise of such a general ability on a particular occasion. The incompatibilist can, after all, readily allow that there are general abilities, such as the ability to speak French in the above example, which one retains at the time one is not exercising it. But she may not grant that a causally determined agent could in fact have exercised such a general ability at a time when he does not in fact do so.

A conclusion one might draw is that there may be a more specific and stronger notion of an ability to do otherwise that is not compatibilism-friendly, and that can't be accounted for by semantics that deny the Fixity of the Past or the Fixity of the Laws. Carl Ginet (1990: chapter 5) has argued that there is reason to think that there are contexts of inference in which we assume such a more specific and stronger notion of an ability to do otherwise, which on his view cannot be accounted for by any such compatibilist semantic proposal.[22] If he is right, the answer to the question: *Is being able to do otherwise compatible with determinism?* depends on which sense you mean.

A key question now arises: Which notion of "could have done otherwise," if any, is required for moral responsibility in the sense at issue in the debate? In effect, Ginet proposes to settle this question by a manipulation argument wherein an agent is manipulated to act in a certain way but still would satisfy the compatibilist sense of "able to do otherwise." This is a valuable suggestion, and it's the one we'll turn to in Chapter 7.

Appendix I: What is a Modal Proposition?

What is a modal proposition? Introductory students are bound to find most discussions of the Consequence Argument technically inaccessible, especially as regards formal notions involving modal propositions and the logical properties of them. A few brief remarks should prove helpful. A modal proposition is about a way (a manner or a mode) in which another proposition obtains. Logical necessity is a modal notion. Consider the unmodalized proposition p:

p = Two plus two equals four.

That proposition, p, is true. But notice that there is a *way*—a manner or mode—in which p is true. It is true and cannot be but true, hence, we can append to this proposition the modal operator, *it is necessary that*, and we generate a distinct proposition which has the original embedded in it:

$\Box$p = It is necessary that two plus two equals four.

By appending the "□" to the original proposition p, we generate a distinct proposition, □p, asserting, not just that p obtains, but that it is necessary that p obtains.

There are various modalities, though the most commonly recognized and manageable ones are logical necessity, represented by the box as indicated above, and logical possibility, represented by a diamond (◊). Other modalities include such notions as belief, knowledge, justification, obligation, and permissibility.

Modal propositions and the logical relations they can enter into have logical properties that distinguish them from their non-modal counterparts. For instance, their truth is not simply a function of the truth of the constituent propositions embedded in them, not in the way that complex propositions in what is known as first-order truth-functional logic are simply a function of their constituents. Consider, for instance, conjunction in a non-modal context. If p is true and q is true, then the conjunction p&q is true, given the semantic rules for assigning values to conjunctions (a conjunction is true just in case all of its ingredient conjuncts are true). But now consider a modal context. It is false that M: Mitt Romney is currently President of the United States (in October 2013). But it is true that ◊M: It is possible that Mitt Romney is currently President of the United States (in October 2013). Had he won the last presidential election, he would be. Note, furthermore, that had he in fact won the election so that the non-modal claim M was in fact true, it would remain true that ◊M, since everything that is actually true is possibly true. Thus, the truth of this modal proposition, ◊M, is not simply a direct function of the truth of the non-modal ingredient, M, embedded in it.

To offer just one more example of how modal contexts differ from non-modal ones, note that the relations between modal propositions give rise to questions that have no place in non-modal contexts. Consider, for example, the modal positions ◊M: It is possible that Mitt Romney is President of the United States (in October 2013), which is true, and ◊B: It is possible that Barack Obama is President of the United States (in October 2013), which is also true. So we have a true conjunction: ◊M&◊B. But can we validly "combine" the two distinct claims of possibility into a *single* possibility claim by way of "agglomeration" and thereby say ◊(M&B)? We cannot. Why? We risk transition from a true to a false claim when, from ◊M&◊B we infer ◊(M&B). The latter tells us that it is possible that the following conjunctive claim is true: that Mitt Romney is President of the United States (in October 2013) *and* that Barack Obama is President of the United States (in October 2013). But, it is not possible that both of these propositions obtain at the same time (at least not under the assumption that the US Constitution has not been altered).

A further helpful point is this: Some modalities need indexing in some manner, for example, to times or persons, or both. For instance, treat the capital letter "J" as representing the modality "is justified in believing that." Let us apply this to some simple proposition. For instance, suppose that Jimmy Olson discovered at the stroke of midnight on New Year's Eve at the turn of the last millennium for incontrovertible reasons that Superman is Clark Kent. So consider the proposition:

r = Superman is Clark Kent.

Applying this to Jimmy Olson (*jo*) on the first day of the year 2000 (*1/1/00*), we get the proposition:

$J_{jo,\ 1/1/00}$, (r) = On New Year's Day of 2000, Jimmy Olson is justified in believing that Superman is Clark Kent.

Grant that $J_{jo,\ 1/1/00}$, (r) is true. But changing the indexing can alter the truth of the proposition, so that, if Lois Lane (*ll*) were substituted for Jimmy Olson, ($J_{ll,\ 1/1/00}$, (r)), the distinct proposition represented here would be false, assuming that our dear Lois remains unaware that her beloved Superman is after all Clark. Likewise, if we preserved the indexing to Jimmy Olson, but changed the time indexing to December 1, 1999, as in $J_{jo,\ 12/1/99}$, (r), we would also get a false proposition rather than a true one.

The modality of concern for our topic, power necessity, concerns the truth of propositions that are not within a person's power to alter at certain times, such as the relation that a person of today stands to the proposition that Caesar crossed the Rubicon in 49 BC. Let us represent the power necessity modality with an operator represented by the capital letter N. Now, indexed to Barack Obama (*bo*), in the year 2013 (*13*), and the proposition that Caesar crossed the Rubicon (q), we get the proposition, $N_{bo,13}$ (q), which can be read as "It is power necessary for Barack Obama in the year 2013 that the proposition, 'Caesar crossed the Rubicon,' obtains." This can in turn be read as: "The proposition, 'Caesar crossed the Rubicon,' obtains, and Barack Obama, in the year 2013, is not free to act in such a way that, if he were to so act, the proposition, 'Caesar crossed the Rubicon,' would not obtain."

Appendix II: Ginet's Challenge to Compatibilist-Friendly Semantics for Ability

Carl Ginet, who early on formulated a version of the Consequence Argument (1966), defends this argument against objections that deny the fixity of the laws and the fixity of the past (1990).

Let's consider first the compatibilist who denies the fixity of the past. Ginet argues that it's intuitive that to be able to do something is to be able to add to the given past, that is, to add some event to the past as it has been given. Now suppose that an agent S does not perform action a at time t, that is, not-a_t, and that there is some event b that occurs before t, b_t, such that:

BT: If it had been the case that a_t, then it would have been the case that not-b_t.

That is, if action a had occurred at t instead, then event b would not have occurred before t. From BT it follows that it was not open to S to make it the case that ($b_t \& a_t$). Let O_{st} stand for "it was open for S at t." The compatibilist under consideration, who Ginet calls the "compatibilist backtracker," will now deny that to be able to do something is to be able to add to the given past. More precisely, the compatibilist backtracker will deny the following principle:

For all S, t, b_t, and a_t, if O_{st} a_t then O_{st} (b_t&a_t).

To this denial Ginet objects that we seem to use this principle in making inferences of which we are confident. For example:

Push-ups: Given the premises that I have done 20 push-ups in the last five minutes and that it is now open to me to do four push-ups in the next minute, I will have done 24 push-ups in six minutes.

The compatibilist backtracker must say that rather than using the principle of the fixity of the given past in such inferences, we use instead:

For all S, t, b_t, and a_t, if O_{st} a_t & X, then O_{st} (b_t&a_t).

The X in inferences like *push-ups* will be:

(1) If it had been the case that a_t, then it would (still) have been the case that b_t.

In some other possible cases, the true conditional, by contrast with (1), is instead:

BT: If it had been the case that a_t, then it would have been the case that not-b_t.

In such cases, it is not open to the agent to add to the given past, and the possibility of such cases makes it the case that the principle of the fixity of the given past is false. The backtracking compatibilist needs to say that in *push-ups* we would need to assume a principle of the form of (1), that if S had done four push-ups in the minute after t, then it would still have been the case that S did 20 push-ups in the five minutes before t.

In Ginet's opinion, the compatibilist backtracker must agree that this account is highly implausible, for in the sort of case at issue, it's implausible to suppose that this sort of backtracking counterfactual is true. Suppose that in *push-ups*, I don't actually do four push-ups in the next minute—I don't do any. We would then need to be confident that in the nearest possible world in which S does four push-ups in the minute after t and the laws of nature are exactly the same as they are in the actual world, it would be true that S did 20 push-ups before t, and thus 24 within six minutes, and no more or less. Ginet argues that it would be difficult on the backtracking view to be confident of this claim, for the reason that any minimal set of changes in the past needed to allow it to be true that S does four push-ups in the minute after t is likely to ramify vastly into the past, in particular if determinism is true. And it may ramify in such a way that the very state of the world at some distant past time together with the same laws of nature would entail that S does not do 20 push-ups before t. For instance, if S can do four push-ups after t, but this would require will-power that S almost never has, a world in which S does 18 push-ups before t might be the one most similar to the actual world.

Ginet also takes on the Local Miracle Compatibilists' objection to the Consequence Argument.[23] The advocate of LMC denies that if p is deducible from the laws of nature, then it is never open to anyone to make it the case that not-p; that is, LMC rejects the Principle of the Fixity of the Laws. Now van Inwagen's case for the inescapability of the laws features examples such as: If it is a law of nature that protons cannot travel faster than the speed of light, then it is open for no one to make protons travel faster than the speed of light (say, by building some sort of machine). As we've seen, David Lewis argues that such examples do not support the principle of the inescapability of the laws. As Ginet formulates it, Lewis argues that van Inwagen-type inferences can be supported by a narrower principle:

> (Y) If p is a law of nature, it is never open to anyone to perform an action that *would be or would cause an event that falsifies* p.

Alternatively expressed, Lewis denies the following:

> (W) It is never open to anyone to perform an action which is such that, had she performed it, a law of nature would not have been a law of nature, or would have had an exception (that is, a law would have been falsified).

The idea, again (as explained Section 3.2), is that S might have acted so that a law of nature would have been falsified without that act being or causing a law-breaking event.

In response, Ginet argues that there are impeccable inferences in which (Y) cannot do the work it would need to do, given Lewis's view. Here is the example Ginet uses to argue this point. Imagine that some time before t, S ingested a drug that quickly causes a period of complete unconsciousness that lasts for several hours. Suppose that, because of the drug, there is true of S a certain proposition of the form:

> At t, S's neural system was in state U.

And suppose it follows from this proposition and the laws of nature that S was unconscious for at least 30 seconds after t. Ginet contends that we are surely entitled to deduce that it was not open to S to voluntarily exert force with her arm in the five seconds after t. But (Y) does not license this inference. For S's voluntarily exerting force with her arm in that five seconds, if it had happened, would not *itself* have been or caused an event that contradicts the laws of nature.

Why not? As Garrett Pendergraft (2011) states it, the relevant proposition at issue, the one that the LMC cannot help herself to in explaining the simple inference that S cannot raise her arm, and the one that would seemingly be underwritten by (Y) is:

> p: If S's neural system is in state U at t, then it is not the case that she voluntarily exerts force with her arm at t+5.

Ginet's point, as it bears on p, is that S's voluntary exertion does not falsify this proposition p, since S's voluntarily exerting force with her arm at t+5 *does not entail that she was in state U at t*. So her voluntarily exerting force with her arm at t+5, *in itself*, does not entail the falsity of p, since it is consistent with p's antecedent being false. So we cannot infer using (Y) alone that it was not open to S to voluntarily exert force with her arm at t+5.

Ginet offers the compatibilist the following reply, which is of a piece with Slote's response we discussed earlier (see Section 3.3). Let

> b_t = at t, S's neural system is in state U.

> a_t = beginning at t+5 seconds, S voluntarily exerted force with her arm for ten seconds.

> Lp = p is entailed by the laws of nature.

> $O_{st}p$ = def It was open to S at t to make it the case that p.

When we perform the inference from:

> $L(b_t$ only if not-$a_t)$ to

> not-O_{st} not-$(b_t$ only if not-$a_t)$

> (and then to not-O_{st} a_t via the principle of the fixity of the given past),

we assume that the nomic necessitation from b_t to not-a_t does not go through S's motivational history in the right way. In particular, the relevant causal path resulting in S's not raising her arm is brought about in a way that takes her motivational or action (and omission) generating agential resources out of play. So in performing such inferences, we're adding extra information (conforming to a further principle).

To this imagined LMC response, Ginet replies that it seems less plausible when one thinks about what it would be like really to know the laws of nature governing the causing of particular actions by their agent's motives and to use this knowledge to manipulate agents. Imagine, for instance, rather than S being rendered unconscious at t+5 due to a drug-induced state, she is instead manipulated by someone into not raising her arm through means perfectly replicating what it would be like for her simply to do so on her own volition (at a determined world). In such a case, the nomic necessitation—that is, the causal pathway—*would* leave in play that agent's motivational resources, just as the LMC (on Ginet's imagined proposal) would demand. Yet it would seem that it would not be open to the agent to do otherwise. To this Ginet might add a "no difference" principle: The manipulation case can be set up so that there is no relevant difference between it and a situation in which the action is causally determined by the laws and past.

Garrett Pendergraft (2011) responds on behalf of the LMC that there may be a compatibilist analysis of "can" that is not subject to a manipulation challenge. But in favor of Ginet's case one might argue that as long as an agent can satisfy The analysis by way of a causal process, and the analysis does not rule out manipulation by fiat, a manipulation case can be set up so that S satisfies the analysis. As we can see, how Ginet's response fares depends on how we assess the manipulation argument. We will turn to this examination in Chapter 7.

Suggestions for Further Reading

Because the literature on the Consequence Argument is so very extensive, and because it is also some of the most challenging work in the free will literature, we believe it is best just to call attention to a small sample of the most central contributions. See:

Beebee, Helen, and Alfred Mele. 2002. "Humean Compatibilism." *Mind* 111: 201–33.
Fischer, John Martin. 1994. *The Metaphysics of Free Will*. Oxford: Blackwell Publishers.
Ginet, Carl. 1966. "Might We Have No Choice?" In Keith Lehrer, ed., *Freedom and Determinism*. New York: Random House: 87–104.
Lewis, David. 1981. "Are We Free to Break the Laws?" *Theoria* 47: 113–21.
Slote, Michael. 1982. "Selective Necessity and the Free-Will Problem." *Journal of Philosophy* 79: 5–24.
van Inwagen, Peter. 1975. "The Incompatibility of Free Will and Determinism." *Philosophical Studies* 27: 185–99.

For a couple of thorough survey articles assessing at an advanced level the state of the art regarding the Consequence Argument, see:

Kapitan, Tomis. 2002. "A Master Argument for Incompatibilism?" In R. Kane, ed., *The Oxford Handbook of Free Will*. New York: Oxford University Press: 127–57.
Speak, Dan. 2011. "The Consequence Argument Revisited." In R. Kane, ed., *The Oxford Handbook of Free Will*. New York: Oxford University Press: 115–30.

For a thoughtful assessment of the (apparent) fall of the classical compatibilist conditional analysis in relation to the wider dialectic and the contested force of the Consequence Argument, one that resonates with our own assessment in the earlier part of this chapter, see:

Vihvelin, Kadri. 2013. "The Abilities and Dispositions of Our Freedom." In *Causes, Laws, & Free Will: Why Determinism Doesn't Matter*. New York: Oxford University Press: chapter 6.

Notes

1 A number of philosophers have proposed helpful refinement to the argument, including John Fischer, 1986, 1994; Ted Warfield, 2000; David Widerker, 1987; Alicia Finch 2013; and Carolina Sartorio 2015.
2 We'll not rehearse the details again here. See our discussion in Section 3.2.
3 What is a "modal proposition"? For readers who might profit from a brief introductory explanation of this issue, please see the Appendix I at the end of this chapter before reading further.
4 The notion of power necessity was developed by Carl Ginet (1980, 1983), and endorsed by John Martin Fischer (1994). In formulating the Consequence Argument, other philosophers have instead made use of slightly different modalities, such as one built from the expression, "has no choice about whether..." or "...is not up to one" or "...is unavoidable for one." These details will not matter for the level of resolution we bring to the discussion in this chapter.
5 Here we are simplifying by assuming that it is unproblematic to combine power necessity with respect to the past and power necessity with respect to the laws into a single premise about power necessity over the past and the laws. Doing so is controversial. To say of power necessity that power necessity over one proposition, p, and power necessity over a second proposition, q, validly generates power necessity of the conjunction of p and q, is to say that power necessity has the logical property of *agglomerativity*. If power necessity is agglomerative, then the principle (Np&Nq) strictly implies N(p&q) is valid.

But the property of agglomerativity is slippery and seems not to apply validly to other modalities, such as obligation. Suppose Joan is obligated by a promise to meet June at noon for lunch on Thursday. Setting aside the indexing, let us represent her obligation as O(r). And suppose also that Joan is obligated to be at a doctor's appointment at the very same time and in a different place that same Thursday. Let us represent this as O(s). So, it is accurate to describe Joan's obligations with the following conjunction: O(r) & O(s). But does Joan have a single obligation (O(r&s)) to meet June for lunch and make her doctor's appointment, an obligation which it is physically impossible for her to satisfy, given that she cannot be in two different places at the same time? It seems not, at least if a constraint on obligation is that it is not physically impossible to comply with it. (See also the appendix to this chapter, where we illustrate that logical possibility is also not agglomerative.)

If, like the notion of obligation, power necessity is not agglomerative, then the first premise of the Consequence Argument as we have formulated it here might be illicit. Power necessity with regard to the past, and power necessity with regard to the laws of nature, might not warrant the inference of power necessity with regard to the conjunction of the past and the laws of nature. If so, then a viable version of the Consequence Argument can only proceed by introducing distinct premises for power necessity over the laws and power necessity over the past. (Furthermore, if it turns out, as some critics have argued, that one can derive a commitment to agglomerativity from the inference principle Transfer, this too might very well create problems.)

6   We also simplify here. We shall treat it as intuitive that if the metaphysical thesis of
    determinism is true, it is power necessary. Moreover, we also shall gloss over a
    further logical detail. The second premise of the argument we present here expresses
    power necessity with respect to the truth of a material conditional: $N((p\&l) \to f)$. But,
    as we have explained (Section 1.4), determinism is best thought of as a metaphysi-
    cally necessary truth about the way the world is (assuming determinism is true). That
    is, determinism is the thesis that $\Box((p\&l) \to f)$. But for present purposes, we can
    understand $((p\&l) \to f)$ as a logical consequence of the proposition $\Box((p\&l) \to f)$, and
    then attend to power necessity with respect to this logical consequence.
7   For a thorough treatment of these issues, see Fischer (1994: chapters 2–6: 23–130). In
    developing this section, we rely heavily on Fischer's assessment of these issues.
8   For a helpful discussion of these two notions of ability and how they figure in ways of
    resisting the Consequence Argument, see Kapitan (2002), whose treatment we rely
    upon in what follows.
9   Some might express this by saying that the laws of nature "supervene" on the actually
    obtaining causal facts. (To explain, if x supervenes on y, then x depends on y, but y
    does not depend on x. This might in turn be captured as follows: There can be no
    change in x without a change in y; but it is possible that there could be a change in y
    without there being a change in x.)
10 To help place in perspective how uncontroversial this notion of a local miracle is,
    think of it this way. On this compatibilist approach, under the assumption that deter-
    minism is true, in this actual world, in each scenario in which a free agent acts as she
    does act, a number of local miracles *actually do occur*! But they are only miracles rel-
    ative to different laws than the ones that actually do obtain in this world. They are
    merely miracles relative to laws obtaining in the possible but non-actual worlds in
    which an agent acts differently than she does in this actual world.
11 For other compatibilists advancing Lewis's basic strategy, see Horgan (1985) and
    Vihvelin (2013).
12 Slote (1982), and also Daniel Dennett (1984), have suggested that the power necessity
    modality has an epistemic element of the sort allegedly at work in Closure. Hence,
    knowledge necessity's modal selectivity infects the power necessity modality in a
    similar manner.
13 For a range of advanced formulations and discussions, see Fischer, 1983, 1986, 1994;
    Ginet, 1966, 1980, 1990; Kapitan, 2002; Lamb, 1977; McKay and Johnson, 1996;
    O'Connor, 1993, 2000; van Inwagen, 1975, 1983, 2002; Widerker, 1987; Wiggins,
    1973.
14 Whereas we have elected to use the notion of power necessity as defined above
    (Section 4.2), van Inwagen proceeds by using the expression "has no choice about."
    The meaning of these expressions are not synonymous, but we will proceed here as if
    van Inwagen's preferred idiom and the modality he builds from it are the same as the
    one we use in this chapter.
15 See note 6 above for a more careful formulation.
16 A word of caution here: In van Inwagen's version of the argument, as we shall set out
    below, the argument does not proceed from step 1 to 2 as we have set it out in this
    paragraph. Instead, before applying Rule α, an intermediate logical operation is per-
    formed on the way the first step is formulated. Then Rule α is applied to that formula-
    tion. We'll explain the motivation for this extra step after setting out the argument.
    Note also that, strictly speaking, what follows from $\Box((P_o\&L) \to P)$ and Rule α is *not*
    that it is power necessary *that it is necessarily true that P is implied by $P_o\&L$*. (Here

we elaborate on a point alluded to in note 6 above.) That is, the following proposition does *not* follow:

$$N[\Box((P_o\&L)\rightarrow P)]$$

This stronger proposition *would* follow from a stronger inference rule. Call it α-strong:

α-strong: $\Box p \vdash \Box Np$

And this stronger rule would state that from the fact that a proposition is necessary, it follows that no one has, or ever had, a choice about whether *that proposition is necessary*. Now, this stronger inference rule might be just as plausible as is Rule α. Nevertheless, it is not the one used in the argument we are currently examining. As for the one that is, Rule α, all it allows us to infer from $\Box((P_o\&L)\rightarrow P)$ is that the following *material conditional*, $(P_o\&L)\rightarrow P$, is power necessary. That is:

$$N((P_o\&L)\rightarrow P)$$

Of course, this material conditional is a logical consequence of the modalized conditional, $\Box((P_o\&L)\rightarrow P)$. And the modalized conditional expresses a metaphysical or broadly logical necessity. But readers should be cautioned against misunderstanding what, strictly speaking, the argument asserts. It is *not* assumed in the argument that, for instance, it is power necessary for a person that the metaphysical thesis of determinism is true—that is, it is not assumed that it is power necessary *that necessarily the past and the laws imply one unique future*. Nor is it claimed in the argument that it is power necessary for any person, with respect to some particular fact, such as that Nixon is pardoned, that it is metaphysically necessary that the fact is implied by the laws and the past. All it claims that is power necessary for any person with respect to any particular fact is that the fact (e.g., P, that Nixon is pardoned for all his crimes while in office) is *materially implied* by the facts of the past and the laws $(P_o\&L)$.

17 This is a point we explained in Section 1.5.

18 For those unfamiliar with the logic used here, the easiest way to see that $\Box((P_o\&L)\rightarrow P)$ and $\Box(P_o\rightarrow(L\rightarrow P))$ are logically equivalent is just to consider what conditions would be required to render the unmodalized propositions $((P_o\&L)\rightarrow P)$ and $(P_o\rightarrow(L\rightarrow P))$ true, and what conditions would be required to render them false. Doing so, one will see that they are the exact same conditions, and so are logically equivalent. Now just assume that the modal necessity operator preserves that relation.

19 See note 5 above for worries about inferring from NP$_o$ and NL that N(P$_o$&L), which have to do with the idea that power necessity ("N") is agglomerative.

20 This indictment seems especially problematic since, as we have noted above, van Inwagen was at pains to avoid the assumption of agglomerativity by taking care to introduce NP$_o$ and NL as distinct steps rather than simply work with the premise N(P$_o$&L).

21 Here we assume some basic knowledge of first-order propositional logic, as we have elsewhere in the text. But as a simple clue to aid one thinking through this the first time, keep in mind that on any interpretation in which p is false, the entire sentence must come out as true, since as a (complex) material conditional, if the antecedent of it is false, then the entire sentence is true. So focus instead on only those interpretations in which p is true, which leaves only two, one in which q is false, and one in which q is true. On each of these remaining interpretations, the complex proposition comes out true.

22 Readers interested in pursuing Ginet's thoughtful reply to these compatibilist views are invited to see Appendix II. We should note, however, that this is very advanced work, and the main points we wish to convey about it are already set out above.

23 There are other objections to LMC that we won't consider in detail here. Helen Beebee (2003), for example, argues that in certain common sorts of cases in which an agent is intuitively able to do otherwise, the local miracle compatibilist is, after all, committed to the causal notion of ability. Peter Graham (2008) responds to Beebee on behalf of the compatibilist, but the issues here turn out to be complex and challenging.

5 Alternative Possibilities and Frankfurt Cases

In this chapter we discuss another of the three decisive influences on the free will debate that originated in the 1960s. As we pointed out in Chapter 3, prior to this time it was generally assumed that the sort of free will at issue in the debate is the freedom to do otherwise, that is, the freedom on a particular occasion both to act and to refrain from acting. It was also generally assumed that moral responsibility required this sort of leeway freedom. But an important article, published by Harry Frankfurt in 1969, changed all of that. There, he argued, by the use of an ingenious type of example, that moral responsibility does not require leeway freedom.

The intuition that moral responsibility for an action requires that the agent could have done otherwise is a powerful one. Indeed, access to alternative possibilities for action would seems to play a significant role in explaining why an agent is morally responsible. For if an agent is to be blameworthy for an action, it seems crucial that she could have done something to avoid being blameworthy—that she could have done something to get herself off the hook (Moya, 2006; Pereboom, 2001: 1; Widerker, 2000). This intuition is aptly expressed by what David Widerker calls the *W-Defense*. About Jones, who breaks a promise and is allegedly morally responsible but could not have done otherwise, he writes:

> Still, since you, [Harry] Frankfurt, wish to hold him blameworthy for his decision to break his promise, tell me *what, in your opinion, should he have done instead*? Now, you cannot claim that he should not have decided to break the promise, since this was something that was not in his power to do. Hence, I do not see how you can hold Jones blameworthy for his decision to break the promise. (Widerker, 2000: 191)

In Carlos Moya's phrasing, to be blameworthy for an action an agent must have an *exempting* alternative possibility, one that, should he avail himself of it, would exempt him from blame (Moya, 2006: 67; cf. Otsuka, 1998). If he is to be praiseworthy for an action, it seems important that he could have done something less admirable. Both classical compatibilists and classical incompatibilists grounded their views about free will precisely in such intuitions. Accordingly, they defended the following principle of alternative possibilities:

(PAP) An action is free in the sense required for moral responsibility only if the agent could have done otherwise than she actually did.

Again, this principle was generally accepted into the 1960s.

But Frankfurt disagreed. His challenge to the alternative-possibilities requirement involves, first of all, examples in which an agent considers performing some action, but a backup, such as a neuroscientist, is concerned that she will not come through. So if she were to manifest an indication that she will not or might not perform the action, the neuroscientist would intervene and make her perform the action anyway. But as things actually go, the neuroscientist remains idle, since the agent performs the action on her own. Here is a version of Frankfurt's original example (Sartorio, 2016):

> A neuroscientist, Black, wants Jones to perform a certain action. Black is prepared to go to considerable lengths to get his way, but he prefers to avoid showing his hand unnecessarily. So he waits until Jones is about to make up his mind what to do, and he does nothing unless it is clear to him (Black is an excellent judge of such things) that Jones is going to decide to do something other than what he wants him to do. If it were to become clear that Jones is going to decide to do something else, Black would take effective steps to ensure that Jones decides to do what he wants him to do, by directly manipulating the relevant processes in Jones's brain. As it turns out, Black never has to show his hand because Jones, for reasons of his own, decides to perform the very action Black wants him to perform.

The idea is that even though Jones could not have avoided the action he performs, he is still intuitively morally responsible for this action. After all, he did it on his own and Black never intervened.

In Frankfurt's diagnosis, this sort of example illustrates a distinction between two types of factors: factors that cause or causally explain the action, and factors that contribute to making the action inevitable even though they do not cause or causally explain the action (Frankfurt, 1969; Sartorio, 2016). In the example above, Black's intentions contribute to making the action inevitable, but they do not cause or causally explain the action, since Black ends up not doing anything at all to produce the action. The factors that cause and causally explain the action are instead the ordinary ones, such as the agent's reasons and deliberation.

Frankfurt argued that the reason the alternative-possibilities requirement seemed initially plausible is that we tend to conflate the two kinds of factors. When we think about cases in which an agent lacks the ability to do otherwise, we tend to assume that the factors that make the action inevitable are also those that cause and causally explain the action. Frankfurt examples are unusual cases in which these two types of factors come apart, and instructively so. In such cases the action is caused and can be causally explained by ordinary factors such as deliberation and sensitivity to reasons, while factors that saliently make the action inevitable are causally idle (Frankfurt, 1969; Sartorio, 2016).

Illustrating and making intuitive the distinction between factors that make the action inevitable and those that cause or causally explain it is one of the three key putative lessons of Frankfurt examples. The two others involve the claim that this distinction is relevant to the nature of moral responsibility in a particular way. One of these is that because we have the intuition that Jones is morally responsible, and access to alternatives is ruled out by factors that make the action inevitable, access to alternatives turns out not to be a requirement for moral responsibility. The other is a thesis about what is relevant to accounting for moral responsibility, given that access to alternative possibilities is ruled out. When we judge Jones morally responsible, we focus just on the actual causal history of his action: what he does do, the reasons he has for doing it, and the deliberative process by which he decides what to do on the basis of his reasons (Frankfurt, 1969; McKenna, 2005b, 2008b; Widerker, 2003). McKenna formulates a response to the W-Defense on the basis of this suggestion, which he calls the L-Reply (2005b, 2008b):

> A person's moral responsibility concerns what she does do and her basis for doing it, not what else she could have done. (2008b: 785)

A profitable way to view this debate is as a contest between the W-Defense and the L-Reply.[1] A role that Frankfurt examples have in this debate is to decide this contest. In analytic philosophy more generally, standoffs of this sort often occur, and one item one might find in the philosopher's toolkit is an example that promises to occasion the intuition that will break the tie.

In the face of this challenge from Frankfurt examples, defenders of the alternative-possibilities requirement will typically concede the first putative lesson, the distinction between inevitability-occasioning and causal factors. But they will not allow that this distinction is relevant to moral responsibility. They claim instead that factors that make an action inevitable will rule out moral responsibility even if they are not causally efficacious. Now, to be successful, a Frankfurt example needs to (1) feature the ruling out of relevant alternative possibilities by factors not also causally efficacious in the production of the action; and to (2) generate the intuition that the agent in the example is morally responsible. In general, when defenders of the alternative-possibilities requirement, after examining a proposed Frankfurt example carefully, do have the clear intuition that the agent is morally responsible, they tend to argue that despite initial impressions the example does feature a relevant alternative possibility after all. When they don't have this intuition, they contend that there is some feature of the actual causal history of the action, such as the agent's causal determination, that undermines this intuition in a principled way. In the remainder of this chapter, we will see how these strategies play out in the more specific types of objections that defenders of the alternative-possibilities requirement have raised.

5.1. Compatibilist and Incompatibilist Source Views

But first we want to make a point concerning how, after Frankfurt's article, various positions in the debate came to be classified. Early on, John Fischer (1982, 1994) correctly pointed out that Frankfurt's argument does not refute the incompatibilist claim that moral responsibility requires that the actual causal history of the action not be deterministic. For it leaves untouched the view that moral responsibility requires that one's action not actually result from a deterministic causal process that traces back to factors beyond one's control—back to causal factors that one could not have produced, altered, or prevented. Note that the above Frankfurt example does not specify that Jones's action is causally determined in this way. If it were specified that his choice is deterministically produced by factors beyond his control, then at least for some the intuition that he is morally responsible might fade away.

This reflection suggests an alternative requirement on the sort of free will required for moral responsibility, one related to the L-Reply:

(Source) An action is free in the sense required for moral responsibility only if its causal history, and in particular its causal source, is of an appropriate sort.

Frankfurt's own compatibilist version of a source account (to be examined in Chapter 9) is one on which the agent's will to perform the action is endorsed by the agent's second-order desires: she must not only will the action, but she must want to will it. In this view, if the action has this sort of causal history, it will have its source in the agent in such a way as to facilitate her moral responsibility for it. And access to alternative possibilities is not required.

The source incompatibilist will affirm that part of what it is to be an appropriate source of an action is that it not be causally determined by factors beyond the agent's control:

(Indeterminism) An action is free in the sense required for moral responsibility only if it is not produced by a deterministic process that traces back to causal factors beyond the agent's control.

A natural, causal interpretation of what it is for a factor to be beyond an agent's control is for it to be outside of her causal reach (Sartorio, 2015).

While leeway incompatibilists would also argue that the actual causal history of a morally responsible action must be indeterministic, they maintain this is so only because an indeterministic history is required to secure alternative possibilities (e.g., Ginet, 1997, 2007). Source incompatibilists, by contrast, contend that the role the indeterministic causal history plays in explaining why an agent is morally responsible is independent of facts about alternative possibilities. On their view, it's that an indeterministic history allows the agent to be the source of her actions in such a way that they are not causally determined by factors beyond her control.

In opposition to source incompatibilism, Fischer once argued that "there is simply no good reason to suppose that causal determinism in itself (and apart from considerations pertaining to alternative possibilities) vitiates our moral responsibility" (1994: 159). Now it is true that one widespread incompatibilist intuition is that if due to causal determination we can never do otherwise, and we therefore could not have refrained from the immoral actions we perform, we could not legitimately be held blameworthy for them. But another common intuition is that if all of our behavior was "in the cards" before we existed, in the sense that things happened before we were born that, by way of a deterministic causal process, inevitably resulted in our actions, we could not legitimately be held responsible for them. By this intuition, if causal factors existed before a criminal was born that, by way of a deterministic process, inevitably issued in his act of murder, then he could not legitimately be blamed for this action. And if all of our actions had this type of causal history, it would seem that we would lack the kind of control over our actions moral responsibility requires.

Still, in the dialectic of the free will debate one should not expect Fischer or any compatibilist to be moved much by this basic source incompatibilist intuition alone to abandon their position. In our view, the best source incompatibilist challenge to compatibilism develops the claim that causal determination presents in principle no less of a threat to moral responsibility than deterministic manipulation by neuroscientists. We shall turn to that challenge in Chapter 7. Nonetheless, what this basic intuition should show at this stage is that there might well be a coherent incompatibilist position that could survive the demise of the alternative-possibilities requirement on moral responsibility (Della Rocca, 1998; Pereboom, 2001).

5.2.   The Flicker of Freedom Defense

Leeway theorists have argued that the alternative-possibilities requirement can withstand the argument from Frankfurt examples. In the next three sections, we will consider and address three objections to this argument: the Flicker of Freedom, Dilemma, and Timing defenses.

We begin the Flicker defense, which concedes the intuition that the agent in the Frankfurt example is morally responsible, but claims that the example features an alternative possibility that explains the intuition. In any Frankfurt example, there must be some factor that the neuroscientist's device is rigged up to detect that could have but does not actually occur, such as the agent's intention to do otherwise (e.g., Fischer, 1994: 134–47; Naylor, 1984; van Inwagen, 1983: 166–80). This factor—a "flicker of freedom," to use Fischer's term—can then serve as the alternative possibility required for moral responsibility. It's not implausible that the formation of an intention to do otherwise, say, should count as the relevant sort of alternative possibility, and so this factor could indeed serve to explain the agent's moral responsibility.

Fischer responds to the Flicker defense by arguing that one can construct Frankfurt examples in which the neuroscientist's device detects some factor that can't plausibly have this explanatory role. One might, for instance, imagine that Jones will decide to kill Smith only if Jones blushes beforehand, and that Black's device will activate only if Jones does not blush by a certain time (Fischer, 1982, 1994). Then Jones's failure to blush by a certain time might be the alternative possibility that would trigger the intervention that causes him to kill Smith. Supposing that Jones acts without intervention, we might well have the intuition that he is blameworthy despite the fact that he could not have done or chosen otherwise, or formed an alternative intention. He could have failed to blush, but as Fischer argues, such a flicker is of no use to the leeway theorist since it is too "flimsy and exiguous" and "insufficiently robust" to play a part in grounding moral responsibility.

But what is it for an alternative possibility to be robust, and why would the robustness of an alternative possibility be crucial? As we've argued, the intuition underlying the alternative-possibilities requirement is that if, for example, an agent is to be blameworthy for an action, it is crucial that she could have done something to avoid being blameworthy. If having an alternative possibility does in fact play a role in explaining an agent's moral responsibility for an action, it would have to be robust in at least the sense that as a result of securing that alternative possibility instead, the agent would thereby have engaged in a voluntary undertaking whereby she would have avoided the responsibility she actually has for the action (McKenna, 1997; Mele, 1996; Otsuka, 1998; Pereboom, 2001; Wyma, 1997). If Jones had failed to blush, he would not in this way have voluntarily avoided responsibility for killing Smith. So failing to blush in the above scenario does not count as a robust alternative.

Robustness also has an epistemic component. Suppose that the only way Joe could have avoided deciding to take an illegal deduction on his tax form—a choice he does in fact make—is by voluntarily taking a sip from his coffee cup, for unbeknownst to him, the coffee was poisoned, so a sip would have killed him immediately; or, for another version, it is laced with the drug that induces compliance with the tax code (Pereboom, 2000, 2001, 2014; cf. Moya 2006: 64, who constructs an example of this form). In this situation, Joe could have behaved voluntarily so as to preclude his choice to evade taxes, which would have precluded the blameworthiness he actually incurred. But whether he could have voluntarily taken the sip from the coffee cup is intuitively irrelevant to explaining why or whether he is blameworthy for his decision. What's missing is that Joe has no inkling that taking the sip would render him blameless. This motivates the epistemic component of the robustness condition: If Joe were blameworthy because he has an alternative possibility in this situation, it must be that he in some sense understood that or how it was available to him.

On the assumption that in any situation taking the morally best option fully available to the agent renders her blameless, here is a proposal (a substantial necessary condition—not a sufficient condition) that accommodates all of these concerns. We state the criterion in terms of blameworthiness by contrast with moral responsibility more generally:

Robustness: For an agent to have a robust alternative to her immoral action A, that is, an alternative relevant per se to explaining why she is blameworthy for performing A, it must be that

(i) she instead could have voluntarily acted or refrained from acting as a result of which she would be blameless, and

(ii) for at least one such exempting acting or refraining, she understood (at some level) that she could so voluntarily act or refrain, and that if she voluntarily so acted or refrained she would then be, or would likely be, blameless. (Pereboom, 2014: 13)

The Frankfurt defender's response to the flicker defense is that Frankfurt examples can be constructed which, although they feature an alternative possibility, that alternative possibility is not robust, and thus cannot serve to explain the agent's moral responsibility for her action. The resulting source view opposes, specifically, the following version of PAP:

(PAP-Robust) An action is free in the sense required for moral responsibility only if the agent has access to a robust alternative to that action.

In addition, we can now characterize leeway views, whether compatibilist or incompatibilist, as those that affirm that for an agent to be blameworthy for an action, she must have available to her a robust alternative possibility, that is, one that satisfies Robustness. Source views, by contrast, deny this. The leeway incompatibilist, whose position will feature prominently in the discussion that follows, holds in addition that the reason causal determination precludes moral responsibility is that it rules out alternative possibilities altogether, but most importantly, those of the robust sort.

5.3. The Dilemma Defense

The Dilemma Defense was initially suggested by Robert Kane and then systematically developed by Widerker (Kane, 1985: 51, 1996: 142–4, 191–2; Widerker, 1995: 247–61; cf. Ginet, 1996). It's an objection raised from the point of view of the leeway libertarian in particular. Here is Widerker's version: For any Frankfurt example, if causal determinism is assumed to hold in the actual sequence that results in the action, then no libertarian can be expected to have the intuition that the agent is morally responsible—it's ruled out by the nature of the actual causal history of the action. If, on the other hand, indeterminism in the actual sequence is presupposed, the scenario will not serve the Frankfurt defender's purpose, for any such case will fall to a dilemma. In Frankfurt examples the actual situation will feature a prior sign, such as Jones's blush, that signals the fact that the intervention is not required. If the prior sign causally determined the action, or if it were associated with some factor that did, the intervener's (or his device's) predictive ability could be explained. However, then the libertarian, again, would not and could not be expected to have the intuition that the agent is morally responsible. If the relationship between the prior sign and the action was not causally deterministic in such ways, then it would be open that the agent could have done otherwise despite the occurrence of the prior sign. And then it's open that the intuition that the agent is morally responsible can be explained by access to an alternative possibility after all. Either way, PAP (or PAP-Robust) emerges unscathed.

5.3.1. The Mele–Robb Example and Hunt's Blockage Strategy

In response, a number of critics have attempted to construct Frankfurt examples that escape this objection, for instance Eleonore Stump (1990, 1996); Al Mele and David Robb (1998); David Hunt (2000, 2005); Pereboom (2000, 2001, 2014); McKenna (2003); Widerker (2006); and Fischer (2010). In one kind of case there are no prior signs to guide intervention, not even non-robust flickers of freedom. One ingenious scenario in this category was developed by Mele and Robb (1998). The example features Bob, who inhabits a world in which determinism is false:

> At t1, Black initiates a certain deterministic process P in Bob's brain with the intention of thereby causing Bob to decide at t2 (an hour later, say) to steal Ann's car. The process, which is screened off from Bob's consciousness, will deterministically culminate in Bob's deciding at t2 to steal Ann's car unless he decides on his own to steal it or is incapable at t2 of making a decision (because, e.g., he is dead at t2).... The process is in no way sensitive to any "sign" of what Bob will decide. As it happens, at t2 Bob decides on his own to steal the car, on the basis of his own indeterministic deliberation about whether to steal it, and his decision has no deterministic cause. But if he had not just then decided on his own to steal it, P would have deterministically issued, at t2, in his deciding to steal it. Rest assured that P in no way influences the indeterministic decision-making process that actually issues in Bob's decision.

Mele and Robb argue that Bob is morally responsible for his decision, and thus it would seem that this case evades the dilemma defense.

One concern for this example is that it involves *trumping preemption* (Schaffer, 2000), and that this notion is incoherent. As the case is set up, Bob's deciding on his own to steal Ann's car trumps and preempts Black's deterministic process. Can we conceive of a mechanism that explains how this could be? Jonathan Schaffer provides a nice example of trumping preemption: Suppose the soldiers are trained to obey the general rather than the major when these two officers issue orders simultaneously (2000). Imagine that the major and the general shout: "March!" at the same time. It's intuitive that only the general's order is causally efficacious, trumping the major's order. However, in this case the trumping preemption has an explanation, so perhaps Mele and Robb owe us an explanation of how trumping preemption might work in their case.

Mele and Robb discuss several potential problems for their scenario, one of which is whether we can make sense of what would happen at t2 if P and Bob's indeterministic deliberative process were to diverge at t2, in particular if Bob's indeterministic process were to result in his deciding not to steal, while P, as the set-up specifies, in his deciding to steal. Here is how they describe the difficulty:

> The issue may be pictured, fancifully, as follows. Two different "decision nodes" in Bob's brain are directly relevant. The "lighting up" of node N1 represents his deciding to steal the car, and the "lighting up" of node N2 represents his deciding *not* to steal the car. Under normal circumstances and in the absence of preemption, a process's "hitting" a decision node in Bob "lights up" that node. If it were to be the case both that P hits N1 at t2 and that x does not hit N1 at t2, then P would light up N1. If both processes were to hit N1 at t2, Bob's indeterministic deliberative process, x, would light up N1 and P would not. The present question is this. What would happen if, at t2, P were to hit N1 and x were to hit N2? That is, what would happen if the two processes were to "diverge" in this way? And <u>why</u>?

And here is the answer they provide:

> We extend Bob's story as follows. Although if both processes were to hit N1 at t2, Bob's indeterministic deliberative process, x, would preempt P and light up N1, it is also the case that if, at t2, P were to hit N1 and x were to hit N2, P would prevail. In the latter case, P would light up N1 and the indeterministic process would not light up N2. Of course, readers would like a story about why it is that although x would preempt P in the former situation, P would prevail over x in the latter. Here is one story. By t2, P has "neutralized" N2 (but without affecting what goes on in x). That is why, if x were to hit N2 at t2, N2 would not light up. More fully, by t2 P has neutralized all of the nodes in Bob for decisions that are contrary to a decision at t2 to steal Ann's car (e.g., a decision at t2 not to steal anyone's car and a decision at t2 never to steal anything). In convenient shorthand, by t2 P has neutralized N2 and all its "cognate decision nodes." Bear in mind that all we need is a conceptually possible scenario, and this certainly looks like one. (Mele and Robb 1998: 104 5)

The aspect of this story that might raise a concern for the libertarian is P's neutralization of N2 and all its cognate decision nodes. The libertarian might contend that P's neutralizing procedure is equivalent to P's causal determination of Bob's decision to steal the car; after all, the neutralization would seem to be a causal process that renders inevitable x's hitting N1 instead. However, Mele and Robb do specify that P's neutralizing activity does not affect what goes on in Bob's indeterministic decision-making process, and if so, it would seem that P would not causally determine the decision. How can we shed light on this difficulty?

Let's examine a strategy that more vigorously exploits the neutralization idea, an approach known as "blockage," which has been developed by David Hunt (2000). Consider two situations (Pereboom, 2001: 15–18):

Situation A: Scarlet deliberately chooses to kill Mustard at t1, and there are no factors beyond her control that deterministically produce her choice. When Scarlet chooses to kill Mustard, she could have chosen not to kill him. There are no causal factors, such as intervention devices, that would prevent her from not making the choice to kill Mustard.

In these circumstances, the leeway incompatibilist would agree that Scarlet could be morally responsible for her choice. But against the alternative-possibilities requirement we can employ the following variant:

Situation B: Scarlet's choice to kill Mustard has precisely the same actual causal history as in A. But before she even started to think about killing Mustard, a neuroscientist had blocked all the neural pathways not used in Situation A, so that no neural pathway other than the one employed in that situation could be used. Let's suppose that it is causally determined that she remain a living agent, and if she remains a living agent, some neural pathway has to be used. Thus every alternative for Scarlet is blocked except the one that realizes her choice to kill Mustard. But the blockage does not affect the actual causal history of Scarlet's choice, because the blocked pathways would have remained dormant.

One might have the intuition that Scarlet is morally responsible for her choice in Scenario B as well, fueled by the supposition that it does not feature any relevant divergence from Scenario A. However, this intuition might be challenged upon more careful reflection on whether in B Scarlet retains free will. An important question about a blockage case is one that Fischer asks: "Could neural events bump up against, so to speak, the blockage?" (Fischer, 1999: 119). If so, there still might be (robust) alternative possibilities in Scenario B. But if neural events can't bump up against the blockage, then, as Kane suggests, it might be that the neural events are causally determined partly by virtue of the blockage, and that we now have "determinism pure and simple" (Kane, 2000: 162).

In response, the blockage defender can point out that in more standard Frankfurt examples the action is also inevitable, but the libertarian's intuition that the agent is morally responsible for it depends on the fact that it does not have an actual causal history by which it is made inevitable. What makes the action inevitable is instead some fact about the scenario that is not a feature of its actual causal history. Thus the action's being inevitable need not make it the case that it is causally determined. But then how is the blockage case different from the standard Frankfurt-style cases? After all, the blockage does not seem to be a feature of the actual causal history of the action either.

Nevertheless, perhaps Kane's charge of determinism can be defended. It might be that two-situation cases of the variety just canvassed are misleading just because it is natural to assume that the actual causal history of an event is essentially the same in each, given that the only difference between them is a restriction that would appear to have no actual effect on the event. But now consider a simple two-situation case modeled on a reflection of Hunt's (Fischer, 1999: 119–20). Imagine a universe correctly described by Epicurean physics (Pereboom, 2001: 17). At the most fundamental level we find only atoms and the frictionless void, and that these atoms fall in a determinate downward direction—except when they undergo uncaused swerves.

> Situation C: A spherical atom is falling downward through space, with a certain velocity and acceleration. Its actual causal history is indeterministic because at any time the atom can be subject to an uncaused swerve. Suppose that the atom can swerve in any direction other than upwards. In actual fact, from t1 to t2 it does not swerve.

A counterfactual situation diverges from C only by virtue of a device that eliminates alternative possibilities and all differences thereby entailed:

> Situation D: This case is identical to C, except that the atom is falling downward through a straight and vertically oriented tube whose interior surface is made of frictionless material, and whose interior is precisely wide enough to accommodate the atom. The atom would not have swerved during this time interval, and the trajectory, velocity, and acceleration of the atom from t1 to t2 are precisely what they are in C.

One might initially have the intuition that the causal history of the atom from t1 to t2 in these two situations is exactly the same. However, this intuition might be undermined by the fact that the restrictions present in D but not in C may change this causal history from one that is essentially indeterministic to one that is essentially deterministic. Because the tube prevents any alternative motion, it might *in fact* rule out any indeterminism in the atom's causal history between t1 and t2. And if the tube rules out any indeterminism in this causal history, it would seem to make it deterministic.

This problem could make it hard to assess moral responsibility in blockage cases. Sympathy for Frankfurt-style arguments is generated by the sense that moral responsibility is largely a function of the features of the actual causal history of an action, to which restrictions that are present yet play no actual causal role are irrelevant. But in a scenario in which such restrictions may indeed be relevant to the nature of the causal history of an action our intuitions about whether the agent is morally responsible might be challenged. This concern may make one less confident when evaluating these difficult kinds of Frankfurt-style cases. Returning to Mele's and Robb's case, it's a key feature of the example that if Black's deterministic process P and Bob's indeterministic deliberative process were to diverge at t2, P would neutralize N2 (which corresponds to not deciding to steal the car) and all its cognate decision nodes. In this respect it resembles a blockage scenario. But blockage scenarios threaten to be deterministic, and thus the Mele and Robb example inherits this challenge. Still, we don't think this challenge is clearly successful against their case.

5.3.2. Pereboom's Tax Evasion Case

Pereboom has also proposed a Frankfurt example designed to respond to the Dilemma Defense (Pereboom, 2000, 2001: 18–19, 2003, 2009b, 2012a, 2014). Its distinguishing features are these: The cue for the neuroscientist's intervention is a necessary condition for the agent's availing herself of any robust alternative possibility (without the intervener's device in place), while this cue for intervention itself is not a robust alternative possibility, and the absence at any specific time of the cue for intervention in no sense causally determines the action the agent actually performs. Here is the case:

> *Tax Evasion (2)*: Joe is considering claiming a tax deduction for the registration fee that he paid when he bought a house. He knows that claiming this deduction is illegal, but that he probably won't be caught, and that if he were, he could convincingly plead ignorance. Suppose he has a strong but not always overriding desire to advance his self-interest regardless of its cost to others and even if it involves illegal activity. In addition, the only way that in this situation he could fail to choose to evade taxes is for moral reasons, of which he is aware. He could not, for example, fail to choose to evade taxes for no reason or simply on a whim. Moreover, it is causally necessary for his failing to choose to evade taxes in this situation that he attain a certain level of attentiveness to moral reasons. Joe can secure this level of attentiveness voluntarily. However, his attaining this level of attentiveness is not causally sufficient for his failing to choose to evade taxes. If he were to attain this level of attentiveness, he could, exercising his libertarian free will, either choose to evade taxes or refrain from so choosing (without the intervener's device in place). However, to ensure that he will choose to evade taxes, a neuroscientist has, unbeknownst to Joe, implanted a device in his brain, which, were it to sense the requisite level of attentiveness, would electronically stimulate the right neural centers so as to inevitably result in his making this choice. As it happens, Joe does not attain this level of attentiveness to his moral reasons, and he chooses to evade taxes on his own, while the device remains idle. (Pereboom, 2000, 2001, 2003, 2009a; David Hunt also suggested such a strategy (2000), and later develops a similar example (2005); and Seth Shabo (2010a) proposes valuable refinements)

In this situation, Joe is intuitively blameworthy for choosing to evade taxes despite lacking a robust alternative possibility.

Note that cases formulated prior to the dilemma defense, such as Fischer's blush example, also feature a necessary condition for doing otherwise; in

Fischer's example, that necessary condition is the blush not ever occurring. So the distinctive characteristic of *Tax Evasion 2* is not the presence of a necessary condition for doing otherwise, but rather a necessary condition for doing otherwise *the absence of which at any specific time will not causally determine the agent to perform the action*. This feature of the example guarantees that at no specific time is the agent causally determined to perform the action, which facilitates the satisfaction of a requirement for moral responsibility on which the libertarian insists. In *Tax Evasion 2*, the necessary condition for Joe's not deciding to evade taxes, i.e., his having the specified level of attentiveness to the moral reasons, is the right kind, because its absence at any specific time indeed does not causally determine his deciding to evade taxes. At any time at which the level of attentiveness is absent, Joe could still make it occur at a later time, and thus he is not causally determined to decide to evade taxes by its absence at the previous time. (Although if there is a deadline, we'll need to think about what happens if he waits to decide until then, an issue that we'll address below.) We want to note, however, that Fischer (2010) develops an intriguing argument that a case similar to *Tax Evasion* but set in a deterministic context provides a strong challenge to the alternative-possibilities requirement.

The *Tax Evasion* case does feature alternative possibilities that are accessible to the agent—Joe's achieving higher levels of attentiveness to moral reasons. And this fact about the example occasions the objection that by voluntarily achieving the specified higher level of attentiveness, Joe would have voluntarily done something as a result of which he would have been precluded from the blameworthiness he actually incurs. Had he voluntarily achieved the requisite level of attentiveness, the intervention would have taken place, whereupon he would indeed have decided to evade taxes, but not in such a way that he would have been blameworthy for this decision. However, this alternative possibility is not a robust one. Joe has no understanding at all of the fact that by voluntarily achieving the requisite level of attentiveness he would not be (or would likely not be) blameworthy. Rather, he believes that achieving this level of attentiveness is compatible with his freely deciding to evade taxes anyway (which would be true without the intervener's device in place), and he has no reason to think otherwise.[2] We can even specify that he believes that if he did achieve this level of attentiveness, he would still be very likely to decide to evade taxes. However, despite his lacking a robust alternative, it seems intuitive that Joe is blameworthy for his actual decision.

An important response to *Tax Evasion* is the contention that Joe's responsibility for his decision is merely derivative of his responsibility for his earlier voluntary refraining from becoming more attentive to moral reasons, for which he does have a robust alternative (Widerker, 2006; for the response below, see Pereboom, 2009a, 2014). The example does allow that Joe could have become more attentive to moral reasons instead—after all, this is the cue for intervention.

A reply to this objection begins with a consideration of the nature of merely derivative moral responsibility. Biff decides to get drunk, understanding that when he is intoxicated he will no longer be able to avoid being abusive to his companions, and then when he is drunk he assaults one of them. In this example, Biff satisfies paradigmatic general conditions on moral responsibility at the time he decides to get drunk, but not when he is drunk and abusive. If he is morally responsible for the assault, it is only derivatively so—derivative, in particular, on his being non-derivatively morally responsible for deciding to get drunk, and his foreseeing that when he is drunk he is likely to be abusive (Ginet, 2000).

Widerker (2006) proposes a challenge to the *Tax Evasion* argument in which he applies the distinction between non-derivative and derivative responsibility to the example, arguing that non-derivative moral responsibility is governed by the alternative-possibilities requirement. He contends that in *Tax Evasion*, Joe, without access to relevant alternatives, is only derivatively blameworthy for his decision:

> [A] problem with Pereboom's example is that, in it, the agent is *derivatively* blameworthy for the decision he made, because he has not done his reasonable best (or has not made a reasonable effort) to avoid making it. He should have been more attentive to the moral reasons than he in fact was – something he could have done. And in that case, he would not be blameworthy for deciding to evade taxes, as then he would be forced by the neuroscientist so to decide. If this is correct, then Pereboom's example is a case of derivative culpability, and hence is irrelevant to PAP, which … concerns itself only with direct or nonderivative culpability. (Widerker, 2006: 173; Ginet anticipates this objection in Ginet, 1996)

Pereboom (2009a, 2014) responds by arguing that there is a sense in which this is a dialectically unsatisfying response to this Frankfurt example, since it explicitly cites a leeway position in support of its verdict about Joe's responsibility. Widerker's thought appears to be that Joe is non-derivatively morally responsible only for not deciding to be more attentive to the moral reasons because only relative to this decision does he have a robust alternative, and hence any responsibility he has for deciding to evade taxes must be derivative of this decision. One might accordingly apply the following alternative-possibilities schema to any case of this sort: the agent is non-derivatively morally responsible for acting or refraining at a particular time only if a robust alternative possibility relative to so acting or refraining is accessible to her then, and all other moral responsibility is derivative of such non-derivative responsibility. However, the concern for the application of this schema is that it will miss the force of a potential counterexample, and will thus risk failing to engage an important objection. At the same time, we haven't ruled out that the alternative-possibilities schema gets things right.

But in judging whether it does, the drawbacks for imposing it on situations like Joe's need to be assessed. It might initially be supposed that there won't be any such drawbacks because intuitions about whether agents are morally responsible do not distinguish between non-derivative and derivative responsibility. It may be intuitive that Joe is responsible for deciding to evade taxes, and not intuitive that he is non-derivatively as opposed to merely derivatively morally responsible. In response, the paradigm for derivative responsibility is provided by the drunkenness example cited earlier. In this illustration, some of the uncontroversial general conditions on non-derivative moral responsibility fail to be satisfied when Biff is drunk, yet they are all satisfied when he decides to get drunk. However, Biff's situation differs from Joe's. Biff has knowingly put himself in a position in which some of the uncontroversial general conditions on non-derivative moral responsibility will not be satisfied at the relevant subsequent times. The same is not the case for Joe. One might object that if an agent can't be sufficiently attentive to moral reasons, one such uncontroversial condition is not satisfied. Yet at any time when Joe is not sufficiently attentive to moral reasons, he understands that it is open to him to become sufficiently more attentive at a later time. As a result, Joe's situation diverges in the crucial respect from paradigm examples of derivative responsibility. In Pereboom's view, this indicates that the application of the alternative-possibilities schema to Joe in the way suggested by Widerker's objection may not be appropriate (Pereboom, 2009a, 2014).[3]

5.4. The Timing Defense

Carl Ginet (1996, 2002), a defender of leeway incompatibilism, has developed a third major type of objection to Frankfurt examples. In his challenge to *Tax Evasion*, specifically to the Pereboom (2000, 2001) version of this example, he argues that at t1, the precise time Joe makes the decision to evade taxes, he might instead have been attending to the moral reasons, and that this alternative possibility is robust:

> For had J taken it, he would at t1 have been refraining from a willing – to do B [to decide to take the illegal deduction] right then – such that by so refraining he would have avoided responsibility for doing B right then and would have been aware that he was avoiding responsibility for doing B right then (that being such an obvious implication of his not doing B right then, of which he of course would have been aware). (Ginet, 2002)

David Palmer (2011) and Christopher Franklin (2011a), both leeway incompatibilists, also raise this type of objection to *Tax Evasion*.

The force of Ginet's objection depends on a component of his (1996) general response to Frankfurt's argument against the alternative-possibilities requirement. Ginet begins with the following schema for Frankfurt examples:

> Black sets up a mechanism that monitors Jones's actions and would cause Jones's doing B by t3 if Jones has not already done B by some deadline t2. We must suppose that had this mechanism been triggered at t2 it would have causally necessitated Jones's doing B by t3 in such a way as to render Jones unable to avoid doing B by t3, and that there was no time at which Jones

knew or should have known about this mechanism. The mechanism is not triggered because Jones does B at t1, before t2. [Let "B" stand for deciding to murder someone, say Smith.]

Ginet argues that in a case of this type Jones will not be responsible for doing B *by t3* "because, owing to the presence of Black's mechanism, Jones could not have avoided it," but "he may be responsible for the obtaining of the temporally more specific state of affairs"—doing B at t1—"which he could have avoided." One might fail, he thinks, to distinguish *Jones's doing B at t1* and *Jones's doing B by t3* because they are morally equivalent in the sense that Jones would be as blameworthy for the first as he would be for the second had Black's mechanism not been present. This feature of the example is what allows our (in his view, mistaken) sense that Jones is blameworthy for making the decision by t3 to be explained by his being blameworthy for making the decision precisely at t1. What accounts for Jones's blameworthiness, in what Ginet thinks to be the right analysis, is his having access to an alternative to doing B at t1, and what he is in fact specifically blameworthy for is doing B at t1.

Pereboom (2012a, 2014) proposes a response to Ginet's objection.[4] He contests the claim that the sense that Jones is blameworthy for doing B by t3, or blameworthy at all, can be explained by his having an alternative possibility to deciding at t1. He begins by presenting a Frankfurt example that fits Ginet's schema:

Tax Cut: Jones can vote for or against a modest tax cut for those in his high-income group by pushing either the "yes" or the "no" button in the voting booth. Once he has entered the voting booth, he has exactly two minutes to vote, and a downward-to-zero ticking timer is prominently displayed. If he does not vote, he will have to pay a fine, substantial enough so that in his situation he is committed with certainty to voting (either for or against), and this is underlain by the fact that the prospect of the fine, together with background conditions, causally determines him to vote (although, to be clear, these factors do not determine how he will vote). Jones has concluded that voting for the tax cut is barely on balance morally wrong, since he believes it would not stimulate the economy appreciably, while adding wealth to the already wealthy without helping the less well off, despite how it has been advertised. He is receptive and reactive to these general sorts of moral reasons: He would vote against a substantially larger tax cut for his income group on account of reasons of this sort, and has actually done so in the past. He spends some time in the voting booth rehearsing the relevant moral and self-interested reasons. But what would be required for him to decide to vote against the tax cut is for him to vividly imagine that his boss would find out, whereupon due to her political leanings she would punish him by not promoting him to a better position. In this situation it is causally necessary for his not deciding to vote for the tax cut, and to vote against it instead, that he vividly imagine her finding out and not being promoted, which can occur to him involuntarily or else voluntarily by his libertarian free will.

Jones understands that imagining the punishment scenario will put him in a motivational position to vote against. But so imagining is not causally sufficient for him to decide to vote against the tax cut, for even then he could still, by his libertarian free will, decide either to vote for or against (without the intervener's device in place). However, a neuroscientist has, unbeknownst to him, implanted a device in his brain, which, were it to sense his vividly imagining the punishment scenario, would stimulate his brain so as to causally determine the decision to vote for the tax cut. Jones's imagination is not exercised in this way, and he decides to vote in favor while the device remains idle.

Suppose that t3 is the last instant that Jones can make a decision to vote prior to the expiration of the two-minute window of opportunity, and he is aware of this, and that he in fact decides to vote at t1, several seconds before t3. Pereboom contends that Jones is intuitively blameworthy for choosing to vote in favor of the tax cut by t3, in spite of the fact that relative to this decision he lacks a robust alternative.

A qualm one might have for *Tax Evasion 2* is that even with the intervener's device in place, Joe is aware that at any particular time, into the indefinite future, he can avoid responsibility for a decision to evade taxes at that time by becoming attentive to the moral reasons instead, and this would count as a robust alternative possibility. The provision in Tax Cut that Jones is committed with certainty to deciding to vote by the last minute he can (t3) is meant to address this type of concern. With this provision in place, it is still true that at any specific time prior to t3 Jones is aware that by vividly imagining the punishment scenario he can avoid responsibility at that instant for deciding to vote for the tax cut, which relative to those specific times would qualify as robust alternatives. However, it is not the case that relative to the entire interval up to and including t3 Jones has a robust alternative. Crucially, his commitment to voting by t3 rules out his not voting at all during this interval by instead spending this time imagining the punishment scenario instead.

Ginet would maintain that because Jones has no alternative possibility to his deciding to vote in favor of the tax cut by t3, he would not be responsible for this particular state of affairs. But in his view Jones is responsible—blameworthy, in particular—for so deciding at t1, and for this he does have a robust alternative. In particular, at t1 he could have refrained from making a decision right then. Recall that in Ginet's conception (1) Jones's making his decision at t1 with the intervener's device in place and (2) Jones's making that decision by t3 supposing the device is not in place are morally equivalent in the sense that he is as blameworthy for the first, and for the same reasons, as he would be the second. This equivalence would allow our sense that Jones is blameworthy for making the decision by t3 to be explained by his being blameworthy for making the decision exactly at t1.

Will this strategy work? Consider the following scenario.[5] Adam has the opportunity to kill Victim by pushing a button which will detonate a bomb which will explode at t4, which he knows will kill Victim instantaneously. Imagine that factors beyond Adam's causal reach causally determine him to decide to push the button in order to kill him, and so to decide at some precise time t1. The leeway incompatibilist will maintain that Adam is not blameworthy for making the decision at t1 to kill his victim. But now suppose that factors beyond Adam's causal reach causally determine him so to decide, but so that it is up to him at which instant during a short interval, beginning at t0 up to and including t3, he makes the decision to push the button. The bomb will explode at t4 no matter which of these instants he makes the decision. Filling out the story, factors beyond Adam's causal reach causally determine him to have a desire to kill Victim so powerful that he will inevitably make this decision at some time in this interval. Adam first has this desire just before t0, and it would persist to t3 were he not to decide before then, and this desire would not alter in strength during the interval. This last instant, t3, is the deadline because Adam believes, correctly, that the bomb is rigged to explode if he decides any later. Adam understands that at which of these instants he decides makes no difference morally, and as a result he is indifferent among them. Suppose he decides at t1. Given incompatibilist sensibilities, leeway or source, he will not be *blameworthy* for deciding at t1 to kill Victim. Rather, he is in a morally neutral sense responsible for deciding at t1 rather than at another instant in the interval.

The reason the leeway incompatibilist must give for Adam's not being blameworthy for deciding at t1 is that he has no (robust) alternative possibility relative to making his decision by t3. According to the leeway incompatibilist it must be the unavailability of some alternative possibility that explains why he is not blameworthy for his choice. In this case, causal determination excludes Adam's blameworthiness, and our leeway incompatibilist holds that, in general, causal determination rules out blameworthiness because it precludes alternative possibilities. The only credible explanation for Adam's not being blameworthy is the unavailability of an alternative to making the decision by t3, and consequently, according to the leeway incompatibilist this unavailability would have to be sufficient for his not being blameworthy at t1.

We can now draw the following consequence from Adam's case for Jones's situation in *Tax Cut*. The leeway incompatibilist won't be able to support the contention that Jones's deciding at t1 to vote in favor of the tax cut with the intervener's device in place is as blameworthy, and for the same reasons, as would be his deciding to vote in favor by t3 without the device in place. For with the device in place, the leeway incompatibilist cannot explain Jones's blameworthiness for making his decision at t1, only his responsibility in a neutral sense for making the decision at t1 rather than at some other available instant. Although, as in Adam's situation, Jones does have an alternative to deciding at t1—for example, continuing to deliberate at t1 and deciding at t2 instead—the availability of this alternative cannot explain Jones's blameworthiness for making his decision at t1. As the case is set up, Jones has no robust alternative to making his decision by t3, and as Adam's scenario shows, for the leeway incompatibilist this has to be sufficient for Jones's not being blameworthy for making his decision at t1. Both Adam and Jones can make their decisions at t2 instead of at t1, but as in Adam's case, Jones's having no robust alternative to deciding by t3 will preclude its being a robust alternative that he decide at t2 instead. But it nonetheless remains strongly intuitive that Jones is blameworthy for deciding to vote for the tax cut at t1, a fact for which the leeway incompatibilist lacks any explanation.

Thus the sense that Jones is blameworthy for deciding to vote in favor of the tax cut can't be explained by his being blameworthy for making his decision at t1 together with the alternatives he has to doing so. On the leeway incompatibilist conception, Jones's blameworthiness for making his decision at t1 would need to depend on his having a robust alternative possibility relative to making the decision by t3. However, for this he has no robust alternative. Consequently, *Tax Cut* issues a challenge to that position, and at least prima facie this Frankfurt example can withstand Ginet's objection.

5.5.   General Abilities to Do Otherwise

Susan Wolf (1990) argues that what is crucially necessary for moral responsibility is a general power to act and to refrain. As we pointed out in our discussion of the Consequence Argument in Chapter 4, incompatibilists will agree that agents can retain general abilities to act and to refrain supposing causal determination. In addition, a number of compatibilists have pointed out that an agent in an appropriately constructed Frankfurt example can retain a general ability or power to refrain from performing the action at issue (Fara, 2008; McKenna, 1997; Nelkin, 2011: 66–76; Vihvelin, 2004; Wolf, 1990). Note that even when Usain Bolt is asleep, he retains the power to run 100 meters in less than ten seconds, despite the fact that his being asleep is currently an impediment to his activating this power. By extension, even if he is causally determined to be asleep and thus not to be running, he retains that power. Similarly, in the standard Frankfurt-style cases the agent would appear to retain the power not to choose to perform the action, despite the fact that she cannot activate the power because of the device.

The idea is that none of these Frankfurt-style arguments undermine the following condition:

> (PAP-Robust-General Abilities) An action is free in the sense required for moral responsibility only if the agent has the general ability to perform a robust alternative to that action.

On Wolf's more specific proposal, which Dana Nelkin develops and endorses, an agent in a Frankfurt case retains what Nelkin calls an *interference-free ability* to refrain from performing the action. That is, the agent possesses the skills, talents, and so on, required for refraining, and nothing *actually* interferes with or prevents the exercise of this power to refrain (Wolf, 1990: 110; Nelkin, 2011: 66–8).

The leeway incompatibilist is apt to raise the following objection. Due to the intervention set-up it seems not to be up to the agent exercise the interference-free ability successfully at the relevant time, and whether this is required for moral responsibility would seem to be what's at issue between leeway and source theorists (Clarke, 2009). The controversy between these opposing sides is whether the agent has access to an exempting alternative possibility, and this is highlighted in Widerker's W-Defense. Despite possessing an interference-free ability to refrain, the agent in the Frankfurt case would appear to lack access to this exempting alternative. If when he decides to kill Smith it's not up to Jones to successfully exercise his interference-free ability to refrain from so deciding, it's plausibly not up to him to avoid the blameworthiness he actually incurs.

5.6. Final Words

Frankfurt's challenge has had a massive and continuing influence on the free will debate. Many participants in the debate, both compatibilist and incompatibilist, are convinced by his argument. But a significant and vocal minority disagrees, and for these theorists the intuition that blameworthiness requires access to an exempting alternative remains strong.

The fact that incompatibilists can and have accepted Frankfurt's argument has several interesting consequences for the free will debate. A resolute source incompatibilism would diminish the importance of two historical differences of opinion between incompatibilists and compatibilists (Kane, 1996: 58–9). One such difference concerns whether "could have done otherwise" should be ana-lyzed conditionally as the classical compatibilist does, for example, as "if she had chosen otherwise she would have done otherwise." As we saw in Chapter 3, compatibilists have contended for the conditional analysis, incompatibilists have argued against it. However, if whether an agent could have done otherwise is not crucial to moral responsibility, then the status of this controversy loses signifi-cance. The second controversy concerns the Consequence Argument. If whether an agent could have done otherwise is not crucial to moral responsibility, how the debate over this argument is resolved becomes less momentous.

A final point: As we've indicated, paradigmatic leeway incompatibilists would advocate an indeterminist condition on moral responsibility only because, as they see it, indeterminism is required for robust alternatives. Source incom-patibilists would also hold that moral responsibility requires that the action's actual causal history have certain indeterministic features, and significantly, they may in addition allow that alternative possibilities for action—not necessarily of the robust sort—are entailed by the actual causal history having these features (Della Rocca, 1998; Pereboom, 2001). Still, on any source incompatibilist view, the aspect of the action that has the important role in explaining why an agent is morally responsible is the nature of the actual causal history of the action, and not the alternative possibilities.

Suggestions for Further Reading

Like the Consequence Argument, the secondary literature devoted to Frankfurt's argument against the alternative-possibilities requirement on moral responsibility is enormous. Here we only offer a small sampling of some of the most important pieces on the topic. See:

Fischer, John Martin. 2010. "The Frankfurt Cases: The Moral of the Stories." *Philosophical Review* 119: 315–36.

Fischer, John Martin. 1994. "Responsibility and Alternative Possibilities." In *The Metaphysics of Free Will*. Oxford: Blackwell Publishers: chapter 7.

Frankfurt, Harry. 1969. "Alternate Possibilities and Moral Responsibility." *Journal of Philosophy* 66: 829–39.

Ginet, Carl. 1996. "In Defense of the Principle of Alternative Possibilities: Why I Don't Find Frankfurt's Argument Convincing." *Philosophical Perspectives* 10: 403–17.

McKenna, Michael. 2008b. "Frankfurt's Argument against Alternative Possibilities: Looking Beyond the Examples." *Noûs* 42: 770–93.

McKenna, Michael. 2003. "Robustness, Control, and the Demand for Morally Significant Alternatives." In David Widerker and Michael McKenna, eds., *Moral Responsibility and Alternative Possibilities*. Aldershot: Ashgate Press 201–18.

Mele, Alfred, and David Robb. 1998. "Rescuing Frankfurt-Style Cases." *Philosophical Review* 107: 97–112.

Naylor, Marjory. 1984. "Frankfurt on the Principle of Alternate Possibilities." *Philosophical Studies* 46: 249–58.

Pereboom, Derk. 2000. "Alternate Possibilities and Causal Histories." *Philosophical Perspectives* 14: 119–38.

Sartorio, Carolina. 2016. *Causation and Free Will*. Oxford: Oxford University Press.

Stump, Eleonore. 1996. "Libertarian Freedom and the Principle of Alternative Possibilities." In Daniel Howard-Snyder and Jeff Jordan, eds., *Faith, Freedom, and Rationality*. Lanham, MD: Rowman and Littlefield: 73–88.

van Inwagen, Peter. 1983 "What Our Not Having Free Will Would Mean." In *An Essay on Free Will*. Oxford: Clarendon Press: chapter 5.

Widerker, David. 1995. "Libertarianism and Frankfurt's Attack on the Principle of Alternative Possibilities." *Philosophical Review* 104: 247–61.

For an anthology devoted just to the dispute over Frankfurt's argument, see:

Widerker, David, and Michael McKenna, eds., 2003. *Moral Responsibility and Alternative Possibilities*. Aldershot: Ashgate Press.

Notes

1   For another interesting reply to Widerker's W-Defense, see Capes (2010).

2   For an argument resisting Pereboom on this point, see Capes (forthcoming). Capes argues that a slightly more permissive notion of robustness allows that an alternative course of action can be robust for a person if she is cognitively sensitive to the fact that, by availing herself of it, she would be at least temporarily blameless.

3   Against *Tax Evasion*, Carlos Moya (2011) objects that the usual standards for exempt-
    ing alternatives are not in place in Frankfurt examples:

> In normal circumstances, with no device lurking, the standards for exempting
> alternatives would have risen to deciding not to evade taxes and not evading them;
> merely attending to moral reasons would not have been enough; but since Joe
> could not have decided and acted that way, the standards lower to the next best
> action he could perform in order to fulfill his moral duties, which so becomes an
> exempting alternative. (2011: 17)

Pereboom (2014) replies that the feature of the context that Moya claims to alter the
standard from the usual one is the unavailability of what would under normal circumstances be an exempting alternative. This conjecture, he argues, is itself motivated by
the alternative-possibilities requirement, which is in contention. The idea is that
Moya's justification is not independent of this requirement, and so his proposal may
not be a satisfying response.

Michael Robinson (2012) develops a further way to resist Pereboom's example by
relying upon the Dilemma Defense, but also borrowing from the Flicker Defense. His
idea is that, in keeping with the Dilemma Defense, agents cannot be assumed to be
causally determined prior to acting freely, and that in the absence of causal determination, an agent will always have a robust alternative, identified at the initial moment of
free action as an alternative that is open to the agent and of which she is reasonably
aware. Robinson concludes that, whenever an agent acts freely, it is always up to her
not to act on her own as she actually does, and this openness is robust, since she will
be aware that by not acting as she does, she'll not be acting wrongly. Pereboom's
response would invoke the specification that for Joe even to begin to choose otherwise would require his greater attentiveness to the moral reasons, and that this is consistent with his not being causally determined, since he could freely choose to become
more attentive.

4   This section is a shortened version of Pereboom (2012a), a slightly revised version of
    which is included in Pereboom (2014: chapter 1).

5   Here, Pereboom revises the example involving Adam relative to Pereboom (2012a;
    2014) due to a helpful comment by Austin Duggan.

6   Strawsonian Compatibilism

We turn in this chapter to P.F. Strawson's seminal 1962 essay, "Freedom and Resentment."[1] As with the topics discussed in the last two chapters, Strawson's contribution profoundly altered the philosophical landscape regarding contemporary work on free will and moral responsibility. One can easily identify in "Freedom and Resentment" at least three distinct arguments for compatibilism. While each of these arguments merits attention, what makes Strawson's essay so important is not captured by attending just to the arguments themselves. It is, rather, the broader context into which these arguments fit. This context involves a conception of moral responsibility's nature that animates Strawson's arguments for compatibilism proper.

Crucially, Strawson was most interested in making clear the role of our moral responsibility practices in our adult interpersonal lives. We are better positioned, as he saw it, to understand what moral responsibility is and what the requirements of it are if we attend to its practical role. This applies to the freedom requirement too. Our care for and commitment to each other as engaged participants in complex social relations with one another reveals how much our seeing each other as morally responsible matters to us. Moreover, this is revealed by attending to our *emotional sensitivities*. Affect matters, Strawson contended. In his view, our demands and expectations that others treat us and others well, and our responses to those who fail to do so, are expressed in our moral emotions, some of which, such as resentment, indignation, and guilt, he understood as *reactive attitudes*. Rather than think of these emotions as mere ancillary byproducts of our thinking and judging people to be morally responsible, these affective proclivities and their manifestations are the most fundamental expressions of these thoughts and judgments. Our understanding people as responsible agents and our holding them responsible for what they do is in this way constituted by these emotions and by the interpersonal social practices in which they find their expression.

Before proceeding to a more careful, scholarly assessment of Strawson's overall case for compatibilism, perhaps it will be useful to invite you to engage in a simple thought experiment to help illustrate what Strawson was getting at. So, before proceeding, consider as vividly as you can a simple case in which you or someone you love, perhaps a grandparent, is wronged by another, maybe maliciously, maybe from mild contempt, or instead as an upshot of mundane indifference. For you, this might be a matter of recalling a real-life case, or instead it might be imaginary. Suppose, for instance, your grandmother is cheated at a checkout counter and manipulated into paying more for a product, perhaps because she is regarded as stupid, foolish, or provincial by the sales person, or maybe because of the color of her skin. Now consider how you would feel, what emotions would be invoked in you, and consider, furthermore, how you would and also how you should be inclined to respond to the person who did this wrong thing. Ask yourself what effect it would have had, and more importantly should have had, on you were you to have come to accept the theor-etical judgment that no one has free will and no one is morally responsible. Would you have, and should you have, altered the way you thought, felt, and acted toward this wrongdoer? Someone rips off your grandma in a checkout line because she is black and unwelcome in their store, and you should now not blame them or think them responsible because no one has free will? Should you withhold any expression of anger? Should you now not scold and denounce them? What Strawson is asking the philosophical community to internalize fully when engaging in theorizing about free will and moral responsibility is what actual role these concepts really play in our lives.

There is a way to theorize about moral responsibility that treats the preceding considerations as either irrelevant or of secondary importance. On this altern-ative approach, the conditions for being and for holding morally responsible are one thing. And true and false judgments or propositions about them can be assessed *irrespective* of the role they play in our interpersonal and emotional lives. Our actual responses to them, being secondary, can be understood insofar as they reliably track (or not) the independent truth of the propositions regarding whether a person (or any person) is morally responsible for what she does.

Perhaps a simple model would be appropriate to illustrate this competitor view. So consider this: Imagine that whether any person is free with respect to and morally responsible for what she has done is a fact that is entirely inde-pendent of our practice of holding morally responsible. But God would also know, with certainty, exactly what any person would deserve for her praise-worthy or blameworthy acts. In this respect, God is a perfect arbiter. Our moral responsibility practices and our emotions, whatever they are, could then be *entirely* off track and disengaged from the truth of the matter, or they could in some way be accurately capturing roughly the independent truth that God would have precisely correct. Whatever the case, given this model, our interpersonal practices are theoretically of secondary importance to understanding the nature of the phenomena. To the extent that we can assess them, our assessment would in the first instance be a matter of their either answering or failing to answer to whatever the independent facts are. Moreover, we could come to discover, at least in principle, that our practices and related emotions are incongruous with these facts (say because no one is really morally responsible) and what we would have reason to do is revise our practices and our emotional proclivities as best we can to live in accord with the truth as we discover it to be. In short, there is the truth about what freedom and responsibility are, and as an independent matter, there is a set of interpersonal practices and emotional responses. In stark opposition to this alternative model, what Strawson hoped to convey in the conception of moral responsibility animating his arguments for compatibilism is that it is not as if our moral responsibility judgments are one thing and our practices of holding responsible and our emotional susceptibilities are another. Rather, our judgments of blameworthiness and praiseworthiness, and our actual blaming and praising, are made appropriate by and gain the entire measure of their meaning from their interpersonal and affective role in our lives. And accordingly, there is a sense in which this grounding is naturalistic—the appropriateness and meaning of moral responsibility judgments is grounded in these actual practices, and not in a realm independent of them.

It would be misleading to report that most or even many contemporary philosophers endorsed Strawson's naturalistic approach to theorizing about free will and moral responsibility. But most working in this arena now accept that to theorize about moral responsibility one must show some deference to the way it relates to our moral emotions and our moral responsibility practices.

We turn now to an examination of Strawson's famous essay and of the constellation of controversies that his paper has instigated. It will be useful to start by situating Strawson's essay within its historical context, since his remarks are especially directed at a distinctive audience and a particular set of theories and arguments that, in his estimation, had missed the mark in thinking clearly about freedom and responsibility.[2]

6.1. Strawson's Audience: Optimists, Pessimists, and Skeptics

Strawson chose an idiosyncratic set of terms to refer to the audience he meant to engage. His choice was, perhaps, unfortunate, since these terms—*optimists, pessimists*, and *skeptics*—tend to confuse rather than illuminate, especially for newcomers to these philosophical issues. The optimists Strawson was referring to were compatibilists; the pessimists were libertarians; and the skeptics were hard determinists (what in contemporary times we would call free will skeptics, including hard incompatibilists). One of the oddities of his choice of terms is that one would have thought that libertarians are better described as optimists. Aren't they the ones that demand especially high metaphysical standards for free will and believe that those standards are met? That seems pretty optimistic! Moreover, why aren't pessimists just the same as skeptics? Isn't being a skeptic about free will and moral responsibility just to be a pessimist about it? Puzzlement vanishes, however, once one bears in mind that the terms *optimist, pessimist*, and *skeptic* are not used by Strawson as terms that describe an attitude toward the nature of freedom and responsibility. They are, rather, terms that describe philosophers' attitudes toward the prospects for continued belief in freedom and responsibility in the face of the possibility that determinism is true. Compatibilists are optimistic about the prospects for freedom and responsibility in the face of determinism. Libertarians are pessimistic about it. It is for this reason that, to defend the legitimacy of freedom and responsibility, libertarians often develop metaphysical theses that in some way insulate these concepts from a scientific world view that could subsume them. Skeptics, in this conception, see no hope and, accepting that determinism or something like it is true, reject the thesis that any one acts freely or is morally responsible.

Strawson charged his philosophical contemporaries—compatibilists and libertarians, as well as hard determinists—with a failure to appreciate properly the facts relevant to understanding moral responsibility's nature. And he proposed to offer a "reconciliation" between them by focusing on the relevant facts and then setting out a set of arguments for compatibilism that were informed by them. To understand his charge that both sides were misguided, it will be helpful to consider the theses and arguments on each side that Strawson took to be inadequate. In each case, his opinion of their failures was expressed with biting jabs. Compatibilists, Strawson complained, argued for their thesis with a "one-eyed utilitarianism" (1982: 79), suggesting that they were blind to or ignorant of other considerations that thus distorted their theorizing. Libertarians, instead, opted for an "obscure and panicky metaphysics" (80) and only were able to offer, as he put it, "an intuition of fittingness—a pitiful intellectualist trinket for a philosopher to wear as a charm against the recognition of his humanity" (79). Well, what were these theses and arguments about which Strawson wrote with such derision?

Consider first Strawson's compatibilist contemporaries.[3] Strawson's main focus was on the classical compatibilists' attention to "the efficacy of the practices of punishment, and of moral condemnation and approval, in regulating behaviour in socially desirable ways" (60). Such efficacy is consistent with the truth of determinism, and the freedom presupposed by this efficacy is just the freedom from being impeded or encumbered from acting as one wants. When one's behavior is the product of being impeded by being coerced, or of being encumbered by innocent ignorance or mistake, there is no efficacy to regulating behavior by way of the pertinent social sanctions. So, in short, blame is justified when there is social utility in applying it, and there is only social utility in applying it when an agent acts freely in the simple compatibilist sense of "acts freely"—that is, when she is doing what she wants unimpeded and unencumbered, from her own intentions and for her own reasons (60–1).

We note here three points about these two classical compatibilist theses:

First, as regards their account of freedom, as we remarked above (Section 3.1), this account of freedom faces difficulties in distinguishing cases in which a person's own wants and desires or other motivational factors are sources of her lack of freedom, as is the case with phobias or compulsive disorders. It will be instructive to consider later on in the chapter whether Strawson's proposal is better able to avoid this problem.

Second, attending exclusively to the efficacy of our blaming and praising practices in terms of social utility overlooks the importance of our engaging in these activities when we are actually involved in our interpersonal lives. It was this that Strawson found especially objectionable about this style of compatibilist argumentation—it's what in Strawson's estimation made their argument a form of one-eyed utilitarianism. Tending exclusively to this dimension of the facts, Strawson protested, suggests to the libertarian adversaries that as compatibilists see it, the significance of blaming is just a matter of social utility. But this really does seem to get things wrong. How so? Recall the case in which a loved one was wronged. Were you to confront the wrongdoer, it would be odd to think that your grounds for blaming him would be that it would be socially beneficial. Your moral anger—your resentment or indignation—oughtn't to be conceptualized as a mere social tool for altering the wrongdoer's conduct. Rather, your emotional response would be, Strawson argued, a vehicle of your sincere expression of your anger and moral disapproval. The moral psychology Strawson invokes, and the theory of moral responsibility he builds upon it, constitutes a proposal that aims to avoid this problem.

Third, and related to the second, a standard criticism in Strawson's time of utilitarian justifications of blame and punishment, praise and reward, is that they are justified solely or mainly in terms of forward-looking considerations. The trouble with using only such resources to justify these practices is that they can yield the wrong results: Sometimes there will be no social utility at all in blaming a genuinely morally responsible wrongdoer (maybe she is just about to drop dead). Other times it would be of greater utility to blame an innocent person rather than the guilty party for some wrongdoing. Strawson, however, seemed not to be animated so much by this concern. Indeed, he granted to his optimist opponents the relevance of the social utility of a system of rewards and punishments. What, as Strawson saw it, seems to be missing in an exclusively utilitarian set of resources for justifying blame and punishment is a backward-looking constraint that links the blame to the blameworthy person, showing how it is that the blame is rendered a fitting response to objectionable conduct. A familiar approach in Strawson's time accounted for this in terms of the wrongdoer's genuinely *deserving* to be the one who is blamed or punished. While Strawson did note the relevance of desert in our responsibility practices, he did not emphasize it. It was, rather, his appeal to considerations of moral psychology that were meant to account for this relation to fittingness (we'll turn to this topic momentarily).

Now consider Strawson's libertarian incompatibilist contemporaries. The burden the classical incompatibilist shouldered was two-fold. One was normative. It was to offer a justification for blaming and punishing. The other was metaphysical. It was to provide an account of free agency that does not involve a causal (causally deterministic) relation between agent and action. Moreover, the sort of metaphysical solution needed to be one amenable to the normative burden—that fact of an agent's possessing and acting from the relevant sort of libertarian freedom must be able to aid in justifying blame and punishment.

Consider first the metaphysical burden. It is natural to associate the libertarian metaphysical view Strawson described as obscure and panicky with the agent-causal view advanced by philosophers like Roderick Chisholm (1964). Chisholm's defense of libertarianism (as discussed in Section 3.4) postulated that free persons are distinct substances who have special causal powers to initiate free actions. He accepted that if a person acts freely, she has the power to be an uncaused mover and so has a power commonly attributed only to God (Chisholm, 1964, in Watson, 1982: 32). Furthermore, Chisholm argued, if persons are free in this way, it is in principle not possible to have a complete science of man (33). It would not be surprising to think that a compatibilist would describe such a view as obscure and panicky. But this is probably too hasty. It seems that Strawson had in mind more generally *any* libertarian theory attempting to make sense of "contra-causal" freedom (Strawson, 79), which was at the time understood as a kind of free action that does not involve causation by prior events or states, including motives and desires.[4]

Next consider the normative burden. Strawson claimed that libertarians were right to recoil at the impersonal one-eyed and forward-looking utilitarian resources for justifying blame and punishment. But he charged that in doing so, they mistakenly appealed to "an intuition of fittingness" that required an exercise of libertarian freedom. What did Strawson mean by "an intuition of fittingness," and what normative work was this supposed to do? One relevant dispute in Strawson's day involved a competitor account to the utilitarian justification of blame and punishment. This competitor was a form of retributivism. The retributivists Strawson had in mind held that blame or punishment was deserved when a person was guilty of wrongdoing. Most importantly, the justification for this judgment of desert was rooted in nothing other than a brute intuition of fittingness: it is just fitting that one who is guilty of freely doing wrong is to be blamed or punished.[5] Notice that, in stark contrast to the utilitarian justification, this strategy is exclusively backward-looking. Blame and punishment's warrant is limited *solely* to its backward-looking relation to the wrong done by a free agent.

Strawson took it as his dialectical burden in opposition to these libertarian incompatibilists to offer a more plausible account of the facts of our human nature as free agents. He also proposed an account of the normative warrant of our blaming and praising practices according to which there is no need for any appeal to intuitions of fittingness and the metaphysical presuppositions about free agency that might appear to go with them.

6.2. Strawson's Assumptions about Moral Psychology

As we have noted, Strawson's arguments for compatibilism are built upon his conception of moral responsibility's nature. This conception arises from assumptions about the moral psychology of normally functioning adult human beings. Hence, it will be instructive to begin an examination of Strawson's own views with a brief sketch of these assumptions. The focal point for his view of our moral psychology is the collection of what he called the reactive attitudes, wherein he attended mainly to moral resentment, indignation, and guilt.

It is best to think of a reactive attitude as a distinctive kind of emotion, one that is a *reaction* to an attitude of another or to an attitude of one's own. A paradigm case is an emotional reaction to an attitude of ill will revealed in immoral action. In such a case, the wrongdoer's attitude serves as a basis for the person who is wronged or a third-party observer to react with an emotion suited to the wrongdoer's attitude of ill will. Strawson focused almost exclusively on negative cases of this sort. He regimented these cases by calling one's reactive anger when it is directed toward someone who has wronged oneself *resentment*, and one's reactive anger to ill will directed toward someone who has wronged another *indignation*. When an agent is herself the source of the ill will at which reactive anger aims, he calls it *guilt*.

What roles do the reactive attitudes play in our psychology? Two are especially pertinent to Strawson's understanding of moral responsibility. First, reactive attitudes are central to the engaged participant stance we adopt toward one another when we regard ourselves and others as members of a moral community, as fellow persons with whom we must get along and as beings who are at least potential objects of our affections and concerns. Call this the *interpersonal stance*. When we authentically engage another as spouse, lover, friend, enemy, coworker, party affiliate, adversary, colleague, or as a stranger whom we assume engages others in similar ways, we adopt the interpersonal stance. Now contrast this with a disinterested stance we can adopt as curious onlookers interested in the goings-on in the environment, whether they concern toasters, aardvarks, or human beings. Call this the *objective stance*. From this disinterested perspective, one is in a sense able to remove or distance oneself from the emotional connections that animate the interpersonal stance. When one responds to one's spouse, for instance, due to her anger or her sorrow, one engages him or her as an intimate whose emotions matter and are liable to affect one's own emotions in fitting ways. But when a therapist or a psychiatrist looks upon the very same episode from the objective stance, the therapist might see it, coolly and in disinterested fashion, as the upshot of certain causes resulting from earlier conditioning or from alterations in brain chemistry. This stance is the one that is also adopted in purely theoretical pursuits such as neuroscience or empirical psychology.

Second, we are inescapably prone to the interpersonal stance and its attendant reactive attitudes. It is not optional. This stance, and experiencing and being susceptible to being targeted by the reactive attitudes, is a feature of our human nature. Like the therapist or psychiatrist, we do have recourse to the objective attitude, even when engaged with those who are closest to us. And we can use this, as Strawson notes, as a shelter from the "strains of involvement" (67). However, while this does afford us the prospect of some distance from or even suspension of the reactive attitudes, the objective stance is not one we are capable of sustaining indefinitely. It would be in a certain way inhuman. Or at any rate this is how Strawson understood the matter.

6.3. Strawson's Theory of Moral Responsibility

Although Strawson never wrote explicitly in terms of a theory of moral responsibility, it is clear from his 1962 essay that he endorsed one, even if only implicitly.

Four key ingredients can be identified in his work, which together comprise his overall view:

First, Strawson was committed to a *quality of will thesis* as regards being responsible for something, such as an action. Fixing upon blameworthiness, when a person is regarded as blameworthy and is subject to a blaming response for what she has done, the basis for her *being* blameworthy for her wrongful conduct is, on Strawson's view, a function of the quality of her will. This, in turn, can be understood in terms of the value of her regard for others as displayed in acting as she did. She showed ill will or a lack of a sufficient degree of good will for whomever she wronged. When her action falls within the domain of morality, she is to be regarded as *morally* responsible for acting as she did.

Second, Strawson was also committed to an *interpersonal theory* of moral responsibility. According to an interpersonal theory, *being* morally responsible for what one does is in some manner dependent upon the practices and norms of those in the moral community suited to hold morally responsible. One cannot, on an interpersonal theory, offer an adequate account of what it is to be morally responsible without making reference to considerations regarding holding morally responsible—and so to the holding-responsible standpoint of others. Such theories stand in contrast to intrapersonal theories of moral responsibility according to which the conditions for being morally responsible need make no reference to norms or practices of holding morally responsible.[6] On Strawson's view, we cannot understand what it is for one to be blameworthy or praiseworthy for her actions but by reference to the sorts of holding-responsible responses her conduct is liable to elicit or render appropriate.[7]

Third, Strawson was as well committed to an *affective theory* of holding morally responsible. For Strawson, when one reacts with resentment to another who acts with ill will, one's emotional response is *itself* a blaming response. It is not that there is her blaming—cast as a judgment about the wrongdoer—and that her resentment is then a further thing over and above her blaming. Resentment is her means of blaming. And while one can experience episodes of emotion and not display it outwardly, in paradigm cases these emotions are overtly expressed and directed at the blamed party. The central point is that the practices of holding morally responsible for blameworthy or for praiseworthy conduct must in some way make reference to the sorts of emotional responses the behavior is liable to elicit or to render appropriate.[8]

Fourth, Strawson argued for a *practice-dependent grounding thesis* according to which being morally responsible is grounded in the practices and norms of holding morally responsible. Holding morally responsible, on this view, is more basic than being morally responsible, and the conditions of being morally responsible are what they are in virtue of the practices and norms of holding morally responsible. As Gary Watson (1987) puts it when explaining Strawson's view, it is not that we hold people morally responsible because they are. Rather, they are morally responsible because we hold them to be so. This thought requires some fine-tuning to be put into a plausible form. It might better be cast in terms of their being morally responsible for a certain domain of conduct because it is *appropriate* to hold them responsible for such conduct. Regardless, the idea is that the metaphysical "in virtue of" facts that serve as the basis for a person's being morally responsible for her conduct are found not in some set of independent facts about persons and their agency but rather in facts about our practices and norms of holding co-members of a moral community to account. Such a deflationary view of the underlying metaphysics of the conditions of responsibility is amenable to a compatibilist thesis. Why? A collection of natural facts about our social practices and norms of holding to account serve to set all of the conditions—including the freedom conditions—for morally responsible agency.

6.4.   Strawson's Arguments for Compatibilism

In this section we canvass Strawson's arguments for compatibilism. In the subsequent section we consider a range of critical reactions to these arguments. One can identify three distinct arguments for compatibilism in Strawson's essay. Two others are also suggested, perhaps not as distinct arguments, but as supporting reasons. For ease of discussion, we will treat them as free-standing arguments.

6.4.1.   The Argument from Exculpation

Strawson's first argument, which is the most complex, might be called his Argument from Exculpation. Incompatibilists contend that if determinism were true no one would be morally responsible for anything. Thus determinism would provide universal grounds for exculpating everyone from moral responsibility. At this point Strawson asks: Given the nature of moral responsibility, would the truth of determinism provide a reason for universal suspension of blaming? To answer this question, he examines how our exculpating pleas function within the context of our actual moral responsibility practices. How do excuses, justifications, and exemptions actually work when they defeat the bases for blaming?

According to Strawson, pleas designed to show that someone is not blameworthy for something she has done divide into two general categories. Some show that a person who *is* a morally responsible agent is not after all blameworthy for some particular seemingly objectionable act. She was pushed or shoved, or was non-culpably ignorant of what she was doing. Or given the circumstances, what she did was after all not objectionable but perhaps even laudatory.[9] Hence, she either had an excuse, or she had a justification.[9] In either case, what is established when these sorts of pleas are warranted is that the agent in question did not after all act from a morally objectionable quality of will. For this reason, blaming her is not warranted. Blaming just is reacting with a pertinent emotion when an action is in fact an expression of ill will or a lack of a sufficient degree of good will.

Yet another category of pleas, exemptions, involve showing that a person is in some respect incapacitated for interpersonal relationships. She is perhaps a small child, or in some way mentally disabled. What is established when such pleas are warranted is that a person is incapable of appreciating or complying with a demand that she act with a sufficient degree of good will. Hence, blaming her by responding to an objectionable quality of will she displays amounts to having an unreasonable expectation.

With the preceding explanation of pleas in place, Strawson's argument can be stated as follows. If determinism were true, it would not provide grounds for excusing or justifying in the ways that the first category does. Determinism would not have as a logical consequence that any particular excuse or justification applies universally. It would not show, for instance, that everyone who ever acted was pushed, or was innocently unaware of what she was doing, and so on. Moreover, no such plea could undermine responsibility *tout court*, since the point of such pleas is only to show that one who *is* a morally responsible agent just happens not to be blameworthy for some act or omission. Any such plea presumes that the agent to whom it applies persists in being a person who remains a candidate for being morally responsible for her conduct. Furthermore, Strawson continues, determinism would not have as a logical consequence that everyone is incapable in some respect of interpersonal relationships and so is exempted from being held morally responsible. It would not show that it would be unreasonable to expect of sane adults that they show sufficient good will toward others.[10] Thus given our exculpating practices and what it is to blame—to react with a fitting emotional response to the ill will of someone who is capable of sufficient good will—determinism would give us no reason to respond as incompatibilists suggest we ought were we to conclude that determinism is true.

Before proceeding, consider briefly in light of this argument how Strawson would handle the problem facing the classical compatibilists' account of freedom. Doing so will bring into relief Strawson's own positive view of freedom. For the classical compatibilists, it seems they cannot explain unfreedom in acting due to defective desires, as in the case of compulsive disorders. Strawson can accommodate such cases under the umbrella of excuses. If the agent acts from a compulsive disorder, it does not reveal an objectionable quality of will, and her regard for others is not impugned. When she *is* able to act so that her actions reflect her regard for others—her ill will or her good will—she is, in Strawson's conception, acting freely.

6.4.2.   The Psychological Impossibility Argument

Strawson's psychological impossibility argument is built upon what he takes to be a simple observation about moral psychology. It is not psychologically possible for us to extinguish or fully suppress our reactive attitudes. Susceptibility to these emotions is a part of our human nature. But when we respond to one who acts with ill will toward us or others with emotions such as resentment and indignation, we are thereby blaming them. Hence, it is psychologically impossible for us to suppress universally our preparedness to blame those whom we take to express ill will. Recall that for Strawson, being blameworthy is just a matter of a sane adult person acting with ill will or a lack of a sufficient degree of good will. If so, then what the incompatibilist would prescribe were we to accept that determinism is true—the squelching of all blame—is something that would be impossible for us to achieve, given our human nature. What they are imagining is a straightforward practical impossibility.

6.4.3.   The Practical Rationality Argument

Strawson argues that even if we were able to choose to suspend fully the reactive attitudes and so extinguish our propensity to blame, we would then have to choose whether to take this route on the basis of what it would be practically rational to do. But choosing to withdraw entirely from the propensity to engage with others by means of these emotions would amount to adopting the objective stance. It would amount to choosing to view all of human kind, including our intimate others, as mere objects—as parts of our natural surroundings that are simply buffeted about by the happenstance of the natural world. As regards these options—persisting in interacting with each other from the interpersonal perspective or instead adopting the objective perspective—Strawson argues that we would have to make any such choice based upon the gains and losses to human life (70). And to this extent, Strawson contends, the cold, impersonal world we would be left with by opting for the exclusively objective stance would hands-down be a far worse option than one in which we persist in caring about and engaging as interpersonal equals with each other.

6.4.4.   The Multiple Viewpoints Argument

The three preceding arguments are the ones perspicuously featured in Strawson's original 1962 essay. But there is reason to think that he was prepared to endorse two others. The first might be formulated as a "multiple viewpoints" argument, and in subsequent work (1985), Strawson developed it explicitly. This argument is meant to explain away the appearance that determinism and more generally an exclusively scientific account of the human condition is incompatible with freedom and moral responsibility. The central idea is that from one viewpoint—that of the interpersonal stance—certain features of the human condition are rendered salient. But from another—the objective stance—those features are not accessible. Instead, from this perspective, what is rendered salient are details about the underlying causal machinery that explains how the spatio-temporal order unfolds. One can mistakenly believe that the truths accessible from the one perspective render false or unwarranted what seems apparent from the other. But the viewpoints and the propositions pertinent to each are not incompatible. Rather, they offer access to different but compatible collections of truths.[11] The following analogy might prove useful: Our ordinary concept of solidity has it that solid objects, such as the surface of a table, are those items that completely occupy a spatial region. But from the vantage point of physics, paradigm examples of solid objects contain a considerable amount of unoccupied space within and among the atoms composing them. While it might seem that a radical result follows—that there are no solid objects—this is not in fact so. Rather, what we should conclude is that our ordinary concept of solidity is distinct from any conflicting concept of solidity that might emerge from physics.

6.4.5.   The Charge of Over-Intellectualizing the Facts

Yet a further claim, clearly expressed in Strawson's original paper, is that all parties to the free will debate over-intellectualize the facts (78). While it might seem difficult to understand how to fashion this as an argument for compatibilism rather than as merely an indictment of opposing views, here is a way. To think that a theoretical discovery like the truth of determinism could undermine the entirety of our moral responsibility practices as a whole, one must maintain that these practices as a whole are such that, as a conceptual matter, they *could* be justified, and so they *should* be justified. And those compatibilists who resist incompatibilism by arguing that the entirety of these practices can be justified and are in fact justified under the assumption of determinism also assume that such justification is needed and is appropriate. But, Strawson proposes, if these practices are given to us by our nature as particular sorts of social and emotional beings, they are not susceptible to such wholesale justification. They would need justification no more than we humans as mammals need justification for the fact that we are creatures with kidneys and a heart. And accordingly, no natural facts, say about the laws of nature, could undermine any appropriate wholesale justification (there being no such thing).

All of this is compatible with the claim that "internal" to these practices, justifications might be called for. Excuses and exemptions serve as such internal justifications; they are ways of getting clear about whether a person really did act from ill will, whether she really was a morally competent agent, whether a particular manner of response is too harsh or lenient. But, in Strawson's view, wholesale justification of the practice would be justification from without, or external, and there is no legitimate demand for it. And accordingly, the problem of free will and determinism evaporates as issuing from a misunderstanding of how the practice of holding morally responsible is rooted in our human nature and the practices it involves. This last thesis lies at the core of Strawson's (1985) claim that his brand of naturalism is sufficient to silence skeptical concerns about our moral responsibility practices.

6.5.   Assessing Strawson's Arguments for Compatibilism

We turn to an assessment of Strawson's arguments for compatibilism. In this section, we shall note several major developments, but will only focus upon a few.

6.5.1.   Assessing Strawson's Argument from Exculpation

Strawson's argument from exculpation is especially vexing, not just because it poses challenging problems of interpretation,[12] but also because there are apparent gaps in it that are hard to reconcile with other claims he makes. Most immediately, consider Strawson's idea that the truth of determinism would not license any global excuse or exemption. Surely Strawson was aware of the dispute between compatibilists and incompatibilists regarding determinism and the ability to do otherwise. A familiar excuse, one that naturally springs to mind in this context, is "he could not have done otherwise." Such a plea does often excuse, and so one might ask why Strawson would not have at least acknowledged this particular plea and taken up the obvious incompatibilist rejoinder that if determinism were true, there is one excuse that would apply universally: No one ever could have done otherwise.

It is a fair criticism of Strawson that he does not take up directly the question of the compatibility of determinism and the ability to do otherwise (e.g., see Ayer, 1980). Nevertheless, there is a charitable interpretation that shows how he would handle this question (McKenna, 2005b). If we understand Strawson as simply claiming that no excuse or justification currently on the books would apply universally if determinism were true, then he would after all be guilty of failing to defend his argument against a transparent objection. But if we instead understand his deeper point to be one about what underlying rationale is implicated in any excuse or justification, then it seems that Strawson has in mind a promising answer to the preceding objection, even if he never spelled it out explicitly. Recall that, as he understands it, what an excuse or justification does is to show that someone does not act with a morally objectionable quality of will. Now, *sometimes* when a person is not able to do otherwise, this inability shows that when she acts, she does not act from a morally objectionable quality of will. In these cases, Strawson can grant, the excuse goes through. But if determinism were true, then the *way* that it would be true that no one can do otherwise (if that would follow) would not entail that no one ever acts from a morally objectionable quality of will. As a result, it would not then show that no one is ever blameworthy. (In this respect, Strawson's view yields a result similar to the one for which Frankfurt argues in his seminal (1969) paper.[13])

Suppose it is granted that Strawson can overcome the preceding objection. There are more pressing problems for his argument from exculpation. Consider the second category of pleas he identifies, exemptions. An exemption invokes the claim that a person is in some respect incapacitated for interpersonal relationships. But here one might reasonably want to know what the capacities are for being able to enter fully into such relationships as a member of the moral community. Think about it from the perspective of a libertarian who believes that persons are free and morally responsible and accordingly possess a distinctive capacity of agency that requires the falsity of determinism. They may first of all agree that being mentally incapacitated in certain ways precludes full participation in interpersonal relationships, and that this yields an exempting condition. But they would in addition contend that determinism, by defeating the free will ability, also yields an exempting condition, and one that universally applies. Normally functioning adult human beings, the libertarian might protest, are not in fact defeated in having the free will ability, but they would be were determinism true.[14] They might press the point by arguing that in the absence of offering some content to what capacities are required for engaging in interpersonal relations as members of a moral community, we are not in a position to judge whether, if determinism were true, an exempting consideration would apply universally.[15]

The preceding objection is not decisive. What it shows is that Strawson's argument for compatibilism is incomplete without further development. Indeed various compatibilists have explored ways of lending support to Strawson on this point. Watson (1987), for instance, has developed the idea that the capacities required are those that enable one to understand what can be communicated to a wrongdoer by way of our reactive attitudes. Such capacities, it might be argued, are not in principle incompatible with determinism.

Strawson claims that within the framework of our moral responsibility practices, there is no exempting condition that would apply universally if we were to learn that determinism is true. But here is a Strawsonian insight that contains the basis for an incompatibilist argument for such a universal exemption. Strawson included seeing someone as "peculiarly unfortunate in his formative circumstances" (66) as a condition for exemption from the class of morally responsible agents. Watson (1987) points out that a person raised in a horribly abusive environment, or under the pressure of powerful indoctrination, might thereby become evil in a way that involves his showing extreme ill will toward others in all of his conduct. And yet, he would be exempted due to this history. The problem is, if such a consideration exempts, why is that? Is it because he is incapacitated for adult interpersonal relationships? His only incapacity would seem to be his being morally objectionable—his being evil. It seems that his having the history he has is the cause of now being a terrible person who acts with ill will. However, the incompatibilist will contend that if determinism is true, *every* person has the history she has, and that history just will be what counts as the source of her later agency, whether she displays any ill will or nothing but good will. In short, if some histories are exempting as ways of giving rise to how a person becomes the person she is and does as she does, then why not all histories? Hence, what we have in light of this objection is a source incompatibilist worry that, contrary to what Strawson contended, is rooted in our ordinary practices of offering various exculpating pleas.

This last concern is of a piece with a collection of puzzling problems compatibilists of various sorts must face, not just those who identify as Strawsonians. Some compatibilists adopt a nonhistorical theory and deny that an unfortunate history can of itself be grounds for exempting. If such a history resulted in some further incapacity in, say, freedom or understanding, then for *this* reason it might exempt. But if a person is made morally terrible by her history, so long as other compatibilist conditions are in place, she remains responsible. This is one way one might modify or extend Strawson's argument (e.g., McKenna, 1998). Other compatibilists instead attempt to distinguish between freedom-and-responsibility-defeating histories and freedom-and-responsibility-enabling histories, and one might defend a broadly Strawsonian thesis along these lines (e.g., Fischer and Ravizza, 1998).

6.5.2. Assessing Strawson's Psychological Impossibility Argument

Strawson's psychological impossibility argument has been the target of considerable critical attention. One immediate reaction to it is to argue that the empirical assumption on which it's founded is beside the point. It might well be, the objection goes, that we are built so that we cannot fail to be disposed to these attitudes and to be motivated to act from them, but this does not serve to indicate that anyone is *actually* free and morally responsible. There might be all sorts of illusions that we are stuck with given our human condition, but our psychology inescapably being a certain way does not render something that is an illusion something that is not one (Smilansky, 2000).

Others, however, have disputed Strawson's claim that we are incapable of suspending the morally reactive attitudes (e.g., Pereboom, 2001; Sommers, 2007). There are well-known examples of human communities that have committed to a considerable detachment from the emotions—both the moral and non-moral ones. So it was with the Stoics, and so it is in certain Buddhist communities. Furthermore, it might be objected, the force of Strawson's psychological impossibility argument gains its force by lumping together all of the morally reactive attitudes and assuming that this class of emotions is quite broad, including love and simple human affection. But in order to refrain from blaming or praising, one needs only withhold attitudes such as resentment and gratitude. Other forms of human affections, such as love, are not implicated in our moral responsibility practices in any direct way. Hence, a more restrictive treatment of the relevant morally reactive attitudes makes it less plausible to think we are psychologically incapable of suspending just this limited class while retaining the wider class of emotions that do not have assumptions about freedom and responsibility embedded in them (again, see Pereboom, 2001; Sommers, 2007).[16]

Another criticism of Strawson's psychological impossibility argument turns on distinguishing between an emotion like resentment as a general type and token instances of them, as actual episodes wherein one manifests, say, a reactive feeling of moral anger toward another. Paul Russell (1992) has argued that Strawson's psychological impossibility argument gains the force it seems to have by eliding this important distinction. While it is true that, as a class of emotions, we are naturally built to be disposed to them, we should not conclude that on any occasion, an episode of these emotions is one that we are incapable of suppressing, especially with respect to its behavioral manifestations. More importantly, we should not conclude that we are incapable to doing so in contexts in which we have reason to believe that our so reacting is not justified. But this then gives rise to the distinct question as to whether there are good reasons that could justify, or instead show as unjustified, pertinent instances of these emotions. Here, one might worry that if determinism is true, such justifications are never possible. Hence we are led to the justificatory question, and on to questions about the putative rationality of these emotions—or more precisely the rationality of acting upon or manifesting these emotions in relevant ways.

6.5.3. Assessing Strawson's Practical Rationality Argument

Consider next Strawson's practical rationality argument. Many critics have taken issue with Strawson's reasoning here. A.J. Ayer (1980), for instance, has argued that one standard of rationality is simply living in accord with the truth, and if the truth of determinism were incompatible with certain beliefs (about what can be deserved if no one can do otherwise), then by one clear standard, it would be irrational to choose to commit to the reactive attitudes were it possible for one to make such a choice. To objections of this sort Susan Wolf (1981) has offered an ironic defense of Strawson's view. Were we to choose to forsake the reactive attitudes in light of the discovery that we are not free, our doing so would be something that would itself be an expression of our freedom as rational agents, that is, acting in accord with what we think we ought to do. Then our very effort to withdraw from the reactive attitudes because we believe ourselves not to be free would itself be an affirmation of ourselves as free agents. This, however, according to Wolf, would be a hollow defense of our rationality. What this would mean is that we cannot consistently choose to live as if we are unfree agents, and thus it would not be rational to do so. But this would not show that we are in fact free. And it would still be true that we would think of ourselves as something we do not want to be.

The preceding dispute operates under the assumption that the costs to human flourishing suggest that, as a matter of practical rationality, we *should* persist in embracing the interpersonal stance and the full spectrum of the reactive attitudes. But others have argued that it is not at all clear that, thinking in terms of the gains and losses to human life, it would be rational to persist in endorsing the reactive attitudes—and in particular those morally reactive attitudes pertaining to blame and punishment (e.g., Pereboom, 2001, 2014; Smilansky, 2000; G. Strawson, 1986). Pereboom (2001, 2014), for instance, rejects Strawson's core claim about the practical rationality of retaining the relevant reactive attitudes. Doing so, he argues, might well be worse in terms of the gains and losses to human life. Rather, it's open that life would be better without them. Ridding ourselves of the propensity to moral anger and to punitive emotions and dispositions, we could still embrace caring and loving relationships, still find meaning in life, and still persist in deliberations about what to do in light of what is most valuable. Granted, the option of a cold, fully objective stance would make it practically irrational to withdraw fully from the stance whereby we hold morally responsible. But we need not do this. We can remain committed to the interpersonal stance while finding it rational to reject just the parts of that stance that presuppose the senses of freedom and moral responsibility that implicate basic desert.

6.5.4. Assessing Strawson's Multiple Viewpoints Argument

Strawson's appeal to considerations of multiple viewpoints is also open to some tough objections. An argument of this sort goes through, minimally, only if it meets two conditions. First the propositions accessible from the differing perspectives cannot be at odds with one another in that they do not yield direct contradictions. Second, there can be no ground available from the one viewpoint that provides reason to adopt the other. But the relation between the objective stance and the interpersonal stance appear to be compromised on both of these fronts, at least as some of Strawson's opponents see it. Most obviously, what can be shown from the objective perspective, under the assumption that determinism is true, is that no one is able to do otherwise, since doing otherwise is not possible given the past and the laws. But from the viewpoint of the interpersonal stance, it does seem that agents are able to do otherwise. Don't we have a straightforward contradiction here? How does the fact that there are distinct stances ameliorate this problem (cf. Nelkin, 2000)? Admittedly, as noted above (Section 5.1), Strawson might be able to resist commitment to a generalized ability-to-do-otherwise condition, but this is work done by another argument, not by the resources of any sort of appeal to multiple viewpoints.

Moreover, the very requirements that the incompatibilists fix upon, it might be argued, are not ones that themselves find their grounds in propositions originally issuing from the objective perspective. It is, rather, elements of the interpersonal stance that provide reason to consider taking up the objective perspective (e.g., Nagel, 1986; Pereboom, 2001, 2014). It is, for instance, because in our moral practices a person's being constrained results in her being excused by virtue of not being able to do otherwise that we then consider whether a proposition of this sort might apply more widely. Or instead, it is because we believe that having one's mind, to use Strawson's own language, "systematically perverted" (65) is a basis for exculpation, that we consider whether a more generic and impersonal set of originating springs of one's mental life and subsequent actions is just as responsibility defeating. In both of these cases, the move to the objective stance is rooted in our interpersonal practices and the reasons taken from within it to excuse or exempt; Wallace (1994) calls this a "generalization strategy." Hence, it seems that the two stances cannot be insulated from each other as innocently as Strawson's approach might suggest.

6.5.5. Assessing Strawson's Charge of Over-Intellectualizing the Facts

Strawson charges his contemporaries with over-intellectualizing the facts. In doing so he made perspicuous his commitment to a version of naturalism along with a rejection of an appeal to metaphysics to settle the free will problem. The central point Strawson advocated as a basis for his indictment is that our practices as a whole do not require justification externally and from without, and that any legitimate type of justification will be internal to the practices themselves. As far as the meaning of notions like responsibility, desert, and guilt, Strawson contended, these notions gain their meaning by virtue of a "complicated web" of attitudes and feelings making up to the moral life (78), and this "structure" or "framework" is just a natural human fact. Hence, he claimed, we do not need any external justification for the "readiness to acquiesce in the infliction of suffering on a wrongdoer" as Strawson would put it (77). Our practices themselves dispose us to so acting, and this is just part of our nature.

These claims of Strawson's appear to be the least defensible, and for reasons similar to those enlisted in Section 5.4. Worries about whether a person genuinely deserves blame or punishment are themselves part of the very system Strawson contends we must accept as a natural fact (Strawson, 1986). But the seeds of the demand for wholesale, external justification derive from an element inside of our conceptual scheme that seems crucial to our understanding of moral responsibility. For as Jonathan Bennett (1980: 24–5) argues, the desert element located in our concept of moral responsibility really does seem to presuppose a set of metaphysical requirements—Bennett calls them Spinozistic—incongruent with Strawson's naturalistic thesis.

There is, moreover, a more general point to make about Strawson's naturalism here in relation to a wider set of philosophical issues. Our moral responsibility practices, to the extent that they involve harming others, are the sorts of practices which it seem we *ought* to be able to justify. Rather than treat them as mere brute, natural facts—metaphysics aside—it would be more satisfying if we had *some* normative account of the justification or warrant for harming others in these distinctive ways (in particular blaming and punishing). So, for instance, both Scanlon (1988, 1998, 2008) and Wallace (1994) embrace much of Strawson's approach to theorizing about moral responsibility's nature. But when it comes to offering an account of the normative basis for our practices, they depart from Strawson's approach. Both, in different ways, attempt to justify our moral responsibility practices, to the extent that, as they saw it, they could be justified, by appeal to a broader set of normative considerations. Scanlon (1988, 1998) argued from appeal to contractualist resources that our responsibility practices (in suitably revised form) could be justified. Wallace (1994), instead, appealed to considerations of fairness.

6.6. Reflecting on Strawsonian Compatibilism

It will be useful to conclude this chapter by contrasting Strawson's contribution to the free will debate with the two others we have just considered in previous chapters. Recall in Chapter 3, in closing our discussion of the debate between classical compatibilists and classical incompatibilists, we explained that the philosophical landscape regarding the free will topic changed radically in the period of the 1960s due to the influence of three striking contributions. The first of these, which we examined in Chapter 4, was the influence of an especially crisp argument for the incompatibility of leeway freedom and determinism. This argument, the Consequence Argument, remains a central topic and point of departure for numerous contemporary philosophers writing on free will. And it is widely regarded by many (perhaps mistakenly, perhaps not) as strongly favoring an incompatibilist diagnosis of the relation between determinism and leeway freedom. The second equally influential contribution, which we examined in Chapter 5, concerns Harry Frankfurt's argument that leeway freedom is not necessary for moral responsibility. If Frankfurt's argument is sound, then the strongest sort of freedom necessary for moral responsibility should be explained in terms of source freedom—a kind of freedom that does not require the ability to do otherwise (leeway freedom).

We note two things about each of these two contributions. First, each is highly focused in the sense that it can be understood in terms of a controversy regarding some specific proposition that has an immediate bearing on assessing the (or a) free will problem. These propositions are, respectively: *the ability to do otherwise is incompatible with determinism* (assessed in Chapter 4), and *the ability to do otherwise is required for moral responsibility* (assessed in Chapter 5). Each of these disputes, being so sharply focused, permit application of well-known tools of analytic philosophy, and each has clearly identifiable implications, making perspicuous what exactly is at stake. Second, these two contributions also are interestingly related. In particular, the soundness of Frankfurt's argument would directly challenge the relevance of the Consequence Argument—at least as it bears on moral responsibility. Moreover, the soundness of the Consequence Argument would make the success of compatibilism turn on the soundness of Frankfurt's argument (or, more generally, on the justifiability of the source conception of moral responsibility). In short, in terms of dialectical relevance, these two theses are interestingly and intimately inter-animated, as is perhaps easily shown by reflecting upon the Basic Leeway Argument for Incompatibilism (as set out in Section 3.3):

1.   If a person acts of her own free will, then she could have done otherwise.
2.   If determinism is true, no one can do otherwise than one actually does.
3.   Therefore, if determinism is true, no one acts of her own free will.

The Consequence Argument offers support for premise 2, while Frankfurt's argument can be used to attack premise 1 (so long as free will is understood in terms of the strongest sense of control required for moral responsibility).

Given the preceding observations, Strawson's contribution, while equally influential (arguably more so), stands in stark contrast with the other two contributions we have considered thus far. How so? The force of Strawson's essay "Freedom and Resentment" *cannot* be understood in terms of a specific line of argumentation for or against any single proposition regarding free will or moral responsibility. Moreover, it is not altogether clear or easy to state how it is that Strawson's overall position bears on any other single point regarding the freedom of the will—such as the thesis that the ability to do otherwise is incompatible with determinism, or the thesis that free will and moral responsibility require the ability to do otherwise. Instead, in this one elegant essay, Strawson made a case for compatibilism by drawing upon a rather broad vision of the overall debate between compatibilists and incompatibilists. And he did so by developing (what was then) a novel way of theorizing about the very nature of moral responsibility. While "Freedom and Resentment" does contain at least three distinct and clearly identifiable specific arguments for compatibilism, and two others also seem to be suggested, these arguments gain their force largely by way of how they flow from the theory of responsibility animating his entire way of rethinking the free will debate. Thus, very much unlike the other two contributions we have considered, Strawson offers a "big picture" assessment of the free will debate which is intended to reorient the way theorists think of the debate itself—of what is at stake and what standards ought to be used to assess the competing theses and arguments.

Suggestions for Further Reading

An especially interesting exchange can be found in a festschrift for Strawson edited by Zak van Straaten, wherein two of Strawson's eminently respected contemporaries, Jonathan Bennett and A.J. Ayer, offer critical papers on "Freedom and Resentment" and Strawson then replies:

Ayer, A.J. 1980. "Free-Will and Rationality." In Zak van Straaten, ed., *Philosophical Subjects: Essays Presented to P.F. Strawson.* Oxford: Clarendon Press: 1–13.
Bennett, Jonathan. 1980. "Accountability." In Zak van Straaten, ed., *Philosophical Subjects: Essays Presented to P.F. Strawson.* Oxford: Clarendon Press: 14–47.
Strawson, P.F. 1980. "Reply to Ayer and Bennett." In Zak van Straaten, ed., *Philosophical Subjects: Essays Presented to P.F. Strawson.* Oxford: Clarendon Press: 260–6.

Other important papers discussing Strawson's "Freedom and Resentment" include:

Russell, Paul. 1992. "Strawson's Way of Naturalizing Responsibility." *Ethics* 102: 287–302.
Shabo, Seth. 2012. "Where Love and Resentment Meet: Strawson's Interpersonal Defense of Compatibilism." *Philosophical Review* 121: 95–124.
Shoemaker, David. 2007. "Moral Address, Moral Responsibility, and the Boundaries of Moral Community." *Ethics* 118: 70–108.
Sommers, Tamler. 2007. "The Objective Attitude." *Philosophical Quarterly* 57: 321–41.
Vargas, Manuel. 2004. "Responsibility and the Aims of Theory: Strawson and Revisionism." *Pacific Philosophical Quarterly* 85: 218–41.
Watson, Gary. 2014. "Peter Strawson on Responsibility and Sociality." In David Shoemaker and Neal A. Tognazzini, eds., *Oxford Studies in Agency and Responsibility, vol. 2: "Freedom and Resentment" at 50.* Oxford: Oxford University Press: 15–32.
Watson, Gary. 1987. "Responsibility and the Limits of Evil: Variations on a Strawsonian Theme." In Ferdinand Schoeman, ed., *Responsibility, Character, and the Emotions: New Essays in Moral Psychology.* Cambridge: Cambridge University Press: 256–86.
Wolf, Susan. 1981. "The Importance of Free Will." *Mind* 90: 386–405.

Here are three book-length treatments that are Strawsonian in important respects and so draw heavily on the insights in "Freedom and Resentment" even if in doing so they depart considerably from Strawson's own view:

McKenna, Michael. 2012. *Conversation and Responsibility.* New York: Oxford University Press.

Russell, Paul. 1995. *Freedom and Moral Sentiment*. New York: Oxford University Press.
Wallace, R. Jay. 1994. *Responsibility and the Moral Sentiments*. Cambridge, MA: Harvard University Press.

Here are two collections of essays devoted just to Strawson's "Freedom and Resentment:"

McKenna, Michael, and Paul Russell, eds., 2008. *Free Will and Reactive Attitudes: Perspectives on P.F. Strawson's "Freedom and Resentment."* Aldershot: Ashgate Press.
Shoemaker, David, and Neal A. Tognazzini, eds., 2014, *Oxford Studies in Agency and Responsibility, 2: "Freedom and Resentment" at 50*. Oxford: Oxford University Press.

Notes

1 All references to Strawson's essay will be to the Watson (1982) reprint.
2 For a discussion of Strawson's essay in its historical context, see the introduction to McKenna and Russell (2008: 1–17).
3 Strawson refers explicitly to the compatibilist P.H. Nowell-Smith's work here (1948, 1954). Nowell-Smith refers in his arguments to the libertarian C.A. Campbell, who in turn targets the compatibilist arguments of R.E. Hobart. These were, in essence, the classical compatibilists and incompatibilists we discussed in Chapter 3.
4 More precisely, Strawson probably had in mind the libertarian view of C.A. Campbell (1951). What is the textual evidence for this? Strawson cited Nowell-Smith's (1954) argument against libertarians, and Nowell-Smith's focus was Campbell. There is textual evidence to suggest that Campbell had in mind something like agent causation in developing his libertarian theory, but it is by no means explicit. What Campbell did clearly seem to have in mind is an ability friendly to the Kantian thesis that a person can act contrary to the determinations of her own motivations and do what is morally right.
5 Here again, the textual evidence that this was Strawson's target is shown by Strawson's citation of Nowell-Smith (1948). In this essay, Nowell-Smith argues against retributivists, and in doing so explicitly discusses their efforts to ground retributivism in intuitions of fittingness (e.g., 1948: 54).
6 In our introductory remarks in this chapter, we sketched an intrapersonal theory to help contrast it with Strawson's. Recall, on this view, there are independent truths, perhaps accessible by God, that our practices could get completely wrong. The sort of intrapersonal theory we sketched there is sometimes referred to as a *ledger theory*, since being responsible for something is like its being true that there is a (positive or negative) mark in a ledger that records one's morally appraisable acts. For the development of such a view, see Haji (1998) or Zimmerman (1988).
7 Here we leave it unsettled how best to interpret Strawson. Most take him to have committed to a dispositional view according to which blameworthiness is a function of what (typically) disposes others to a blaming response (e.g., see the introduction to Fischer and Ravizza (1993: 18–19) and Wallace (1994)). And some who have interpreted him this way advise instead a normative reading according to which blameworthiness is a function of what renders a blaming response appropriate (ibid.). However, we believe Strawson's essay can also be read this way and that the text is

indeterminate between these two interpretations. Regardless, we also prescribe a normative view as the correct one, if indeed any version of an interpersonal theory is true.

8 On an affective theory of holding morally responsible, we can make sense of blaming someone in the absence of experiencing one of these emotions. But in such cases, we would do so by reference to the fact that in some manner such behavior still is liable to elicit an emotional response. Or instead, such behavior would render it fitting or appropriate to respond with a pertinent emotion (Wallace, 1994).

9 Excuses show that one is not to blame for a wrong done. Justifications show what one did was not wrong.

10 Here we take some interpretive liberties by skating over one formulation of Strawson's argument that would render it highly implausible. Strawson at one point characterizes exemptions as reasons that show a person to be "psychologically abnormal" (68). He then remarks that no universal plea could show everyone to be abnormal. This invites a reading of his argument that makes it ripe for easy refutation. On its face, it appears that he is making the point that abnormality is statistically at odds with applying to all cases. Of course this is true, but it would not follow that every person *could not* suffer from a condition that as a matter of statistical fact only few actually suffer. In our estimation, Strawson should not be read in this way, but we grant that the text invites this reading. For a defense of our interpretation of Strawson on this point, see McKenna (2005b).

11 In this respect, Strawson's argument is similar to one Daniel Dennett subsequently advanced in "Mechanism and Responsibility" (1973), in which Dennett draws upon Strawson's 1962 paper.

12 See note 8 above.

13 See McKenna (2005b) for a development of this point.

14 This way of expressing the criticism is roughly the one set out by David Wiggins (1973).

15 Several philosophers have raised this concern regarding Strawson's argument, including Bennett (1980), McKenna (1998), Russell (1992), Watson (1987), and Wiggins (1973).

16 For one who resists this way of criticizing Strawson, see Seth Shabo (2012). Shabo, fixing upon the emotion of love, argues that one cannot compartmentalize one's emotions so as to withhold some of the morally reactive attitudes (like a propensity to resentment) without thereby being at odds with a loving attitude as well.

7 Three Source Incompatibilist Arguments

This chapter marks a point of transition. In the first half of this book we introduced the free will debate and then considered its recent history. Chapter 1 was devoted to getting clear on key concepts and related terminology. Chapter 2 introduced the free will problem, casting it as a collection of related problems. Chapter 3 focused upon the classical compatibilist and incompatibilist views from the history of philosophy, concentrating especially on the early twentieth century. Then in the next three chapters, we examined the three most influential contributions shaping the contemporary landscape. All of them originated in the 1960s. Collectively they set the stage for the current debates about free will and moral responsibility. We are now prepared to consider the free will debate in its most recent form.

To make this transition, it will be helpful to reflect upon the emerging dialectical burdens faced by compatibilists and incompatibilists, especially in light of two of those three recent historical influences: the Consequence Argument and Frankfurt's Argument against the alternative-possibilities requirement on moral responsibility. Doing so will reveal the importance of arguments for incompatibilism that do not hinge on questions regarding the freedom to do otherwise.

7.1. The Emergence of Source Theories

So, how should we understand the dialectical burdens of the current contestants in the free will debate? Recall the distinction, introduced in Chapter 2 (Section 2.3), between leeway freedom and source freedom. Leeway freedom crucially features an ability to do otherwise and is understood in terms of a Garden of Forking Paths Model of freedom. On this model, an agent's freedom essentially involves distinct possibilities for acting or refraining from acting, resulting in alternative paths into the future, and the agent's exercising control by settling which path is realized. Source freedom crucially features an agent's being the causal origin of an action and is understood in terms of a Source Model of freedom. On this model, freedom essentially involves the agent's having a certain role in the causal history of an action, a role that secures the agent's control by her being in some way its causal origin. As we set it out in Chapter 3, the dominant center of attention within the framework of the classical debate was the compatibility of leeway freedom and determinism. This in turn can be understood in terms of efforts either to advance or instead resist what we called (Section 3.3) the Basic Leeway Argument for Incompatibilism (BLI), which we shall rephrase just slightly as follows:

1. If a person acts of her own free will, then she is able to do otherwise.
2. If determinism is true, no one is able to do otherwise.
3. Therefore, if determinism is true, no one acts of her own free will.

Given the classical focus upon Leeway Freedom, the dispute over BLI amounted to a dispute over the second premise. Now, as we explained (Section 4.1), it seemed that classical compatibilists and classical incompatibilists were nearing a stalemate over whether determinism is compatible with an agent's ability to do otherwise. It was in this context that the Consequence Argument played a pivotal role. It at least appeared to lend substantial support to the incompatibilist side. As we argued in Chapter 4, the soundness of the Consequence Argument is not settled. But it is fair to say that it does help support the simple, intuitive thought that determinism rules out the ability to do otherwise (and so rules out leeway freedom), as BLI would have it.

While the Consequence Argument offers support to the second premise of BLI, as explained in Chapter 5, Frankfurt's argument against the Principle of Alternative Possibilities (PAP) served to cast the first premise of BLI into doubt.[1] Frankfurt's argument has been the center of so much controversy in part because it occasions a major shift in the basic strategies for advancing both compatibilism and incompatibilism. Suppose it was established that Frankfurt's argument is sound. This would show that leeway freedom is not required for free will and moral responsibility. This result would render the Consequence Argument irrelevant to the heart of the free will debate—or at least the free will debate cast in terms of the conditions necessary for moral responsibility.[2]

But now, if Frankfurt's Argument were to show that leeway freedom is not essential to free will, and if it hence rendered the Consequence Argument otiose, it would thereby make especially salient another sort of freedom that *is* required for moral responsibility. This would be source freedom. Call those philosophers who accept Frankfurt's argument, or some other argument to the same conclusion, *source theorists*. Source theorists contend that in theorizing about free will, understood as a condition necessary for moral responsibility, we must tend just to a source model of freedom and reject an account of freedom that essentially involves the freedom to do otherwise. *Leeway theorists*, by contrast, oppose Frankfurt's argument and other arguments for the same conclusion. They are committed to the thesis that free will requires the ability to do otherwise.

One might at first think that source theories are the exclusive domain of compatibilism, since Frankfurt himself and various others following his lead used his argument in the service of advancing a broader compatibilist thesis. But source theories are not the exclusive domain of compatibilists. All Frankfurt's argument is designed to establish is that a certain sort of freedom is *not* required for moral responsibility; it says nothing about how to account for the sort of freedom that *is* required. A significant number of incompatibilists have endorsed Frankfurt's argument, accepting that we must attend to source freedom in our theorizing about free will and moral responsibility. They also argue that the sort of source freedom required for moral responsibility is incompatible with determinism. Accordingly, source theorists divide into *source compatibilists* and *source incompatibilists*.[3] They are united in accepting Frankfurt's argument (or some argument to the same conclusion) and thus taking the Consequence Argument and similar variants to be beside the point. Contemporary leeway theorists, by contrast, divide into *leeway compatibilists* and *leeway incompatibilists*.[4] They agree on taking seriously the centrality of the Consequence Argument, or an appropriately similar argument, as at the heart of their dispute. To complicate matters a bit more, Seth Shabo (2010a) usefully distinguishes two kinds of source incompatibilism: (1) the *compromising* view defended by Kane (1996), for whom robust alternative possibilities are required for moral responsibility because—but only because—they are required for ultimate sourcehood; and (2) the *uncompromising* view, held by most of the other source incompatibilists, according to which robust alternative possibilities are not required for ultimate sourcehood. Rather, the only alternative possibilities required on this view are those that are entailed by the falsity of determinism (Della Rocca, 1998; Pereboom, 2001).

Given the preceding dialectical "redistricting" occasioned by Frankfurt's argument, one can now begin to appreciate how the newly emerging dialectical burdens have changed. Leeway theorists remain committed to tending to the Consequence Argument. As a result, that argument has remained a significant influence on philosophers currently advancing some version of a leeway theory of freedom—whether they are incompatibilists or compatibilists. Given this perspective, incompatibilists should assume the burden of defending some variant of this argument, or instead some relevantly similar argument that promises to do better. Compatibilists shoulder the burden of rejecting it. But what about the dialectical burdens of source theorists of various sorts? In one respect source compatibilists have a dialectical advantage over leeway compatibilists: They do not have to take on the burden of explaining the freedom to do otherwise under the assumption that determinism is true. Still, they must offer some positive account of source freedom all the ingredients of which are compatible with determinism.

Given the source view, incompatibilists need to show why we should think that determinism rules out a relevant kind of source freedom. In light of the source incompatibilists' burdens, they are apt to endorse what earlier (Section 3.3) we called the Basic Source Argument for Incompatibilism (BSI):

1. A person acts of her own free will only if she is its ultimate source.
2. If determinism is true, no one is the ultimate source of her actions.
3. Therefore, if determinism is true, no one acts of her own free will.

As with the Basic Leeway Argument, BSI is also open to resistance from compatibilists. Compatibilists, after all, will offer their own variations on what counts as being an adequate source of one's own agency. Hence, just as an argument like the Consequence Argument served as a resource to aid in supporting BLI, source incompatibilists need some argumentative resources to supplement BSI. The remainder of this chapter will be devoted to considering three distinct arguments for source incompatibilism. In each case, one can see how the argument lends support to BSI.

The first argument we will consider is the Ultimacy Argument for Incompatibilism, which aims to establish as a condition on free and morally responsible actions that they ultimately originate from exercises of one's own agency and not in causal conditions external to her. The second argument, the Direct Argument for Incompatibilism, is designed to show that under the assumption of determinism, non-responsibility for the remote past and the laws of nature transfers through to non-responsibility for what one does. The third argument, the Manipulation Argument for Incompatibilism, contends that causal determination is no different in any relevant respect from a form of manipulation that clearly undermines an agent's freedom and moral responsibility.

7.2.   The Ultimacy Argument for Incompatibilism

In this section, we will consider two ways of formulating an Ultimacy Argument. In either form, the argument is most frequently cast not in terms of free will but instead in terms of moral responsibility. It is natural to understand the force of the argument in terms of problems for the freedom condition(s) for moral responsibility. Accordingly, we will take some interpretive liberties here by casting versions of the argument in terms of the freedom required for moral responsibility.

We'll begin by formulating what an incompatibilist advocate of the Ultimacy Argument takes ultimacy to be. Note that there are relatively familiar folk conceptions of what it is for a person to be the initiator of a course of action and what it is for her to shape herself. These notions might be used to develop a characterization of ultimate sourcehood. We often look to identify one person rather than another as the one who initiated some course of action or some event. "Whose idea was this?" often expresses our interest here. And there is also the familiar expression of being a "self-made" person, perhaps as someone who "picked herself up by her own bootstraps," as the saying goes. These folk conceptions are not themselves clearly incompatibilist notions. Still, one can see how they might capture some sense of identifying a person as the ultimate source by contrast with courses of action or ways of acquiring character that are out of an agent's control in some uncontroversial sense. Call this the *folk notion of ultimacy*. Such a notion falls short of what the incompatibilist seeks in the ultimacy argument.

For a precise specification of what the incompatibilist does seek, consider what would credibly be involved in an agent's performing a free act. Agents do not exercise voluntary control in the production of *all* of their motivational and other action-generating states and processes. That they could exercise such control over all such internal ingredients causally antecedent to an action would be too stringent a requirement on freedom and responsibility. Accordingly, to capture a plausible sense of ultimacy for free acts, it cannot be that *each* condition that brings about a free action is such that the agent is the ultimate initiator of it. It must be instead that an agent voluntarily contributes *some* substantive necessary condition to that action.

With these considerations in mind, consider the following proposal for an incompatibilist formulation of ultimacy (McKenna, 2008d: 192):

> U: An agent is the ultimate source of her action only if she voluntarily contributes some substantive necessary condition, C, to that action such that there are no sufficient conditions for the occurrence of the action that obtain independently of her agency.

Will this do? Not if Frankfurt-examples are consistent with an agent being the ultimate source of her action, as source incompatibilists typically contend. Consider any Frankfurt-example in which the neuroscientist's device ensures that the agent will perform an action if she does not do so on her own. So long as there is a successful example in which there is such a factor independent of the agent's contribution C that ensures that she will performing that same act, a condition like U will fail as a way to specify ultimacy.[5] What needs to be added is that any sufficient condition for the occurrence of the action that obtains independently of her agency is not also a sufficient condition of her actual contribution to C. So here is a proposal that arguably avoids this problem:

> U2: An agent is the ultimate source of her action only if she voluntarily contributes some substantive necessary condition, C, to the conditions that actually bring about her action, and there are no sufficient conditions for her actual contribution to C that obtain independently of her agency.

We shall treat U2 as a satisfactory way of specifying an incompatibilist ultimacy condition on directly free action.[6]

We turn now to a first way of formulating an Ultimacy Argument.[7] Assume that a person acts as she does when she is (allegedly) free due to her state of mind at the time. She might act from passion, out of anger, on calm cool reason, but whatever it is, her agency is engaged by virtue of features of her mental economy. When she is in control, her mental life produces her actions in a non-deviant fashion. Just to simplify matters (and for no other reason), suppose we think of reasons on the classic Humean model as belief–desire pairs. If an agent, Ann, acts to steal a loaf of bread, there is some combination of belief and desire that is Ann's reason why she so acts, a reason we can abbreviate as BD. If she is morally responsible for stealing the bread, and if she acted freely in doing so, then it seems that both her responsibility and her freedom are due to her reason,

BD, that is, are due to the way she is mentally. But if she is not morally responsible for at least some crucial aspect of the way she is mentally at the time at
which she acts, then she is not morally responsible for her action, since her
action is due to the way she is mentally. What would be required for her to be
morally responsible for BD? Well, she would have to be responsible for her
freely acquiring BD. So the way she was mentally in the acquisition of BD
would have to be the product of something she did freely and for which she is
morally responsible. But then there must have been some other belief–desire
pair, BD′ that non-deviantly led to her acquisition of BD, and for her to be
morally responsible for BD, she must be morally responsible for BD′. And so
on, *ad infinitum*.

It turns out that, on this version of the Ultimacy Argument, a person is
morally responsible for her actions only if she freely chose and brought about
her own self. But this is impossible; therefore, so is morally responsible agency.
Consider Galen Strawson's version of this argument (1994: 5):

1.   Nothing can be *causa sui*—nothing can be the cause of itself.
2.   In order to be truly morally responsible for one's actions one would have to
     be *causa sui*, at least in certain crucial mental respects.
3.   Therefore, nothing can be truly morally responsible.

As explained above, to remain focused on the topic of freedom, we will cast
these arguments explicitly in terms of freedom. So, consider then this slight
amendment to Strawson's argument:

1*.   Nothing can be *causa sui*—nothing can be the cause of itself.
2*.   In order to be free in the strongest sense required to be truly morally
       responsible for one's actions one would have to be *causa sui*, at least in
       certain crucial mental respects.
3*.   Therefore, nothing can be free in the strongest sense required to be truly
       morally responsible.

This version of the Ultimacy Argument is very ambitious. Note that determinism
does not play any role in the argument at all. Hence, it is not an argument for
incompatibilism in the traditional sense, since it does not say that *determinism* is
what rules out freedom and moral responsibility. Rather, the very concept of
moral responsibility, at least in the "true" basic-desert-involving sense, is incoherent. It has the seeds in it of a demand that is metaphysically impossible to
achieve (for finite beings). So, let us label this version of the Ultimacy Argument
an *impossibilist* version.[8] We can take this argument for impossibilism about
freedom and responsibility to feature the thesis that free and morally responsible
agency is impossible due to the very concept of responsibility (or freedom), and
not because of any fact about the universe (such as that it is deterministic).

How convincing is this version of the Ultimacy Argument? In our view, the
second premise is problematic. It masks an especially important assumption that

many involved in the free will debate would want to resist, as Randolph Clarke
has pointed out (2005: 13–14).[9] What Strawson assumes in endorsing the second
premise of this impossibilist version of the Ultimacy Argument is this:

> P: You act freely in the sense required for you to be truly morally respons-
> ible for what you do only if you act freely in the sense required for you to be
> truly morally responsible for the way you are mentally (as it bears on what
> you do).

But P can be challenged. Suppose, as in the case of Ann above, she steals the
bread due to BD. BD captures how she was mentally at the time at which she
acted. In order for it to be that Ann freely steals the loaf of bread, must it be, as P
requires, that she acts freely with respect to the way she is mentally in that she
possesses BD? If it must be, an argument needs to be given, one that goes beyond
the Ultimacy Argument. One might contend that even if it is not up to Ann how
she is mentally—that is, whether she freely possesses BD—it is up to her whether
she acts on BD. This criticism is especially forceful for incompatibilists with libertarian leanings who hold that in the absence of determinism persons might be
free and responsible. According to them, it could very well be that at a certain
time, a person has no direct control over how she is mentally, over what beliefs
and desires she has, but it can be causally open to her that she act on some belief–
desire pair and also causally open that she refrain from acting on that belief–
desire pair, and she might exercise direct control in acting or in refraining.

A similar criticism of the argument is also available to the compatibilist (e.g.,
McKenna, 2008d: 191; Mele, 1995: 225). On a compatibilist view, Ann might
very well be directly free with respect to acting on her belief–desire pair even if
she is not directly free with respect to her possession of that belief–desire pair.
Think of it this way, the compatibilist might say: Among the many causally
related events that will unfold in the history of the world, a person's development will result from prior causes. She will come to have various states of mind
that will be the product of factors that are beyond her control, including genetic
traits, parental influence, and the vagaries of luck. At some point, in the inter-
stices of various causally related events, this agent will act in such a manner that
she will exercise control over her conduct. From conditions that lack control,
control will arise.

Is there a less ambitious version of an Ultimacy Argument that might advance
a source incompatibilist thesis? The ingredients of such an argument can be
found in the writings of a number of incompatibilists. Recall this quotation from
Paul Edwards (from Chapter 3):

> "You are right," he [the hard determinist] would say [to the compatibilist],
> "in maintaining that some of our actions are caused by our desires and
> choices. But you do not pursue the subject far enough. You arbitrarily stop
> at the desires and volitions. We must not stop there. We must go on to ask
> where *they* come from; and if determinism is true there can be no doubt

about the answer to this question. Ultimately our desires and our whole character are derived from our inherited equipment and the environmental influences to which we are subject at the beginning of our lives. It is clear that we had no hand in shaping these." (Edwards, 1958, in Hook, 1958: 121 [our brackets])

From this insight Edwards proceeds to argue that, under the assumption that determinism is true, no one is free and morally responsible. In more recent times, Saul Smilansky has advanced a similar line of argument. According to Smilansky, if determinism is true, then all of our conduct is just part of the "unfolding of the given" (2000: 284). Assuming determinism, anything a person does is but an outgrowth of factors that are ultimately beyond her control, since the origin of her conduct is found in sufficient causal springs obtaining before she was even born (45). Hence, no one is the ultimate source of her actions if determinism is true.

To facilitate discussion, it will be useful to have before us a formulation of the Edwards–Smilansky-type argument set out in premise and conclusion form. So consider this version of the Ultimacy Argument (as set out by McKenna, 2008d: 192):

1. A person acts freely in the sense required for true moral responsibility only if she is the ultimate source of her action.
2. If determinism is true, no one is the ultimate source of her actions.
3. Therefore, if determinism is true, no one acts freely in the sense required for true moral responsibility.

Notice that this version of the Ultimacy Argument is an incompatibilist version, and it is not as demanding as Strawson's impossibilist version. It leaves open that if determinism is false, it might be possible to satisfy the requirement of ultimacy, and so for agents to act freely.[10]

This version of the Ultimacy Argument is problematic for reasons having to do with how we understand the notion of ultimacy. Suppose we interpret this argument so that we understood the occurrence of the word "ultimate" along the lines specified in U2. If so, the problem with the argument is that it is question-begging. It is obvious that U2 cannot be satisfied if determinism is true, and a demand for it as a condition of freedom and responsibility, as is expressed in premise 1 above, just is an expression of the truth of incompatibilism. Incompatibilism is thus assumed as a premise in the argument. And it is obvious how a compatibilist would respond. She would grant premise 2 as obviously true and deny premise 1.

One might instead consider interpreting the notion of ultimacy along the lines of the folk notion noted above. An incompatibilist could then treat it as a substantive matter to be established by philosophical argument that, so understood, determinism is incompatible with being an ultimate source of one's actions. But so interpreted, the argument would be vulnerable from two different lines of attack. First, a compatibilist might resist the first premise of the argument and contend that being a mediated rather than an ultimate cause of action is sufficient for freedom and responsibility. It would just be that the nature of the mediated cause is rich enough to capture the many features of agency marking off persons as sophisticated creatures by contrast with other beings whose resources for causal efficacy in the natural order are by comparison more impoverished. Second, a compatibilist might instead reject the second premise of the argument and attempt to offer a compatibilist-friendly account of ultimacy. Such a compatibilist could grant, as premise 1 contends, that an important condition upon acting freely is that one act from resources of her own agency that she had some hand in shaping for herself, but that this is consistent with a deterministic history of a sort that falls far short of a condition like U2.[11]

In our estimation, what the preceding assessment of the incompatibilist version of the Ultimacy Argument shows is that for incompatibilists to advance a compelling version of it, what they need is a substantive, non-question-begging, defense of a proposal for what ultimacy is such that it would help render both premises 1 and 2 of the argument true. This, it seems, would require a different style of argument that would yield a conclusion for a thesis like U2. If so, then such a source incompatibilist defense would really rest on this distinct argument. As readers will soon learn, in our estimation the best candidate argument to do this work is a Manipulation Argument for Incompatibilism—which we take up in Section 4.

Before moving on to the next argument for source incompatibilism, we pause to clarify something that should be of use to many studying this literature. It is important to distinguish between philosophers who are committed to an *ultimacy thesis*, such as U2, and philosophers who are committed to some version of the Ultimacy Argument. Robert Kane (1996: 73–8), for instance, is committed to an ultimacy thesis, and so is Derk Pereboom (2001: 4; 2014: 4). But neither is committed to arguing for a thesis by way of an Ultimacy Argument. As it happens, both instead appeal to a manipulation argument.

7.3.   The Direct Argument for Incompatibilism

We turn to the *Direct Argument*, first advanced by Peter van Inwagen (1983). The Direct Argument for incompatibilism is so named, as van Inwagen explained, because it aims to establish an incompatibility between moral responsibility and determinism without taking the indirect route of trying to show that something necessary for moral responsibility—such as the freedom to do otherwise—is incompatible with determinism (van Inwagen, 1983: 183–4).[12] In this way, it aims to secure moral responsibility's incompatibility with determinism directly. In deference to van Inwagen's intentions, we will follow his lead and forgo any attention to the freedom condition for moral responsibility in setting out the argument.[13]

The Direct Argument's structure mirrors the structure of the Consequence Argument, but instead of transferring powerlessness over the past and the laws to powerlessness over their consequences, it transfers nonresponsibility for the past and the laws to nonresponsibility for their consequences. As a first pass, we'll borrow from van Inwagen's pithy formulation of the Consequence Argument (1983: 16, quoted in Chapter 4), modifying it by substituting the notion of nonresponsibility for not being up to us. So, consider this equally pithy expression of the Direct Argument:

> If determinism is true, then our acts are the consequences of the laws of nature and events of the remote past. But we are not responsible for what went on before we were born, and neither are we responsible for what the laws of nature are. Therefore, we are not responsible for the consequences of these things (including our present acts).

This formulation of the Direct Argument masks significant and interesting complexity, just as van Inwagen's similar formulation of the Consequence Argument did. Here too van Inwagen and other philosophers have developed the argument in impressive ways, sorting through this complexity in admirable detail. We shall now explore these issues, but not quite with the same level of detail and scrutiny we did when assessing the Consequence Argument.

To begin, we need a more developed expression of the argument. The Direct Argument invokes a compelling pattern of inference applied to modal propositions about nonresponsibility (rather than about power necessity, as in van Inwagen's more precise formulation of the Consequence Argument). Nonresponsibility can be understood in terms of what a person is not even partly morally responsible for. No one is, for instance, even partly morally responsible for the truths of mathematics, or the fact that water is composed of hydrogen and oxygen. Intuitively, the pattern of inference drawing upon these modal propositions about nonresponsibility can be expressed as follows:

> If a person is not even partly morally responsible for certain facts, and if she is not even partly morally responsible for the fact that these facts have a particular consequence, then she is not even partly morally responsible for the consequence either.

In short, nonresponsibility transfers from one fact to consequences of it. Here is an example that van Inwagen offered to help show the appeal of this pattern of inference, which we can refer to as *Snakebite* (1983: 187):

> If John is bitten by a cobra on his thirtieth birthday, and no one is even partly morally responsible for this fact, and if a consequence of his being bitten is that he dies, and no one is even partly morally responsible for this distinct conditional fact, then no one is even partly morally responsible for John dying.

This general pattern of inference is applied to determinism to yield an appealing source incompatibilist argument. The argument requires the assumption that determinism is true, and the assumptions of nonresponsibility for the past and nonresponsibility for laws of nature. Given these assumptions, here is a simplified sketch of the argument:

1. No one is even partly morally responsible for either the facts of the remote past or the laws of nature.
2. No one is even partly morally responsible for the fact that the facts of the remote past in conjunction with the laws of nature imply that there is only one unique future.
3. Therefore, no one is even partly morally responsible for the facts of the future.

According to the Direct Argument, if determinism is true, no one is even partly morally responsible for how the future will unfold, including how one acts. In short, determinism is incompatible with moral responsibility.

In this section, we will make do with the preceding formulation and will forgo a fully developed version of the Direct Argument, which is, as van Inwagen puts it (1983: 185), "inscriptionally identical" with the advanced version of the Consequence Argument (which we set out in Section 4.4). However, two formal details of the more advanced expression of the argument will prove useful to explicate here. First, the modal operator of nonresponsibility, NR, when applied to a proposition, p, for an agent, S, and a time, t, is represented as follows: $NR_{S,t}(p)$, and can be understood in English as:

> p and agent S at time t is not even partly morally responsible for the fact that p.

In relevant contexts, the indexing to agents and times can be dropped, as in NRp, and then can be read as:

> p and no one is even partly morally responsible for the fact that p.

Treating the first conjunct as elliptical, this can be shortened to:

> No one is even partly morally responsible for the fact that p.

Second, the argument employs a closure inference principle that is the analog to the Transfer principle deployed in the Consequence Argument. Van Inwagen refers to this closure principle as Rule B, but it is often referred to as the Principle of the Transfer of Non-Responsibility, or just *Transfer NR*, and it is a formalized way of expressing what we set out above as an intuitive expression of the pertinent pattern of inference. It can be formulated as follows:

TNR: $NRp, NR(p \rightarrow q) \vdash NRq$

In English, TNR reads:

1. No one is even partly morally responsible for that fact that p.
2. No one is even partly morally responsible for the fact that p implies q.
3. Therefore, no one is even partly morally responsible for the fact that q.

With these resources in place, we turn to a treatment of several of the most pressing objections to the Direct Argument.

The most familiar strategy for resisting the Direct Argument is by way of showing that it is invalid because the inference rule TNR is invalid. To get this result, what a critic needs is an example of this form:

$$NRp \ \& \ NR(p \rightarrow q) \ \& \ \sim NRq$$

That is, what is needed is a case in which a person is not even partly morally responsible for p, is not even partly morally responsible for the fact that p implies q, but *is* morally responsible for q.[14] Now consider the following example developed by Mark Ravizza as applied to moral responsibility for the consequences of one's actions:

> Imagine that Betty plants her explosives in the crevices of a glacier and det-onates the charge at T1, causing an avalanche that crushes the enemy for-tress at T3. Unbeknownst to Betty and her commanding officers, however, the glacier is gradually melting, shifting, and eroding. Had Betty not placed the dynamite in the crevices, some ice and rocks would have broken free and crushed the enemy base camp at T3. (Ravizza, 1994: 72–3)

Call this example *Avalanche*. Avalanche is exactly a case that satisfies the requirements specified for a direct counterexample to Transfer NR:

- Betty is not morally responsible for the condition of the glacier prior to T3.
- Betty is not morally responsible for the fact that, if the glacier is in that con-dition prior to T3, then the enemy base camp is destroyed at T3.
- Betty is morally responsible for the destruction of the enemy base camp.

Ravizza in coauthored work with Fischer (Fischer and Ravizza, 1998: chapter 6), made use of examples such as this one to mount a sustained assault on the Direct Argument. How might the advocate of the Direct Argument respond?

Note two things about Avalanche. First, it is a case about moral responsibility for the consequences of one's actions and so not a case of moral responsibility for the action itself, such as responsibility for the decision to destroy the enemy camp. Second, it involves a "two path" case. There is one path leading to a certain result and then a distinct path to that same result. The former path it can be granted is one for which no one is morally responsible. But the other allows for the possibility of a distinct "responsibility-conferring" path. Each of these features of the case appears to give the advocate of the Direct Argument room for a reply.

Consider first the fact that the example involves moral responsibility for consequences. A defender of the Direct Argument might point out that moral responsibility for consequences is always in some way derivative of moral responsibility for action (or omission), and it is not surprising that a Transfer NR principle not restricted to actions (and omissions) could be easily discredited by examples like Avalanche (Pereboom, 2001). What matters, however, is whether nonresponsibility for past and laws, and nonresponsibility for their leading to an agent's acting as she does, lead to nonresponsibility for those very actions. A case like Avalanche leaves this basic source incompatibilist worry entirely unaddressed.

A critic of the Direct Argument might reply by constructing examples concerning responsibility for basic actions, such as decisions, that have the same structure and so would threaten a version of Transfer NR restricted to actions (e.g., Fischer and Ravizza, 1998: 157–8). The resources for doing so are, as it turns out, familiar. Consider this Frankfurt-type example:

> Imagine that Betty deliberates and decides to destroy the enemy basecamp by T3. Unbeknownst to her, there is a nefarious demon who will cause Betty to so decide if at the very moment Betty actually decides she were not to do so. As it happens, Betty decides on her own.

This has the same structure as a counterexample to a pertinent version of Transfer NR as applied to actions:

- Betty is not morally responsible for the presence and the intentions of the demon.
- Betty is not morally responsible for the fact that, if the demon is present, she, Betty, will decide by T3 to destroy the enemy camp.
- Betty *is* morally responsible for deciding by T3 to destroy the enemy camp.

True, critics of Frankfurt's argument who dispute the coherence of this style of example will not be persuaded by this counter-reply. But set that aside here.[15] It seems that such an example has the right structure to show that pertinent versions of a Transfer NR principle, even ones restricted to basic actions (and omissions), are invalid.

Now consider the fact that the examples employ two-path cases. An advocate of the Direct Argument might object that the examples differ in a dialectically relevant sense from the way in which, if determinism is true, an agent's putative free acts and omissions are ensured. McKenna (2001) and Eleonore Stump (2000) have developed this way of resisting Fischer and Ravizza's criticism of the Direct Argument. Here is how McKenna puts the objection:

> [If] determinism is true, then the manner in which the facts of the past and the laws of nature entail one unique future is *not* analogous to the manner in

which one set of independently existing causally sufficient conditions (for example, an erosion) ensure a subsequent event also ensured by *some distinct set* of independently existing sufficient conditions (i.e., Betty's action). Assuming determinism, the pertinent facts (consisting in the deterministic order of things) are not *independent* of an agent's reasons for action, *they constitute them*! Therefore, at a deterministic world involving a typical case regarding a judgment of moral responsibility, the case is relevantly like a one-path, *not* a two-path case. (McKenna 2001: 45)

Both McKenna and Stump thus propose a suitable revision to Transfer NR to one-path cases. Here is an informal statement of such a principle, which should suffice for present purposes:

> If a person is not responsible for a certain fact, and if this fact identifies at some particular time the sole causal antecedent of the path to the bringing about of a further fact, and if the person is not responsible for any part of the path between the two facts, then the person is not responsible for the further fact either.[16]

Call this Transfer NR-Revised (TNR-R). Will TNR-R or some similar variation suffice to aid in advancing a defensible version of the Direct Argument? Fischer (2004: 200–1) has replied by suggesting that we might be able to identify even in one single causal path two sets of properties or processes, one of which is responsibility-conferring even if the other is only at best *controversially* (as the incompatibilist would see it) not responsibility conferring. Hence, we could thereby generate counterexamples even to TNR-R. But this way of resisting the Direct Argument hinges upon delicate issues about how one set of properties that are responsibility-conferring might be superimposed upon the set in virtue of which an action is ensured as an upshot of determinism's truth. Can we really think of the actual instantiation of the (allegedly) responsibility-conferring properties in a deterministic case *as distinct from* the properties in virtue of which an act is determined? This is not clear (McKenna, 2008c: 366–7). Fischer's reply seems to rely on presuppositions that are too esoteric when weighed against the apparent intuitive appeal expressed in TNR-R of the idea that a person is not responsible for something if she is not responsible for the only path that results in its coming about.

Fischer, however, offers a distinct reply to efforts to restrict a version of TNR to one-path cases. Such efforts, he charges, appear to be question-begging against the compatibilist because they do not "employ a principle that is broadly appealing" (2004: 203). Is this a fair charge? Perhaps it is. We will explore this charge, but if it is question-begging, and if it does not employ a principle that is broadly appealing, it is hard to see how that would be so. To explain, recall that van Inwagen claimed that the initial appeal of TNR was due to the fact that it seemed to be confirmed by examples like *Snakebite*, and there are numerous others that one might cite as well. Another van Inwagen offered went basically as follows:

No one is responsible for the fact Plato died in antiquity. Nor is anyone responsible for the fact that if Plato died in antiquity, he never met Hume. Therefore, no one is responsible for the fact that Plato never met Hume.

Call this case *Plato*. There are many other cases like it one might construct. It is such cases that—*at least apparently*—make appealing a principle like TNR. Of course, Fischer's objection is not that TNR is not broadly appealing but rather than TNR-R is not, and that the latter's appeal really just begs the question against the compatibilist (that is, its appeal is exhausted in an intuition supporting incompatibilism). But suppose it were pointed out to unbiased, impartial inquirers who might come to see the initial appeal of TNR by way of examples like *Snakebite* and *Plato* that when there are two paths to a certain result, the principle does not seem to work. Suppose, for instance, that it were pointed out that in a revised case like *Two-Path Snakebite* TNR fails. In *Two-Path Snakebite* just prior to John's being bitten, Leonard secretly poisoned John so that he would die soon thereafter. Such an audience, seeing that two-path cases create problems, might readily think that a natural move is to restrict the principle, since so restricted, it captures their pattern of inference rather innocently when reasoning about cases like *Snakebite* and *Plato*. If this is correct, then it at least *seems* that a principle like TNR-R is not after all question-begging. If so, the Direct Argument survives as a serious threat to compatibilism.

Thus far, we have explored the strategy of producing counterexamples to TNR as a means of resisting the Direct Argument, and this has led to proposed revisions such as TNR-R. A slightly different strategy, developed by McKenna (2008c), seeks to undermine TNR or revisions like TNR-R not by adducing counterexamples (of the form NRp & NR(p→q) & ~NRq), but by calling into question the initial appeal of any such principle as one that can be employed in an argument for an incompatibilist conclusion. Consider *Snakebite* and *Plato*, which were offered as innocent examples confirming the appeal of TNR. Notice that in each example the transfer of nonresponsibility from one fact to consequences of it never in any way involves a causal chain passing through an agent when she is acting competently and unimpaired in her exercise of well-functioning agential resources (by standards that would be agreeable to both compatibilists and incompatibilists alike). In *Snakebite*, for instance, a poisonous snake bites John and he dies from it. There is no fact about which no one is responsible that leads to any agent acting in any normal way at all.

With the preceding observation in place, consider the history of a putatively free agent at a determined world as a compatibilist might see it. However the facts of the remote past and the laws unfold, they will include a history that results in this agent—let's call her Ann—coming into existence. As her life progresses, she will acquire various skills and abilities, eventually coming to be able to deliberate and form intentions. At some point, Ann will exercise her freedom in a normal way. From conditions that lack freedom, a free agent will emerge, one whose actions can be candidates for assessment in terms of moral responsibility. So consider Ann's first free act (FFA)—free at least as the compatibilist would see it—and one for which she is (allegedly) responsible. Suppose an incompatibilist critic were to deploy a TNR principle by pointing out that just prior to FFA, she was not morally responsible for the state she was in. And, assuming determinism is true, she was not morally responsible for it being the case that, given that prior state (and the laws), she would subsequently perform that act FFA. Hence, the incompatibilist would conclude, she is not morally responsible for FFA. In response, a compatibilist would be right to claim that without *independent backing for a principle like TNR*, the incompatibilist is not entitled to deploy it here without begging the question against the compatibilist. It is a transparent fact about what compatibilism comes to that, at some point, an agent's first free and responsible act will arise from antecedent conditions over which she had no control and for which she was not responsible.

What this suggests, McKenna has argued, is that prior to the incompatibilist applying TNR to a case like the above case of Ann by way of an argument like the Direct Argument, she first needs confirming instances of how the principle can apply that are not question-begging instances. Cases like *Snakebite* and *Plato* will not do, since they are plainly beside the point. They are not in any way about effects of prior nonresponsibility facts on normally functioning exercises of agency.

Some critics of McKenna's assault on the Direct Argument (e.g., Haji, 2010; Schnall and Widerker, 2012) have countered by pointing out that there are various familiar cases of nonresponsibility transferring from one fact to another implied by the first, where the latter involves exercises of normal deliberative agency, cases that are not question-begging regarding the present dispute between compatibilist and incompatibilists. These cases, these critics contend, could be used as credible confirming instances of a TNR principle. In one (Schnall and Widerker, 2012: 29–36), a commanding officer in the military reprimands a subordinate, Jones, for lying about being sick and missing work. The officer happened to see someone frolicking on the beach, Smith, who looked like Jones, and with this good evidence at hand, proceeded to issue Jones a severe reprimand. This appears to be a solid confirming instance of TNR:

> The officer is not responsible (in the sense of being blameworthy) for the fact that he sees someone who looks like Jones on the beach (and so comes to believe it is Jones in a way that is not epistemically culpable), nor for the fact that if he sees someone he believes to be Jones on the beach, then he reprimands Jones. So, finally, he is not responsible for (unjustly) reprimanding Jones.

Call this case *Reprimand*. Will examples such as *Reprimand* suffice to meet McKenna's challenge? In our estimation, it seems that they will not. While we can simply grant the judgments of nonresponsibility (in the sense of not being blameworthy) in *Reprimand* and in similar cases are all true, the question is whether there is special reason to postulate a principle like TNR to explain the reasoning about them. There are familiar principles regarding nonculpable ignorance that are common ground between compatibilists and incompatibilists, and all that is needed is a principle of this sort to explain a nonresponsibility judgment for the officer's reprimanding of the innocent Jones.[17]

What is needed as a way of providing confirming instances of TNR is a kind of case in which *all* of the familiar compatibilist-friendly conditions for moral responsibility (and let us also assume, blameworthiness) are in place, and yet, prior facts of nonresponsibility transfer through to facts about how the agent exercises her well-functioning agency. In the process of opposing the Direct Argument, McKenna (2008c: 380) actually suggested a promising strategy for the incompatibilist to pursue. She could invoke a case in which an agent is manipulated into being in a state that is qualitatively identical to the state a normally functioning agent might be in at a determined world when she acts in such a way that, by compatibilist standards, she would be regarded as free and morally responsible (even blameworthy) for acting as she does. In such a case, many would claim that an agent so manipulated does not act freely and is not morally responsible. Such examples could be used as a source of support, confirming the validity of an inference such as TNR. But this suggests that the argumentative work of the Direct Argument would in effect really be carried by a distinct way to reach a source-incompatibilist conclusion, a manipulation argument. We will now turn to an examination of this type of argument.

7.4.   The Manipulation Argument for Incompatibilism

Manipulation arguments for incompatibilism begin with an example in which an agent is covertly manipulated into acquiring a psychic structure on the basis of which she performs an action. The proponent of the argument contends that the featured agent thereby satisfies what might be called a Compatibilist-Friendly Agential Structure (CAS), which provides minimal conditions a compatibilist would take to be sufficient for acting freely. Such an example is meant to elicit the intuition that, due to the nature of the manipulation, the agent does not act freely and is not morally responsible for what she does. It is then argued that any agent's coming to be in the same psychic state through a deterministic process is no different in any responsibility-relevant respect from the pertinent manner of manipulation. The conclusion is that CAS is inadequate. The claim is that no candidate CAS will turn the trick; free will and moral responsibility are incompatible with determinism.

To illustrate, consider Richard Taylor's formulation of a manipulation argument. Taylor targeted a classical compatibilist account of freedom according to which one is free so long as her volitions are not impeded in acting as she wants to act. About such a view, he wrote:

> But if the fulfillment of these conditions renders my behavior free—that is to say, if my behavior satisfies the conditions of free action set forth in the theory of soft determinism—then my behavior will be no less free if we assume further conditions that are perfectly consistent with those already satisfied.

We may suppose further, accordingly, that while my behavior is entirely in accordance with my own volitions, and thus "free" in terms of the conception of freedom we are examining, my volitions themselves are caused. To make this graphic, we can suppose that an ingenious physiologist can induce in me any volition he pleases by pushing various buttons on an instrument to which, let us suppose, I am attached by numerous wires. All of the volitions I have in that situation are, accordingly, precisely the ones he gives me. By pushing one button, he evokes in me the volition to raise my hand; and my hand, being unimpeded, rises in response to that volition. By pushing another, he induces the volition in me to kick, and my foot, being unimpeded, kicks in response to that volition. We can even suppose that the physiologist puts a rifle in my hands, aims it at a passerby, and then, by pushing the proper button, evokes in me the volition to squeeze my finger against the trigger, whereupon the passerby falls dead of a bullet wound.

This is the description of a man who is acting in accord with his inner volitions, a man whose body is unimpeded and unconstrained in its motions, these motions being the effects of his inner states. It is hardly the description of a free and responsible agent. It is the perfect description of a puppet. (Taylor, 1974: 45)

Note that the particular compatibilist account of CAS that Taylor was aiming to discredit falls far short of the more robust theories currently on offer (theories we shall canvass in later chapters), but his strategy is suggestive of how more recent proposals could be contested. Taylor is not alone in invoking manipulation to discredit a compatibilist proposal. Kane (1996: 65), for instance, argues similarly by invoking the unsettling utopian societies of Aldous Huxley's *Brave New World* and B.F. Skinner's *Walden Two* to suggest that the citizens in these societies would satisfy Frankfurt's (1971) conditions for compatibilist free will. Yet, Kane argued, they would lack the deeper sort of freedom constitutive of genuine free will.

Thus far we have written in terms of manipulation arguments—plural. This is to make perspicuous that there are different instances of a general form. Let's refer to the argument form as *the* manipulation argument. So, treating "X" as a placeholder for different ways of manipulating an agent, consider *The Manipulation Argument (TMA)*:

1. If an agent, S, is manipulated in manner X to perform act A from CAS, then S does not A freely and is therefore not morally responsible for A-ing.
2. Any agent manipulated in manner X to A is no different in any relevant respect from any normally functioning agent causally determined to do A from CAS.
3. Therefore, any normally functioning agent causally determined to do A from CAS does not A freely and therefore is not morally responsible for A-ing.

Different instances of TMA will arise in relation to: (1) different candidate cases of manipulation, and (2) different compatibilist proposals for CAS.[18]

How will compatibilists respond to TMA, and to the various particular versions of manipulation arguments? Given the variability of (1) and (2), there is no one-size-fits-all compatibilist reply to the full range of manipulation arguments. Whether a compatibilist is positioned to resist either the first or second premise of a particular manipulation argument will depend on the details of the manipulation case and on the content of her account of CAS. To reject the first premise of a manipulation argument is to adopt a *hardline reply*, since it involves taking on directly the hard burden of resisting the (often) intuitively plausible judgment that a suitably manipulated agent does not act freely and is not morally responsible. To reject the second premise of a manipulation argument is, by contrast, to adopt a *softline reply*, since it permits that an agent manipulated in the way featured by the argument does not act freely and is not morally responsible (McKenna, 2008a). Instead, it involves showing how it is that an agent who is merely determined to act as she does differs in some relevant way from an agent so manipulated.

Despite that fact that there is no one-size-fits-all reply to manipulation arguments, McKenna has argued that compatibilists have good reason to adopt a general policy with respect to them: When reflecting upon the manipulation argument—that is, TMA, the argument form—compatibilists should adopt a defeasible policy of inclining toward a hardline reply to various instances when doing so is a viable option (McKenna, 2004: 216–17; 2008a: 143–4). This, however, might seem counterintuitive. Hardline replies apparently involve bullet-biting, at least in response to carefully constructed examples that really do appear to capture the conditions for compatibilist freedom. Softline replies allow intuitions about freedom-destroying manipulation cases to go undisturbed. So why advise compatibilists to incline toward hardline replies? Why look for bullets to bite? McKenna grants that compatibilists might win battles by adopting a softline reply to particular instances of manipulation arguments, pointing out how their respective accounts of CAS are not satisfied by various cases of manipulation. The strategy is to allow that the manipulated agents in question are not free and responsible and then to argue that the agents so manipulated are different with regard to what is involved in being a free agent at a determined world. But the trouble with this dialectical maneuver (as we will illustrate in the discussion to follow) is that it is open to the incompatibilist to parry with a simple adjustment to her case of manipulation, one that accommodates the compatibilist in such a way that the compatibilist's preferred account of CAS *is* satisfied. Thus, in adopting a softline reply to pertinent instances, compatibilists just forestall the inevitable, which is a revised case of manipulation, and a new instance of a manipulation argument for which compatibilists will not have the option of a softline reply—for which, they'll *have* to face the music and take on directly a hardline reply.

We turn now to an examination of Pereboom's (1995, 2001, 2014) version of a manipulation argument, which is often referred to as the *Four-Case Manipulation Argument*. Pereboom attacks a version of CAS that is a conjunction of four influential contemporary compatibilist proposals. For ease of discussion, let us refer to this conjunctive account as *CAS**. Given CAS*, the manipulated agent featured in Pereboom's argument is not constrained by any irresistible desires and does not act out of character (Ayer, 1954); he acts upon first-order desires with which he identifies at a higher order (Frankfurt, 1971); he is responsive to reasons in a way that displays a stable, sane pattern (Fischer and Ravizza, 1998); and when he acts, he has the general capacity to regulate his behavior in light of moral reasons (Wallace, 1994).[19] In proceeding in this manner, Pereboom intends to target more than extant compatibilist proposals; all compatibilist comers are open to the same treatment. Whatever further compatibilist proposals one might come up with could just be conjoined to CAS*.

An innovation of Pereboom's way of advancing a manipulation argument is that he does not just work from one manipulation case. Rather, he employs a series of them, three, in such a way that the first in the series involves a kind of manipulation that is very different from the kind of causal process that would be expected to unfold at a deterministic world of the sort that ours might be. He then marches through two more cases so that each case comes closer and closer to a case in which an agent acts as she does in a world at which determinism is true. In doing so, he employs a generalization strategy of treating like cases alike. In transition between the cases, he argues that there is no freedom-and-responsibility-relevant difference between the modes of manipulation, so that if we are to treat the first case as one in which the manipulated agent is not free and responsible, that will carry over to the next in the series, and so forth, with the fourth and last merely being a case in which determinism is true. This generalization strategy is used to back up the second premise in Pereboom's argument— that is, it is meant to show that the highlighted means of manipulation, even in an extreme case such as his first, are no different in any relevant respect than is the means of causation at work under the assumption of determinism.

Here is a truncated summary of each case as set out in his earlier (2001) formulation:

> *Case 1*: Professor Plum was created by a team of neuroscientists, who can manipulate him directly through radio-like technology, but he is as much like an ordinary human being as is possible, given his history. The scientists "locally" manipulate him to undertake a process of reasoning, directly producing his every state moment by moment, which leads to the killing of White for egoistic reasons. (112–13)

The manipulation is such that Plum fully satisfies CAS* when he murders White. Of course, we are to have the intuition that, due to the extremity and pervasiveness of the manipulation, Plum does not act freely and is not morally responsible for killing White.

> *Case 2*: Plum is like an ordinary human being, except he was created by a team of neuroscientists who, although they cannot control him directly, have

programmed him from the outset to weigh reasons for action so that he is often but not exclusively egoistic, with the result that in the circumstances he is causally determined to undertake the process that results in his killing White. (113–14)

Again, Plum satisfies CAS*. As for the time lag between the neuroscientists' manipulations and Plum's act, there is no relevant difference, Pereboom argues, between this case in which all of the programming takes place at the beginning of his existence and Case 1 where the manipulation is direct and moment by moment. Treating like cases alike, we are to have the intuition that Plum does not act freely and is not morally responsible for killing White.

> *Case 3*: Plum is an ordinary human being, except that he was determined by the rigorous training practices of his home and community so that he is often but not exclusively rationally egoistic (exactly as egoistic as in Cases 1 and 2). His training took place at too early an age for him to have had the ability to prevent or alter the practices that determined his character. In his current circumstances, Plum is thereby caused to undertake the … process … that results in his killing White. (114)

Yet again, Plum satisfies CAS*. Case 3 is a common sort of case that we would find in the actual world. But the causal inputs, Pereboom reasons, are just less weird causes as in comparison with the sort highlighted in Case 2. Otherwise, there is no relevant difference. So, treating like cases alike, we are to have the intuition that Plum does not act freely and is not morally responsible for killing White.

> *Case 4*: Physicalist determinism is true, and Plum is an ordinary human being, generated and raised under normal circumstances, who is often but not exclusively rationally egoistic (exactly as egoistic as in Cases 1–3). Plum's killing of White comes about as a result of his undertaking the relevant process. (115)

Once again, Plum satisfies CAS*. And since Case 4 differs from Case 3 merely by virtue of the fact the deterministic causes apply universally rather than locally as regards the details of Plum's upbringing, there again seems to be no relevant difference between the cases. So, Pereboom argues, treating like cases alike, we should conclude that Plum in Case 4 does not act freely and is not morally responsible for killing White. Ergo, CAS* is refuted.

According to Pereboom, by way of his manipulation argument and his march from Cases 1 through 4, he is able to exploit Spinoza's strategy of making salient the hidden causes of human actions so as to show how, once they are revealed, the illusion of control dissipates:

> Men think themselves free, because they are conscious of their volitions and appetite, and do not think, even in their dreams, of the causes by which they

are disposed to wanting and willing, because they are ignorant of [those causes]. (Spinoza, 1677, v. 1, 440)

Seeing that being causally determined (Case 4) really is just like, in all relevant respects, being manipulated moment by moment by a team of neuroscientists (Case 1) helps crystallize the incompatibilist intuition that determinism destroys free and responsible agency.

Several critics have opted for a softline reply to Pereboom. Worries about his first two cases have led some to think that the manipulated agents in them fall far short of satisfying anything like CAS*. For instance, some have worried that in Case 1, with Plum manipulated moment by moment, Plum's agency is bypassed altogether. There just is no unified agent acting at all (Baker, 2006; Demetriou, 2010: 601–5; Fischer, 2004: 156; Haji, 1998: 24; Mele, 2005a: 78).

In resisting these softline critics, McKenna (2008a: 148–52) has argued that further embellishments to Pereboom's Case 1 can be innocently added to it with the result that we can with confidence believe that there *is* a Plum as a unified agent who acts. It is just that Plum in Case 1 so acts as a result of numerous "micro" interventions that "steer" Plum in certain directions rather than others while leaving Plum's identity and agency intact—eventually resulting in the killing of White.[20]

More recently, Pereboom has proposed a different tactic as a way of answering these softline replies to his argument. Bear in mind that the basis for the critics' objections all had to do with the *pervasiveness* of the actual moment-to-moment manipulation of Plum, which led these critics to think that there was no agent Plum at all, or instead that the agent Plum was not acting at all (e.g., Baker, 2006; Demetriou, 2010). In reply, in his more recent formulation of his argument (2014: 76), in Case 1 Pereboom gives the team of neuroscientists the same *ability* to manipulate moment by moment, but he now arranges the example so that the team only exercise that ability very sparingly, allowing it to be that Plum acts mostly on his own without any intervention from the neuroscientists at all. Indeed, in his most recently revised version of Case 1, Pereboom has it that the team only intervenes at *one* crucial juncture, thereby affecting the result that Plum chooses to kill White for egoistic reasons. As Pereboom puts it:

> In this particular case, they [the team of neuroscientists] do so by pressing a particular button just before he begins to reason about his situation, which they know will produce in him a neural state that realizes a strongly egoistic reasoning process, which the neuroscientists know will deterministically result in his decision to kill White. (2014: 76)

This revision, assuming it is still successful in eliciting a judgment of unfreedom and nonresponsibility, sidesteps the preceding softline objection.

Either of the proposals for defending Pereboom's Case 1, McKenna's or Pereboom's, is an illustration of the point we made just above: As a general overall strategy, a softline compatibilist reply is unstable, since it leaves a compatibilist wishing to resist a manipulation argument vulnerable to a slight modification by her opponent to the disputed example. Such a modification by the proponent of the manipulation argument just builds in the compatibilist condition that in an earlier iteration the softline critic found to be lacking. What this seems to suggest is that for compatibilists to answer well-executed versions of manipulation arguments, they have to be prepared to take on a hardline reply. In this case, it would seem that they need to be able to resist Pereboom's plausible claim that in Case 1 Plum does not act freely and is not morally responsible.

How might a compatibilist proceed? Reflecting upon Pereboom's Case 1 —especially the earlier (2001) formulation in which Plum is actively and pervasively manipulated moment-by-moment—it is hard to imagine how a compatibilist could mount a credible case for resisting the intuitively appealing contention that Plum does not act freely and is not morally responsible. To begin, as McKenna (2008a; 2014) has noted, the compatibilists' burden here need not be to establish that Plum in Case 1 *does* act freely and *is* morally responsible. Since Pereboom's appeal to the case was meant to elicit an intuitive reaction of unfreedom and nonresponsibility, and since it really is reasonable for the compatibilist to grant that, on its face, the example does illicit such an intuitive reaction, it is too tall of an order for the compatibilist to be expected to show that Plum really does act freely and is morally responsible. Instead, it should be enough, McKenna argues, for the compatibilist *to cast credible doubt* on the judgment that Plum does not act freely and is not morally responsible. Thus, all the compatibilist needs to do is show that it is not clearly established that Plum is not free and is not responsible for killing White.

McKenna (2008a; 2014) has attempted to do so as follows.[21] First, consider pertinent agential and moral properties of Plum *as displayed in Case 4*. In this case, Plum is just as much like an ordinary moral agent as any one of us. His phenomenology is just as sophisticated. He is capable of feeling incredible remorse, or instead ambivalence about killing White, or alternatively, delicious pride. Furthermore, we can suppose that Plum had a rich history of moral development just like any psychologically healthy person who emerges from childhood into adulthood. We can also allow that Plum is an agent who lives up to the kind of emotional complexity of the sort Strawsonians highlight. He is capable of resentment and gratitude, moral indignation and approbation, guilt and pride, and he is richly sensitive to the significance of these morally reactive emotions in his relations with others. He is, in this way, a full-fledged member of the moral community, one whose standing enables the kinds of interpersonal relations out of which adult moral life arises. Now, if all of this is true of Plum in Case 4, it must be granted that *it can equally as well be true of Plum in Case 1*. The point of attending to these details is to help elicit the intuitions that are friendly to compatibilists—to bring forth the sense that a determined agent of the sort Plum is in Case 1 is a complex agent just like any person we might come across in the course of our daily lives (as would be the case for Case 4).

Second, consider the initial attitude both compatibilists and incompatibilists are entitled to adopt toward Plum in Case 4. Naturally, the compatibilist is not entitled to insist that it be granted that Plum in Case 4 *does* act freely and *is* morally responsible. That is precisely what is in dispute in considering Pereboom's argument. Nor, for this reason, should the compatibilist expect that the intuitions that she seeks to elicit in Case 4—by focusing on salient agential and moral properties—speak commandingly in favor of compatibilism. All the compatibilist can expect is that an open-minded inquirer, one who is undecided and so agnostic by the prospect that determinism rules out freedom and responsibility, could be moved to see the plausibility of compatibilism. But equally to the point, incompatibilists cannot assume at the outset that Plum in Case 4 is not free and is not morally responsible, nor ought they to expect that the initial intuition about Plum in Case 4 is that, clearly, he does not act freely and is not morally responsible. Again, that is what is in dispute, and assuming this at the outset would be patently question-begging. Thus, the stance toward Case 4 that an incompatibilist such as Pereboom is dialectically obligated to take in executing his argument is the same one that a compatibilist like McKenna must take. Both must allow that in Case 4 it is an open question whether Plum acts freely and is morally responsible for killing White.

Third, armed with the two preceding considerations, McKenna attempted to turn Pereboom's strategy against him. Pereboom begins with Case 1 and, seeking to elicit an incompatibilist intuition in response to the disturbing manipulation featured in it, marches through to his Case 4, thereby drawing an incompatibilist conclusion. McKenna (2014) grants that Pereboom does gain *some* intuitive advantage in favor of incompatibilism by calling attention in Spinozistic fashion to hidden causes revealed in Case 1 and transferring through to Case 4. That has to be weighed on the scales when evaluating the overall strength of Pereboom's argument. Nevertheless, McKenna proposed that the compatibilist move in the opposite direction, and this too must be weighed in the scales. Begin with Case 4. By calling attention to the salient agential and moral properties of Plum in Case 4, McKenna sought to elicit the intuition among an audience of undecided, open-minded inquirers that it is not clearly the case that determinism rules out free will and moral responsibility. It is at least a plausible contention. Since, by Pereboom's own lights, Case 3 differs in no relevant respect from Case 4, and since we are also instructed by Pereboom to treat like cases alike, the compatibilist should treat Case 3 just as we treat Case 4. Likewise we should treat Case 2 no differently than we treat Case 3, and finally we should treat Case 1 no differently than we treat Case 2. Hence, we get the result that we should treat Case 1 no differently than we treat Case 4.[22]

To clarify: How, exactly, should we treat Case 1, according to this hardline compatibilist strategy? We should transfer through to Case 1 the initial undecided open-minded attitude of agnosticism that perhaps Plum in Case 4 does act freely and is morally responsible. That is, given this strategy, and the initial dialectical attitude the compatibilist is entitled to in Case 4, the compatibilist is in no position to conclude that in Case 1 Plum *does* act freely and *is* morally responsible. She's only entitled to conclude that it is not clear that Plum does not act freely and is not morally responsible. And she is entitled to conclude this much by way of carrying over the intuitive weight regarding Case 4 that she seeks initially to elicit from an undecided audience by inviting them to focus carefully on the rich agential and moral properties that Plum in Case 4 has—all of which, it can be granted, carry over just as much to Plum in Cases 3, 2, and 1.

Fourth, to help cement this hardline compatibilist response to Pereboom, McKenna took one further step to help lessen the jarring counterintuitive suggestion that, perhaps, an agent like Plum in Case 1 does act freely and is morally responsible. The central idea is that there are actual cases which are in many respects just like the imaginary outlandish manipulation cases featured in an argument like Pereboom's, and these cases are not all that uncommon. Here, our intuitions do not seem to favor an incompatibilist diagnosis. As Nomy Arpaly has pointed out, when reflecting on the nature of different manipulation cases, there are all sorts of real-life cases where persons undergo spectacular changes as a result of things like religious conversions, the birth of a child, one's hormones drying up, and so on (Arpaly, 2006: 112–13). Indeed, there's no end to the number of naturally occurring real-life cases of "manipulation" in which massive and unexpected alterations disrupt people's lives in ways that dramatically reconfigure their psychic constitutions: People suffer traumatic accidents; have a loved one die in their arms unexpectedly; are crushed during their youth by the weight of violent parents. Yet, if these types of changes leave the adult person otherwise sane, rational, and stable in ways that would allow satisfaction of pertinent compatibilist conditions on free action (such as those specified in CAS*), very few are inclined to think that these kinds of "manipulation" cases undermine a person's free agency and her responsibility. They are just regarded as the (often) tragic contingencies out of which these people manage to fashion their moral personalities and thereby come to be the kinds of agents they are.

In reply to McKenna, Pereboom (2008b; 2014) has argued that if we get clear on the dialectically appropriate state that should be expected of those whose intuitions ought to be informative, we shall see that cases like Case 1 and Case 2 should still have the effect of recommending an incompatibilist diagnosis as regards Case 4. According to Pereboom, the dialectically appropriate audience to target:

> affirms that determinism provides a reason for giving up the responsibility assumption, but claims that so far the issue has not been settled. Its advocate would say about an ordinary case of an immoral action, in which it is specified that the action results from a causally deterministic process that traces back beyond the agent's control, that it is now in question whether the agent is morally responsible. Call this the *neutral inquiring* response. By this response it is initially epistemically rational not to believe that that the agent in an ordinary deterministic example is morally responsible, and not to believe that he is not morally responsible, but to be open to clarifying considerations that would make one or the other of these beliefs rational. (Pereboom, 2008b: 162)

So, according to Pereboom, the appropriate initial response toward his Case 4 by members of the pertinent target audience is the *neutral inquiring response*. But what kind of clarifying considerations would be of use for such an audience? Pereboom writes:

> adducing an analogy in which one's intuitions are clearer might itself count as the relevant sort of clarifying consideration. In a situation in which the neutral inquiring response to an ordinary determined agent is at first epistemically rational, it may be that an analogous manipulation case functions as a clarifying consideration that makes rational the belief that the ordinary determined agent is not morally responsible. (162)

As Pereboom sees it, intuitions about a case like Case 1 or Case 2 are clearly friendly to incompatibilism, and these cases provide the right sort of analogy to Case 4 to help clarify the rationality of one's beliefs. This is so, even granting that attention to the agential and moral properties of Plum in Case 1 (carrying over from Case 4) do lend some weight to a compatibilist diagnosis.[23]

The dispute between Pereboom and McKenna—that is, the dispute between us, your co-authors—appears to hinge primarily upon these two interrelated questions: In light of cases like Case 1 and Case 2, has the neutral inquiring audience been given sufficient reason to move away from an open-minded agnosticism and toward an incompatibilist conclusion? Or does the hardline compatibilist have sufficient resources to maintain that, once set out, it remains rational for such an audience to remain neutral—thus persisting in treating it as an open question whether determined agents are free and responsible?[24] We will not pursue the matter here, except to note that McKenna thinks Pereboom is deluded, and Pereboom thinks McKenna is bat-shit crazy.

One further question we have not pursued here is whether the sorts of closer-to-real-life cases McKenna and Arpaly identify should carry greater or instead lesser weight (as in contrast with more remote cases) in assessing what it would be rational for a neutral inquiring audience to believe. McKenna (2008a; 2014) thinks that we should assign greater probative value to the closer-to-real-life cases, which (no surprise) are friendlier to a compatibilist diagnosis. Pereboom (2008b; 2014) thinks we should assign greater probative value to the more esoteric cases like his Case 1. He points out that we do not ordinarily bring to bear on our judgments of responsibility any theory about the general causal nature of the universe that might threaten their rationality. The Spinozistic concern is that in ordinary cases such judgments will have been shaped by a supposition of indeterministic free will. The local and remote manipulation cases may be artificial, but the artificiality is required to make the deterministic causation salient, while for the ordinary cases the concern is that it is not, and thus is readily suppressed. On this issue, Dana Nelkin concurs:

> One might argue that their unrealistic quality helps ensure that we are focused on the stipulated features, and that we aren't implicitly but unconsciously

relying on background assumptions that we bring to ordinary life. In this way, the intuitions are arguably *more* reliable than the real life ones. (2013: 125)

7.5.   Closing Remarks on Arguments for Source Incompatibilism

In this chapter we have focused upon three arguments for a source incompatibilist conclusion. As we see it, the most compelling of these is (some instance of) the Manipulation Argument. The Ultimacy Argument, we claimed, was to be distinguished from an incompatibilist-friendly ultimacy thesis of the sort incompatibilists like Kane (1996) or Pereboom (2001; 2014) have endorsed. The Ultimacy Argument, in our opinion, is not compelling if it works with a folk notion of ultimacy, and it is question-begging if it makes use of a more precise notion of ultimacy, one that has built right into it a requirement of indeterminism. The Direct Argument, we contended, while initially attractive, seems to rely upon an inference principle like Transfer NR that needs supporting by way of uncontroversial instances of it. But the best candidates for such instances look to be those figuring centrally in Manipulation Arguments for Incompatibilism. Thus, as regards the dispute between source compatibilists and source incompatibilists, a good deal turns on the force of a manipulation argument like Pereboom's Four Case Manipulation Argument.

We hasten to note, however, that all three of these arguments for source incompatibilism are not the exclusive domain of source incompatibilists. A leeway incompatibilist such as Ginet (1996) or van Inwagen (1983) can also profit from them. Leeway incompatibilists are committed to an ability-to-do-otherwise condition on free will and moral responsibility, and accordingly, they seek to establish their incompatibilism on the basis of the Consequence Argument. But as Shabo (2010a) points out, allegiance to an alternative-possibilities condition is consistent with *also* endorsing an incompatibilist source requirement on free will and moral responsibility. It thus is open to incompatibilist defenders of an alternative-possibilities condition to seek grounds for their incompatibilism in consideration regarding causal sources of action, and as Shabo points out, this is in fact Kane's (1996) strategy.

Finally, we should also note that there is one further discussion in the literature that also points in the direction of a source incompatibilist conclusion, one we have elected not to develop in this chapter. As we saw in Chapter 6, in an influential article Gary Watson (1987) explores the presuppositions of Strawsonian compatibilism, and in particular whether, as Strawson (1962) contended, all of the typical excusing or exempting conditions really are friendly to a compatibilist diagnosis. One of those excuses was *being unfortunate in formative circumstances*. Watson examined that sort of excuse (exemption) by considering carefully a particularly disturbing application of it, the case of Robert Alton Harris (which we considered in our Introduction). Harris committed two horrible, cold-blooded murders. When hearing about it we are inclined in

Strawsonian fashion to blame him and to want to punish him harshly, as is evidenced by our strong negative reactive emotions. But, Watson notes, when we really do examine carefully the life-history of a case like Harris's, which involved cruelty and misery from birth onwards, our reactive emotions begin to soften, and our resentment is mixed with sympathy. There is a concern here that learning of the sources of even an extremely evil person's history can issue in an exempting or at least a mitigating stance, which results in a challenge to a compatibilist diagnosis. Indeed, incompatibilists might contend that it suggests a different path to a source incompatibilist conclusion, one that is not built on imaginary thought experiments about teams of neuroscientists manipulating agents, but by way of actual, real-life cases.

Suggestions for Further Reading

For an excellent book devoted to assessing all of these arguments for incompatibilism, as well as others, see:

Haji, Ishtiyaque. 2009. *Incompatibilism's Allure*. Peterborough, Ontario: Broadview Press.

Here we offer a sampling of works related to each of the three distinct arguments:

The Ultimacy Argument

Clarke, Randolph. 2005. "On an Argument for the Impossibility of Moral Responsibility." *Midwest Studies in Philosophy* 29: 13–24.
McKenna, Michael. 2008d. "Ultimacy & Sweet Jane." In Nick Trakakis and Daniel Cohen, eds., *Essays on Free Will and Moral Responsibility*. Newcastle: Cambridge Scholars Publishing: 186–208.
Smilansky, Saul. 2003. "The Argument from Shallowness." *Philosophical Studies* 115: 257–82.
Strawson, Galen. 1994. "The Impossibility of Moral Responsibility." *Philosophical Studies* 75: 5–24.

The Direct Argument

Fischer, John Martin, and Mark Ravizza. 1998. "The Direct Argument for Incompatibilism." In *Responsibility and Control: An Essay on Moral Responsibility*. Cambridge: Cambridge University Press: chapter 7.
McKenna, Michael. 2008c. "Saying Goodbye to the Direct Argument the Right Way." *Philosophical Review* 117 (3): 349–83.
Ravizza, Mark. 1994. "Semicompatibilism and the Transfer of Non-Responsibility." *Philosophical Studies* 75: 61–94.
Shabo, Seth. 2010b. "The Fate of the Direct Argument and the Case for Incompatibilism." *Philosophical Studies* 150: 405–24.
van Inwagen, Peter. 1983. "What Our Not Having Free Will Would Mean." In *An Essay on Free Will*. Oxford: Clarendon Press: chapter 5.

Warfield, Ted. 1996. "Determinism and Moral Responsibility are Incompatible." *Philosophical Topics* 24: 215–26.

Widerker, David. 2002. "Farewell to the Direct Argument." *Journal of Philosophy* 99: 316–24.

The Manipulation Argument

Baker, Lynne R. 2006. "Moral Responsibility without Libertarianism." *Noûs* 40: 307–30.

Demetriou, Kristin. 2010. "The Soft-Line Solution to Pereboom's Four-Case Argument." *Australasian Journal of Philosophy* 88: 595–617.

Fischer, John Martin. 2011. "The Zygote Argument Remixed." *Analysis* 71: 267–72.

Frankfurt, Harry. 1975. "Three Concepts of Free Action II." *Proceedings of the Aristotelian Society* supp. vol. IL: 113–25.

Locke, Don. 1975. "Three Concepts of Free Action I." *Proceedings of Aristotelian Society* supp. vol. IL: 95–112.

Kearns, Stephen. 2012. "Aborting the Zygote Argument." *Philosophical Studies* 160 (3): 379–89.

Matheson, Benjamin. Forthcoming. "In Defense of the Four-Case Argument." *Philosophical Studies*.

McKenna, Michael. 2008a. "A Hard-line Reply to Pereboom's Four-case Argument." *Philosophy and Phenomenological Research* 77 (1): 142–59.

Mele, Alfred. 2006b. "My Compatibilist Proposal: Objections and Replies." In *Free Will and Luck*. New York: Oxford University Press: chapter 7.

Mele, Alfred. 2005a. "A Critique of Pereboom's Four-Case Argument for Incompatibilism." *Analysis* 65: 75–80.

Pereboom, Derk. 2008b. "A Hard-line Reply to the Multiple-Case Manipulation Argument." *Philosophy and Phenomenological Research* 77 (1): 160–70.

Pereboom, Derk. 2001. "Problems for Compatibilism." In *Living Without Free Will*. Cambridge: Cambridge University Press: chapter 4.

Pereboom, Derk. 1995. "Determinism al Dente." *Noûs* 29: 21–45.

Todd, Patrick. 2012. "Defending (a Modified Version of the) Zygote Argument." *Philosophical Studies* 164 (1): 189–203.

Todd, Patrick. 2011. "A New Approach to Manipulation Arguments." *Philosophical Studies* 152 (1): 127–33.

Notes

1 Admittedly, Frankfurt's argument was designed to attack the proposition that moral responsibility requires the ability to do otherwise. But as we use the term "free will" to identify the strongest sense of freedom required for moral responsibility, this slight refocusing of Frankfurt's argument is innocent enough.

2 Philosophers might legitimately persist in debating the apparent incompatibility between leeway freedom and determinism irrespective of the matter of moral responsibility. And here we do not wish to deny that this is in its own right an interesting topic worthy of being regarded as *a* genuine free will problem. But it still would be a distinct problem from one that is animated in terms of the conditions for moral responsibility.

3 Source compatibilists include Harry Frankfurt (1971), John Martin Fischer (1994), John Martin Fischer and Mark Ravizza (1998), Ishtiyaque Haji (1998), Michael McKenna (2013), and Carolina Sartorio (2016). Source incompatibilists include David Hunt (2000, 2005), Derk Pereboom (2000, 2001, 2014), Seth Shabo (2010a, 2011), and Eleonore Stump (1990, 1996).

4 Leeway compatibilists include Bernard Berofsky (1987, 2012), Joseph Campbell (1997, 2007), Daniel Dennett (1984, 2003), Michael Fara (1998), Terry Horgan (1979, 1985, 2015), Edward Nahmias (2011), Dana Nelkin (2008, 2011), Michael Smith (2003), and Kadri Vihvelin (2004, 2013). Leeway incompatibilists include Randolph Clarke (1993, 2003), Carl Ginet (1966, 1990), Robert Kane (1985, 1996), Peter van Inwagen (1983), Timothy O'Connor (2000), and David Widerker (1995, 2003).

5 Thanks to Carolina Sartorio for pointing this out. Some might wish to quibble here by arguing about the essential conditions for act-identity, maintaining that an act as the product of Frankfurtian ensuring conditions could not be numerically identical with one that was the upshot of a free agent's own unimpeded exercising of her agency. This might be a viable alternative argumentative strategy, but we instead offer a simpler and more elegant proposal that avoids these complications.

6 For a similar proposal see Sartorio (2016).

7 In this and the next three paragraphs, we draw heavily from McKenna (2008d: 189–91).

8 Recall, as we explained earlier (Section 2.1), impossibilism is the thesis that it is not metaphysically possible for anyone to have free will regardless of whether determinism is true or false.

9 See also Mele (1995: 222).

10 This version of the Ultimacy Argument is very close to, or maybe can be thought of as being basically identical with, the Basic Source Incompatibilist Argument (BSI).

11 For an attempt to advance the latter compatibilist response to an incompatibilist version of the Ultimacy Argument, see McKenna (2008d, 2014).

12 Another familiar name for the argument is the *Transfer of Nonresponsibility Argument.*

13 Nevertheless, we wish to note here that the argument's plausibility strongly suggests that if the argument goes through and nonresponsibility for past facts and laws "transfers through" to nonresponsibility for what one does, it is implicitly due to the undermining of some freedom or control condition on moral responsibility. This observation is consistent with van Inwagen's main motivation for constructing this argument, which was more precisely to avoid questions about the compatibility of determinism and a *particular* candidate condition for moral responsibility: the ability to do otherwise. Van Inwagen discharged a distinct argument for that incompatibility by way of the Consequence Argument (discussed in Chapter 4). And his main motivation for the Direct Argument was to circumvent those who might be convinced (misguidedly to his mind) that Frankfurt's argument (discussed in Chapter 5) was sound and so the ability do to otherwise is not necessary for moral responsibility. Those who were so convinced would, when considering the issue of moral responsibility, be unmoved by the Consequence Argument even granting it was sound. All of this, however, is consistent with thinking that if determinism is incompatible with moral responsibility, it is grounded in some freedom or control condition for moral responsibility *other than* a (contested) ability-to-do-otherwise condition.

14 Note that this is essentially what McKay and Johnson (1996) produced in their assault on the Transfer principle (at work in the Consequence Argument) with their counterexample—the example involving refraining from tossing a coin. (See our discussion in Section 4.5.) This might not be immediately clear, since their example was meant to show that powerlessness is not agglomerative. But, as we explained, the principle of agglomerativity for powerlessness can be derived from the Consequence Argument's Transfer principle in conjunction with an unimpeachable logical principle. So the counterexample McKay and Johnson produced to agglomerativity for powerlessness was *also* a counterexample to Transfer, thereby proving Transfer invalid.

15 There is a delicate point about the dialectic that we will not develop in the main body of the text but is worth just noting. The reason we can safely set aside the incompatibilist objections of those unconvinced by the role of Frankfurt-style examples is that such critics are bound to find an argument like the Consequence Argument compelling as it pertains to moral responsibility. They will thus be less invested in drawing upon an argument like the Direct Argument to establish their incompatibilism. By contrast, the interlocutor who is more interesting here, given the relevance of the Direct Argument to the wider controversy, is the incompatibilist who finds Frankfurt's argument compelling, who thus thinks the Consequence Argument is thereby rendered beside the point (as regards moral responsibility), and who seeks another style of argument for an incompatibilist conclusion. This sort of incompatibilist—a source incompatibilist—is not in a position to object to the above means of resisting the Direct Argument by complaining that Frankfurt-examples are unsuccessful.

16 This is roughly identical to McKenna's proposed Transfer NR*** (McKenna, 2008c: 368).

17 For an excellent treatment of this issue and a thoughtful reply to Schnall and Widerker, one developing the reply we have suggested here, see Loewenstein (forthcoming).

18 TMA is the only argument form we will consider. But Mele (2008) distinguishes three different forms. The first, which he calls a *straight manipulation argument*, is basically the form we have set out. The second form, a *manipulation argument to the best explanation*, replaces the second premise as we have set it out with a best-explanation premise of roughly the form, "the best explanation that S is not free and morally responsible when manipulated in manner X into A-ing is that S is causally determined." The third form, an *original design argument* of the sort Mele himself has developed (2006b), works not from a case of an already existing agent who is manipulated, but from an agent who is originally designed to perform some act, A. Although there are important differences between these forms, what we have to say about TMA carries over to these others as well.

Pereboom (2001; 2014) appeals to a best explanation in prosecuting his argument, and Mele (2006b: 141–4) takes issue with Pereboom on this point. Below, we will set out Pereboom's argument, but in doing so, in the interests of simplicity, we will interpret Pereboom's argument as an instance of the TMA form. Thus, we will set aside his appeal to a best explanation as well as his (2014: 82–6) reply to Mele on the viability of this strategy.

19 Ayer's proposal is basically the classical compatibilist view examined in Chapter 3. We'll examine the other compatibilist thesis in subsequent chapters. For present purposes, readers can simply grant that Pereboom accurately identifies the three other compatibilist proposals (Frankfurt's, Fischer and Ravizza's, and Wallace's).

20 These interventions need be no different in force or severity than the sort influencing our behavior due to changes in hormone levels or fluctuations in blood sugar.

21 This and the next four paragraphs are drawn from McKenna (2014).

22 For further development of McKenna's argument, see also Daniel Haas (2012). See also Pereboom's (2014: 99–101) reply to Haas.

　　Also, Fischer (2011) has responded to another manipulation argument, Mele's (2006b) zygote argument, in a similar fashion.

23 See Daniel Haas (2012) for a defense of McKenna on this point, and Pereboom (2014) for a reply to Haas.

24 Yet a further question, not discussed here, is whether the force of a manipulation argument is sufficient for an incompatibilist conclusion even under the less demanding assumption that manipulation at least mitigates moral responsibility. Patrick Todd (2011) has argued that mere mitigation rather than a full judgment of nonresponsibility is enough to threaten compatibilism. However, both Justin Capes (2013) and Hannah Tierney (2013) have argued that compatibilism is consistent with thinking that determinism can mitigate, since it might be that forms of freedom and responsibility incompatible with manipulation could be greater or more enhanced than forms that are instead compatible with it. Andrew Khoury (2014) explores a different way of replying to Todd, which instead focuses upon the fact that implicit in mitigation is a concession that the manipulated agent is responsible (to some degree). For some reservations about Khoury's strategy, see Tierney (2014).

8   Contemporary Compatibilism

Seven Recent Views

We turn in this chapter to contemporary compatibilism. There is a striking difference between contemporary compatibilist proposals and the range of contemporary libertarian proposals. As we will explain in Chapter 10, there are three distinct ways to advance a libertarian theory: event causal, noncausal, and agent-causal. While each has been developed in interestingly different ways, viable libertarian proposals all clearly fall into one of those three camps. By contrast, there is such an array of contemporary compatibilist strategies that it is challenging even to think about how to sort them into manageable categories. For this reason, in this chapter, we will consider seven compatibilist proposals, commenting only briefly on each. Then in the next chapter, we'll focus in more detail on three particularly prominent compatibilist strategies, one developed in terms of reasons-responsiveness, another in terms of a mesh between different elements internal to an agent's psychological architecture, and a third advancing a contemporary defense of leeway freedom.

Before proceeding to specific compatibilist theories, it will be useful to consider a few important factors influencing recent work. The first three sections below are devoted to this task.

8.1.   The Dispute between Historical and Nonhistorical Compatibilists

One variable affecting contemporary compatibilism concerns whether free will and (or) moral responsibility are essentially historical.[1] Until recently, the default assumption had been that compatibilism is a nonhistorical thesis (e.g., see Double, 1991: 56–7). The idea was that for the compatibilist it should not matter how a person came to be the way she is. All that should matter is whether, given that a person is a certain way when she acts, she does so from resources that are freedom-conferring. Thinking that the manner of acquiring pertinent freedom-conferring resources of agency should also matter invites the worry that determinism *itself* could be the sort of history that is freedom-defeating. Despite this default assumption, in recent times, several influential compatibilist proposals have accepted a historical requirement (e.g., Fischer and Ravizza, 1998; Haji, 1998; Mele, 1995, 2006b). The general strategy is to point out that *some* historical requirements on freedom or responsibility are compatible with determinism. Moreover, the historical compatibilist can argue, a historical constraint is well-motivated for reasons entirely independent of the compatibilism/incompatibilism debate. The main motivation comes from reflection on a range of cases.

Suppose that a person is kidnapped and indoctrinated into a cult by brainwashing, which results in a dramatic alteration of her personality (some readers might recall the real-life case of Patty Hearst). Imagine that the outcome of the process is a person who, by credible nonhistorical compatibilist standards, would satisfy the conditions for acting freely. Many would nevertheless argue that such a person does not act freely and is not morally responsible because the history leading up to her being that way corrupts her agency. Compatibilists who take this position contend that requiring that an agent *not* have such a history (a negative requirement), or instead requiring that she *does* have a history that involves acquiring certain beliefs and values under her own steam (a positive requirement), is consistent with determinism being true. Such compatibilists will claim that the conditions on freedom need to be supplemented with a historical condition.

Because examples like the one above involving brainwashing are so disturbing and seem to be so clearly freedom-and-responsibility-undermining, it is perhaps surprising that numerous compatibilists have resisted arguments for a historical conclusion and have opted for a nonhistorical thesis (e.g., Arpaly, 2003, 2006; Berofsky, 2006; Double, 1991; Frankfurt, 1975; McKenna, 2004; Watson, 1999; Wolf, 1987). The best known advocate of the nonhistorical position is Harry Frankfurt. Consider this often-quoted passage:

> To the extent that a person identifies himself with the springs of his actions, he takes responsibility for those actions and acquires moral responsibility for them; moreover, the questions of how the actions and his identifications with their springs are caused are irrelevant to the questions of whether he performs his actions freely and is morally responsible for performing them. (Frankfurt, 1975, as appearing in 1988: 54)

Frankfurt would be prepared to say about our kidnapped and brainwashed person that if she satisfied his proposed nonhistorical compatibilist conditions for acting freely in the way required for moral responsibility, then she really does act freely and is morally responsible for what she does in the aftermath of her indoctrination.

We'll not develop the controversy further here except to note how this debate intersects with strategies compatibilists have for resisting various instances of the Manipulation Argument. Recall McKenna's (2008a) diagnosis of the policy compatibilists should adopt toward responding to manipulation arguments (discussed in Section 7.4). Where possible, he claims, compatibilists should tend toward a hardline reply because softline replies are unstable. Able incompatibilist defenders of manipulation arguments are poised to revise their examples in response to softline replies, thereby incorporating into revised manipulation examples the ingredient previously found lacking in the context of a softline reply. A cost of this strategy for compatibilists, we noted, is that it involves resisting the intuitively plausible thesis that agents in pertinent manipulation cases are not free and not responsible.

It is at this juncture that the historical compatibilist can push back against McKenna's advice. She can point out that she has a *principled* basis for adopting a softline reply to many of the far more intuitively disturbing manipulation cases, like those that involve brainwashing and invasive manipulation. Such cases violate a historical condition on freedom and responsibility (Fischer and Ravizza, 1998; Haji, 1998; Mele, 1995, 2006b). Historical compatibilists can concede that when faced with well-executed manipulation cases that build in the pertinent historical details, they will after all have to take a hardline stance. But, these historical compatibilists can argue, manipulation cases that build in enough historical details turn out to be far less troublesome. It is just not by comparison as counterintuitive in such cases to think that such agents might after all be free and be morally responsible.

8.2. The Influences of Strawson on the Justification of our Blaming Practices

As we explained, P.F. Strawson paid special attention to our practices of holding morally responsible (Chapter 6). Drawing upon a broad form of naturalism, Strawson claimed that because these practices and the emotions animating them are natural facts of our social lives, they do not need any external rational justification. Hence, any special metaphysical condition for responsible agency as a requirement for engaging in these practices is misguided. Indeed, it involves over-intellectualizing the facts about our responsibility practices (Section 6.4.5). While few have agreed with Strawson that we should leave the matter there and treat our responsibility practices *simply* as natural facts, a significant number have accepted Strawson's general approach by taking it that the primary focus when theorizing about freedom and responsibility should be our practices of holding responsible—not a set of conceptually prior questions about the metaphysics of the agents held responsible. What Strawson got right, according to these philosophers, is that we do not need any external justification involving special metaphysical facts about the nature of persons that could underwrite our practices. But, contra Strawson, that is consistent with an *internal* constraint on these practices requiring a *normative* justification for holding others responsible (e.g., Russell, 1992, 2013). The justification is taken to be internal rather than external because it is a feature of the practices themselves that blaming and punishing, as well as other forms of holding responsible, presuppose fair treatment, or deservingness, or something of the sort. That is, they have general aptness conditions for their application, conditions that, if unsatisfied, *would* (contra Strawson) be reason to think that these practices are unjustified.

Some contemporary philosophers (Scanlon, 1998, 2008; Wallace, 1994) have thus advanced compatibilist theses by attending to the normative burdens of

Seven Views of Contemporary Compatibilism 181

justifying our practices of holding morally responsible, especially blaming and punishing. The general strategy is to identify an adequate justification for, say, blaming, and then ask what presuppositions about agency are entailed by a justification of this sort. On such a view, it would be misleading to claim that there are *no* metaphysical requirements at all on free and responsible agency. Rather, whatever requirements there are will hinge on the normative conditions needed to justify our practices of holding responsible. Suppose, for instance, that a justification for blaming was advanced in terms of fairness. A plausible condition on blaming might be that those blamed were able to understand moral demands, because otherwise it would be unfair to hold them to account for wrongdoing. It would then be a requirement of responsible agents, flowing from considerations of fairness, that they are able to understand moral demands. The question would then become: Do we have any reason to think that all (or most) persons are unable to understand moral demands, and is there any reason to think that determinism is incompatible with persons being so constituted?

8.3. The Proliferation of Senses of Moral Responsibility

We turn now to the proliferation of distinct kinds of moral responsibility identified within our moral responsibility practices. Until fairly recent times, the default assumption was that moral responsibility was one kind of thing, and the debate about the (strongest sense of) freedom required for that one kind proceed from there. But in his highly influential article, "Two Faces of Responsibility," Gary Watson (1996) identified two kinds of moral responsibility: *attributability* and *accountability*. Moral responsibility in the attributability sense, on Watson's view, concerns evaluations of what is revealed about an agent or her character in acting as she does, about what she stands for or cares about. Such a responsibility-evaluation, according to Watson, is different from what is involved in evaluating an agent's conduct in ways that involve *holding her to account* for how she acts. In this stronger sense, her being responsible warrants (at least some) others treating her in certain ways, in making demands for apology, reparation, and so forth. More recently, David Shoemaker (2015) has argued that there is a further kind of moral responsibility distinct from the attributability and the accountability notions: *answerability* (cf. Bok, 1998; Smith, 2004). Answerability concerns responsibility for one's judgments as revealed in one's agency, and presupposes that an answerability-responsible agent is able to answer for her exercising of her judgment-sensitive capacities. Others have proposed different ways of carving up the domain of moral responsibility (that do not seem to map clearly onto the distinctions drawn above), including Scanlon (1998, 2008), whose views we will discuss below.[2]

There are more minimal senses of moral responsibility as well. On Moritz Schlick's (1939) proposal, for instance, the point of blaming and praising is to reduce the incidence of bad action and to increase the frequency of good action. As we saw in Chapter 6, P.F. Strawson pointed out that such a forward-looking "optimist" conception does not capture our entire actual practice of holding morally responsible, and in particular misses the component connected with the reactive attitudes. But we can identify Schlick's notion with yet another sense of moral responsibility.

The freedom or control conditions implicit in these different senses of moral responsibility are liable to differ. This gives rise to the question of just what sort of moral responsibility is at issue in the free will debate. Especially relevant to compatibilism is the fact that some of the senses of responsibility recently identified, for example, the attributability sense and the one that Schlick has in mind, seem to have minimal freedom requirements that are *obviously* compatible with determinism—so much so that it would be odd to think that there is even on the face of it any reason to think that determinism could pose a threat to this sort of freedom. In light of this, we think it is most useful to proceed under the assumption that the relevant sense of moral responsibility at issue in the free will debate is the accountability sense. This is the sense in which a morally responsible agent is liable to the sanctioning responses of others holding her to account for her conduct by way of blaming and punishing and so exposing her to harms of various sorts. It is the sense that seems to presuppose the need for relatively robust freedom requirements, and so it is most likely to give rise to potential philosophical problems as to whether and how such freedom can be satisfied.

Even once the sense of moral responsibility relevant to the free will debate(s) is limited to accountability, there are further difficulties zeroing in on what is at issue between compatibilists and incompatibilists. Some contend that the traditional free will debate should be conceived as limited *only* to whether we have the free will required for a basic desert-entailing sense of moral responsibility (e.g., Pereboom, 2001, 2014). In this desert-entailing sense, a person is morally responsible and blameworthy for an action only if she deserves blame for it in a basic sense. Basicness in this context is a matter of an agent's deserving blame *just because* she culpably acted wrongly and not for any further reasons, such as those that follow from a consequentialist or a contractualist moral theory. Hence, even restricting attention to moral responsibility in the accountability sense, if the justification offered by a compatibilist for blaming is by appeal to normative considerations of a consequentialist or contractualist sort, some will object that the compatibilist misses the mark or changes the subject. Of special importance here—so the charge goes—is that the freedom required for justifying accountability-blame by way of these non-basic-desert-based resources is much easier to come by and obviously compatible with determinism. Hence, it is not plausible to think that freedom in that sense, relying on these justificatory resources, should have any bearing on the traditional free will problem (e.g., Pereboom, 2007: 86).

8.4.   Dennett's Multiple-Viewpoints Compatibilism

In *Elbow Room: The Varieties of Free Will Worth Wanting* (1984), Daniel Dennett defends compatibilism in a way inspired by important developments in the philosophy of mind. More recently, in *Freedom Evolves* (2003), Dennett has drawn more extensively on his work on consciousness in *Consciousness Explained* (1991) and the nature of evolution in *Darwin's Dangerous Ideas* (1995).

In *Elbow Room*, Dennett argued for the legitimacy of folk psychological notions in the explanation of intentional action. His view invokes a range of stances adopted toward a system, including the most basic physical stance, the intermediate design stance, and the mentalistic intentional stance. The adoption of a stance is justified by its effectiveness in understanding, predicting, and interacting with the system. Key to free will is the intentional stance. According to Dennett, even a thermostat can be interpreted from this stance as a very limited intentional system since its behavior can usefully be predicted by attributing to it adequate beliefs and desires to display it as acting rationally within some limited domain. For example, the thermostat *desires* that the room's temperature (or the engine's internal temperature) not go above or below a certain range. If it *believes* that it is out of the requisite range, the thermostat will respond appropriately to *achieve* its desired results.

One might worry that a thermostat does not really have intentions, by contrast with titmice, toddlers, or college sophomores. According to Dennett, this concern starts one down the wrong path (1973: 155). To seek a clean distinction between some metaphysically authentic intentional beings from simulacra like thermostats presupposes that there is more to any intentional system than adopting a stance toward it as an intentional system. If that stance genuinely pays off—if it facilitates a fruitful exchange, allows for helpful predictions, allows one to engage rationally with it—then it wins the status of an intentional creature. No special metaphysical tag is needed. Hence, for Dennett, the propriety of adopting the intentional stance toward a system is settled pragmatically in terms of the utility of its application in interacting with the system. Along with this thesis goes Dennett's claim that folk psychological explanations (appealing to the intentional stance) are entirely consistent with more basic design and physical stances, the former appealing to the intentions, not of the system, but of its designer, the latter appealing only to the basic mechanistic processes that cause the system from moment to moment to move from one physical state into another. Once a system becomes sufficiently complex, as with even a chess playing computer, the intentional stance will become indispensable for successful interaction (1973: 154).

Just as the decision to adopt toward a system the intentional stance is a pragmatic one, so too is it a pragmatic decision to adopt toward a system the stance that it is a morally responsible person. Dennett calls this latter stance the *personal stance* (1973: 57–8). As with the intentional stance, there is nothing metaphysically deep required to interpret legitimately a system as a person (no special faculty of the will, for instance). Such systems are legitimately regarded as morally responsible agents if interpreting them according to the personal stance pays off (1984: 158–63). And just as the physical stance—which may be deterministic—is compatible with the intentional stance, it is also compatible with the personal stance. Furthermore, Dennett argues that it is practically impossible to interpret and predict the kinds of complex systems under consideration purely from the physical stance. Hence, the physical stance will never supplant the personal stance. We persons involved in the everyday commerce of interacting with each other need the personal stance; it is not threatened by the specter of determinism. Call his view *Multiple Viewpoints Compatibilism*.

Dennett is also clear that holding agents responsible is to be justified on consequentialist grounds (1984). Furthermore, there are no metaphysical facts about moral responsibility independent of this consequentialist justification of holding responsible. In Dennett's view, there is no such thing as basic desert, and thus no free will of the sort that is required for basic desert responsibility. In this respect, his view is similar to some of the skeptical views we will discuss in Chapter 11.

What is free will on Dennett's account? First, he contends that leeway freedom is *compatible* with determinism, and he endorses Slote's rejection (see Section 4.3.3) of the Consequence Argument (Dennett, 1984: 123). While Dennett does not offer an analysis of the ability to do otherwise, he does provide a general explanation of leeway freedom for free agents at determined worlds in terms of the evolution of intentionally complex beings "designed" to be able to avoid some outcomes and seek others (2003: chapter 3).

Despite arguing that leeway freedom is compatible with determinism, like Frankfurt (1969) Dennett contends that leeway freedom is not necessary for moral responsibility. But he finds Frankfurt's manner of arguing unpersuasive for the reason that it crucially depends on esoteric examples (1984: 132). His strategy is instead to show that our practical interests in freedom and responsibility are not informed by considerations of the ability to do otherwise in the precise sense that incompatibilists have thought of it (holding fixed the past and the laws). One example he uses to defend his position is the case of Luther, who when standing at the church doors, claimed that he "could do no other" (1984: 133). This argument, however, is open to an objection. The incompatibilist can take Luther's case to be one in which, if he were free, he literally could have done otherwise, but given his moral convictions, he would not have done otherwise; he was resolute.

Suppose Dennett is correct that the crucial sense of freedom for moral responsibility does not require leeway freedom, regardless of his manner of arguing for the point. How does he set out an account of source freedom? For Dennett, free will consists in the ability of a person to control her conduct on the basis of rational considerations through means that arise from, or are subject to, critical self-evaluation, self-adjusting, and self-monitoring. That is, free will involves *responsiveness to reasons*. Dennett notably provides a series of valuable observations about how this sort of control might have naturally arisen from less sophisticated sorts of creatures through a process of evolution (2003). (We will defer discussion of reasons-responsiveness here. It will be taken up in detail in the next chapter.)

What of the source incompatibilists' arguments, especially the manipulation argument (discussed in Chapter 7)? As regards the condition of ultimacy—as something the manipulation argument aims to prove—Dennett means to put the incompatibilist on the defensive (2003: chapter 4). Ultimacy requires indeterminism in the decision-making process, and Dennett argues that there is no way to show that there is a defensible place for it; its presence cannot aid in enhancing freedom as is required by libertarians. So it should be jettisoned as a plausible condition on a kind of freedom worth wanting. As for the manipulation argument, he charges incompatibilists with argumentative trickery by appealing to what he calls "intuition pumps" (1984: chapter 1). Intuition pumps, according to Dennett, are examples designed to sway our philosophical intuitions, but are themselves philosophically suspect. Such examples involve cases of (apparently) normally functioning agents being manipulated, for example, as if like a puppet hooked up to some wires (1984: 8–10). Dennett is suggesting here that real human agency is not like this—and it is laughable to think that it is. In this respect, Dennett is prepared to adopt unqualifiedly what we described (Section 7.4) as a softline reply to manipulation arguments, since, in his view, there is always going to be a relevant difference between a manipulated agent and a normal agent acting at a determined world, one whose design is the product of a long evolutionary history. But this response might be questioned. If a world is determined, it seems at least in principle possible to imagine artificial ways of replicating the causes of local chunks of that world, or all of it. And if this can be imagined as a coherent conceptual possibility, what reason is there for thinking that we cannot test our concepts of freedom and responsibility by appeal to manipulation cases that make use of these thought experiments?

8.5. Wolf's Reason View and Nelkin's Rational Abilities View

In *Freedom within Reason* (1990), Susan Wolf develops a position in the free will debate that she called the Reason View. According to the Reason View, moral responsibility requires "the ability to act in accord with Reason" (67). This ability, Wolf argues, is compatible with determinism. More recently, in *Making Sense of Freedom and Responsibility* (2011), Dana Nelkin has advanced her own version of a good-reasons-tracking theory, which Nelkin calls the Rational Abilities View:

> Stated most simply, the view is that one is responsible for an action if and only if one acts with the ability to recognize and act for good reasons. (3)

Nelkin also argues that the ability in question is compatible with determinism.

Both Wolf and Nelkin are thereby committed to an intriguing asymmetry. First, the freedom required for moral responsibility when one acts for good reasons does not require the ability to do otherwise. If an agent recognizes good reasons and acts for their sake, she thereby exercises an ability to recognize and act for good reasons. Hence, praiseworthiness does not require leeway freedom. But when an agent fails to act for good reasons, moral responsibility requires that she is able to recognize and act for good reasons *instead*. Thus, blameworthiness *does* require leeway freedom.

Consider this much-discussed example Wolf uses to advance the part of her asymmetry thesis that concerns praiseworthiness:

> Two persons, of equal swimming ability, stand on equally uncrowded beaches. Each sees an unknown child struggling in the water in the distance. Each thinks "The child needs my help" and directly swims out to save him. In each case, we assume that the agent reasons correctly—that child does need her help—and that, in swimming out to save him, the agent does the right thing. We further assume that in one of these cases, the agent has the ability to do otherwise, and in the other case not. (Wolf, 1990: 81–2)

Wolf contends that both agents are morally responsible and praiseworthy. Nelkin concurs (2011: 21). Wolf considers a competing perspective—the Autonomy View, as she calls it—that requires the ability to do otherwise for moral responsibility (82). On this conception, only one of the two swimmers is morally responsible for saving the child. But Wolf finds this implausible: "For there seems to be nothing of value that the first agent has but the second agent lacks. Both examples are examples of agents' thinking and doing exactly what we want agents to think and do" (82).

As for the other half of the asymmetry thesis, concerning blameworthiness, Wolf uses as a foil a view she calls the Real Self View (1990: 85–9). We'll examine these positions in detail in the next chapter. For present purposes, it is enough to note that the Real Self View explains free agency in terms of the architecture of an agent's internal mental states when her internal subsystems are working in harmony. When an agent's real self is manifested in her actions, she acts from desires or motivations that at a deeper level she wants or values. When she acts in this way, she acts freely. As Wolf sees it, the problem with views of this sort is that an agent could act from values that are truly hers and reflect who she is, but if she is blinded to the wrongness of her values or if is she is incapable of acting contrary to them when she sees that they are wrong, then she is intuitively not morally responsible for what she does. For Wolf, the crucial missing requirement is that the values or deep desires a person acts from and that reflect who she really is must be ones that she is psychologically capable of aligning with The True and the Good (75), or, as Nelkin would put it, with good reasons. Hence, an agent who does not act for good reasons must be psychologically capable of doing so. The upshot is that blameworthiness requires the ability to do otherwise.

Wolf's and Nelkin's asymmetry thesis gives rise to the possibility of a puzzling metaphysical result, as Nelkin notes (2011: 18). Suppose the Consequence Argument is sound, and that thus leeway freedom is incompatible with determinism. Suppose as well that an adequate compatibilist account of source freedom was identified and shown to be immune to source incompatibilist arguments (such as those canvassed in Chapter 7). The upshot would be that praiseworthiness and the freedom required for it would be compatible with determinism, but blameworthiness and the freedom required for it would be incompatible with determinism. While this might be welcome news to the likes of Henry Kissinger or Bill Cosby, most would take it as an unwelcome result and treat it as grounds to think that something was awry with the reasoning leading to this asymmetry. So Wolf and Nelkin face two questions. First, in the context of blameworthy conduct, is their case for the compatibility of determinism and leeway freedom convincing? Second, is the ability they identify in the context of praiseworthiness, requiring only source freedom, immune to the arguments for source incompatibilism?

To assess Wolf's and Nelkin's arguments for the compatibility of determinism and leeway freedom, it will be instructive to consider a challenge to their thesis that blameworthiness requires leeway freedom (see, e.g., Fischer and Ravizza, 1998: 59–60). The challenge should be familiar by now. Take any ordinary case that would satisfy Wolf or Nelkin of an agent who is blameworthy for performing an act. Grant that in doing so *some* abilities bearing on her agency and her exercising of it play a grounding role in her being blameworthy. Now inject this case into the context of a Frankfurt example. Recall the one we drew upon in Chapter 5:

> A neuroscientist, Black, wants Jones to perform a certain action. Black is prepared to go to considerable lengths to get his way, but he prefers to avoid showing his hand unnecessarily. So he waits until Jones is about to make up his mind what to do, and he does nothing unless it is clear to him (Black is an excellent judge of such things) that Jones is going to decide to do something other than what he wants him to do. If it were to become clear that Jones is going to decide to do something else, Black would take effective steps to ensure that Jones decides to do what he wants him to do, by directly manipulating the relevant processes in Jones's brain. As it turns out, Black never has to show his hand because Jones, for reasons of his own, decides to perform the very action Black wants him to perform. (Sartorio, 2016)

A lesson defenders of Frankfurt's argument wish to draw from examples like this is that an agent can act freely and be responsible for what she does even if she is unable to act otherwise. Hence, whatever sort of freedom plays a grounding role in an agent's being morally responsible for what she does, it is not one that involves the ability to do otherwise. Since any candidate case of blameworthy action on a view like Wolf's or Nelkin's is a candidate for being "Frankfurted," it appears that they are wrong that blameworthiness requires leeway freedom. Hence, they should instead accept a symmetrical source compatibilist view of the freedom conditions for moral responsibility.

Nelkin offers a thoughtful reply to this challenge. Key to her view, as we saw in Section 5.5, is *the interference-free conception of ability*. Setting it out helps make clear her proposed account of leeway freedom. On Nelkin's view, following Wolf (1990: 110), a blameworthy agent has an ability to X:

> if (i) the agent possesses the capacities, skills, talent, knowledge and so on which are necessary for X-ing, and (ii) nothing interferes with or prevents

the exercising of the relevant capacities, skills, talents, and so on. (Nelkin, 2011: 66)

Nelkin maintains that in a typical Frankfurt example involving blameworthy action when a character like Jones acts on his own and Black remains inactive, Jones retains the ability to do otherwise. Why? Because Black remains inactive when Jones acts, and so Jones retains the relevant abilities, and nothing actually interferes with them. Nelkin explains that the ability at issue here is not to be confused with the more permissive notion of a general capacity, which clearly a person can retain even when something is actually preventing her from exercising it—such as the ability to type even when on a desert island with no keyboards about (67). So, Nelkin contends, there is a *more finely specified notion of ability* beyond a mere general capacity that agents retain in Frankfurt examples, and if they retain this ability, they retain leeway freedom. In particular, "they have the skills, talents, and knowledge, but they also have unimpeded use of their bodies and uncluttered piers in their sights" (67). Moreover, Nelkin notes, getting to the heart of her disagreement with defenders of Frankfurt's argument, "The circumstances provide all that they might need to act [otherwise], but for a counterfactual intervener" (67 [our brackets]).

We will not consider here the dispute between Nelkin and Frankfurt defenders (see our brief assessment of the controversy in Section 5.5). Instead, consider the distinct question as to whether Nelkin's notion of ability is compatible with determinism. Taking up this question (2011: 72–6), Nelkin explains that what it amounts to is whether, under the assumption of determinism, when an agent performed an action, determinism would interfere with her doing otherwise (74). To this, Nelkin retorts that it would be no more interfering than indeterminism would be (74–5). She then pursues a novel tactic, first advanced by Ned Markhosian (1999), to defeat the impression that determinism should be thought of as interfering at all. Nelkin argues that agents as substances can be causes, and this is compatible with determinism (Chapter 4).[3] This, Nelkin contends, helps to dispel the impression that an agent's being determined to do A interferes with her ability to do something other than A (171).

It is unclear, however, that Nelkin's appeal to agents as substance causes in deterministic contexts is adequate to show how an agent is able to do otherwise and, in the context of Nelkin's own treatment, how it is that an agent is not impeded from her doing otherwise. It is plausible on Nelkin's agent-causal proposal that determinism should not be thought of as forcing or impeding an agent in her acting as she is *actually* causally determined to act. But granting Nelkin's agent-causal thesis, when an agent agent-causes her doing A on the supposition of determinism, it remains true that there are prior causes determining her to agent-cause her act of A-ing. So, it would seem true that in some sense she is impeded from doing anything other than A. We leave this as a question that is worth pursuing.

Finally, we turn briefly to the question of whether Wolf's and Nelkin's account of praiseworthiness can withstand the challenges of source incompatibilism.

One resource Nelkin develops that distinguishes her view from Wolf's is her appeal to agent causation. With it, she argues that an *agent* can be a genuine source of her actions, and this defeats a familiar "disappearing agent" objection (to be discussed in Chapter 10) that indeterministic or instead deterministic event-causes of actions exclude the agent as a contributor to her own actions.

What of the Manipulation Argument (Section 7.4)? Consider Wolf's example set out above of the swimmer who could not but help the drowning child. Suppose that this swimmer was manipulated in a manner similar to the agent Plum in, say, Case 2 of Pereboom's Four-Case Argument. Here, Nelkin (2011: 55–7) takes a hardline reply and develops further McKenna's "work-backwards" strategy (see our discussion of hardline replies and McKenna's reply to Pereboom in Section 7.4). Moreover, Nelkin argues that Pereboom-like cases in which an agent like Plum is manipulated into acting well and responding to good reasons are not intuitive in favor of incompatibilism. So it seems Nelkin would reason similarly about the case at hand, Wolf's swimmer who is unable to do otherwise but who is so caused by way of a Pereboom-like manipulation scenario. (For Pereboom's reply, see, 2014: 102–3.)

8.6.   Mele's Action-Theory Theory

A familiar classical compatibilist view is an austere one that invokes as little as possible beyond the basic features of agency.[4] The classical compatibilists in Hobbes's and Hume's time used only blunt instruments to fashion such a view (see Section 3.1.1). All they seemed to employ was the notion of a desire or want, and the negative condition that it be unimpeded. But despite these sparse resources, their strategy was a philosophically elegant one. Postulate no more than the features of agency itself. They need be no fancier than the sort at play with normally functioning human persons. There is little reason to imagine that determinism is incompatible with these features. Next, to capture *free* agency, append some negative conditions that secure that sometimes that basic sort of agency can function unhindered by coercive or compulsive forces. This is enough for free will on such a view. Add no more metaphysical constraints, nothing further to show how it gels with determinism. Leave compatibilism at that; simple is better.

In *Autonomous Agents* (1995), Alfred Mele, who is agnostic between compatibilism and libertarianism, develops a contemporary form of compatibilism that shares with the classical compatibilist such a strategy of theoretical austerity. Mele's contemporary version drew upon a finely tuned set of conceptual tools to capture more clearly the contours of the springs of action. He made use of philosophy's matured understanding of action theory, an understanding to which he himself contributed (e.g., Mele, 1992). He then appended to his account of agency as little as possible in order to generate a form of compatibilism that speaks to the contemporary dialectic. Call his proposal *The Action-Theory Theory*.

In his 1995 publication, Mele did not fashion compatibilism in terms of free will and determinism, but instead in terms of *autonomy* and determinism.

Nevertheless, he understood autonomy to be among the concepts in discussions of moral responsibility (1995: 4). Mele understood autonomy as the capacity for self-rule, and he looked to more basic features of self-control to explain the phenomenon.

What does Mele have in mind by self-control? The opposite of weak will or akrasia. He draws upon his account of weakness of will to help shed light on weak will's opposite, self-control. According to Mele, weakness of will arises when one's motivational states become misaligned with one's judgments about the best (or better) course of action (1995: 7). Because evaluations of things one desires can be out of line with the strength of one's desires for those things, one's best judgments sometimes are in disharmony with one's strongest desires (desires that play a causal role in action) (25). It is in such cases of conflict that the self-controlled as opposed to the weak-willed agent is able to resist acting upon her currently strongest desire and instead act in accord with what she judges it best to do (80). This is possible since agents with the sophistication of normally functioning persons can employ strategies like promising themselves rewards for resisting temptation, or directing their attention to less desirable features of the path more strongly desired, and can generally exploit less episodic and more stable motivation to exercise self-control. In so doing, they can bring their motivational condition into line with their best judgments (81–3).

According to Mele, an agent can be both determined *and* exercise the resources to act with self-control. Determinism is thus compatible with self-controlled agency. But it is Mele's contention that even an optimally self-controlled agent can fall short of autonomous agency (1995: 121–7). For this reason he concludes that more has to be added to his account of self-control to get all the way to autonomous agency. Notice that, up until this point, Mele's theory appeals *only* to features of agency at work in the theory of action. These include such notions as best judgments, strongest desires, intentions, the ability to promise oneself rewards, the distinction between more and less episodic motivational factors, and questions about the potential conflict between best judgment and motivational desires.

How is it that on this view self-controlled agency is *not* itself sufficient to capture autonomous agency? Because the beliefs, values, and principles that inform one's deliberation and conduct might be instilled in a person in some autonomy-undermining manner. Such cases arise via various sorts of manipulation, through brainwashing or hypnosis, or even a history of rigorous indoctrination during youth (recall the example of brainwashing mentioned above in Section 8.1). The key element in an agent's *not* having had, for instance, unsheddable principles and values instilled and sustained in an autonomy-undermining manner is that the way in which the agent acquired them did *not* bypass an agent's critical capacities to assess the principles and values for herself (1995: 166–73). In non-bypassing cases, the agent had the opportunity to embrace or shed them. Accordingly, Mele postulates a *negative historical constraint* on autonomous agency: An agent acts autonomously if she acts with self-control, has beliefs that foster deliberation, is able to deliberate effectively, and so long as she was not caused to endorse and then sustain unsheddable values or principles by means that bypassed her capacities for critical evaluation (1995: 193).

Mele argues for his historical thesis by invoking pairs of examples in which one agent does not have an objectionable history and the other does, where it seems that only this factor and no other explains our intuition that one agent is free and responsible (or instead autonomous) and the other is not. Mele's most frequently discussed case is that of Ann and Beth (1995: 145; 2006: 164–5). Here is our compressed retelling of the cases:

> Ann is an extremely productive college professor who is by stipulation autonomous. She devotes her life almost exclusively to her work. Beth is an equally talented colleague who has many interests, not just her work. Beth's dean wants Beth to be like Ann. So he hires a team of psychologists capable of "new-wave brainwashing" (1995: 145) to capture Beth in her sleep and without her knowledge eradicate her hierarchy of values and install instead a hierarchy that is just like Ann's. Beth turns out to be in the relevant respects a "psychological twin" of Ann (145). Afterwards, Beth begins to act just as Ann does. The question is, when Beth acts, does she do so autonomously? Since Beth is just like Ann, and since, by hypothesis, Ann acts autonomously, if we judge that Beth does not act autonomously, it must be due to her unusual history.

Mele's proposed diagnosis of what explains the difference is just as set out in the preceding paragraph: Beth fails to satisfy a negative historical condition. When she acts in ways that please the dean, her history *includes* (rather than lacks) a process of value-acquisition that bypasses her ability to acquire and then sustain her values under her own steam.

In *Free Will and Luck* (2006b: chapters 6–7) Mele revisited his 1995 compatibilist proposal, defending it against various incompatibilist arguments. In doing so, he shifts to writing in terms of freedom and moral responsibility rather than autonomy. He makes short work dispensing with the Consequence Argument and the prospects for leeway freedom (2006b: 138). As discussed earlier (Section 5.3.1), Mele defends Frankfurt's argument, and so, as it bears on his compatibilist proposal, he advises a source compatibilist position (2006b: 138).

What about arguments for source incompatibilism? Mele replies (138–44) to Pereboom's Four-Case Manipulation Argument.[5] One of his objections involves a softline reply in response to Pereboom's Case 1, arguing that Plum in Case 1 is "out of the control loop" (142), and so his agency is simply not engaged. Recall that we considered such a reply (Section 7.4) and argued that Pereboom had the resources to reply in a way that addresses Mele's objection but still retains the force of the manipulation case. But set this dispute aside. Note that Mele's historical proposal is illustrative of how historical compatibilists can appeal to principled resources for adopting a softline reply to a range of manipulation arguments (a point we note above in Section 8.1). If, for instance, the case of Beth were to be imported into a manipulation argument, supposing Beth's agency is not defective in other ways after the intervention, a nonhistorical compatibilist would be forced to take a hardline reply. Mele's historical compatibilists would not, and it would be a tall order to do so, since the case of Beth seems to strongly illicit a judgment of nonresponsibility.

But what of manipulation arguments drawing on examples that incorporate Mele's proposed historical conditions? Here, Mele introduces a manipulation argument that zeroes in on this question, setting out a case designed to suit the needs of historical compatibilists, namely *The Zygote Argument* (2006b: 188–9). The argument features the goddess Diana, who purposefully creates a zygote that eventually becomes Ernie. At some point in his life, Ernie performs an act, A, and this is just exactly as Diana planned it given her detailed knowledge of the universe upon initially creating Ernie's zygote. Here is Mele's statement of the argument:

1. Because of the way his zygote was produced in his deterministic universe, Ernie is not a free agent and is not morally responsible for anything.
2. Concerning free action and moral responsibility of the beings into whom zygotes develop, there is no significant difference between the way Ernie's zygote comes to exist and the way any normal human zygote comes to exist in a deterministic universe.
3. So determinism precludes free action and moral responsibility.

According to Mele, what a compatibilist should say about Ernie is that he acts freely and is morally responsible for his action (193). This is a hardline reply. Crucially, Ernie satisfies the historical conditions Mele commends compatibilists to endorse, since other than Ernie's unusual start in life, he can have a history just like any other normal person living out his life at a determined world. Accepting that Ernie might after all be free and be morally responsible for his action is plausibly far less costly than would be accepting that agents like Beth, apprehended and brainwashed, act freely and are morally responsible. And this provides one strong incentive for compatibilists to advance a historical theory.

8.7. Scanlon's Contractualist Compatibilism

Next, we shall consider T.M. Scanlon's work on moral responsibility (1988, 1998, 2008). While Scanlon's views have changed over time, and while his attention sometimes varies between the different kinds of moral responsibility he identifies—attributive or instead substantive responsibility—he is clearly committed in all of his work to compatibilism. In his earlier book *What We Owe to Each Other* (1998), Scanlon explicitly sets aside the more traditional compatibilist strategy of attending to the metaphysics of causation or of human agency as a way of executing an argument for compatibilism (251). Instead, he proposes to show that determinism's apparent threat to both attributability-responsibility and substantive-responsibility can be diffused by attending to how freedom of choice and voluntariness of action are relevant to judgments of moral responsibility (251). Scanlon then accounts for this relevance by way of his contractualism.

Very briefly, Scanlon's argumentative strategy unfolds as follows. First, he distinguishes between *attributability* responsibility and *substantive* responsibility. As for attributability responsibility, Scanlon writes:

> To say that a person is responsible, in this sense, for a given action is only to say that it is appropriate to take it as a basis for moral appraisal of that person. (1998: 248)

On Scanlon's view, such responsibility only renders one eligible for positive and negative appraisal, since one can be morally responsible for morally indifferent actions (248). Nevertheless, moral praise and blame, when fitting, pertain to the attributability sense of responsibility (1998: 250). Substantive responsibility instead has to do with obligations or duties moral agents can come to bear. About this kind of responsibility, Scanlon writes:

> These judgments of responsibility express substantive judgments about what people are required ... to do for each other. (248)

This sort of responsibility, as Scanlon puts it, is particularly sensitive to the choices a person makes. Why? If the moral burdens she comes to bear are an upshot of her own choices, this can diminish the force of objections she may have against bearing these burdens (249).

With these two notions of responsibility in place, Scanlon proceeds to assess the reasons supporting (and defeating) judgments of either sort of moral responsibility. In neither case, he argues, would determinism give reason to reject these judgments (nor would a more permissive thesis making room for probabilistic causal laws, which he calls the Causal Thesis).

Let's focus more carefully on Scanlon's treatment of substantive responsibility. The scope of what we are morally responsible for in the substantive sense, according to Scanlon, is often dependent upon our choices. Why should this be? To begin, choice has value, instrumental, representative, and symbolic (251–6). Hence, we have reason to want outcomes "to depend on the way we respond when presented with alternatives" (257). So we seek the justification of moral principles that places a value on this. But now, with the introduction of the value of choice in moral principles settling the scope of substantive responsibility, isn't there the threat that determinism (or the Causal Thesis) would be in conflict with this value? Doesn't choice require a genuine ability to do otherwise, and isn't it in conflict with determinism? Scanlon argues that the moral question of what substantive burdens a person should take on is to be settled by whether a person would have a legitimate complaint others could not reasonably reject were she to object to being shouldered with these burdens. But then, so long as she is provided with *reasonable* options within the context of the expectations of the moral community, however she chooses, poorly or well, there is no more or less that is reasonable for her to demand of that moral community.

An example Scanlon uses to illustrate this is of a reckless woman who is harmed by ignoring adequate warnings and thus being exposed to toxic chemicals at a clean-up site. She bears the burdens of her harms to herself and so is substantively responsible for her own condition because the community took very reasonable and extensive steps to warn her. In the face of these warnings, she chose poorly. In such a context, choice still has its value even in the face of determinism's truth, and so choice can still settle questions regarding the scope of our substantive responsibility. As Scanlon puts it:

> Choice can still retain its value even if it is caused, ultimately, by factors outside of us … so long as these factors operate "through us." (262)

This, in compressed form, is Scanlon's (1998) argument for the compatibility of determinism and substantive responsibility.

At this juncture, a critic might resist as follows: It may be true that by contractualist reasoning the distributions of burdens are best allotted by means that give weight to the value of choice. As an upshot of this, those who bear considerable burdens as a result of choosing poorly might not have a complaint against others that they have these burdens to bear; their substantive responsibilities are allotted in a justified way. But in a context in which, because determinism is true, these agents do not possess a more basic kind of freedom as to how they choose and thus what burdens they come to bear, there is a deeper sense, as some might see it, in which they do not deserve the lot they find for themselves in life. While this does not undermine the justification Scanlon offers, the threat is that the allotment of our substantive responsibilities is in some sense just a matter of luck. It is not grounded on anything deeper about our own nature.

Now consider, Scanlon's treatment of attributability responsibility and with it the aptness of blame and praise. Here, we turn to Scanlon's more recent book *Moral Dimensions: Permissibility, Meaning and Blame* (2008), in which he expands upon and also departs to a certain degree from his earlier treatment. Scanlon takes up the Strawson-inspired strategy noted above (Section 8.2) whereby exploring the normative grounds for our holding-responsible practices will shed light on the presuppositions about free and responsible agency. In the course of developing an interpretation of the ethics of blame, he proposes to "examine why blame might be thought to be appropriate only for actions that are undertaken freely, and explain why moral blame … does not presuppose free will" (6). In this passage and others, it appears Scanlon means to advance compatibilism by bypassing altogether a freedom condition on action. But at other points it seems he only means to take aim at a "strong kind of freedom" (123) rather than one that would be compatible with determinism. We'll assume the latter in what follows.

Scanlon argues that the blameworthiness of an action is a function of its meaning, and its meaning indicates "something about an agent's attitudes that impairs his or her relations with others" (6). Blaming is in turn a matter of understanding one's relations with a person as modified in a way rendered appropriate by the meaning of that person's action (6). When, for instance, a person betrays a friend by speaking disparagingly about her out of turn, this action reveals something about the person's attitudes toward the friend that impairs their relationships by normative standards of friendship. The betrayed friend, in modifying her understanding of her relation with this person in ways that are appropriate or deserved, *thereby* blames that person.

Why doesn't blameworthiness require free will? Because a blameworthy person's objectionable attitudes as revealed in her actions are reason-providing for another's modifying her relations with the person. If the betraying friend really does display objectionable attitudes toward the betrayed friend, the betrayed friend is given reasons to adjust her assessment of the so-called friend, regardless of how "free" the friend is in acting as she does.[6] There is, thus, no special freedom requirement of an "opportunity to avoid" blame as a normative constraint on the aptness of blaming (2008: 186–7). Furthermore, the appropriate, fitting, or deserving forms of treatment constitutive of blaming only involve modifications to one's regard and treatment of the blamed person that are not owed unconditionally (187), as a contractualist might think of it. If a poor attitude of a blameworthy person makes a response by a blamer appropriate, it only involves modifications that are not unconditionally owed to others by principles no one could reasonably reject. Hence, a blamer is permitted to so respond regardless of any putative robust freedom requirements.

As Scanlon acknowledges, if the ethics of blame as he understands it were to justify harsher treatment, then perhaps it *would* seem reasonable to ratchet up the freedom requirements in a way friendly to incompatibilism (190). At this juncture, it is worth considering two related points bearing upon the topics discussed above (Section 8.3). First, it is not clear whether and if so how Scanlon's notion of attributability-responsibility (which appears *not* to be designed to capture what Watson meant by the term *attributability*) overlaps with the core notion of accountability-responsibility identified in the previous section. It is that latter notion, we claimed, that is most relevant to questions of free will. One worry is that we are just talking about different things. So it is not surprising that Scanlon is able to specify transparently compatibilist-friendly freedom conditions.

But set this worry aside. Suppose there is enough overlap between Scanlon's proposed notion of attributability-responsibility and the Watsonian notion of accountability-responsibility that we can take Scanlon's proposal as a genuine contender for how we ought to understand responsibility in that overlapping domain. There arises a second problem. Many incompatibilists, such as Pereboom (2001, 2014), claim that only the basic desert-entailing moral responsibility is genuinely at issue in the free will debate, and this is so even when attending to the narrower notion of accountability-responsibility. There is a question about this shared domain as to whether Scanlon's proposal is such a notion, or is at least the *same sort* of desert-entailing notion that these incompatibilists have in mind. Scanlon now embraces a limited basic desert-based theory as it pertains to his notion of attributability-responsibility (2008: 188–9; 2013), and he thus departs from his prior (1998) rejection of desert-based theories. But he emphasizes that on his view of blame, *what* is deserved is not to be understood in terms of the goodness of harming a blameworthy person (188) or the permissibility of significantly harming her or allowing her to be significantly harmed (189). All basic desert involves is the fittingness of modifying one's relation with a blamed person, in particular the withdrawing of good will upon being wronged (Scanlon, 2013). He is clear that he does not think that punishment can be justified on the grounds of basic desert. Here, what Scanlon has in mind by basically deserved blame is gentler—far gentler—than the sort of deserved blame other desert-entailing theorists have in mind. Thus, Scanlon does not endorse standard compatibilism about basic desert-entailing moral responsibility. His view is intermediate between such a compatibilism and some of the skeptical views we will discuss in Chapter 12.

It is, however, doubtful that Scanlon would take a charge of departure from standard compatibilism to be unwelcome. The same applies to the previously noted criticism of his treatment of substantive responsibility (that the distribution of burdens are ultimately a matter of luck). Scanlon remarks that if our ordinary notions of blame and the justification for the responsibilities people come to shoulder depart from his theory of responsibility, then his proposal is to be regarded as a revisionist one. As he puts it, "I am quite content with this result" (1998: 294).

8.8. Wallace's Fairness-Based Compatibilism

In *Responsibility and the Moral Sentiments* (1994), R. Jay Wallace argued for compatibilism by appeal to fairness as informing the normative constraints on holding morally responsible. He then drew conclusions about the conditions of agency presupposed by these constraints, arguing that they are compatible with determinism. Like Scanlon, Wallace adopts a Strawson-inspired approach by setting aside questions about the metaphysics of agency as a starting point for theorizing. Instead he seeks an internal justification of our practices of holding responsible. These inform us about the relevant conditions of free and responsible agency. There is also a more specific appeal to a Strawsonian strategy found in Wallace's argument for compatibilism. Recall Strawson's Argument from Exculpation (Section 6.4.1). Strawson first identified distinct kinds of exculpating pleas and then sought the underlying rationale that rendered them applicable. In light of this rationale, determinism, Strawson argued, would not provide grounds for invoking any exculpating considerations of either kind. Hence, it gives us no reason to think that it would undermine freedom or responsibility. Wallace advances an argument with a similar structure. He attempts to show that the normative basis for the appropriate application of these various exculpating pleas does not presuppose any conditions of agency incompatible with determinism.

Seeking to improve upon Strawson's own way of focusing on certain emotions, Wallace distinguishes the morally reactive attitudes of resentment and indignation from other attitudes and emotions. According to Wallace, a reactive attitude of resentment or moral indignation has as its object a certain sort of belief: that a person has violated an obligation to which she is held (1994:

33–40). To hold an agent morally responsible (and blameworthy) for an action is to respond to her, or to believe that it would be appropriate to respond to her, with the morally reactive emotion of resentment or moral indignation, one that has the sort of content specified here.

By giving content to the morally reactive attitudes, Wallace shows how they can be subject to critical evaluation by objective standards. If, for instance, it turns out that the belief serving as a basis for a morally reactive attitude is false, that is, if the person in question did not violate the obligation in question, then the rational basis for the attitude is shown to be undercut. Hence, the attitude should be forsworn. Given this characterization of the morally reactive attitudes, Wallace next turns to the Strawsonian issue of when excuses or exemptions are appropriate.[7] According to Wallace, in the case of excuses it depends on whether the agent in fact *did* violate the obligation to which others hold her (1994: 118–53). In the case of exemptions it turns on whether the agent possesses the general capacities to understand and act upon the moral demands placed on her by such obligations (1994: 154–94). In each case, it is a normative principle of fairness that informs our excusing or exempting practices. In the case of excusing practices, the fairness principle is one of desert: One does not deserve to be blamed for violating a moral obligation that she did not violate, hence it would be unfair to do so. In the case of exempting practices, the principle is one of moral reasonableness: It is unreasonable to demand of a person that she comply with moral demands if she simply hasn't the capacities or resources to do so, hence it would be unfair to do so.

Wallace proceeds to argue that neither of these moral principles is threatened by determinism. Determinism would not show that no one ever violates moral obligations, nor would it show that everyone is incapacitated to understand or comply with the demands involved in moral obligations. The upshot is that Wallace's compatibilist account of freedom in the context of blameworthy action is, first, that an agent acted in such a way that she violated an obligation, and, second, that she possessed a general capacity to comply with moral demands despite the fact that she failed to do so.

Furthermore, Wallace argues that excuses that appear to presuppose the demand for an ability to do otherwise, and hence, leeway freedom, such as, *I could not have done otherwise*, are excuses that cannot be generalized. They work when they do *only* by showing that an agent did not violate a moral obligation in acting as she did (1994: 152–3). Factors other than her disregard for a moral obligation explain her action—for example, she was forced to do something at gunpoint, or was physically unable to get to the emergency phone because her leg was broken, and so on. So it seems that Wallace shares with Frankfurt the view that leeway freedom is not needed for moral responsibility, but by way of a different argument. Only source freedom is required.

Note the similarities between Scanlon's and Wallace's positions. Each appeals to the normative conditions on holding responsible and blaming, and each uses these to identify conditions on agency, in each case showing that these conditions are friendly to a compatibilist diagnosis. Both also explain the relevant norms by way of a broader set of ethical commitments, which for Scanlon issues from his contractualism and for Wallace issues from considerations of fairness. Nevertheless, there are important differences. One is that Wallace restricts his account of holding morally responsible to the morally reactive emotions and their appropriate expression, whereas Scanlon (2008: 128–31) takes these emotions to be but one factor in the larger spectrum of attitudinal modifications that involve blame. This is because, for Scanlon, understanding one's relations with another to be modified in response to the other's objectionably impairing their relationships encompasses more than what is involved in manifesting or finding fitting a negative moral emotion.

Another difference concerns the nature of blame, and the resulting strength of the normative warrant needed for justifying it. Scanlon explicitly denies that he thinks of blame as a kind of sanction (2008: 184–5). He even grants that if it were, it would seem plausible to require a condition of fair opportunity to avoid (184), which could help support the rationale for incompatibilist freedom conditions. Wallace (1994: 51–2), by contrast, makes clear that he thinks of blame as of a piece with a spectrum of sanctioning responses. This, in turn, suggests a further interesting difference between Wallace and Scanlon. In the previous section, a worry was raised about whether the sense of desert-entailing moral responsibility Scanlon endorsed was the same sort that various incompatibilists take to be central to the free will debate. The worry was, first, that the kind of responsibility Scanlon focused on (attributability in Scanlon's sense of the term) was different from what animates other theorists (accountability in Watson's sense of the term), and, second, that the modes characteristic of deserved blame for Scanlon were not very burdensome for the one blamed, and so perhaps he does not really engage incompatibilists. Wallace, on the other hand, is clearly interested in the accountability sense of moral responsibility. He also understands blame in a way that imposes harms, and while he does not justify this so much in terms of basic desert but instead fairness, it seems he is more in the ballpark of the sort of desert-entailing accountability-responsibility that is the focus of concern for incompatibilists.

But what of Wallace's positive account of the freedom required for morally responsible agency? Does it provide robust resources to silence the incompatibilist worries that Scanlon sought to avoid? As we noted, Wallace only requires source freedom. His view does not require that, at the time of action, an agent must be able to do otherwise, given the particular conditions she is in. Hence, as he sees it, he can avoid the challenges of the Consequence Argument. All he requires is a general capacity to comply with moral reasons when one fails to do so, and for him this involves a compatibilist-friendly general capacity to do otherwise in some sense, one that is uncontroversially compatible with determinism. But one might worry that this is not enough to satisfy further considerations of fairness that are of a piece with those to which Wallace is committed. An agent might do morally wrong, violate a moral obligation to which she is and ought to be held, possess the relevant general capacities, and yet be covertly made to do so by means that are beyond her control, as in a manipulation case.

Some would think that if this were so, it would be unfair to sanction such an agent by way of a blaming response. What seems to be needed, then, for Wallace to defeat such worries about charges of unfairness is further development, beyond an appeal to any general capacity, of the sort of source freedom actually exercised by a morally responsible agent in acting as she does when she does wrong. A source compatibilist might contend that some covert ways of generating an agent's action (as in certain manipulation cases) are incompatible with freedom, while other deterministic casual histories are not. This is how a historical compatibilist would argue. Or a source compatibilist might contend that such histories are sufficient for freedom even given the covert causes. This is the route a nonhistorical compatibilist would take.

It is worth considering, in light of the worry raised in the last paragraph, where Wallace stands on manipulation cases and the historical versus nonhistorical approach to theorizing responsibility (see Section 8.1). He does address manipulation cases, but under the rubric of systematic behavior control or conditioning (1994: 155). His principle of distinguishing those exempt from morally responsible agency is informed exclusively by whether the persons in question are incapacitated to understand and comply with the demands of moral obligations. Therefore, it looks as if Wallace is committed to a nonhistorical position, although he never discusses the debate in these terms. To the extent that any nonhistorical position is susceptible to manipulation cases of the sort sketched above (Section 8.1), it seems that Wallace's is as well. Hence, he must adopt that same style of response as Frankfurt's: It doesn't matter how an agent comes to be the way she is, so long as relevant freedom conditions are satisfied at the time she acts.

8.9. Russell's Strawsonian-Inspired Critical Compatibilism

In *Freedom and Moral Sentiment* (1995), and then in a series of more recent papers (e.g., 2000, 2002b, 2004, 2013), Paul Russell advances a form of compatibilism that places emphasis on a capacity for moral sense. This capacity enables free and morally responsible agents to appreciate and be responsive to the moral sentiments, and most notably the reactive attitudes central to Strawson's compatibilist project. Here is Russell's pithy formulation of, as he explicitly labels it, *the condition of moral sense*:

> The responsible agent must be able to feel and understand moral sentiments and reactive attitudes. (2004: 203)

Recall that the crucial element in Strawson's account of being morally responsible is understood in terms of the quality of a person's will (Section 6.3). But a critical examination of Strawson's compatibilist proposal (e.g., Russell, 1992; Watson, 1987) revealed that Strawson needed to provide some credible explanation of the salient capacities that bear on competent participation in adult

interpersonal relations (Section 6.5.1). This in turn would settle the proper extension of the moral community—and so of the class of morally responsible agents.
When a person is blameworthy because she acts from a morally objectionable
quality of will, what are the capacities implicated in her conduct that help ground
our sense that she is accountable for acting from such a will?

Strawson was far too confident in thinking *only* in terms of quality of will.
Russell's (2004) proposal, as a plausible extension of Strawson's compatibilism,
is that the pertinent capacity is a capacity to appreciate and be responsive to the
moral sentiments of others, and of one's own—say, in terms of emotions like
guilt and pride. Just as fear (that is not irrational) reveals a salient understanding
of genuine danger, so too exercises of moral sense reveal a salient understanding
of the moral affections, demands, and expectations of others. One who lacked
this sense altogether, such as a psychopath or instead a very young child, would
be incapacitated for exercises of agency that could be expected of adult members
of a moral community. Although Russell does not propose any argument that
this crucial capacity is compatible with determinism, he operates under the not-
implausible presupposition that it is.

The preceding problem for Strawsonian compatibilism—identifying the capacities required for participation in the moral community—was rendered all the
more pressing given that Strawson's naturalistic claims animating his psychological impossibility argument seemed inadequate (Section 6.5.2). How so? The
mere fact that we are naturally disposed to attitudes of a certain type does not
itself show that we can set aside questions regarding the appropriateness of token
instances of them as actually manifested in thought and action. It is for this
reason that Russell's defense of Strawsonian compatibilism is only a qualified
defense. Russell is plausibly *the* philosopher alive today who has given full voice
to Strawsonian compatibilism as a view that remains a live option.[8] Nevertheless, he has made very clear that his defense is a limited and critical one (1992,
2013). He rightly rejects Strawson's more sweeping naturalistic attempts to
refute free will skepticism by relying on the inevitability of our human propensity to the reactive attitudes like resentment and indignation. True, we are so
susceptible, but that only allows for a *type-naturalism* that can refute a *type-
skepticism* whereby it is claimed that we are not justified in even being disposed
to the *having* of these types of attitudes. This does nothing to refute a *token-
skepticism* according to which, in the instances where we manifest tokens of
these types, there is reason to believe that doing so is not ever justified. According to the token-skeptic, implicit in the actual expression of these attitudes is the
presumption that the agents at whom they are directed are free, and there are
reasons to believe that no one is free in the required way.

The proper way to answer these skeptics, Russell argues (1992), is by way of
Strawson's "rationalistic" arguments that attempt to show that we have no good
reason to excuse or exempt all human agents (see Chapter 6, Sections 4.1 and
5.1). But it is exactly here that one needs to know what relevant capacities our
excuses and exemptions are really tracking (or, as the skeptics would put it,
attempting to track). Russell's Strawson-inspired proposal is cast in terms of a

moral sense, which involves a capacity to appreciate the reactive attitudes. What matters, then, when we respond to the quality of a morally responsible agent's will depends upon whether that agent has a moral sense, one that is effective in helping to modulate an agent's conduct in the world and most notably in her interpersonal relations with others.

Russell's proposal provides for an interesting point of comparison with Wallace's (1994) view, as we have set it out here. While both are clearly Strawson-inspired views, their differences reveal different paths as regards how one thinks about the crucial capacities for moral agency and the related scope of moral responsibility. Note that Wallace restricts his account of the capacities bearing on free will and responsibility to a general ability to grasp and comply with moral and nonmoral obligations. In doing so, he explicitly limits the scope of moral responsibility in Kantian fashion to the domain of deontic notions (cast in terms of obligations, rights, duties, permissibility, impermissibility, right, wrong, and so on). Russell (2013), by contrast, has a more inclusive sense of capacity that is meant to be alive to the wide range of considerations that our ethical sentiments and emotions can track. This interestingly is revealed in Russell's 1995 book, which was devoted to understanding Hume's views about freedom and responsibility and showing their relevance to the contemporary free will debate.[9] On the Humean view, what our moral sense tracks is not limited just to morality conceived in terms of obligations and related concepts, but instead also encompasses attention to traits of a person liable to elicit pleasurable or painful qualities of mind (1995: 179–80).

A difference that emerges, then, between Russell and Wallace has to do with the capacities presupposed by the intended domain of our responsibility concerns. Freedom understood in terms of capacities to comply with obligations might be more stringent than when understood in terms of the full range of ethical concerns that Russell is willing to include, such as being a creepy person or acting unvirtuously. Acting with a moral sense alive to these considerations might not impose the same sorts of burdens in terms of freedom. One important question for Russell is how permissive on his view free and responsible agency is. We have evaluated a range of compatibilist proposals, Wallace's included, but also Scanlon's and Dennett's, in terms of their relevance to desert-entailing moral responsibility. There is a plausible case to be made for the view that desert-entailing moral responsibility and the freedom it presupposes should be limited to moral wrongdoing, a deontic notion. Why? Some would argue that one can basically deserve the hard treatment associated with blaming only if she does morally wrong. If so, there is a worry that Russell's Strawsonian-inspired compatibilism does not engage directly the controversies at the heart of the free will debate.[10]

Set the preceding considerations aside. A further interesting aspect of Russell's compatibilist proposal is that it is critical of compatibilism despite being an endorsement of it—hence the label *Critical Compatibilism*. In this respect, Russell (2002b) distances himself from Strawson's (1962) explicit allegiance to optimism. As the Strawsonian optimist sees it, determinism poses no threat at all to our responsibility practices. Now, Russell agrees with compatibilists in rejecting free will and moral responsibility skepticism. Our moral responsibility practices require a capacity for agency that includes a moral sense, and we agents retain such capacities even if determinism is true. But even while rejecting skepticism, we nevertheless have reason to be pessimistic at, as Russell puts it, the horizon (2002b). The reason is that we cannot be the ultimate originators of our actions. They were ultimately settled for us in the distant past. Looking at the horizon of our own conditions in the natural world, we come to see that no conclusion of the compatibilists' can silence the powerful thought that our place in the world and our playing out our part in the moral community as we do is relevantly beyond our control or just a matter of luck. Russell's view here is provocative insofar as it makes considerable concessions to the moral responsibility skeptic (see Chapter 11) despite not sharing her thesis in an unqualified way. This pessimism at the limit, Russell holds, should not warrant anything as dramatic as "Pascalian despair"; it is, rather, just disconcerting (2002b: 251).

8.10.   Bok's Practical-Standpoint Compatibilism

In *Freedom and Responsibility* (1998), Hilary Bok advanced a form of compatibilism by way of what might be called a *standpoint argument*.[11] According to Bok, there is a legitimate standpoint at which judgments of responsibility arise. This is distinct from a standpoint at which questions of determinism would be settled. Responsibility or freedom concepts at work within this former viewpoint are not threatened by the possibility that determinism is true. The relevant standpoint arises by distinguishing, in Kantian fashion, between the practical and the theoretical points of view. The former is the stance of practical deliberation, and has as its goal figuring out how one ought to act, which goals to set, how to plan one's life, by considering and weighing reasons. The latter standpoint is concerned to describe and explain events as resulting from antecedent conditions (Bok, 1998: 62–5). According to Bok, while both libertarian and compatibilist notions of free will *are* found within the range of the "ordinary" concept of freedom, the one that matters to the free will debate is the one that a practical agent would have good reason to adopt (1998: 100). It is not that only one of these standpoints captures the "real" truth about what the concept of free will is. It's that one is pertinent to agency in a way that the other is not. Bok thus seeks to settle the free will problem by focusing on the role of the concept of freedom from the point of view of a deliberator engaged in settling practical issues.

Given her practical standpoint approach, Bok maintains that the sort of freedom of use to deliberators concerns possibilities restricted in scope to those consistent with what an agent understands to be practically possible from her limited epistemic perspective (1998: 108). These possibilities are much looser than the sort required by libertarian free will, the latter requiring attention only to possibilities given a precisely specified past and holding fixed the actual laws of nature. Bok's favored possibilities allow an agent to reason about alternative courses of action conditional upon her choosing in one manner as opposed to another. Hence, Bok embraces a conditional analysis of free will. For an alternative to be genuine, it need not be open given precisely the same past and laws of nature. It need only be genuine given the coarser facts about the conditional relation between an agent's will and subsequent conduct likely to arise from it. If she chooses in one fashion, then she'll act in one way; if she chooses in another, then she'll act in a different way (1998: 120).

So Bok embraces leeway freedom in order to capture the freedom-relevant condition for moral responsibility. Her appeal to a conditional analysis of regulative control, however, leaves her open to the same sort of criticism leveled against the classical compatibilist's conditional analysis (see Section 3.2). It would, however, be unfair to dismiss Bok's practical standpoint compatibilist theory simply because the particular analysis of freedom she relies on is suspect. It might be true that traditional conditional analyses are in trouble, but other treatments of agential ability remain. So perhaps Bok could defend leeway freedom without the classical compatibilists' conditional analysis. (We'll explore efforts to do this in the next chapter.) Thus, Bok's position remains very much alive despite worries about the details of her proposed analysis of leeway freedom. The important philosophical point, on Bok's approach, is that the demands of the practical standpoint invite a looser notion of possibility, and so of ability, than the sort that is at work when formulating precise definitions of determinism, or when attempting to fashion libertarian notions of free will. Some looser notion of agential possibility might allow a compatibilist to say that all the possibility that is needed for leeway freedom is something like epistemic possibility, "for all I as a practical agent know" possibility.

How does Bok justify the import of this compatibilist notion of freedom? In her view, it is justified by our practical interest in improving the qualities of our wills, which are reflections of ourselves, fashioners of the people we will become (1998: 123–66). We care, when we deliberate, to evaluate possibilities in terms of how we acted in the past and how we might improve our conduct and ourselves in the future. A compatibilist notion of freedom will help us to do the work of improving our characters and fashioning ourselves. It will allow us to conceive of what it is within our general range of capacities to do, and to evaluate our options in terms which lead to our improvement.

Bok's justification for a compatibilist-friendly notion of freedom is surprisingly forward-looking. We care about the relevant notion of freedom since we care about future improvements to our wills and characters. This is in deep conflict with the spirit of approaches, such as Strawson's (see Section 6.1), that have dismissed such consequentialist sorts of justification of free will (e.g., Smart, 1963) as unable to capture the intimate connection between an agent and her responsibility for what she had done. For an agent's regret or guilt to be a genuine expression of her attitude toward her conduct and those whom she wronged, it had better be a response to what she did in the past, and not merely a vehicle for improving herself in the future.

Here we offer two comments. First, as with our assessment of Scanlon's views, there is a concern that the sense of moral responsibility Bok has in mind is not aligned with the sort pertaining to the traditional free will problem. The natural way to understand accountability-responsibility is in terms of backward-looking considerations, ones in virtue of which a blaming or praising response is taken to be appropriate, and, importantly deserved *just because* of the way an agent acted. The reason-giving resources that justify blaming on Bok's legitimately-called-to-moral-improvement view, having the forward-looking orientation they have, are not suited to treat questions of responsibility as settled by attending just to what a person has done and what she deserves because of that. Second, the sort of conditional freedom Bok identifies for this sense of freedom is clearly compatible with determinism in a way that is entirely unproblematic (Pereboom, 2007: 72). In a deterministic environment, one's self-assessment and others' assessments of one can be useful means of causally influencing a person in morally laudatory ways that will shape her subsequent behavior. But as we have explained above (Section 8.3), many incompatibilists see any conception of freedom that is so clearly compatible with determinism as orthogonal to the philosophical puzzles related to the (strongest) sort of freedom necessary for moral responsibility.

8.11. A Continuum Ranging from Normative to Metaphysical Approaches

We began this chapter by noting that the many contemporary compatibilist views currently in circulation defy easy categorization. Here we note one interesting way of sorting contemporary compatibilist proposals. Rather than think of distinct categories, we propose a continuum of views that emphasize at one end almost exclusively normative considerations and forgo attention to action-theoretic and metaphysical considerations. At the other end of the spectrum, we find approaches that tend almost exclusively to issues in the theory of action and to related metaphysical questions. This appears to be on display in the seven previous sections. Scanlon's view, for instance, seems to be at the most extreme normative end of the spectrum, while Mele's appears to be located at the most extreme action-theoretic and metaphysical end of the spectrum. Plausibly, Wolf and Nelkin are squarely in the middle. While Bok, Russell, and Wallace are closer to Scanlon than to Mele, Dennett is closer to Mele than to Scanlon. We turn in the next chapter to three general compatibilist strategies, two of which seem also to fall somewhere between these two extremes, mesh theories and reasons-responsive theories. A third, devoted to leeway compatibilism, is located at the action-theoretic and metaphysical end of the spectrum, perhaps even at a point further along than Mele's.

Suggestions for Further Reading

Given that we have covered so many compatibilist proposals, we limit our recommendations in this section just to the major works by the central authors for each of these views:

Dennett's Multiple Viewpoints Compatibilism

Dennett, Daniel. 2003. *Freedom Evolves*. London: Penguin Books.

Dennett, Daniel. 1984. *Elbow Room: Varieties of Free Will Worth Wanting*. Cambridge, MA: MIT Press.

Dennett, Daniel. 1973. "Mechanism and Responsibility." In Ted Honderich, ed., *Essays on Freedom and Action*. London: Routledge and Kegan Paul.

Wolf's Reason View and Nelkin's Rational Abilities View

Nelkin, Dana. 2011. *Making Sense of Freedom and Responsibility*. Oxford: Oxford University Press.

Nelkin, Dana. 2008. "Responsibility and Rational Abilities: Defending an Asymmetrical View." *Pacific Philosophical Quarterly* 8: 497–515.

Wolf, Susan. 1990. *Freedom within Reason*. Oxford: Oxford University Press.

Wolf, Susan. 1980. "Asymmetrical Freedom." *Journal of Philosophy* 77: 157–66.

Mele's Action-Theory Theory

Mele, Alfred. 2006b. *Free Will and Luck*. New York: Oxford University Press.

Mele, Alfred. 1995. *Autonomous Agents*. New York: Oxford University Press.

Scanlon's Contractualist Compatibilism

Scanlon, T.M. 2008. *Moral Dimensions: Permissibility, Meaning, Blame*. Cambridge, MA: Belknap Harvard Press.

Scanlon, T.M. 1998. *What We Owe to Each Other*. Cambridge, MA: Harvard University Press.

Scanlon, T.M. 1988. "The Significance of Choice." In Sterling M. McMurrin, ed., *The Tanner Lectures on Human Values*. Cambridge: Cambridge University Press: 1–35.

Wallace's Fairness-Based Compatibilism

Wallace, R. Jay. 1994. *Responsibility and the Moral Sentiments*. Cambridge, MA: Harvard University Press.

Russell's Strawsonian-Inspired Critical Compatibilism

Russell, Paul. 2013. "Responsibility, Naturalism, and the Morality System." In D. Shoemaker, ed., *Oxford Studies in Agency and Responsibility*, vol. 1, Oxford: Oxford University Press: 184–204.

Russell, Paul. 2004. "Responsibility and the Condition of Moral Sense." *Philosophical Topics* 32: 287–306.

Russell, Paul. 1992. "Strawson's Way of Naturalizing Responsibility." *Ethics* 102: 287–302.

Bok's Practical-Standpoint Compatibilism

Bok, Hilary. 1998. *Freedom and Responsibility*. Princeton, NJ: Princeton University Press.

Notes

1 The distinction between historical and nonhistorical theories can be understood by considering the difference between things that are essentially historical and things that are not (see Fischer and Ravizza, 1998: 171–3). A simple example is a sunburn. A sunburn is a burn caused by the sun. Without that history, a burn is not a sunburn but an injury of some other kind. Another simple example is a genuine rather than a counterfeit dollar bill. Examples of nonhistorical properties are things like being a sphere or having a broken leg. If something is spherical, it does not matter how it came to be that way; it has the shape it has. Likewise for a broken leg.

2 It is a point of contention whether there are multiple senses of moral responsibility or instead just one. Angela Smith (2012) has argued for a monistic thesis as against the pluralists.

3 This calls for a brief explanation of a rather complicated metaphysical point about the nature of causation, or more precisely, the nature of the items that can stand in causal relations. (We cannot do justice to the issue here.) A widespread assumption is that causation is a relation between events (where events are thought of as changes occurring in time that involve substances or objects—like an acid's being poured onto the surface of a car, which causes the car's paint to dissolve). It is regarded as a relative outlier thesis that things themselves—as substances—can be causes. Of course, a familiar libertarian approach claims that persons are unique among items in the natural world in that they are undetermined substances with causal powers. (We covered this libertarian view briefly in Section 3.4, and readers will also find a more detailed treatment of it in Chapter 10.) But Nelkin argues both that substance causation is pervasive in nature and not just limited to persons as agents, and that causation of this sort is compatible with determinism.

4 In this section, we rely on McKenna (2009a).

5 Readers will recall that we covered Pereboom's argument in Section 7.4. We invite readers to revisit our presentation of the argument there if they need a reminder about the details of the argument.

6 Scanlon can say (2008: 180–1), when conventional compatibilist constraints on freedom are violated, like duress or coercion, there is reason to think the person does not have an objectionable attitude.

7 As readers might recall from discussion of Strawson (Section 6.4.1), excuses involve specific pleas that one is not responsible for some bit of conduct, such as "I did not see you there." Exemptions involve pleas that a person is not competent to function as a morally responsible agent, such as, "She did not understand what she was doing. She is severely mentally ill."

8 Recall, we noted in Chapter 6 that while Strawson has dramatically influenced contemporary debates about freedom and responsibility, few contemporary philosophers defend his basic compatibilist proposal. In a qualified way, Russell does.

9 Indeed, Russell (1995) argues against orthodoxy that Hume's views are far more aligned with Strawsonian compatibilism than with the traditional classical compatibilism of the Schlick/Ayer variety.

10 To be clear, we only wish to acknowledge this line of reasoning. We do not necessarily endorse it. One of us, McKenna (2012), has explicitly argued against it.

11 In this section, we rely on McKenna (2009a).

9   Contemporary Compatibilism

Mesh Theories, Reasons-Responsive Theories, and Leeway Theories[1]

Three of the most widely discussed contemporary compatibilist theories are mesh theories, reasons-responsive theories, and leeway theories. Mesh theories account for free will in terms of a well-functioning harmony between different elements within an agent's psychic structure. Reasons-responsive theories account for free will in terms of an agent's somehow being sensitive to reasons in the production of an action. Leeway theories focus primarily upon advancing a contemporary account of leeway freedom. In this chapter, we focus on these three approaches.

9.1.   Mesh Theories: An Initial Characterization

A lean theory of freedom advanced by classical compatibilists like Hobbes and Hume had it that a person acts freely just in the case there are no impediments to her doing what she wants (see Section 3.1.1). If a person is chained up or threatened at gunpoint, or has an epileptic seizure, she does not act freely. But if she is doing what she wants, she does. A further conditional requirement was also typically included, to the effect that the agent would do otherwise had she wanted to do otherwise. All of this is compatible with the truth of determinism. The appeal of this proposal was its simplicity. It required no special metaphysical extras beyond the normal functioning of human agency.

A shortcoming of the classical compatibilist's proposal (as noted in Section 3.1.1) is that an agent's lack of freedom may arise precisely from her own desires. Desires arising from compulsive disorders, phobias, addictions, or psychotic episodes could all be attributable to a person, and yet when she acts upon them unencumbered by any external impediments—when they are causally efficacious in leading her to action—it seems that she is not at all free. In essence, they impair the agent, and yet they do so from sources that in some sense count as elements of her own psychological constitution.

Can a compatibilist correct the failure of this classical compatibilist strategy while preserving its basic intuitive appeal—that freedom is most fundamentally a matter of the unimpeded operation of normally functioning human agency? One option is to show that defective desires or intentions in the production of action result from defective subsystems or processes within the overall architecture of an agent's psychology. When the relevant subsystems or processes misfire, break down, or are out of sync with each other, the desires and intentions they cause are alien to the agent, just as external impediments are. By analogy, a car can be impeded by a roadblock, but it can also be impeded when its own internal systems come into a state of disharmony rendering it inoperable. A theory of action should be able to identify various psychological processes of agents that uniquely figure into the intentional actions of which normally functioning persons are capable. When the ingredients mesh in a harmonious way, then the agent acts unimpeded; her actions and the desires or intentions causing them are a free outcome of her own agency. Call any such theory a *mesh theory*.

Various philosophers have opted for some version of a mesh theory.[2] We shall focus primarily on Harry Frankfurt's. His is the first and most influential, and others have formulated their versions by reference to the relative strengths and weaknesses of his. We'll then consider Gary Watson's and Michael Bratman's alternative proposals.

9.2. Frankfurt's Hierarchical Mesh Theory

Frankfurt begins with the fundamental notion of desire. *First-order desires* are desires that have actions as their objects (1971). Frankfurt then identifies an agent's *will* with her *effective* first-order desires, those that move her "all the way to action."[3] Many creatures have first-order desires. But, Frankfurt points out, persons also have reflexive capacities to adopt attitudes about their own attitudes. A *second-order desire* is a desire that one have a first-order desire. For example, an agent might desire to want to help the poor when she actually doesn't want to help them. More generally, *higher-order desires* have as their objects not actions, but instead desires of a lower order. But for Frankfurt, what is characteristic of persons is a particular kind of higher-order desire. A *second-order volition* is a second-order desire for a first-order desire to be one's will, for a first-order desire to move her all the way to action. That is, one has a second-order volition when one wants to will some action and not merely to want to have a desire without willing it. Persons, Frankfurt contends, are distinctive in their ability to have higher-order volitions.

Frankfurt develops a hierarchical mesh theory of freedom on the basis of these distinctions. Treating the symbol "→" as representing the relation "bring about,"[4] consider the following template for understanding the agency of persons in non-deviant cases:

second-order volition → will → action

Frankfurt distinguishes two types of freedom that concern action and two types of freedom that concern the will. In general, for an action to be free, nothing can impede the relation between willing the action and the action (1971: 19–20). The first type of action-related freedom requires that nothing impede the actual relation between will and action. The second type requires in addition that the agent is free to act otherwise; specifically, that nothing would impede her acting otherwise were she to will to act otherwise (24). Freedom pertaining to the will is treated in a parallel way. In general, for an agent's will to be free, nothing can impede the relation between second-order volition and will (20–1). The first type requires that nothing impede the actual relation between second-order volition and will. The second requires in addition that the agent is free to make some other first-order desire her will instead; specifically, were she to have a different second-order volition, her will would follow suit.

Frankfurt thus distinguishes four types of freedom. Two implicate considerations regarding *leeway* among alternatives, and two implicate only considerations regarding the actual *source* of an agent's action. And here are the four technical terms Frankfurt assigns to each:[5]

	Concerning action	Concerning the will
Source:	acting freely	(acting of one's own) free will
Leeway:	freedom of action	freedom of the will

Many nonhuman animals are able to act freely and with freedom of action. But because only persons are capable of having second-order volitions (19), only they are able to act of their own free will and with freedom of the will.

One further qualification is needed. To explain the freedoms that concern the will, it is not enough that the relation between second-order volition and will be unimpeded. As Frankfurt observes, it is possible that one second-order desire conflicts with another second-order desire, just as first-order desires conflict with each other. One might ask whether it might then be indeterminate whether in willing in accord with a second-order volition, an agent is really acting of her own free will or with freedom of the will. Accordingly, what Frankfurt requires in addition is that the agent decisively *identifies* herself with one of her first-order desires by means of a second-order volition. The second-order volition that yields this identification will come to constitute what at a higher order of reflection *she* wants her will to be. This will be so regardless of whether it does in fact come to be her will.

Frankfurt takes no stand as to whether, in his terminology, freedom of the will is compatible with determinism. Alluding to the debate over whether determinism is compatible with the ability to do otherwise, he writes that it is a "vexed question just how 'he could have done otherwise' is to be understood."[6] Regardless, Frankfurt (1969) has famously argued that moral responsibility does not require the ability to do or to will otherwise (see Chapter 5, which is devoted to Frankfurt's argument for this conclusion). Rather, what is required is only that, in his terminology, an agent act freely and of her own free will. These two freedoms, Frankfurt contends, are compatible with determinism.

To illustrate these freedoms, Frankfurt introduces the case of the *willing addict*, whose first-order desire for a narcotic is irresistible, and so constitutes his will (24). This addict also identifies with his addictive first-order desire by means of a second-order volition. His second-order volition is that his first-order desire for the drug be and remain effective in leading him to action. Thus when he takes the narcotic, he does so freely, and of his own free will, since he acts upon the will that, at a higher order, he wants to have. However, due to his addictive first-order desire, he is not free to have any other first-order desire be his will other than the one that is. As a result, he lacks freedom of the will. Despite this, Frankfurt contends, when he does take the drug, because he does so freely and of his own free will, he is morally responsible for doing so.

In light of the above treatment, here is the necessary and sufficient condition Frankfurt proposes for the freedom required for moral responsibility:

> OFW: A person acts of her own free will if and only if her action issues from the will with which she identifies by means of a higher-order volition.

Susan Wolf (1990) has labeled Frankfurt's theory a *Real Self* view, since the core idea is that free and morally responsible agency is a matter of actions issuing from one's real or deep self. The idea is that when the desire that moves an agent to action is not one with which she identifies in the way Frankfurt specifies, her conduct is alien to her. She is then impeded by another desire in a manner analogous to how classical compatibilists held that external impediments, like shackles, impede agents.

9.3.   Three Challenges to Frankfurt's Hierarchical Theory

Frankfurt's argument against the alternative possibilities requirement (Chapter 5) has had a considerable influence on contemporary work on free will and moral responsibility. We will set these matters aside here, as we have already discussed them. In this chapter, we will examine three aspects of Frankfurt's positive theory of source freedom as expressed in OFW.

9.3.1.   Manipulation Arguments

One objection to Frankfurt's theory focuses upon the sufficient condition specified in OFW. Don Locke (1975), Derk Pereboom (1995, 2001), and Robert Kane (1996) have challenged Frankfurt by devising manipulation arguments (see Section 7.4) featuring examples tailor-made to satisfy Frankfurt's compatibilist conditions. In each case, an agent is covertly manipulated into acquiring the specified mesh of second-order volition, will, and action. Yet, due to the pervasive nature of the manipulation, it is contended that the agent does not act (or will) freely and is not morally responsible.

More recently, Fischer and Ravizza (1998), Haji (1998), and Mele (1995, 2006b) have pressed the point as it bears on Frankfurt's commitment to a *non-historical* theory. To illustrate, consider Mele's (1995: 145–6) case of two agents, Ann and Beth (discussed in Section 8.6). Ann comes to be who she is under her own steam. But Beth, who was not anything like Ann, is unknowingly converted overnight by a team of neuroscientists into a psychological duplicate of Ann. Suppose that Ann then acts freely and is morally responsible for what she does in virtue of her satisfying the sufficient conditions Frankfurt proposes. Frankfurt is forced to say that when Beth acts just as Ann does, Beth acts freely and is morally responsible for her conduct immediately following the manipulation. But, Mele argues, this is the wrong result, and to the extent that we are inclined to say that Ann is morally responsible while Beth is not, we have evidence that our concept of moral responsibility has an *historical* dimension lacking in Frankfurt's OFW (Mele 1995: 146, 2006b: 170–2).

In response to such historical worries, Frankfurt remains defiant (1975), affirming nonhistoricism together with its *prima facie* counterintuitive implications:

> What we need most essentially to look at is, rather, certain aspects of the psychic structure that is coincident with the person's behavior.... It is irrelevant whether [the causes to which we are subject] are operating by virtue of the natural forces that shape our environment or whether they operate through the deliberate manipulative designs of other human agents. We are the sorts of persons we are; and it is what we are, rather than the history of our development, that counts. (Frankfurt 2002: 27–8 [our brackets])

A number of philosophers find the price Frankfurt is willing to pay too high, and thus conclude that either there must be a compatibilist-friendly way to distinguish between freedom-destroying histories and freedom-allowing ones, or compatibilism must be shelved. Whether that is the correct conclusion, what is clear is that Frankfurt's exclusive reliance on the resources of his mesh theory forecloses his ability to append a compatibilist-friendly historical requirement to OFW.

9.3.2.   Accounting for Freedom with an Unharmonious Mesh

A second type of objection to Frankfurt's theory focuses on the necessary condition specified in OFW (e.g., Haji, 2002; Pereboom, 2001: 106, n. 34). Consider another case of Frankfurt's, the case of the *unwilling addict* (17–18). The unwilling addict's will is not the will she wants because she has a second-order volition to will to refrain from taking the narcotic, and this is a second-order volition that constitutes identification. When she takes the narcotic anyway, she therefore does not act of her own free will, as OFW tells us. But how can Frankfurt distinguish this case from that of the *weak-willed non-addict*, who judges it best, all things considered, that she not take the narcotic, and in light of her judgment about what is best, forms a second-order volition for her will to be constituted by her first-order desire not to take the narcotic. Nevertheless, she has a first-order desire to take the narcotic, which, while not irresistible, is quite strong. In this case it seems that she can take the drug of her own free will and be morally responsible for her action. But given OFW, since she is acting contrary to the will she identifies with by way of a second-order volition, she *ipso facto* does not act of her own free will. However, this would seem to count against OFW. For it would seem better to deny that OFW gets the necessary conditions for acting of one's own free will and for being morally responsible right than to conclude that the weak-willed non-addict does not act of her own free will and is not morally responsible.

Frankfurt could retreat to a revised and weaker version of OFW, i.e.:

> OFW-sufficient: A person acts of her own free will *if* her action issues from the will with which she identifies by means of a higher-order volition.

This, unlike OFW, offers only a sufficient and not also a necessary condition for acting of one's own free will. But he then lacks an account for free will and moral responsibility in the case of weakness of will. For weak-willed actions do not issue from the will with which the agent identifies by means of a higher-order volition, and yet weak-willed agents apparently can act of their own free will in the sense required for moral responsibility. The problem is especially puzzling in light of Frankfurt's remark that his model "lends itself in fairly obvious ways to the articulation and explication of ... weakness of the will" (1987, as reprinted in 1988: 165). More worrisome, if some distinct account of freedom could explain how a weak-willed agent might act of her own free will and be morally responsible, it would very likely provide an appealing basis for explaining an agent's freedom even when her will is aligned in Frankfurt's preferred manner. This in turn would cast doubt, not on the truth, but on the explanatory relevance of OFW-sufficient.

9.3.3. Explaining Identification

A third objection to Frankfurt's theory is that a crucial ingredient in OFW—identification—obscures rather than illuminates the nature of free will. Watson was the first to press this point (1975). Faced with the prospect of potential conflicts among higher-order desires, as explained above (Section 9.2), Frankfurt appealed to the notion of identification via an agent's decisive commitments. He thereby claimed to specify which desires are truly one's own and thus implicated in one's free will, and which desires are alienated from oneself. But, Watson asks:

> What gives these volitions any special relation to "oneself"? It is unhelpful to answer that one makes a "decisive commitment," where this just means that an interminable ascent to higher orders is not going to be permitted. This *is* arbitrary. (1975 as reprinted in Watson, 2003: 349)

Several of Frankfurt's subsequent papers include attempts to offer a satisfactory answer to Watson's challenge.

In one response, Frankfurt specifies that identification involves two ingredients: an *unopposed* second-order volition to act in accord with a first-order desire, and a *judgment* that any further deliberation would be unnecessary (1987, as reprinted in 1988: 168–9). Later, Frankfurt appealed to the distinction between *activity* and *passivity* (1992b as reprinted in 1999: 87). When a person is active, she determines what her will shall be, thereby rendering pertinent desires internal. When her will is being acted on by desires, those desires are external to her and she is passive with respect to them (1994 as reprinted in 1999: 132–3). On yet another proposal, *satisfaction* does the work (1992a as reprinted in 1999: 105). Satisfaction requires,

> no adoption of any cognitive, attitudinal, affective, or intentional stance. It does not require the performance of a particular act; and it also does not require any deliberate abstention. Satisfaction is a state of the entire psychic system—a state constituted by the absence of any tendency or inclination to alter its condition. (104)

In this passage, Frankfurt clearly departs from his earlier (1987) judgment requirement. Satisfaction, it seems, is to be understood merely negatively in relation to a person, construed as a "psychic system."[7]

Frankfurt's reliance on satisfaction offers a reply to another objection to his notion of identification closely related to Watson's. In his treatment of Frankfurt's earlier work, David Velleman (1992) contends that a person, if she is to be the *agent* of her actions, must stand in the right kind of relation to her desires. Otherwise, she is merely a passive witness to their place in the causal nexus of her psychic life. Many libertarians appeal to the notion of agent causation at this point, which they conceive as involving causation fundamentally by the agent as a substance, in a way that precludes reduction to event causation (see Chapter 10). Velleman, like Frankfurt, wants to avoid such a move. But, in keeping with Watson's challenge to Frankfurt, Velleman objects that invoking the notion of identification in the absence of further clarification is merely a label for the problem of accounting for an agent's involvement in the efficacy of her desires in the right way, which is the very problem that needs to be solved (1992: 474). Velleman himself proposes that we functionally identify the agent with a master-desire or motive, in particular, the desire to act in accord with the best reasons (1992: 478–80). Frankfurt, however, as revealed in the above quotation, opts for a different strategy. An agent is not to be identified with any element within a psychic system, such as a master desire; the agent *is* the system. When, on Frankfurt's view, is the system properly functioning as an agent? This is to be answered exclusively in terms of the negative condition of satisfaction: when there is an absence of any tendency or inclination to alter its condition.

Much rides on Frankfurt's notion of identification. Without it, he arguably has no reply to Watson's original challenge. With it, he cements his real self view; it is the very basis by which the agent, qua real self, gets into the act, as Velleman would require. It thus seems unsatisfying for Frankfurt to offer no more than the assertion of a negative condition on an agent as a psychic system—satisfaction—as the only ingredient beyond the interplay of desires.

A considerable amount of interesting philosophical work has been devoted to providing further support for Frankfurt's notion of identification.[8] We'll not pursue that matter further here.

9.4.   Watson's Structural Mesh Theory

Not long after Frankfurt presented the initial formulation of his hierarchical theory, Gary Watson proposed an alternative model (1975). Like Frankfurt, Watson was interested in accounting for free agency in terms of a mesh between different elements within an agent's psychic structure. He offered a model based on a Platonic conception wherein judgment and evaluation can be a source of motivation. Watson contends that the proper way to account for an agent who acts freely and who identifies with the sources of her agency is not in terms of a mesh located in hierarchies of desires. It is, rather, a mesh between different systems within an agent: her *motivational system*, which is influenced by elements such as one's appetitive desires; and her *valuational system*, whereby an agent judges what she takes to be valuable, good, or desirable (1975, as reprinted in Watson, 2003: 346–8). A free agent is one whose motivational system works in harmony with her valuational system (347). On Watson's account, if anything is to do the work of identification, it is an agent's valuational system (350). The valuational system can, however, be plagued by motivations that oppose the agent's values; these motivations can result in an agent acting unfreely by acting contrary to what she values.[9]

One advantage Watson claims for his mesh theory over Frankfurt's is that it more accurately captures the nature of practical judgment (350). Agents normally deliberate about what to do, and about what it is best to do, not what first-order desires they would like to be the ones on which they would act. Watson seems plain right about this, though perhaps there is some reason to retain a commitment to a hierarchical ingredient in a mesh theory (e.g., Bratman, 2005, as reprinted in 2007: 213–16). In particular, some deliberation is distinctively devoted to questions of self-formation captured by such expressions as "making something of oneself."

While Watson's mesh theory differs from Frankfurt's in the ways just noted, there are also several points of similarity, which invite some of the same objections raised against Frankfurt's view. Watson's proposal is equally susceptible to challenges of manipulation cases as is Frankfurt's, and Watson has explicitly registered his concurrence with Frankfurt's defiant stance against this challenge (Watson, 1999, as reprinted in Watson, 2004: 211–13). Some might also think that the same worry applies regarding an act's status as free when it does not issue from a harmonious mesh. If the harmony is not only sufficient but necessary for exercises of free will, we get the result that there is no weakness of will insofar as this requires *freely* acting contrary to one's judgment of what it is best to do. However, this seems not to be regarded by Watson as a problem. He has argued for skepticism about weakness of will on just the point that agents do not freely act contrary to their evaluative judgments about what is best to do (Watson, 1977). Nevertheless, though Watson does not develop the point, it appears that on his view the harmony is *not* necessary. As he sees it, unfree agents are not those who merely do not act in accord with their valuational edicts, but rather are unable to do so (1975, as reprinted in Watson, 2003: 347–8). Finally, as Velleman has pointed out (1992: 472), Watson's appeal to a valuational system is susceptible to the same sort of objection that he (Watson) put to Frankfurt. Why take an agent's judgment issuing from her valuational system to be the source of who she is, what she identifies with, and hence, the spring of her free action? Watson himself anticipates this objection, though he does not offer any suggestions as to how to overcome it (1987, as reprinted in Watson, 2004: 167–9).

9.5.   Bratman's Planning Theory

In a series of papers, Michael Bratman has embraced the problem framed by the controversy between Frankfurt and Watson (e.g., see Bratman, 1997, 2003, 2004, 2005, 2007).[10] Bratman offers a distinctive answer to Velleman's (1992) challenge that identification be explained in a way that satisfactorily accounts for an agent's role in action (Bratman, 2003). He draws upon his planning theory of intentions, a theory that accounts for intentions as embedded in larger plans. An agent's actions are intentional in virtue of plans into which her intentions fit. My intention to head to the local pub, for instance, is understood as an intention in relation to my plan of meeting my friends there for an evening of good cheer. Here we have a kind of meshing of one element, an intention, within wider aspects of agency, a plan. While this is not itself a matter of hierarchy, it is sug- gestive that at a more primitive level of agency, mere planning agency, a kind of mesh is required for agents to get about in the world, to make today's activities gel with tomorrow's travel plans, and to make tomorrow's travel plans conform with the unexpected contingencies that tomorrow might turn up. We can then account for morally responsible agency by building upon these resources (Bratman, 1997).

Turning directly to the question of what psychic elements have agential authority to speak for an agent, for her identifications, Bratman looks, not as Frankfurt does to higher-order desires, nor as Watson does to evaluative judg- ments, but instead to higher-order intentions construed as self-governing policies of practical reasoning (Bratman, 2004, as reprinted in 2007: 239). These policies involve an agent's diachronic commitments to managing her life in ways that allow her to be effective in carrying out other plans and intentions. A commit- ment to work hard after dinner, for example, will constrain other potential plans. It will be given a ranking priority that will help the agent organize and control her life over considerable stretches of time. Such a self-governing policy will be hierarchical, though in a way that differs from Frankfurt's. It will be hierarchical insofar as it will govern (by constraining or fostering) other plans that are liable to arise in the course of a life (240–3). But, why will such a self-governing policy, as opposed to other candidate features of agency such as higher-order desires or valuations, have the authority to speak for the agent? Bratman's answer is that it will bind the agent's activities across time with the same threads that bind her identity across time (243–9).

How does Bratman's proposal fare in response to the objections put to Frankfurt's and Watson's accounts? He can respond differently to relevant cases of manipulation. Bratman's theory is transparently historical. Along with other historical compatibilists, he can say that agents manipulated as, for example, Mele's Beth is, are not free or responsible. Is Bratman able to account for an agent's freely acting contrary to her identification-conferring higher-order policies, that is, in the context of an unharmonious Bratmanian mesh? Or is he forced to conclude that in such cases the agent never acts freely and is never morally responsible? It is unclear. We'll not pursue the matter, but note that Bratman, like Frankfurt and Watson, faces the burden of addressing this charge.

What of the criticism that identification is left unaccounted for? On this point, it appears that Bratman has made progress. By linking the conditions of identification to conditions of agency, we get what he calls a nonhomuncular account of the agent's playing a role in her agency. One might contend that the advantage by which Bratman is able to make progress also gives rise to an objection. His view relies on a particular formulation of a Lockean account of personal identity, one in which certain higher-order self-governing policies are crucial to constituting an agent's identity. An agent who would reject relevant policies and act contrary to them would appear to do so only at the expense of suffering an identity-destroying change.[11]

9.6. Reasons-Responsive Theories: An Initial Characterization

Recall the problem facing classical compatibilist accounts of freedom noted above—they had inadequate resources to explain how freedom can be undermined from within an agent's own mental life (Section 9.1). As we've seen, mesh theories aim to correct for this deficiency by the complexity of psychological structure internal to the agent. A distinct strategy that also attempts to account for freedom in terms of the unimpaired functioning of normal human agency instead asks whether the relationship between agent and action involves a sufficiently rational link. Is the agent, by way of the motivational states and deliberative processes leading to action, sufficiently sensitive to rational considerations? An agent acting on compulsive disorders, phobias, addictions, or psychotic episodes (all problems for the classical compatibilist) might not be suitably sensitive to rational considerations, to the reasons she has to act. The compulsive hand-washer washes her hands when she has a good reason to do so, but also when she has no good reason to do so, and even when she has an overwhelmingly good reason not to do so. Her behavior is disjointed from a spectrum of reasons that would otherwise lead to the free, unimpaired exercise of her deliberative agency. Views that account for free will and moral responsibility by sensitivity to reasons are called *reasons-responsive theories*.

Reasons-responsive theories have roots in the Aristotelian idea that the human being is a rational animal, one that when mature can appreciate and be sensitive to good reasons about how to live well, and how to make informed decisions.[12] In recent times, a number of philosophers have adopted some version of a reasons-responsive theory, usually but not always in defense of compatibilism.[13] We have already canvassed three theses that can broadly be construed as reasons-responsive theories. One was Dennett's multiple viewpoints compatibilism. As we explained (Section 8.4), according to Dennett, free will consists in the ability of a person to control her behavior in light of rational considerations, something that complex beings as evolved intentional, conscious systems eventually are able to do. Although he did not develop a reasons-responsiveness theory of moral responsibility in detail, he was clearly committed to the general thesis. Two other philosophers we've already considered also defend a reasons-responsive theory, Wolf (1990) and Nelkin (2011). Their respective views are distinctive insofar as responsiveness is understood in terms of a domain of reasons in accord with which an agent should aim to act. For Wolf, this is understood in terms of the True and the Good. For Nelkin, it is understood in terms of good reasons.

In the upcoming sections, we will focus primarily on Fischer and Ravizza's reasons-responsive theory, as theirs is the most comprehensive, has been the most influential, and has instigated a vast secondary literature.

9.7. Fischer and Ravizza's Reasons-Responsive Theory

Fischer and Ravizza advance a version of the reasons-responsive view they call *semicompatibilism* (1998: 51). This is the thesis that determinism is, or at least might be, incompatible with leeway freedom, but is compatible with source freedom. They characterize each of these freedoms in terms of control. *Regulative control* requires the ability to do otherwise; *guidance control* does not. Instead, guidance control is a source notion characterized in terms of the agent's rational capacities, in particular her responsiveness to reasons. Regulative control and leeway freedom are not required for moral responsibility, they argue, since Frankfurt's argument against the alternative possibilities requirement is successful.

On its face, a reasons-responsive view is ill-suited for theorists who endorse Frankfurt's argument. A natural way to specify that an agent is responsive to reasons is that her actions are motivated by the reasons relevant to her situation and available to her, and if there had been such reasons sufficient for refraining from an action, she would have refrained instead and thus would have acted otherwise. But in Frankfurt examples (Chapter 5), agents seem not to be responsive to reasons in this way. If sufficient reasons for refraining from the action had been presented to them, these agents would not be able to act otherwise, due to the presence of the intervener or intervention device. But Fischer and Ravizza contend that, despite this hurdle, Frankfurt's argument can be wedded to a reasons-responsiveness analysis.

How so? The freedom an agent exercises in a Frankfurt example is solely a matter of guidance control, and this control is a matter of the actual sequence of events leading to action. It is irrelevant what alternative courses of action are open to such an agent. To give what Fischer and Ravizza call an *actual-sequence* analysis of guidance control (53), we need to focus on the psychological processes of the agent that are actually causally implicated in her bringing about her action—Fischer and Ravizza call these the *mechanism* of her action (39). They propose that we attend first of all to the actual-sequence mechanism and the properties it has. Some of these properties will be dispositional or modal properties (53). It will be true to say of the agent's mechanism, that, if sufficient reasons to do otherwise had been presented, *and if the mechanism had operated unimpeded*, then it would have responded differently.

But notice, to test the truth of these counterfactuals we have to examine possible worlds in which the pertinent mechanism operates unimpeded. The worlds we examine won't feature Frankfurt's intervening device. The result is that in a Frankfurt example, an *agent* per se is *not* responsive to reasons: Due to the presence of the intervener's device she cannot do otherwise in the presence of good reasons to do otherwise. But the idea is that we can still say that the agent acts with guidance control, *insofar* as she acts from a *mechanism* that is responsive to the relevant reasons. Thus, on this view, the agent is reasons-responsive only by virtue of such a reasons-responsive mechanism.

Crucial to Fischer and Razizza's theory is that responsiveness to reasons comes in degrees. A mechanism is *strongly reasons-responsive* if it would always respond in accord with sufficient reasons, so given sufficient reasons to do otherwise, it would invariably respond with an alternative action (41). This, however, is too strong as a requirement for the freedom relevant to moral responsibility. When agents act badly, they often do not act on sufficient reasons. And in one kind of case of weakness of will, an agent fails to act on reasons that she recognizes as sufficient. Thus the strong notion would rule out responsibility for much immoral action and for weak-willed action.

By contrast, a mechanism is *weakly reasons-responsive* if it would respond differently to at least one reason to do otherwise. Thus, it would at least sometimes respond in accord with sufficient reasons, so given sufficient reasons to do otherwise, it would at least sometimes respond with an alternative action (44). Fischer endorsed this criterion for moral responsibility early on (e.g., 1987, 1994) but he came to recognize that it is too weak. Insane agents who by no means act from mechanisms that are appropriately responsive to reasons might well act from mechanisms that are sensitive to some minimal range of sufficient reasons to do otherwise. An agent might even act from a mechanism responsive to quite a range of sufficient reasons, but the range might reveal no sane or stable pattern (65–8). What is required, Fischer and Ravizza argue, is action from a *moderately reasons-responsive* mechanism (69–76).

The account of moderate reasons-responsiveness Fischer and Ravizza set out has two key elements, a *receptivity* component and a *reactivity* component. Receptivity is the capacity to recognize and evaluate a spectrum of reasons for action, while reactivity is the capacity to act in accord with such recognition and evaluation of reasons. Significantly, Fischer and Ravizza's proposal involves an asymmetry. Guidance control, they contend, requires *regularly receptivity* of a mechanism to reasons, but only its *weak reactivity* to reasons. To capture the spectrum of reasons to which an agent's mechanism must be regularly receptive, they specify that that spectrum exhibit a pattern of rational stability (70–1). It must also pass a sanity test, such that a third-party inquirer could come to understand the pattern of reasons the agent would accept (71–2). Also, some of the reasons must be minimally moral, which is needed to rule out smart animals, very young children, and, perhaps, psychopaths (76–81). As for reactivity, Fischer and Ravizza argue that it is sufficient that an agent act from a mechanism such that there is just one possible world in which that mechanism operates and the agent reacts differently to a sufficient reason to do otherwise (73). They also argue that "reactivity is all of a piece" (73). That is, a mechanism's reacting to a sufficient reason to do otherwise in some possible world establishes that mechanisms of this type have the general capacity to react differently to any sufficient reason to do otherwise.

There is one further essential element in Fischer and Ravizza's specification of moderate reasons-responsiveness, and thus in their preferred notion of guidance control. In order for an agent to exercise this sort of control, the mechanism on which she acts must *be her own*. This ownership condition is meant to ensure that the agent's mechanism is not alien to her, that it was not, for example, installed by means of brainwashing or covert electronic manipulation. Ownership features three conditions. First, the agent must come to view herself, when acting from relevant mechanisms, as an agent, capable of shaping the world by her choices and actions. Second, she must see herself as an apt target of others' moral expectations and demands as revealed in the reactive attitudes. Third, the beliefs satisfying the first two conditions must be based, in an appropriate way, on the individual's evidence (238).

Fischer and Ravizza's ownership condition introduces a historical element into their account. This distinguishes their view from, for example, Frankfurt's nonhistorical theory, and allows them to argue that in relevant cases of manipulation, such as that of Mele's Beth discussed above (Section 3.1, and Section 8.6), the agent is not morally responsible.

9.8.   Three Challenges to Fischer and Ravizza's Theory

There are a few features of Fischer and Ravizza's complete theory of moral responsibility we will not take up here, since we have devoted considerable attention to these topics already. One is their contribution to the debate over Frankfurt's attack on leeway freedom (e.g., Fischer, 2002). Another is their effort to establish the resilience of the Consequence Argument (e.g., Fischer, 2004; Fischer and Ravizza, 1998; Ravizza, 1994). A third is their objections against the source incompatibilists' Direct Argument. In this section, we will focus instead on three important challenges to their position.

9.8.1.   Receptivity and Reactivity

Patrick Todd and Neal Tognazzini contend that there is a missing element in Fischer and Ravizza's account of receptivity (Todd and Tognazzini, 2008). As Fischer and Ravizza formulate the view, it is possible that an agent act from a mechanism that is regularly receptive to a number of reasons to do otherwise, but is *not* receptive to the *actual* moral reasons to do otherwise that are present in her context of action—the agent, by way of her mechanism, is incapable of recognizing the force of these pertinent reasons. Todd and Tognazzini would appear to be right to argue that such an agent is not morally responsible. Indeed, their worry is of a piece with what motivates philosophers like Wolf (1990) and Nelkin (2011) to explain reasons-responsiveness in a way that secures sensitivity to good reasons. Accordingly, Todd and Tognazzini propose an amendment to Fischer and Ravizza's view: Receptivity should include not just an appropriately sane pattern of reasons-recognition, but also receptivity to the *actual* moral reasons bearing on her context of action.

Now consider reactivity. Fischer and Ravizza claim that, so long as an agent's mechanism is reactive to just one sufficient reason to do otherwise in some possible world, this confirms their "reactivity is all of a piece" thesis according to which the agent, via her mechanism, has the general capacity to react differently to any reason to do otherwise. But this seems to allow for guidance control cases in which an agent is patently unfree (e.g., McKenna, 2005a; Mele, 2000, 2006a; Russell, 2002a; Watson, 2001). For instance, Mele offers the case of an agoraphobic incapable of leaving his house even to attend his daughter's wedding, though he would leave it if it were set on fire (2000, 2006a). Fischer and Ravizza's thesis would specify that this agoraphobic has the general capacity to react differently to any reason to leave the house, which would appear incorrect. The upshot is that what Fischer and Ravizza need, as McKenna has put it (2005a), is not regular receptivity and weak reactivity, but instead regular receptivity and weak*er* reactivity (see also Pereboom, 2006b). This allows them to make room for cases in which a blameworthy agent recognizes sufficient moral reasons to do otherwise but does not act on them. In response to these objections (especially Mele's formulation), Fischer has conceded the point and now accepts the proposed emendation (2005: 154 n. 3).

9.8.2.   Mechanisms and Agents

Fischer and Ravizza admit that they have no principle for mechanism individuation whereby, when we "hold fixed" the mechanism across possible worlds, we can identify that very same mechanism in other possible worlds. They instead rely upon an intuitive notion of sameness (Fischer and Ravizza, 1998: 40). Several critics have objected to this element of their account (Judisch, 2005; McKenna, 2001; Shabo, 2005; Watson, 2001). At a crucial juncture, Fischer and Ravizza consider an objection that focuses on a non-addict who acts from a particular mechanism in taking a drug and who would refrain from doing so only due to certain especially strong reasons not to take it. He would refrain because he would get more "energy or focus" in the face of these strong reasons (1998: 74). The drug user, the objection contends, is not reactive to most reasons not to take the drug, and so is not morally responsible for taking it, despite the fact that he would respond to an especially strong incentive. This would then suggest—contrary to Fischer and Ravizza—that reactivity is *not* all of a piece, and thus that reactivity to *some* reasons to do otherwise does not confirm a mechanism's general capacity to react to *all* reasons to do otherwise. Fischer and Ravizza's reply is to claim that, while such cases are possible, in the scenario in which such an agent gets more energy or focus, a different mechanism is at work (74). However, the worry is that they have no principled basis for mechanism individuation, and thus it is hard to see what could license their contention (McKenna, 2001). Why couldn't an agent act from the same mechanism and get more energy or focus only in the presence of (for example) especially strong reasons? Indeed, this seems to describe Mele's case of the agoraphobic.[14]

On the matter of mechanism individuation, Ishtiyaque Haji's similar reasons-responsive compatibilist theory compares favorably (1998). Haji also develops an actual sequence, reasons-responsive view, and considers which aspects of an agent are to be held fixed in settling whether, in acting as she did, she was appropriately reasons-responsive. He proposes that what we hold fixed is an agent's proximal desire, the one immediately preceding action, and also the motivational base from which this desire gains its relative strength (1998: 75–8). In the case of Mele's agoraphobic, we would get the right result: Set the house on fire and you're bound to alter his motivation base. Nevertheless, when evaluating whether he is reasons-responsive in remaining in his house and not attending his daughter's wedding, holding fixed his actual desires and motivational base (and thinking about this as at least partially constitutive of his mechanism), if no reasons would persuade him to leave, it seems his phobia can be regarded as freedom-defeating, which yields the proper result.

Some might see haggling over the details of mechanism individuation as involving minutia with little bearing on Fischer and Ravizza's larger enterprise. That would be a mistake. The viability of their view depends on this notion. Without it, they cannot give a mechanism-based account of reasons-responsiveness. But by their own lights, they cannot, as some have advised they should (e.g., Ginet, 2006), fall back on an agent-based account without having to concede that agents in Frankfurt examples are not reasons-responsive. And without the contention that agents in Frankfurt examples are reasons-responsive, they cannot analyze guidance control (source freedom, as we would put it) just in terms of reasons-responsiveness.

There are two options for Fischer and Ravizza and other reasons-responsive theorists, if the costs of retaining a mechanism-based theory are too high. One is to agree to an *agent-based* reasons-responsive theory and also to commit to leeway freedom as a requirement on moral responsibility. Nelkin's and Wolf's positions (Section 8.5) count as examples of such a view. More recently, in coauthored work with David Brink, Nelkin has developed in more detail the conditions of reasons-responsiveness along these lines—while also explaining receptivity and reactivity features in ways that resemble Fischer and Ravizza's approach (Brink and Nelkin, 2013). For those convinced by Nelkin's rejection of Frankfurt's argument and her defense of leeway freedom, this looks to be a viable way to advance a reasons-responsive theory.

An alternative strategy (McKenna, 2013; Sartorio, 2016) argues that an agent-based reasons-responsive theory is after all consistent with Frankfurt examples. This would require showing, contrary to what Fischer and Ravizza contend, that agents in Frankfurt examples (rather than their mechanisms of action) are reasons-responsive. We will turn to those strategies below.

9.8.3.   Counterfactuals and their Relevance to Source Freedom

One intriguing recent debate concerns a dispute between *source compatibilists* like Fischer and Ravizza, who rely only upon source freedom, and contemporary *leeway compatibilists* such as Michael Smith (2003), Kadri Vihvelin (2004), and Michael Fara (2008), who argue that the freedom to do otherwise is required for moral responsibility. (We will consider Vihvelin's view in a later section.) An especially contested topic concerns the status of the sorts of counterfactuals Fischer and Ravizza employ to analyze the reasons-responsiveness of a mechanism. On their view, to test a mechanism for reasons-responsiveness in Frankfurt examples, we go to possible worlds in which the intervener is not present and ask whether, supposing sufficient reasons to do otherwise were put to the agent and the pertinent mechanism were operative, the agent would respond differently. These leeway compatibilists, however, contend that the truth of such counterfactuals confirm that an *agent* acting freely in a Frankfurt example *is* able to do otherwise.[15] They argue that the counterfactual intervention merely functions as a *would-be mask* of that ability, and an ability or disposition being merely counterfactually masked allows the ability to persist. In a Frankfurt example, were the agent about to do otherwise, the intervention would occur, at which time the agent would be prevented from exercising the ability to do otherwise and may even be correctly said to lose it. But when the agent is acting as she does, and the intervener remains dormant, that agent retains the ability to act otherwise, and thus has leeway freedom.[16]

Randolph Clarke (2008) argues that although there may be such general abilities an agent in a Frankfurt example retains, there is another key capacity she lacks. While the agent may retain the general ability to do otherwise, due to the presence of the intervener it is *not up to her* to exercise this ability. The salient question, then, is what is really at stake in this dispute—is it an agent's having a general ability to do otherwise, or its being up to the agent in a context to exercise such an ability? (We touched on this briefly in our chapter on Frankfurt's argument—Section 5.5.)

9.9. McKenna's and Sartorio's Agent-Based Reasons-Responsive Source Theories

Michael McKenna (2013) and Carolina Sartorio (2016) have each developed agent-based, reasons-responsiveness theories, while, unlike Nelkin, retaining allegiance to source compatibilism. Each offers arguments to show how in the context of a Frankfurt example an agent can be reasons-responsive—and most crucially—*reactive* to reasons to do otherwise. The hurdle for both McKenna and Sartorio is that, as Fischer and Ravizza would put it, in a Frankfurt example an agent will not be reactive to sufficient reasons to do otherwise because even if such reasons were present and the agent was receptive to them, the agent would *not* react otherwise by acting any differently. The intervener would take over.

McKenna (2013) attempts to avoid this problem by distinguishing between an agent's reacting otherwise by acting differently in a Frankfurt example and reacting otherwise by *not* acting upon the reasons she otherwise would act upon. The former is ruled out in a Frankfurt example, but, McKenna argues, the latter is not. To explain, recall the case of Black, Jones, and Smith. Suppose that, as things happen, Jones shoots Smith on his own while Black waits secretly in the wings, doing nothing. Now add further details about Jones's reasons-responsiveness. Suppose that Jones is an aptly reasons-responsive agent in the manner that accords roughly with the requirements Fischer and Ravizza identify (setting aside the mechanism route). Among the reasons to which Jones would be responsive include Smith's having his child with him at the time—let's suppose this might easily have been the case. Were Smith's child with him, and were Black not present, Jones would not shoot Smith, as Jones would respond to a reason not to shoot Smith (sparing the child a horrible experience). As Fischer and Ravizza see it, *with* Black present, Jones—the agent—is *not* reasons-responsive because he would *not* react to this reason (not to shoot Smith) by *acting* otherwise. Black would cause Jones to shoot Smith. But McKenna proposes that in the scenario in which Black intervenes, Jones *is* differentially reactive to reasons to do otherwise, and this is so even if it is not manifested in Jones's acting otherwise. How so? The presence of the reasons including worries about Smith's child are such that Jones *does not* react to them by acting for his own reasons to kill Smith. Indeed, this is so whether or not Black is present. That is a kind of reactivity—not one leading all the way to action—but reactivity all the same.

Sartorio (2016) has proposed what seems to be a simpler and more elegant way to avoid the problem Fischer and Ravizza identify for agent-based, reasons-responsive, source compatibilist theories. She argues that the absence of a reason can be part of the actual cause of why an agent acts as she does. As such, contra Fischer and Ravizza, it is not true that, for an agent to be responsive and reactive to reasons to do otherwise in the context of a Frankfurt example, it must be that if those reasons were present she would have reacted otherwise. It is enough that the *absence* of the reasons plays a causal role in an agent's *actually* acting as she does. So, for instance, on Sartorio's view, given the supplemented case of Jones proposed in the previous paragraph, when Jones shoots Smith on his own in the actual sequence while Black remains inactive, Jones is actually reactive to the reason: Smith's being accompanied by his child. How so? The absence of this reason is one of the actual causes of Jones shooting Smith, and it is by virtue of causation by the absence of this reason that Jones is reactive to it.

9.10. Contemporary Leeway Theories

We turn now to contemporary proposals that focus primarily on establishing the compatibility of determinism and leeway freedom. Thus far, we have already discussed several compatibilist theories that endorse a leeway freedom condition and offer some argument for the compatibility of leeway freedom and determinism. These include the views advanced by Scanlon (1998), Bok (1998), Dennett (1984, 2003), Wolf (1990), Nelkin (2011), and Watson (1975). These views, however, do not take up the project of arguing for compatibilism about leeway freedom by focusing directly on a distinct set of metaphysical and semantic issues that are characteristic of the type of position we will now consider.[17] Views in this class include those of Michael Smith (2003), Kadri Vihvelin (2004, 2013), and Michael Fara (2008).[18] Because Vihvelin's is most thoroughly developed, we will examine it in some detail in the next section.

This strategy returns to a collection of traditional topics familiar to classical compatibilists like Hume and later Schlick, Ayer, and Hobart. Take the topic of laws, for instance. One strategy for advancing compatibilism is to offer a deflationary Humean view of the laws according to which they are generalizations regarding how the course of events actually unfolds. Or consider the classic compatibilist move of showing that causation is distinct from coercion or compulsion, so that coming to understand the causes of one's intentions is not a matter of discovering what forces or compels those actions.

One strategy for defending leeway compatibilism involves attending to two metaphysical issues. A first concerns the metaphysics of causation and the natural laws that pertain to causal relations. Compatibilists shoulder the burden of explaining how these laws, understood within a deterministic system, and the nature of causation itself, are not freedom-defeating. A second metaphysical issue concerns the nature of abilities of free agents and how they might be realized and exercised in deterministic contexts. Are they to be understood as powers, dispositions, or in terms of intrinsic states of an agent? Along with these two metaphysical issues, a further task is to offer a credible semantics that shows how we can make ability-to-do-otherwise claims consistent with claims about the causal determination of all actions. Another project draws upon these resources to identify the point where the Consequence Argument and others like it fail.

Some compatibilists, for example, Oisin Deery (2015), Terry Horgan (2015), and Eddy Nahmias et al. (2004), have joined to the preceding project the further recommendation of attending to the phenomenology of agency. They argue that in view of the phenomenology, understanding of our agency as free is best explained in terms of our ability to choose among options, and this provides reason to accept leeway compatibilism.

9.11. Vihvelin's New Dispositionalism

Vihvelin develops a sophisticated compatibilist theory of free will that revives a conception that had largely been set aside for half a century, one that attempts to reconcile causal determination with our being able to do otherwise from how we in fact act. As we saw in Chapter 3, this tradition, developed with intensity during the first half of the twentieth century by philosophers such as G.E. Moore, R.E. Hobart, and A.J. Ayer, features a family of compatibilist conditions on free will. Most prominently, these philosophers, following Hobbes, Locke, and Hume, advocate a conditional account of the ability to do otherwise. In Hume's version, to be free in the sense at issue, an agent must satisfy the following criterion: "by liberty, then, we can only mean a power of acting or not acting according to the determinations of the will—that is, *if we choose to remain at rest, we may; if we choose to also move, we also may*" (*Enquiry Concerning Human Understanding*, §8). G.E. Moore advanced a view of this type, arguing that to say that I could have acted otherwise is to claim that *I would have acted otherwise if I had so chosen*. The satisfaction of this condition is compatible with causal determination: even if I am causally determined to act as I do, it might still be true that I would have acted otherwise if I had so chosen to act.

Again, such conditional analyses of "could have done otherwise" were contested in the mid-twentieth century by C.D. Broad (1934), C.A. Campbell (1951), and especially forcefully in the 1960s by Roderick Chisholm (1967) and Keith Lehrer (1968, 1976). As a result of these criticisms, and of Frankfurt's challenge to the alternative possibility requirement for free will and moral responsibility (see the discussion below), compatibilist positions of this type were almost completely abandoned. More specifically, compatibilists largely rejected the alternative possibilities requirement on free will, and instead advanced a view in which this requirement has no role.

The following is the most prominent type of objection to the conditional analysis. Suppose Brown does not at some time t jump in the sea to save a drowning child, and we say:

(1) Brown could have jumped into the sea at t.

A proponent of conditional analysis proposes that (1) is equivalent to:

(2) If Brown had chosen to jump into the sea at t, he would have jumped into the sea at t.

(Variants of (2) substitute for "chosen": "willed," "tried," "set himself," or "wanted.") Chisholm argues that this sort of analysis is subject to a counterexample of the following form. Suppose that the sea is very cold, and Brown knows it, and as a result it is psychologically impossible for him to choose to jump into the sea. But we might suppose that if he did choose to jump, he would actually jump. Thus here (2) is true, and yet it is intuitive that (1) is false—Brown could not have jumped into the sea. The conclusion is that (2) is not a correct analysis of (1).[19]

Vihvelin criticizes these kinds of objections using her core positive idea: that abilities to do otherwise are to be characterized in terms of intrinsic dispositions, that is, dispositions of agents that consist in intrinsic properties—by contrast with extrinsic or relational properties—that agents have. Because the essential features of such intrinsic dispositions are not analyzed conditionally, her view gains immunity to the assault on conditional analyses. An impressive feature of Vihvelin's development of this position is her defense of its explanatory power: In various key respects, it admirably does the work it needs to do in order to count as a contending theory.[20]

In her analysis, Vihvelin distinguishes between narrow and wide abilities. A narrow ability to A, where A-ing is some type of action, is, as Vihvelin puts it, a matter of "what it takes" to A (2013: 11). What it takes to A, she holds, includes whatever skills, competence, or know-how are required to A—and to do it without too much luck. A narrow ability also involves "the psychological and physical capacity to use" the required skills or exercise the competence or know-how. Usain Bolt can run 100 meters in ten seconds, but lacks a narrow ability to do so if he is asleep. Having a wide ability to A is having a narrow ability to A and being in circumstances amenable to the exercise of that ability. One must have the means and the opportunity to A, and there must be nothing external that stands in one's way. Despite being able to run 100 meters in ten seconds when in propitious circumstances, Bolt lacks a wide ability to do so now if he's asleep on swampy ground.

Vihvelin proposes a specific definition for the sort of ability required for free will:

> LCA-PROP-Ability: S has the narrow ability at time t to do R in response to the stimulus of S's *trying to do* R if, for some intrinsic property B that S has at t, and for some time t' after t, if S were in a test-case at t *and* S tried to do R *and* S retained property B until time t', then in a *suitable proportion of these cases*, S's trying to do R and S's having of B would be an S-complete cause of S's doing R. (187)

This is a complex characterization. Some of the complexity arises from the fact that free will does not require success in every possible case in which the agent tried to do otherwise. Hence, Vihvelin specifies that she succeeds in a suitable proportion of test cases.

There are a number of pertinent questions one might ask about this proposal. One objection we would like to highlight is due to Clarke (2014a),[21] and it begins by pointing out that the way it secures compatibility with determinism is by something close to a conditional specification after all. So suppose that an agent acts badly, and the leeway compatibilist claims that despite being causally determined, he could have refrained instead. On Vihvelin's proposal, this is to say that for some intrinsic property the agent had at the time of action t, and for some time t' after t, if he were in a test-case at t and tried to refrain and retained that intrinsic property until time t', then in a suitable proportion of these test cases his trying to refrain and having the intrinsic property would be a complete cause of his refraining. But just as on the conditional compatibilist proposal above we can ask what happens if the agent cannot choose otherwise, we can wonder what results if the agent lacks the ability to try. So suppose she can't actually try to refrain due to some psychological disorder, but in a suitable proportion of test cases in which she does try, the refraining is caused in the right way. Then Vihvelin's analysis specifies that she has the narrow ability, even though it's intuitive that due to her disorder she doesn't.

A further key feature of Vihvelin's work is the set of criticisms of Frankfurt's attack on the alternative possibilities requirement for free will and moral responsibility.

Vihvelin develops an original strategy to oppose Frankfurt's argument. She divides Frankfurt-style examples into two sorts: Bodyguard cases are those in which the trigger for the neuroscientist's intervention is the subject's trying or beginning to do otherwise than the action at issue—it's something the agent *does*; while in Preemptor cases the intervention is triggered by some event that occurs earlier than trying or beginning to perform the action at issue, and it is not something the agent does. Vihvelin argues that in all Bodyguard cases the agent has a relevant alternative, namely the beginning or trying to do otherwise, while in Preemptor cases the intervener will always be sufficiently remote so as to preserve the agent's ability to do otherwise. Many extant cases, we believe, fall to this dilemma.[22]

Furthermore, according to Sartorio, the kind of example that Pereboom (2000, 2001, 2014) and Hunt (2000, 2005) have been developing since the late 1990s is not impugned by either strategy (Sartorio classifies an example of this kind as a Bodyguard case, Kittle as a Preemptor example). Again, its distinguishing features are these: The trigger for intervention is a necessary condition for the agent's availing herself of any robust alternative possibility (without the intervener's device in place), while this trigger itself is not a robust alternative possibility (and the absence at any specific time of the cue for intervention in no sense causally determines the action the agent actually performs). In response to Vihvelin's criticism of Bodyguard cases, the agent's availing herself of the necessary condition for not performing the action is not a robust alternative to the action in question, for the reason that availing herself of that necessary condition would not exempt her from responsibility for the action in question—it would not have gotten her off the hook. (We discussed an example like this, due to Pereboom, in detail in Chapter 5, Section 3.2.)

Vihvelin's leeway compatibilist proposal is a detailed attempt to revive the spirit of classical compatibilism. Further proposals of this sort are likely to appear in the near future, and to become the focus of intense discussion.

Suggestions for Further Reading

As with the previous chapter, we have covered a lot of ground. To begin, we'll simply list the most familiar pieces representative of the major positions we have covered:

Bratman, Michael. 1997. "Responsibility and Planning." *Journal of Philosophy* 1 (1): 27–43.

Fischer, John Martin, and Mark Ravizza. 1998. *Responsibility and Control: An Essay on Moral Responsibility*. Cambridge: Cambridge University Press.

Frankfurt. Harry. 1971. "Freedom of the Will and the Concept of a Person." *Journal of Philosophy* 68: 5–20.

Haji, Ishtiyaque. 1998. *Moral Appraisability*. New York: Oxford University Press.

Vihvelin, Kadri. 2013. *Causes, Laws, & Free Will: Why Determinism Doesn't Matter*. New York: Oxford University Press.

Watson, Gary. 1975. "Free Agency." *Journal of Philosophy* 72: 205–20. Reprinted in Watson, Gary, ed., 1982. *Free Will*. New York: Oxford University Press.

For an extremely impressive collection of critical essays devoted to Frankfurt's work, see the festschrift organized by Sarah Buss and Lee Overton:

Buss, Sarah, and Lee Overton. 2002. *Contours of Agency: Essays on Themes from Harry Frankfurt*. Cambridge, MA: MIT Press.

For further development of the views of Frankfurt, Watson, and Bratman, see their books, consisting of collections of previously published articles:

Bratman, Michael. 2007. *Structures of Agency*. New York: Oxford University Press.

Frankfurt, Harry. 1999. *Necessity, Volition, and Love*. Cambridge: Cambridge University Press.

Frankfurt, Harry. 1988. *The Importance of What We Care About*. Cambridge: Cambridge University Press.

Watson, Gary. 2004. *Agency and Answerability*. New York: Oxford University Press.

For numerous essays by Fischer responding to his critics and developing further his reasons-responsive theory, see his three books containing many of his articles on these topics:

Fischer, John Martin. 2012. *Deep Control: Essays on Free Will and Value*. New York: Oxford University Press.

Fischer, John Martin. 2009. *Our Stories*. New York: Oxford University Press.

Fischer, John Martin. 2006. *My Way*. New York: Oxford University Press.

For thorough critical discussions of Fischer and Ravizza's (1998) proposal, see:

Ginet, Carl. 2006. "Working with Fischer and Ravizza's Account of Moral Responsibility." *Journal of Ethics* 10: 229–53.

Russell, Paul. 2002a. "Critical Notice of John Martin Fischer and Mark Ravizza *Responsibility and Control: A Theory of Moral Responsibility*." *Canadian Journal of Philosophy* 32: 587–606.
Watson, Gary. 2001. "Reason and Responsibility." *Ethics* 111: 374–94.

For another intriguing way of developing a reasons-responsive compatibilist view, one that we did not develop in this chapter, see:

Arpaly, Nomy. 2006. *Merit, Meaning, and Human Bondage*. Princeton, NJ: Princeton University Press.
Arpaly, Nomy. 2003. *Unprincipled Virtue*. New York: Oxford University Press.

For efforts to advance an agent-based reasons-responsive source compatibilist theory (rather than a mechanism-based one like Fischer and Ravizza's) see:

McKenna, Michael. 2013. "Reasons-Responsiveness, Agents, and Mechanisms." In David Shoemaker, ed., *Oxford Studies in Agency and Responsibility*, vol. 1. New York: Oxford University Press: 151–84.
Sartorio, Carolina. 2016. *Causation and Free Will*. Oxford: Oxford University Press.

For efforts to advance an agent-based reasons-responsive leeway compatibilist theory, see:

Brink, David, and Dana Nelkin. 2013. "Fairness and the Architecture of Responsibility." In David Shoemaker, ed., *Oxford Studies in Agency and Responsibility*, vol. 1. Oxford: Oxford University Press: 284–313.
Nelkin, Dana. 2011. *Making Sense of Freedom and Responsibility*. New York: Oxford University Press.

Notes

1 In Sections 1 through 7 of this chapter, we draw from McKenna (2011).
2 See, for example, Bratman, 1997, 2002, 2004, 2007; Doris, 2002; Dworkin, 1970, 1988; Frankfurt, 1971; Velleman, 1992, 2002; Watson, 1975.
3 We'll use this formulation of *will* in discussing Frankfurt's work, though his formulation is slightly misleading: An agent's will might be frustrated. Something might impede an agent from acting on it (1988: 20). Thus, it is inaccurate to describe it as an *effective* first-order desire, one that *does* move an agent all the way to action. Frankfurt might formulate what he has in mind this way: An agent's will is either her effective first-order desire, or one that, in the absence of external impediments, would be effective. We are indebted to Ishtiyaque Haji for this point.
4 The natural way to understand the relation is in terms of causation. But Frankfurt rejects a causal theory of action (1978), despite his compatibilist pedigree. So, let "bring about" be neutral between causation and some other manner of "moving an agent all the way to action."
5 Nailing down Frankfurt's account of freedom is notoriously difficult given the language he used to formulate it. The chart we offer seems to make the best sense of his

two most often quoted paragraphs in his "Freedom of the Will and the Concept of a Person" (1988: 23–4).

6 Although, see the last two paragraphs in the same essay, where Frankfurt writes "the freedom of the will appears to be neutral with regard to the problem of determinism" (25).

7 Insofar as satisfaction does not require performance of an action, it stands to clarify what he does *not* have in mind by activity when drawing the distinction between activity and passivity (Frankfurt, 1992b). How so? Being active with respect to one's desires is not a matter of acting; it is, instead a matter of what one cares about. As regards what is antecedently important to a person, which is revelatory of a person's cares, Frankfurt writes, "it must not be subject to his own immediate voluntary control" (1992b as reprinted in 1999: 93).

8 See the essays by Bratman (2002), Moran (2002), and Velleman (2002), as well as Frankfurt's replies in the edited collection by Buss and Overton (2002).

9 In subsequent work, Watson added an important qualification to his understanding of valuing as it issues from an agent's valuational system. It is not to be understood, Watson tells us, in terms of judging good. That is too rationalistic (1987, as reprinted in Watson, 2004: 168). What we value can depart from what we regard as (objectively) valuable. Perhaps what will turn the trick is "caring about something because (in as much as) it is deemed to be valuable" (168). Nevertheless, this can fall shy of what "might be sanctioned by a more general evaluational standpoint" (168).

10 By including Bratman's work in a section on compatibilism about free will and moral responsibility, we take some liberties. Bratman rather understands his treatment of identification to speak to the topic of autonomy and explicitly indicates that caution is needed to infer from conclusions about this topic similar conclusions about morally responsible agency and the contested freedom it requires (Bratman, 2005: 51). Nevertheless, it is natural to see how Bratman's work could be appropriated to the problem both Frankfurt and Watson address regarding freedom and responsibility.

11 We owe this point to Thomas Reed, a graduate student at Florida State University.

12 For one who draws upon these resources to argue that Aristotle has a worked-out theory of responsibility, see Irwin (1980: 132–7). Although Irwin does not use the label "reasons-responsive" to describe what he takes Aristotle's theory to be, he might as well have done so.

13 See, for example, Arpaly (2003, 2006); Dennett (1984); Fischer (1994); Fischer and Ravizza (1998); Gert and Duggan (1979); Glover (1970); Haji (1998); McKenna (2013); Nelkin (2011); Pettit and Smith (1996); Sartorio (2016); Smith (2003); Vihvelin (2013); and Wolf (1990). Pereboom (2014, 2015a) defends a reasons-responsive view of a conception of moral responsibility that does not invoke desert.

14 Fischer resists McKenna's criticism (2004 as reprinted in 2006: 239–42). Space does not permit further pursuit of this point.

15 Their reasons here are similar to those deployed by Nelkin in advancing her interference-free conception of ability (see our discussion in Section 8.5).

16 Fischer (2008) has responded to Vihvelin, and Vihvelin has countered (2008).

17 Nelkin's (2011) position might be taken as an exception to this claim.

18 We include among this class of leeway compatibilists Beebee (2000, 2003); Berofsky (2012); Campbell (2007); Horgan (1985, 2015); Lewis (1981); and Vihvelin (2004, 2013).

19 We discussed this criticism at length (Section 3.2) when assessing classical compatibilism.

20 There are two other philosophers who began to advance accounts of this sort about a decade ago, around the same time that Vihvelin (2004) first proposed a view of this type: Michael Smith (2003) and Michael Fara (2008). Smith's position isn't as sophisticated as Vihvelin's, and it remains undeveloped. Fara's view is impressive, but Fara has left philosophy and will not pursue the position further. Vihvelin's is now the best-developed position of this sort, and it is a serious and major contender among compatibilist views.

21 Randolph Clarke, "Free Will and Abilities to Act," presented at a symposium on Vihvelin (2013) at the University of Southern California, September 2014.

22 Vihvelin's argument against Preemptor cases has been disputed by John Fischer (2008), Simon Kittle (2014), and in a forthcoming article by Carolina Sartorio. While Vihvelin's book features a resourceful defense of her view against Fischer, this defense is in turn ably contested by Kittle and by Sartorio.

10 Contemporary Incompatibilism

Libertarianism

According to libertarian views, we human beings have the ability to act freely in the sense relevant to free will. Crucial to an action's being free in this sense is that it not be causally determined by factors beyond the agent's control. Recent times have witnessed the explicit differentiation of three major versions of libertarianism, the event-causal, non-causal, and agent-causal types. In this chapter, we will present each of these views together with their problems and prospects.

10.1. Three Kinds of Libertarianism

In the event-causal libertarian view, actions, conceived as agent-involving events—as agents acting at times—are caused solely by prior events, such as an agent's having a desire or a belief at a time, and some type of indeterminacy in the production of actions by appropriate events is held to be necessary for the kind of free will required for moral responsibility (Balaguer, 2010; Ekstrom, 2000; Franklin, 2011b; Kane, 1996). On other formulations, actions are indeterministically caused by states or property instances. This position has an ancestor in the Epicurean view according to which a free decision is an indeterministically caused swerve in the otherwise downward path of an atom (Lucretius 50 BCE/1982).

In agent-causal libertarianism, free will of the sort required for moral responsibility is accounted for by the existence of agents who as substances have the power to cause actions without being causally determined to do so (Chisholm, 1964, 1976; Clarke, 1993, 2003; Griffith, 2010; Kant, 1781/1787/1987; O'Connor, 2000, 2009; Reid, 1788; Taylor, 1966, 1974). A first crucial agent-causal libertarian claim is that the causation involved in an agent's acting freely does not reduce to causation among events. What secures the failure of this reduction is that it is the agent *fundamentally as a substance* that has the power to cause decisions. A second crucial claim is that when an agent acts freely, she is not causally determined by factors beyond her control to cause it. Determinism is compatible with agent causation (Markosian, 1999; Nelkin, 2011), but according to agent-causal libertarianism, for a decision to be free it's necessary that the agent not be causally determined to cause it.

A third kind of libertarianism is non-causal (Bergson, 1889/1910; Ginet, 1990, 1996, 2007; Goetz, 2008; McCann, 1998). Henri Bergson was an early proponent of this sort of position. In his view, although actions occur in time, the temporal properties of conscious agency do not resolve into the kinds of magnitudes required for the applicability of causal laws. An attempt to theorize scientifically about conscious agency will inevitably involve invoking physical concepts that do not in fact apply to it, but are merely metaphorical, and as a result causal theories of conscious agency are only metaphorical as well. More generally, the mental is *sui generis*, and as it really is, it is not subject to scientific theorizing, and is not causal in nature. This non-causality, on Bergson's account, makes room for actions to be free. Contemporary non-causal theorists, such as Carl Ginet, Hugh McCann, and Stewart Goetz, don't tell a similar story about how it might be that certain actions have non-causal account, although their views might nonetheless have their roots in the nineteenth-century project to distinguish the human sciences from the natural sciences, and in this way to insulate distinctively human features of reality from the natural scientific conception.

Among philosophers with broadly naturalist sympathies—that is, those attracted to a scientific view of the world—event-causal libertarianism is usually regarded as the most attractive of these three positions. The notion of an uncaused event and the idea of a substance-cause seem non-naturalistic to many participants in the debate. We'll begin with the event-causal view, set out the most influential family of objections against it, and then see whether the non-causal and agent-causal libertarian alternatives are viable.

10.2. Two Event-Causal Libertarian Accounts

We will now examine two prominent versions of event-causal libertarianism. The first is Mark Balaguer's (2010) elegantly simple account, and the second is Robert Kane's (1996) more complex story.

Note first that event-causal libertarian accounts differ with respect to the point in the causal history of an action at which causal determination must be absent. Chris Franklin (2011b) argues that the causal relation between the events that proximally cause the agent's decision and that decision must be indeterministic for the decision to be free. More specifically, the correct place to situate the indeterminism is between the non-actional mental states that potentially lead to action, such as the beliefs and desires that constitute the agent's reasons, on the one hand and decision and overt action on the other (2011b: 202). The intuitive idea is that for non-derivatively free actions, the agent's freedom consists in the action's being up to her once the reasons have been considered. Other sorts of event-causal libertarianisms, such as the "Valerian" libertarianism that Mele once proposed, locate the indeterminacy prior to the moment of choice, for example in the considerations that come to the agent's mind. One concern for that type of view is that the agent is evidently not in control of this kind of indeterminacy.

In his *Free Will as an Open Scientific Problem* (2010), Mark Balaguer develops a position of the sort Franklin specifies:

> The view does not involve any sort of irreducible agent causation, but it does hold that undetermined L-free decisions are (ordinarily) causally influenced by – indeed, probabilistically caused by – agent-involving events, most notably, events having to do with the agent having certain reasons and intentions. (2010: 67)

He defines several notions in setting out this position. The paradigm case of a free act is a *torn decision*, one for which the reasons and motivations that cause it are equally balanced:

> *A torn decision*: A decision in which the agent (a) has reasons for two or more options and feels torn as to which set of reasons is stronger, that is, has no conscious belief as to which option is best, given her reasons; and that (b) decides without resolving the conflict – that is, the person has the experience of "just choosing." (2010: 71)

Balaguer does not claim that all free decisions are torn decisions, only that torn decisions are useful as representative examples of free decisions, and, in addition, that lessons drawn from considering them transfer to cases in which a decision is not torn but yet undetermined. The characterization of a torn decision facilitates his conception of *L-freedom*, that is, libertarian freedom:

> If an ordinary human torn decision is wholly undetermined, then it is *L-free* – that is, it is not just undetermined but also appropriately nonrandom, and the indeterminacy increases or procures the appropriate nonrandomness. (2010: 78)

His notion of *appropriate nonrandomness* combines authorship and control: "In order for a decision to be L-free, it has to be authored and controlled by the agent in question: that is, it has to be her decision, and she has to control which option is chosen" (2010: 83). Lastly, he defines the notion of *torn-decision indeterminism*—TDW-indeterminism:

> *TDW-indeterminism*: Some of our torn decisions are wholly undetermined at the moment of choice, that is, the moment-of-choice probabilities of the various reasons-based tied-for-best option match the reasons-based probabilities, so that these moment-of-choice probabilities are all roughly even, given the complete state of the world and the laws of nature, and the choice occurs without any further input, that is, without anything else being significantly causally relevant to which option is chosen. (2010: 78)

Thus in the case of a torn TDW-indeterminist decision there is no mismatch between the underlying probabilities for the various options at the time of the decision and the probabilities for those options at that time based on the agent's consciously available reasons.

To illustrate his account, and to facilitate objections, Balaguer sets out his example of Ralph, who makes a specific torn decision (2010: 72, 80):

> Stated in ordinary language, Ralph is deciding whether to stay in Mayberry or move to New York. Favoring the move to New York are his desire to play for the Giants, and his desire to star on Broadway. Favoring staying in Mayberry are his desire to marry Robbi Anna, and his desire to manage the local *Der Wienerschnitzel*. Suppose Ralph makes the torn decision to move to New York – he just decides to move to New York.

Because this account is event-causal libertarian, it's important to see how Ralph's story is to be told in event-causal terms. More specifically, since on this view control is a causal matter, and all the relevant causation is by events, the purely event-causal specification will allow us to test whether the view can secure the sort of control required for free will and moral responsibility. In Ralph's story, events E1–E4 are the events, and thus the causal factors, that are relevant to which decision, E5 or E6, will result:

> E1: Ralph's desiring at $t1-tn$ to play for the Giants,
> E2: Ralph's desiring at $t1-tn$ to star on Broadway,
> E3: Ralph's desiring at $t1-tn$ to marry Robbi Anna,
> E4: Ralph's desiring at $t1-tn$ to manage the local *Der Wienerschnitzel*,
> E5: Ralph's deciding at tn to move to New York,
> E6: Ralph's deciding at tn to stay in Mayberry.

In the actual situation,

> E1 and E2 probabilistically cause E5,

and E5 thereby satisfies a key condition on free action.

In *The Significance of Free Will*, Robert Kane defends a more complex version of event-causal libertarianism. In his view, the paradigm type of action for which an agent is morally responsible is one of moral or prudential struggle, in which there are reasons for and against performing the action in question. The production of an action of this sort begins with the agent's character and motives, and proceeds through the agent's making an effort of will to act, and issues in the choice for a particular action. The effort of will is a struggle to choose in one way given countervailing pressures, and results from the agent's character and motives. For a free choice, this effort of will is *indeterminate*, and consequently, the choice produced by the effort will be *undetermined*. Kane illustrates this specification by an analogy between an effort of will and a quantum event:

> Imagine an isolated particle moving toward a thin atomic barrier. Whether or not the particle will penetrate the barrier is undetermined. There is a

probability that it will penetrate, but not certainty, because its position and momentum are not both determinate as it moves towards the barrier. Imagine that the choice (to overcome temptation) is like the penetration event. The choice one way or the other is *undetermined* because the process preceding it and potentially terminating in it (i.e. the effort of will to overcome temptation) is *indeterminate*. (Kane, 1996: 128)

The effort of will is indeterminate in the sense that its causal potential does not become determinate prior to the occurrence of the choice. There are various possibilities, consistent with the laws of nature, for how this causal potential can be resolved. Thus when it is resolved, the choice that does in fact occur will be undetermined. Kane warns against construing his view so that the indeterminacy occurs after the effort is made: "One must think of the effort and the indeterminism as fused; the effort is indeterminate and the indeterminism is a property of the effort, not something that occurs before or after the effort." He contends that if an agent is morally responsible for a decision, it must be free in this sense or else there must be some such free choice that is its sufficient ground, cause, or explanation (1996: 35). Kane illustrates this conception by his example of a businesswoman on her way to work—let's call her Anne—and the assault victim she encounters. Anne experiences an inner struggle between her moral conscience, which counsels her to stop and help the victim, and her career ambitions, which urge her not to miss her meeting. When the struggle is resolved in favor of Anne's decision to stop and help the victim, Kane supposes that the effort of will from which the decision results is indeterminate, and that consequently the decision in undetermined, and that this secures freedom of action and moral responsibility.

In a recent article (2016), Kane sets out this key element of his position in an illuminating way in response to Franklin's requirement for the location of indeterminism. In Kane's view, the indeterminism is not located between, on the one hand, non-actional mental states that potentially lead to decision and overt action, and on the other hand, decision and overt action, contrary to Franklin (2011b: 202). Kane maintains that freedom is primarily freedom of the will, not freedom of action. For him, freedom of the will essentially involves multiple goal-directed processes, formed over extended periods of time, which result in competing efforts of will. These competing efforts are then resolved indeterministically—in the central sort of case, either could have resulted in an action holding fixed the exact past and the laws.

10.3.   Luck Objections to Event-Causal Libertarianism

A prominent family of objections to libertarianism develops the idea that a non-deterministic history of an action precludes an agent's being morally responsible for it. A classical presentation of this type of concern is found in Hume's *Treatise of Human Nature* (1739). There he argues, as we saw in Chapter 3 (Section 3.1), more specifically, that if an action is not causally determined, it will not have sufficient connection with the agent for her to be morally responsible for it. Some objections that reflect the Humean concern are called *luck objections* (Clarke, 2005; Mele, 1999, 2006b), for the reason that they attempt to show that on the libertarian view at issue whether the action occurs is a matter of luck— good or bad—and thus it is not sufficiently in the control of the agent for her to be morally responsible for it.

Alfred Mele and Ishtiyaque Haji advocate and develop a version of the luck objection that targets the event causal view according to which free actions must be proximally and indeterministically caused by appropriate agent-involving events. Suppose that in an event-causal libertarian world W an agent A makes decision D at t, that is, A-involving events E proximally cause decision D at t. Because the history of D is indeterministic, there is another world, W*, which features exactly the same events antecedent to t as those that precede E's causing D at t in W, but without D occurring at t. But then the fact that D did come about then would seem to be a matter of luck. The occurrence of agent-involving events—and only events are causally relevant—prior to t are compatible with D's occurrence and with D's non-occurrence. So it would seem that D is not sufficiently under the control of the agent for moral responsibility in particular.

Peter van Inwagen's "rollback objection" (van Inwagen, 2002: 171–5) is another version of the luck objection. Here is Balaguer's statement of this challenge:

> Suppose that some agent S is torn between two options, A and B, and eventually chooses A in a torn-decision sort of way. And now suppose that God "rolls back" the universe and "replays" the decision.... If the decision is undetermined in the manner of TDW-indeterminism, then if God "played" the decision 100 times, we should expect that S would choose A and B about 50 times each. (2010: 92)

Balaguer concludes that in this situation it would at least initially seem to be a matter of chance or luck what she chose, and to the extent that this is right, it seems that S didn't author or control the decision. At the very least, it seems that the element of chance or luck here diminishes S's authorship and control. One way of thinking about the rollback objection is that it has as its core component the luck objection Mele and Haji develop, while the addition of the rollback story brings out the lucky nature of the situation in a particularly forceful way.

Van Inwagen (1983: 132–4) and Mele (1999: 277) develop another kind of story that serves to enhance the sense of luck, one involving a "randomizing" manipulator. Here is a version of such a story (Pereboom, 2014; cf. 2001). Imagine that Ralph*'s abilities, character, and motivations are exactly like Ralph's. And Ralph* too makes the decision to move to New York. But Ralph* differs in that the advent of his choice involves a randomizing manipulator who spins a dial which will land on one of two positions. The dial's landing on a position is the crucial indeterministic component of the neural realization of the choice to perform the action, and it replaces the crucial indeterministic component in Ralph's neural processes. The position the dial lands on thus makes the key difference as to which decision Ralph* makes. If the dial settles on one position, Ralph* makes one choice, and if it lands on the other, he makes the other. Suppose, in addition, that Ralph*, just like Ralph, has reasons for making the choice, he chooses for these reasons, he wants to choose for these reasons more than any others, he is not being coerced or compelled in choosing. It nevertheless appears that the indeterminacy of the sort exhibited by Ralph*'s decision does not provide for moral responsibility for the choice, and this is intuitively because he lacks the control over his decision that moral responsibility demands. However, there would seem to be no relevant difference between Ralph and Ralph*, and so it appears that Ralph also lacks this sort of control. In each case, it would be the indeterminacy and its exact location that undermined control.

Pereboom advances another challenge in the same family, one that he calls *the disappearing agent objection*. It's related to a more general objection to event-causal theories of action (Brent ms.; Hornsby, 2004a, 2004b; Nida-Rümelin, 2007; Velleman, 1992), one that targets basic desert moral responsibility rather than agency (which we discuss in Section 11). It involves the notion of an agent *settling whether a decision occurs*. How do agents typically do this? Suppose Mary is deliberating about which flavor of ice cream to buy, chocolate or strawberry. She would typically settle which flavor-buying decision occurs by settling which flavor to buy. This is in accord with Mele's view that "in deciding to A, one settles upon A-ing (or upon trying to A), and one enters a state—a decision state—of being settled upon A-ing (or upon trying to A)" (Mele, 1992: 158–9). With this understanding in place, here is the objection:

> *The disappearing agent objection*: Consider a decision that occurs in a context in which the agent's moral motivations favor that decision, and her prudential motivations favor her refraining from making it, and the strengths of these motivations are in equipoise. On an event-causal libertarian picture, the relevant causal conditions antecedent to the decision, i.e., the occurrence of certain agent-involving events, do not settle whether the decision occurs, but only render the occurrence of the decision about 50% probable. In fact, because no occurrence of antecedent events settles whether the decision occurs, and only antecedent events are causally relevant, *nothing* settles whether the decision occurs. Thus it can't be that the agent or anything about the agent settles whether the decision occurs, and she therefore will lack the control required for moral responsibility for it. (Pereboom, 2014; cf. 2001, 2004, 2007)

The concern raised is that because event-causal libertarian agents will not have the power to settle whether the decision occurs, they cannot have the role in action that secures the control that moral responsibility demands. One way of thinking about the disappearing agent objection is that it also has as its core component the luck objection Mele and Haji raise, and then adds a supposition about what would dissolve the responsibility-undermining luck that the scenario involves. Such luck would dissolve if only it involved an agent with the power to settle which decision occurs. Given an initial expectation that the scenario will involve the decision's being settled by an agent, the fact that this turns out to be missing shows up as a disappearing agent.

10.4. Applying the Objections

These objections can straightforwardly be directed against the supposition that Balaguer's account can secure the control required for moral responsibility. What do they look like when applied to his Ralph example? The events that are causally relevant are:

> E1: Ralph's desiring at $t1-tn$ to play for the Giants,
> E2: Ralph's desiring at $t1-tn$ to star on Broadway,

and,

> E3: Ralph's desiring at $t1-tn$ to marry Robbi Anna,
> E4: Ralph's desiring at $t1-tn$ to manage the local *Der Wienerschnitzel.*

Let's suppose that what actually results is:

> E5: Ralph's deciding at tn to move to New York,

E1–E4 do not settle whether E5 occurs, because the occurrence of E1–E4 renders the occurrence of E5 only 50 percent probable. E1–E4 are compatible with the nonoccurrence of E5—in fact, the nonoccurrence of E5 is 50 percent probable, given E1–E4. So the occurrence of E5 would seem to be a matter of luck. Moreover, nothing in the scenario settles whether E5 occurs. Thus neither the agent nor anything about the agent settles whether E5 occurs. So it appears that on this event-causal libertarian view, using Balaguer's categories, torn decisions cannot be appropriately nonrandom, and the indeterminacy in question cannot increase or procure the appropriate nonrandomness. Moreover, authorship is missing given that such control is required for authorship.

In his defense of his event-causal account, Balaguer considers several versions of the luck objection. In his response to the rollback version, he contends that "in each of the different plays of the decision, it is *Ralph* who does the choosing" (2010: 93). More generally, in his view:

> the most we could hope for, vis-à-vis authorship and control is that it be *Ralph* who does the just-picking.... Ralph chooses – consciously, intentionally, and purposefully – without being causally influenced by anything external to his conscious reasons and thought. Thus it seems that in this case, we do get the result that it is Ralph who does the just-choosing. And so it also seems that in

this scenario, we procure as much authorship and control for Ralph as we can, given that he is making a torn decision. (2010: 97)

But first, if, in accord with the event-causal libertarian position,

Ralph decides to move to New York

is analyzed as:

Ralph-involving events E1–E2 probabilistically cause Ralph-involving event E5,

Then the luck objections retain their original force. But Balaguer argues that he can evade this concern by focusing on what the agent does: "if the just-choosing were done by anything other than the *agent*, then she would lose authorship and control" (2010: 97). However, if Ralph's just-choosing is what secures the requisite control, and control is fundamentally causal in nature, then what is required is that a causal relation is obtained between Ralph as agent and the decision. However, the event-causal libertarian allows only causal relations among events, and not a causal relation between agent and event.

Kane also sets out a line of defense against the luck objection. First, he points out that decisions can be undetermined and yet have many features indicative of agent control and moral responsibility. Undetermined decisions can still be made voluntarily, intentionally, for reasons, knowingly, on purpose, and as a result of the agent's efforts. Agents might not be coerced or compelled if their actions are indeterministic (Kane 1996: 179, 1999: 237–9). Thus an action's having an indeterministic causal history is consistent with significant control in action, and, Kane contends, with control sufficient for moral responsibility.

One might object that while indeterminism allows for these features of control in action, compatibilists can appeal to the same features as a defense against the objection that causal determination rules out the control required for moral responsibility. Because incompatibilists deny that causally determined action can feature enough control for responsibility, one might question whether Kane's first strategy can be successful. In accord with this observation, the critic can argue that while the event-causal view can secure *as much* control as compatibilism does, still, agents would have *no more control* over their actions than they would if determinism were true, and such control isn't enough for moral responsibility (Clarke, 2003; Pereboom, 2001, 2014).

This objection might be clarified by turning to Kane's UR (for "ultimate responsibility"), which specifies his key conditions for moral responsibility. UR has two elements (1996: 35). The first is that to be ultimately responsible for an event, an agent must have voluntarily been able to do otherwise. The second is that to be ultimately responsible for an event, an agent must be responsible for any sufficient ground or cause or explanation of the event. If actions are undetermined events, then the first component of UR might be satisfied, and agents could have the required leeway for alternative actions. For Kane the second component is grounded in a more fundamental requirement about the origination of action:

> (Q) If the action did have such a sufficient reason for which the agent was not responsible, then the action, or the agent's will to perform it, would have its source in something that the agent played no role in producing ... ultimately responsible agents must not only be the sources of their actions, but also of the *will* to perform the actions. (1996: 73)

But this requirement yields a threat to Kane's position. First, (Q) has the consequence that agents cannot be responsible for decisions that are undetermined because they are not produced by anything at all, since then agents clearly cannot be the source of the will to perform them. Between decisions that are undetermined because they are not produced by anything at all, and those that are causally determined by factors beyond the agent's control, lies a range of decisions for which factors beyond the agent's control contribute to their production but do not determine them, while there is nothing that supplements the causal contribution of these factors to produce them. By analogy, according to the standard interpretation of quantum mechanics, antecedent events causally influence which quantum event will occur from among a range of possibilities by fixing the probabilities governing this range, but these antecedent events do not causally determine which of these possible quantum events will occur. Similarly, antecedent events might influence which decision an agent will make without determining any particular decision. However, the concern is that if there are factors beyond the agent's control that influence a decision's production without causally determining it, while there is nothing that supplements the contribution of these factors to produce the decision, then its production features only a combination of the first two types of responsibility-undermining factors. If causal factors beyond an agent's control, instead of causally determining a single decision, simply leave open more than one possibility, and the agent plays no further role in determining which possibility is realized, then it would seem that we have no more reason to think she has the control required to be morally responsible than in the deterministic case (Pereboom, 2001).

In response to this type of objection, Kane argues that in one respect the indeterminism in his event-causal libertarianism diminishes control, but that indeterminism is required to enhance it in another respect: "indeterminism is functioning as a hindrance or obstacle to [the businesswoman's] realizing one of her purposes—a hindrance or obstacle in the form of resistance within her will which has to be overcome by effort" (2007: 178; 2015). Adding in the indeterminism in the way he specifies enhances control because it provides for plural voluntary control:

> The ability to bring about whichever of the options they will, when they will to do so, for the reasons they will to do so, on purpose rather than by

mistake or accident, without being coerced or compelled in doing so, or otherwise controlled by other agents or mechanisms. (Kane, 2011a: 389)

This point makes sense as a response to the no-enhanced-control objection.

Still, the objector might now point out that so far Kane lacks a response to the various versions of the luck objection, and thus the plural voluntary control that remains is insufficient for moral responsibility. In response, Kane might argue that there is an additional resource for responding to the luck objection available to him. Mele (2006a) suggests a related view that escapes the luck objection as he sets it out, one on which by earlier character-forming decisions, for which the agent is morally responsible, she can significantly affect the probabilities that govern her decision. More generally, through their past behavior such agents shape present practical probabilities, and in their present behavior agents shape future practical probabilities. Mele calls this view "daring soft libertarianism." Along the same lines, Kane might propose that choices are produced by efforts of will, and efforts of will are explained in part by the agent's character, but the character that explains an effort of will need not be a factor beyond the agent's control. For this character could in turn be produced partly by the agent's free choices.

But this type of account is vulnerable to the following objection. Consider the first free choice an agent makes. Her character cannot explain how this choice might be free and responsible, since it could not have been produced in part by other free choices the agent makes. However, she cannot be free and responsible in the second choice either. Suppose the first choice was character-forming. Because the agent cannot be responsible for the first choice, she also cannot be responsible for the resulting character formation, and thus she cannot be responsible for the second choice either. Since this type of reasoning can be repeated for all subsequent choices, an agent that meets Kane's specifications can never be morally responsible for a choice she makes (Pereboom, 2001, 2007).

10.5.   Adding in Higher-Order States

One might propose to solve the luck problem within the event-causal framework by specifying that the event- or state-causal etiology of a decision for which an agent is morally responsible must feature agent-involving states such as values or standing preferences, thereby making it intuitive that the agent does in fact settle whether the decision occurs. In Laura Ekstrom's version of event-causal libertarianism (2000, 2003), a decision for which an agent is morally responsible must result by a normal causal process from an undefeated authorized preference of the agent's, where such preferences are non-coercively formed or maintained, and are caused by, but not causally determined by considerations brought to bear in deliberation. In her view, these conditions on the formation of preferences intuitively tie them to who the agent is, and preclude causal determination of preferences by factors beyond the agent's control.

Ekstrom argues that indeterminacy need not make preferences and decisions purposeless, that it need not render them accidental, and that it does not preclude rational explanation. But the luck objection can be raised here as well. Imagine that in some situation, an agent can decide either morally or out of self-interest, and she considers reasons for each choice, and this results in a motivational balance between the two options. And in addition, she has both moral and self-interested undefeated authorized preferences. We can now ask: With this balance of motivations and preferences in place, what settles whether her self-interested or her moral preference wins out, whether the self-interested or moral decision occurs? When one of the preferences is efficacious, this would seem to happen without anything about the agent settling that it is, and thus which actually occurs would appear to be a matter of luck. Adding in the agential requirements on formation of preferences appears not to make it intuitive that she settles which decision occurs, which would be required if she is to be responsible for her decision.

10.6. Agent-Causal Libertarianism

It's natural to turn to agent-causal libertarianism if one is impressed by the luck problem for the event-causal alternative. Recall the disappearing agent version of the luck objection to event-causal libertarianism. Suppose a decision occurs in a context in which the agent's moral motivations support that decision, and her prudential motivations favor her refraining from making it, and these motivations are equally balanced. On the event-causal libertarian position, the causal conditions pertinent to the decision, the occurrence of certain agent-involving events, will not settle whether the decision will occur. Because no occurrence of antecedent events will settle whether the decision will occur, and only antecedent events are causally relevant, nothing will settle whether the decision will occur. So it can't be that the agent or anything about the agent settles whether the decision will occur, and for this reason she lacks the control required for moral responsibility for it.

What would need to be added to the event-causal libertarian account is involvement of the agent in the making of her decision that would facilitate her settling whether the decision occurs, which would allow the control in deciding required for moral responsibility. Agent-causal libertarianism proposes to satisfy this requirement by introducing the agent as a cause, not merely as involved in events, but rather fundamentally as a substance. Supposing the agent was reintroduced merely as involved in events, the disappearing agent objection could be reiterated. What the agent-causal libertarian adds instead is an agent who possesses a causal power, fundamentally as a substance, to cause a decision—or more inclusively as O'Connor (2009) specifies, "the coming to be of a state of intention to carry out some act"—without being causally determined to do so, and thereby to settle, with the requisite control, whether this state of intention will occur. Agent-causal libertarianism was advocated by Immanuel Kant (1781/1787/1987) and Thomas Reid (1788) in the eighteenth century, and then developed in more recent times by Roderick Chisholm (1964, 1976), Richard Taylor (1966, 1974), Timothy O'Connor (2000, 2009), Randolph Clarke (2003), and Meghan Griffith (2010).

10.7.   Agent-Causal Libertarianism and Luck Objections

Suppose an agent is deliberating about whether to buy a chocolate ice-cream cone or to refrain from doing so. On one attractive version of the libertarian agent-causal view, the agent-as-substance can either settle on the action or on the refraining. Her settling on the action is the forming of her intention to perform it, which in this case amounts to her decision to perform it (O'Connor, 2000; cf. Mele, 1992; sometimes intentions are formed without decisions being made; Mele, 1995). Crucially, by settling on the action, the agent-as-substance *causes* the decision to perform it, and thereby settles that this decision will occur.

One significant objection is that this agent-causal position is as vulnerable to luck objections as event-causal libertarianism is. So, for example, Mele (1999, 2006b) and Ishtiyaque Haji (2004) contend that a luck objection has as much force against the claim that agent-causal libertarianism provides the control required for moral responsibility as it does against the proposal that event-causal libertarianism yields this sort of control. One way to support this contention is by first noting that when an agent A agent-causes decision D at time t, an event of the following type occurs:

G: A's causing D at t.

As Mele and Haji argue, given exactly the same conditions antecedent to t as those that precede A's agent-causing D, and given the indeterminism of the libertarian view, G might not have occurred. So then in some other possible world, W*, the causal antecedents of G in the actual world are present, but D fails to occur. Thus the fact that G did come about would seem to be a matter of luck. They argue that this consideration provides reason to conclude that on the agent-causal libertarian position, D is also not sufficiently under the control of the agent.

The agent-causal libertarian will need to agree that given the causal conditions prior to G, G and D might not have occurred. However, she will argue that what the agent-as-substance in W does *most fundamentally* is to cause D, and the proposal is that it is in the causing of D that her responsibility-conferring control is located. The substance-causal relation is embedded in event G, and thus G will not be what is most fundamentally caused. On Mele's and Haji's objection, we imagine that only the events that occur prior to G in W also occur in W*. But the agent-causal libertarian maintains that the crucial control is not exercised by way of these prior events, but by the agent-as-substance. If in addition to the events that precede G we specify that in both W and W* the agent-as-substance's exercises her agent-causal power but that D occurs in W and not in W*, this will be so because the agent-as-substance causes D in W but causes the decision to refrain from the action in W*. Thus it wouldn't appear to be a matter of luck that D occurs in W (Pereboom, 2014).

Meghan Griffith (2005) employs an epistemic analogue of this line of reasoning in her response to Peter van Inwagen's challenge to agent-causal libertarianism. Van Inwagen (2000) argues that on the supposition that I am an agent-cause, if in some situation I know the objective probability of my remaining silent is 0.57, and of my speaking and not remaining silent is 0.43, I fail to be in a position to promise to you that I will remain silent. My failing to be in a position to make this promise indicates that on the agent-causal view I lack the sort of control required for responsibility for remaining silent. Griffith argues that while on the event-causal conception this kind of reasoning is plausible, on the agent-causal position it is not. For even if the causally relevant agent-involving events issue in these probabilities, I as agent-as-substance have the power to definitively determine whether the decision to remain silent will occur by causing it, and knowledge of how I will exercise my agent-causal power would put me in a position to make a promise. In these circumstances I could come to know which decision I will make, even if full mastery of the causally relevant agent-involving events alone will not yield this knowledge.

Another sort of luck argument might be pressed against the agent-causal libertarian. When an agent-as-substance causes a decision, an event of the following type occurs:

G: A's causing D at t.

But such an agent could not cause events of type G, for it's absurd to claim that the agent-as-substance causes herself to cause a decision. Since this agent could not cause events of type G, she cannot be responsible for them. And because the agent cannot be responsible for such events, she cannot be responsible for the choices embedded in them. If an agent cannot be morally responsible for her causing of her choices at times, neither can she be responsible for her choices.

Ginet (1997: 91) presents a version of this objection against O'Connor's agent-causal libertarianism. In O'Connor's view, in a case of agent causation, *the agent's causing at t an event e* is not itself an event which has a sufficient causal condition. Consequently Ginet sees him as vulnerable to the objection that this more complex event will be an undetermined event over which, according to the agent-causal theorist's own objection to event-causal libertarianism, an agent cannot have sufficient control for moral responsibility.

Roderick Chisholm's (1971) reply to this type of concern is that when an agent causes a choice by an exercise of her agent-causal power she does indeed cause an event of type G, for which she can be morally responsible. When an agent acts freely, what she does most fundamentally is to cause a decision to act. She can be morally responsible for this decision because she causes it by her agent-causal power, and such causing supplies the control required for moral responsibility. Less boldly, note that it is a *logical consequence* of the agent's causing a decision that an event of type G occurs. It would thus follow logically from the fact that at *tn* Ralph agent-causes his decision to move to New York that the more complex event *Ralph's causing at tn a decision to move to New*

York occurs. So at least we can say that by causing D, the agent brings about G as a logical consequence of causing D.

But even on Chisholm's bolder view, it wouldn't be the agent's causing G that fundamentally explains why G is an event for which she is responsible, but rather the fact that G embeds the responsibility-conferring relation, her agent-causing D at t. The crucial lesson is independent of the additional causal claim. On the agent-causal libertarian's view, what's metaphysically fundamental is that the agent substance-causes the decision, and even if the more complex event of type G that embeds this agent-causal relation turns out to be uncaused, it features, as a component, an instance of causation that supplies the control required for moral responsibility.

10.8.   Agent Causation and Rationality

Another issue for agent-causal libertarianism concerns whether it can incorporate the influence of reasons on action and decision. On Donald Davidson's widely accepted account, reasons influence an action by causing it. Given that reasons are analyzed as agent-involving events, and that the influence of reasons on action is causal, actions would be event- and not substance-caused, at least in this respect. Actions for which agents are morally responsible are typically rational actions, and so such responsible actions would in one respect need to be event- rather than substance-caused. This objection poses a challenge to an agent-causal account of morally responsible action.

Clarke (2003) and O'Connor (2000) have each proposed accounts that address this objection. On Clarke's integrated account of agent causation, an action for which the agent has responsibility-conferring control will be caused by two distinct factors, a complex of beliefs and desires, which includes reasons for action, and the agent-as-substance. This two-stream account allows Clarke to endorse Davidson's causal view of reasons for action and to accept agent causation. A crucial question that arises for this account is whether the agent-as-substance as cause of a decision and the causing of this decision by the belief–desire complex are sufficiently integrated for the substance-causing to be rational. An intuitive way to think of agents as rational is as influenced by reasons in making decisions. So one might ask: On Clarke's account, is the agent-as-substance influenced by the belief–desire complex that constitutes her reasons, or is she not? If she isn't, then the account appears vulnerable to an objection Galen Strawson (1986) raises, that the agent-as-substance is non-rational in her causing of the decision. If the agent-as-substance is influenced by the reasons, then either this influence is causal or non-causal. The non-causal option conflicts with Clarke's Davidsonian position on the role of reasons. But he seems to want to deny the causal option insofar as it involves reasons causally influencing the agent-as-substance. He says, for example, that "a substance cannot be an effect" (Clarke, 2003: 158). Yet there would seem to be a significant motivation to hold that if agents are substance-causes they can be causally influenced by reasons.

Clarke's proposed solution is that it is a matter of natural law that the propensities of the reasons to cause actions are the same as the propensities of the agent-as-substance to cause actions (2003). One issue for this strategy is that a natural law of this sort would seem to be in a sense brute, since there would appear to be nothing about the agent-as-substance per se that explains why its propensities to cause actions match those of the reasons. A second issue is that the agent-as-substance, in causing an action, would then seem to lack the right sort of relation to reasons. Intuitively, this agent must be influenced by reasons in causing an action. However, on Clarke's integrated view, it would appear that there could be no such influence, but rather only a correspondence of propensities of the reasons on the one hand and the agent-as-substance on the other by virtue of a natural law that's brute in the sense just specified.

Hence what seems to be needed is an explanation for how the agent-as-substance could be causally influenced by reasons. O'Connor proposes an account of this kind, one that employs Fred Dretske's (1993) distinction between structural and triggering causes. To illustrate the distinction, the structuring cause of the bomb's explosion is the process by which the bomb is made, while its triggering cause is what detonates it. In O'Connor's view, reasons are structuring causes of a decision by virtue of structuring the propensities of the agent-causal power, while the agent-as-substance, in her exercise of this structured power, is the decision's triggering cause. The result of the causal structuring by reasons is the alteration of the propensities of the agent-causal power toward a range of effects:

> While nothing produces an instance of agent-causation, the possible occurrence of this event has a continuously evolving, objective likelihood. Expressed differently, agent-causal power is a structured propensity towards a class of effects, such that at any given time, for each causally possible, specific agent-causal event-type, there is a definite objective probability of its occurrence within the range (0,1), and this probability varies continuously as the agent is impacted by internal and external influences.... [T]he effect of the influencing events is exhausted by their alteration of the relative likelihood of the outcome, which they accomplish by affecting the propensities of the agent-causal capacity itself. (O'Connor, 2009: 197–8)

The core of O'Connor's account is that the reasons structure the agent-causal power by changing the objective probabilities of its propensities toward effects—toward intention-formations and decisions. Andrei Buckareff (forthcoming) argues that on this view reasons are causally relevant but are not causally efficacious when the action occurs, and this may be a cost of the view.[1]

To this account Pereboom (2014) objects that agent-causal libertarianism cannot accommodate the claim that the propensities of the agent-causal power are governed by probabilities specified in this way. To answer the disappearing agent version of the luck objection, the causal power exercised by the agent must be of a different sort from that of the causally relevant events, and on the occasion of a free decision, the exercise of the agent-causal power must be distinct from the exercise of the causal powers of these events. The disappearing agent objection shows that causal powers of the events are not the sort that can provide the decision-settling control needed for moral responsibility. In fact, O'Connor says:

> We insist upon the importance of the distinction between (the persisting state or event of one's having) reasons *structuring* one's agent-causal power in the sense of conferring objective tendencies towards particular actions, and reasons *activating* that power by producing one's causing a specific intention. On the view I have described, nothing other than the agent himself activates the causal power in this way. To say that I have an objective probability of 0.8 to cause the intention to join my students at the local pub ensures nothing about what I will in fact do. I can resist this rather strong inclination just as well as act upon it. (O'Connor, 2009: 213)

But if the propensities of the reasons and those of the agent-causal power toward the relevant range of effects are exactly the same, then either the causal powers of the reasons and of the agent-as-substance are identical after all, or else this identity of propensities is an unexplained coincidence.

One might also object that if the propensities of the agent-causal power were structured by objective probabilities, the agent would lack the control in action required for moral responsibility in the basic desert sense (Pereboom, 2014). Suppose God created us as agent-causes whose distinctive causal power featured two propensities, one for self-interest and the other for morality. Each of these propensities is structured by equal and unalterable objective probabilities, so that, over our lifetimes, we can expect half of our decisions when self-interest conflicts with morality to be self-interested and half moral. Even if the agent on any such particular occasion could choose either the self-interested or the moral option, from the incompatibilist point of view the agent would not be blameworthy in the basic desert sense for the overall pattern, in particular for the lifetime's immoral half. And it would seem that if an agent isn't blameworthy for the pattern, she isn't blameworthy for the instances that make up the pattern.

It might be replied that this verdict results from the probabilities being unalterable.[2] But suppose we change the case so that agents are in addition governed by a probabilistic law that specifies a 50 percent probability over a lifetime that a subject agent-cause her moral conversion, whereupon 100 percent of the subsequent actions in situations of conflict between morality and self-interest will be moral. Even then, from the incompatibilist point of view, the agents in this world would not be blameworthy for the pattern of immoral actions they may perform, and thus, it would seem, not for the instances that make up the pattern. More complex cases can be constructed, but the verdict would appear to be the same.

10.9.   Contrastive Explanations and an Expanding Agent-Causal Power

Another kind of challenge to agent-causal libertarianism is that it cannot deliver on a number of different demands for contrastive explanation. One such objection, first stated by C.D. Broad (1952) and then developed by Ginet (1990, 1997), claims that this account precludes a contrastive explanation for the timing of an action, why it occurred at the exact time it did and not at some other time. Ginet argues that in addition, contrastive explanations for the exact kind of action performed are also ruled out:

> The agent per se cannot *explain* why the event happened precisely when it did rather than at some slightly different time. Only some difference between the agent at one time and the agent at the other times, some temporally located property, could do that. Nor, it might be added, can the agent per se explain why that particular sort of event rather than some other sort happened just then. (Ginet, 1997: 93–4, 1990: 13–14)

From the unavailability of these kinds of contrastive explanations Ginet concludes that the parallel sort of causation must be absent as well:

> What sense can it make, then, to say that the agent as such is the cause of the occurrence of that particular sort of event rather than some other sort, and is the cause of its occurring at that particular time rather than at some other time? (Ginet, 1997: 93–4)

O'Connor responds by arguing that "a full explanation of why an agent-caused event occurred, will include, among other things, an account of the reasons upon which the agent acted," and that as a result, the agent-causal theory has resources to explain the timing of such an event (O'Connor, 1995b: 184). In his reply, Clarke invokes his integrated two-causal stream view, on which one cause of a free action is an event, for example, the agent's acquisition of certain reasons, and that such an event has the potential to explain an action's occurring at a certain time rather than another (Clarke, 1996: 298–9; cf., 2003). However, we've just seen that Clarke's integrated account of how agent-causes can act on reasons faces a serious objection: The way reasons-causation and agent-causation are integrated is by brute law, where one would think a substantive explanation would be required. O'Connor's solution to this problem—and arguably the only plausible alternative available—is to build the relevant capacity to act on reasons into the agent-causal power as a component. It might be described as a power of an agent fundamentally as a substance to cause a decision upon consideration of reasons, and on the basis of certain reasons, without being causally determined to do so. On this proposal, instead of Clarke's distinct pair of causal powers, those of agents as substances and reasons as events, we have a single, albeit complex, causal power that can do the requisite explanatory work.

O'Connor provides a specific account about how the propensities of the agent-causal power are structured by reasons, and we've noted reconciliation problems with this feature of his position.

To the idea that an appeal to reasons can serve to meet the demand for contrastive explanations he sets out, Ginet objects that there are cases in which an agent causes an event at one particular time rather than at some other time, but reasons can't explain why:

> My reason for picking up the phone does not explain why I picked it up precisely when I did rather than a few seconds earlier or later, and I need not have had any reason for choosing that precise time rather than a slightly different earlier or later one. It is possible that there was nothing at all that explains why the one thing was the case rather than any alternative.... But in that case, it seems natural to infer, there was nothing that *caused* the one rather than any alternative. (Ginet, 1997: 94–5)

Similarly, for the "sort of event" problem,

> My reason for picking up the telephone was that I wanted to make a call. But that reason does not explain why I used my left *rather than* my right hand to pick it up, and indeed I need not have had any reason for using one hand rather than the other. (Ginet, 1997: 94)

However, here the agent-causal libertarian can also build the capacity that underwrites the contrastive explanation into the agent-causal power: It's also a power, fundamentally as a substance, to cause a choice of a particular sort and at a particular time, without being causally determined to do so. This agent-causal power itself would then explain how the agent might cause the right-hand choice by contrast with the left-hand choice, and cause this choice at t1 rather than at some other time, all without invoking reasons. So why did he make the right-hand choice at t1 and not the left? The answer is: because he exercised his agent-causal power at t1 to make a right-hand choice rather than exercising it to make the left.

One might raise the concern that the strategy of building new elements into the agent-causal power in response to demands for contrastive explanation is too facile. The assumption on the agent-causal libertarian's part would be that this power can be expanded without cost to respond to any such demand. But the concern is that as the power inflates, the sense increases that what is being invoked is in fact a kind of *deus ex machina* with dubious explanatory value. The agent-causal libertarian might respond that once the agent-causal power is on board, it's legitimate to supply it with what's required to act rationally and to act in particular ways at particular times. After all, these are just ordinary agential capacities, and it's to be expected that whatever it is that causes actions would possess them.

10.10.   Is Agent-Causation Reconcilable with the Physical Laws?

The coherence of agent-causal libertarianism is perhaps in doubt, but it has not been decisively undermined. Pereboom (1995, 2001, 2014) argues, however, that we have empirical reasons to conclude that it's improbable that we are agent causes of the sort set out by this view. These reasons concern whether agent-causal libertarianism can be reconciled with our best physical theories. On agent-causal libertarianism, when an agent decides freely, she causes the decision without being causally determined to do so. But if the decision results in changes in her brain or in the rest of her body, she at some point would affect the physical world distinct from herself as agent-cause. However, on our best physical theories the physical world is law-governed. Suppose first that the physical laws are causally deterministic (Kant, 1788/1996: Ak V: 97–8). This is what Kant maintains, but on his agent-causal picture, when an agent makes a free decision, she causes the decision without being causally determined to do so. But on the causal route to action that begins with this decision, alterations in the physical world, for example in her brain or some other part of her body, are produced. But it would seem that we would at this point encounter divergences from the deterministic laws. For the alterations in the physical world that result from the undetermined decisions would themselves not be causally determined, and they would thus not be governed by deterministic laws. One might object that it is possible that the physical alterations that result from free decisions just happen to dovetail with what could in principle be predicted on the basis of the deterministic laws, so nothing actually occurs that diverges from these laws. But this proposal would, at least *prima facie*, involve coincidences too wild to be credible. For this reason, it seems that agent-causal libertarianism is not reconcilable with the physical world's being governed by deterministic laws.

Recent expositors of agent-causal accounts, Clarke (1993, 2003) and O'Connor (2000, 2009) in particular, propose that quantum indeterminacy can advance the reconciliation project. On one interpretation of quantum mechanics, the physical world at the micro-level is not deterministic, but is governed by laws that are fundamentally merely statistical or probabilistic. Suppose, as is controversial, that significant quantum indeterminacy percolates up to neural indeterminacy at the level of decision. This constitutes a *prima facie* case for the claim that agent-causal libertarianism is reconcilable with the laws of physics. Still, wild coincidences would seem to arise on this proposal. Consider the class of possible human actions each of which has a physical component whose antecedent probability of occurring is approximately 0.32. It would not violate the statistical laws in the sense of being logically incompatible with them if, for a large number of instances, the physical components in this class were not in fact realized close to 32 percent of the time. Instead, the import of the statistical law is that for a large number of instances we can *expect* physical components in this class to be realized close to 32 percent of the time. But if agent-caused free action were compatible with what according to the statistical law is highly likely, then for a large enough number of instances the possible actions in our class would have to be freely chosen close to 32 percent of the time. Then, for a sufficiently large number of instances, the possible actions whose physical components have an antecedent probability of 0.32 would almost certainly be freely chosen close to 32 percent of the time. However, if the occurrence of these physical components were settled by the decisions of libertarian agent-causes, then their actually being chosen very close to 32 percent of the time would result in a coincidence no less wild than the coincidence of possible actions whose physical components have an antecedent probability of about 0.99 being chosen, over a sufficiently large number of instances, close to 99 percent of the time. The suggestion that agent-caused free choices would not diverge from what the statistical laws predict for the physical components of our actions runs so sharply counter to what we should expect as to render it incredible (Pereboom, 1995, 2001, 2014).

If the libertarian agreed, she might propose that there are indeed departures from the probabilities that we would expect given the physical laws, likely to be found in the brain. Roderick Chisholm (1964) suggests a position of this sort. Steven Horst (2011) points out that physics, at least as we presently find it, features no departure-free laws when they are construed as describing actual motions. The law of gravity, for example, will only result in exactly accurate predictions of motions if there are no other forces, such as electromagnetism, at play. The better view, according to Horst, is to interpret the laws as governing causal powers, which in the case of fundamental physics, are plausibly forces. On this conception, laws do not primarily describe motion, but rather characterize causal powers. Horst argues that this conception of the laws is friendly to a libertarian conception of free will, since any law should be understood as in principle open to the existence of powers not described by that law, and the agent-causal power would be a candidate.

An objection to this proposal is that we would seem to have no evidence that departures from the known physical laws occur, say in the brain. The libertarian could reply that we have phenomenological evidence that we are indeterministically free (Deery et al., 2013), and this yields evidence that the divergences in question in fact occur. Nothing we know rules out the claim that we are undetermined agent-causes and there exist such divergences, and it may be wise for the libertarian to develop this approach.

10.11.   Is Libertarian Agent Causation Required for Agency?

According to Martine Nida-Rümelin (2007) and Helen Steward (2012), libertarian agent causation is required not just for moral responsibility, but for agency itself. Here is how we understand the general concern about agency that gives rise to these views. On the Davidsonian model of agency, action is caused by mental states or events, and not fundamentally by agents as substances (Davidson, 1963). As Velleman casts this view:

There is something the agent wants, and there is an action that he believes conducive to its attainment. His desire for the end, and his belief in the action as a means, justify taking the action, and they jointly cause an intention to take it, which in turn causes the corresponding movements of the agent's body. Provided that these causal processes take their normal course, the agent's movements consummate an action, and his motivating desire and belief constitute his reasons for acting. (Velleman, 1992: 461)

But this state-causal picture appears to be mistaken. As John Bishop puts it:

Intuitively, we think of agents as carrying out their intentions or acting in accord with their practical reasons, and this seems different from (simply) being caused to behave by those intentions or reasons. (Bishop, 1989: 72)

Velleman thinks that borderline cases of action, such as weak-willed action, qualify as action while simply being caused by reasons, but what he calls *full-blooded action* appears to conflict with the state-causal model:

In full-blooded action, an intention is formed by the agent himself, not by his reasons for acting. Reasons affect his intention by influencing him to form it, but they thus affect his intention by affecting him first. And the agent then moves his limbs in execution of his intention: his intention doesn't move his limbs by itself. The agent thus has at least two roles to play: he forms an intention under the influence of reasons for acting, and he produces behavior pursuant to that intention. (Velleman, 1992: 462; cf. Hornsby, 2004a, 2004b, Brent, ms)

Thus here, just as for the event-causal model of free will and moral responsibility, we have a disappearing agent problem. Now, just as for the free will case, the event or state causalist might attempt to answer this disappearing agent problem by providing an account of the role of the agent in event- or state-causal terms. Such an account explicates the distinctive role of the agent in action by certain core desires (Velleman, 1992) or standing preferences (Ekstrom, 2000, 2003), with which the agent, in its role in acting, can be identified. On Velleman's account, the role of the agent is played by a *desire to act in accord with the reasons* (1992: 478–9), and this attitude is enough to supply the agent's role in acting:

Although the agent must possess an identity apart from the substantive motives competing for influence over his behavior, he needn't possess an identity apart from the attitude that animates the activity of judging such competitions. If there is such an attitude, then its contribution to the competition's outcome can qualify as his – not because he identifies with but rather because it is functionally identical to him. (Velleman, 1992: 480)

A potential problem for Velleman's proposal can be illustrated by the phenomenon of torn decisions (Pereboom, 2015b). In the case of Ralph's decision to stay in Mayberry or move to New York, it seems that it can't be a desire to act in accord with the reasons that settles which decision occurs, since in Balaguer's (2010) example the reasons are in equipoise. But it's evident that the agent can settle which action and decision occur. So it appears that the role of the agent can't be played by a desire to act in accord with reasons. And here agent causation, as in the disappearing agent problem for event-causal accounts of free will, would seem to yield a solution.

But so far we don't have a reason for adopting the libertarian version of agent causation. For agent causation is, arguably, compatible with the causal determination of action (Markosian, 1999, 2010; Nelkin, 2011; Pereboom, 2015b). Nida-Rümelin (2007) contends, however, that full-blooded agency, understood as involving *active* causation of intention, precludes causal determination. And Steward (2012) argues that the sort of settling required is incompatible with causal determination, and that libertarian agent causation is essential to agency:

> If determinism were true, the matters in question would already be settled, long before it even occurred to me that I might, by acting, come to settle any of them. And surely it is a condition of being truly able to settle something that it has not already been settled in advance of one's potential intervention. If determinism were true, then, I would not be able to settle matters that it is essential for me to be able to settle, if I am to be an agent. And so, if determinism were true there could not be agents and there could not be actions. (Steward, 2012: 39)

Steward allows that we have a weak notion of settling that does not require indeterminism:

> One might perhaps speak, for instance, of the fall of the third domino's having settled that the fourth would fall, even in a context in which one took it for granted that the fall of the fourth was already guaranteed by the fall of the first (or indeed by events and circumstances occurring long before the fall of the first). (2012: 41)

But weak settling is insufficient for action (2012: 41–69), and this claim has intuitive pull.

However, Steward's argument restricts the determinist to a state or event-causal theory of action, and the concern she raises is that such an account crucially features "the disappearance of the agent" (2012: 62–9). But Steward does not address deterministic agent causation, and it is arguably enough to yield the requisite notion of settling (Pereboom, 2015b). A profitable way to conceive of settling is as a kind of difference-making. Carolina Sartorio (2013) proposes a determinism-friendly event-causal account of the sort of difference-making required for moral responsibility, and it can be modified to yield a deterministic agent-causal account of the kind of settling required for agency. On Sartorio's proposal, moral responsibility requires difference-making in the sense that the actual sequence leading to the action makes an agent responsible for that action *only if the absence of that actual sequence would not have made the agent responsible for the action.* More generally, she proposes (Sartorio, 2016) that moral responsibility is a causal notion, and that causes make a difference to their effects in that they make a causal contribution to their effects not matched by any contribution that their absences would. Similarly, the advocate of deterministic agent causation can propose:

> (S-AC) An agent settles whether an action occurs only if she agent-causes it, where the absence of her agent-causing the action would not have caused that action. (Pereboom, 2015b)

Stated in terms of David Lewis's (1973) semantics for counterfactuals, an agent settles whether an action occurs only if she agent-causes it, and in the closest possible worlds in which she does not agent-cause the action, the absence of the agent-causing would not have caused that action. (S-AC) does not require that the agent be able to do otherwise, and thus it can be satisfied by an agent even if she is causally determined to act as she does.

10.12. Non-Causal Theories

Perhaps the difficulties we've noted for libertarian views can be avoided if one denied that free agency is governed by any sort of causal law, whether deterministic or probabilistic. This would be the case if free agency wasn't causal at all. We noted earlier that on Bergson's view, the mental is *sui generis*, and, as it really is, it is not subject to scientific theorizing, and so it is indeed not causal in nature. Considerations of this type gave rise to the conviction that neither agents nor reasons can be causes, and this thought is part of what motivates contemporary non-causal theories. More generally, the second half of the nineteenth century and the first half of the twentieth witnessed an attempt to distinguish the human and natural sciences, and a non-causal view of agency was one feature of this attempt. It's not clear whether more recent non-causalists have this aim in mind. But a common contemporary theme is that a non-causal view is a particularly promising way to account for free will.

Recent non-causal theories of agency, such as those developed by Carl Ginet (1990), Hugh McCann (1998), and Stewart Goetz (2008), feature specific and different accounts of how it might be that certain actions could be free. On Ginet's theory, for a basic action—one which does not consist in one or more mental events causing other mental events—to be free, it must have an agent as a subject, it must be uncaused, and it must have an actish phenomenological feel. McCann requires that it must be uncaused and intrinsically and fundamentally intentional. In Goetz's conception, it must be uncaused and meet a teleological requirement, and because McCann's intrinsic intentionality is teleological as well, these views are similar in an important respect.

Perhaps the most important test for any libertarian theory is its capacity to respond adequately to the various versions of the luck objection. As we pointed out in the account of agent causation, to fix the problem disclosed by the luck objection, and the disappearing agent version in particular, what arguably needs to be added to the libertarian account under consideration is involvement of the agent in the production of her decisions that would allow her to settle which decision occurs. To answer the luck objection the agent-causal libertarian thus appeals to the controversial notion of substance-causation. But one might contend, as Ginet specifically does, that a non-causal position fares at least as well. On his proposal, an agent's substance-causing basic actions would have no advantage over her *simply performing* such acts, where "performing" can be analyzed non-causally—in terms of the agent's being the subject of the act and an actish phenomenological feel (Ginet, 1990). This position has the advantage of avoiding an appeal to the controversial notion of substance causation.

Here is Ginet's position on free action set out in detail (1997, 2007):

1. Every action either is or begins with a simple mental action, a mental event that does not consist of one mental event causing others.
2. A simple mental event is an action if and only if it has a certain intrinsic phenomenological quality, that is, an "actish" quality.
3. A simple mental event's having this intrinsic actish phenomenological quality is sufficient for its being an action, but not for its being a free action.
4. A simple mental free action must, in addition, not be causally necessitated by antecedent events (Ginet, 1996), and not even probabilistically caused by antecedent events (2007).

Ginet's account holds out the promise of a solution to the problem posed by the disappearing agent objection without resorting to the controversial notion of substance-causation.

The leading sort of objection to non-causal accounts of free will and moral responsibility is that these notions require control, and control is fundamentally a causal notion (Clarke, 2003; O'Connor, 2000). The non-causalist will of course deny this, and claim that his conditions are sufficient for the requisite control. But a concern one might have about non-causal views generally is that they project a sense of control by using causal language, while at the same time disavowing causal notions.

In view of this concern, Pereboom (2014) sets out a dilemma for non-causal theories. When advocates of non-causalism use *prima facie* causal language to express the purportedly non-causal relation, either causation is being invoked, or if it is not, the control required for moral responsibility is absent. Let us examine Ginet's view as a test case. He remarks:

[Making] It was up to me at time T whether that event would occur only if I *made it the case that it occurred* and it was open to me at T *to keep it from occurring*. (2007: 245)

"Made it the case that it occurred" is *prima facie* causal language. For arguably, the making-happen relation is a causal relation, perhaps the paradigmatic causal relation. Plausibly, causation just *is making something happen or producing something*? As Clarke specifies:

> An event that nondeterministically causes another brings about, produces, or makes happen that other event, though it is consistent with the laws of nature that the former have occurred and not have caused the latter. (2003: 33)

Even Ginet, just prior to the above quotation, remarks:

> To suppose it is possible for there to be indeterministic causation is to suppose that causation does not reduce, Humean fashion, to universal regularity but is rather a brute relation among particular events, a relation of *production*, a relation that may be impossible to specify in non-synonymous terms. (2007: 244)

Moreover, "*Keep it from occurring*" also appears causal—the keeping-from-occurring relation would seem to be a causal relation. Thus a challenge for the non-causalism of Ginet's account is that when he says "I made it the case that the event occurred," this seems equivalent to "I caused the event to occur," for the reason that to report that A caused B is really just to report that there is a relation of production from A to B.

David Lewis proposes another characterization of causation that calls into question non-causalism in a similar way:

> We think of a cause as something that makes a difference, and the difference it makes must be a difference from what would have happened without it. (Lewis, 1986)

But Ginet's [Making] would appear to be equivalent to: It was up to me at time T whether that event would occur only if at T I made it the case that it occurred, and at T I made the difference as to whether it would occur. But then, given a "difference making" account of causation, the event's occurring and its being up to me whether that event would occur would also amount to my causing it.

To develop this concern, it is valuable to examine Ginet's reason for rejecting an argument (which he formulates) for the conclusion that an uncaused action cannot have been up to the agent:

1. For any event e that has actually occurred, it was up to the agent S whether e occurred only if S made it the case that e occurred.
2. For any event e, S made it the case that e occurred only if S caused e to occur.
3. If S caused e to occur, then e was not uncaused.
4. Therefore, an uncaused action cannot have been one such that it was up to the agent whether it would occur.

Ginet subsequently writes:

> The false premise is (2).... For it seems evident to me that, given that an action was uncaused, all its agent had to do to make it the case that she performed that action was to perform it. If my deciding to vote for the motion, for example, was uncaused, then it follows that nothing other than me made it the case that I decided to vote for the motion, and it also follows that I made it the case that I so decided: I did so simply by deciding. (Ginet, 2007: 247)

However, in the sentence: "all its agent had to do to make it the case that she performed that action was to perform it," "make it the case" would appear to be causal, and (2) would then seem true.

McCann's position (1998: 180) is also vulnerable to this kind of objection. His view specifies that an agent's exercise of active control has two features. A basic action must be:

1. a spontaneous, creative undertaking on the part of the agent, and
2. intrinsically intentional. The intentionality of a basic action is a matter of its being intrinsically an occurrence that is meant, by the individual undergoing it, to be her doing.

The specification that the basic action is a spontaneous, creative undertaking is suggestive of the agent's making it the case that the basic action occurs, which also risks invoking the causal relation. The same would seem true for the notion of intrinsic intentionality. For it wouldn't appear to make sense to say that a basic action is intrinsically intentional while denying that it is made to occur by the agent or that the agent makes the difference whether it occurs. How could one intend an action and do so successfully without making it happen, or without this process making the difference as to whether it would happen?

But suppose we can make sense of these positions not invoking causation at all. Objecting to McCann's view in particular, Clarke argues: "Where intentionality is divorced from an appropriate causal production, it does not seem that it can, by itself, even partly constitute the exercise of active control" (2008, 2003: 20–1). This objection finds support in one's sense that McCann's conditions (1) and (2) could not be satisfied if it is specified that the agent neither makes the basic action occur nor makes the difference whether it occurs. For how could an action be a spontaneous and creative undertaking on the part of the agent, or an agent's doing, without her making it happen or making the difference whether it will happen? But if it's agreed that the agent does indeed have a making-happen and a difference-making role, the account would appear to be causal after all.

A hypothesis for why non-causalism is nevertheless coherent is that falling under general laws, whether they are deterministic or probabilistic, is essential to the causal relation. This view was held by Bergson, by the Neo-Kantians who developed non-causalist positions in the late nineteenth and early twentieth centuries, and one also finds it in Donald Davidson's (1970) anomalous monism about mental events. In opposition to this tradition, Michael Tooley (1990, 1997) contends that there can be instances of causation that do not fall under any general law, deterministic or probabilistic. Kant (1781/1787/1987) in effect argues that this is at least a *prima facie* conceptual possibility.

Suppose that the non-causalist claimed that if a "making happen" relation is not law-governed, it does not qualify as causal. How substantive, as opposed to merely verbal, would this contention be in the context of the present debate? If what the non-causalist is proposing is that the relation between the subject and the action is a making-happen or a difference-making relation that is non-causal only because it is not governed by any sort of causal law, one might respond that he is invoking the sort of singular relation that Tooley defends, even though he won't call it a causal relation. If this is in fact so, the dispute between the two sides, in particular between the non-causalist and the agent-causalist, would threaten to be merely verbal. To join the issue, following David Chalmers's (2011) recommendation for resolving merely verbal disputes, it would be advisable to drop the term "causal" from the discussion, and speak instead of "making happen" and "difference-making." But it would then appear that causalists and non-causalists could agree that the relation between agent and a free basic action is a making-happen or a difference-making relation, which would seem to be the core issue in the controversy.

Suppose we abandon language involving the term "cause" and restrict ourselves to talk of making happen and difference-making. We can then ask the indeterminist non-causalist whether she agrees that in the case of a free action, the agent makes the action happen or makes the difference whether the decision happens. If the response is positive, then the next question to ask is whether agents making actions happen or making the difference whether actions happen reduces to agent-involving events making actions happen or making the difference whether actions happen. If so, then the problem of the disappearing agent arises again. If not, then it appears we are left with the view that agents-as-substances make actions happen or make the difference whether actions happen. But then there would be no substantive difference between the agent-causal and "non-causal" positions.

10.13.   The Cost of Rejecting Libertarianism

We believe, along with many libertarians, that the best prospect for libertarianism is an agent-causal version, and one that rejects the project of reconciling the account with our best physical theories. In addition, one might adduce non-evidential reasons to opt for such a view. Daniel Speak (2004) argues that those who have cautiously rejected libertarianism about free will on evidential grounds have perhaps overlooked an important feature of justification: a pragmatic and axiological component. Faith in a moral order is laudable, and it sometimes requires belief when it is not adequately supported by the evidence alone—that is, when the evidentialist about justification view recommends that we refrain from believing. For example, our belief that life is worth living may not be adequately supported by the evidence, but we should nevertheless maintain it partly on axiological, in this case moral, grounds. Speak contends that if human agents had libertarian free will, they would possess a kind of dignity that they would lack if they were not free in this sense. Abandoning a belief in libertarianism thus arguably has a serious moral cost, which should be included in determining whether we should believe that we are free in this sense. Libertarians tend to be strongly committed to incompatibilism, and so the force of this pragmatic argument for accepting libertarianism would depend on the practical palatability of the incompatibilist alternative, free will skepticism. To this position we now turn.

Suggestions for Further Reading

Libertarian theories of free will have occupied a prominent place in the history of philosophy. For three especially notable defenses, see:

Bergson, Henri. 1889/1910. *Essai sur les données immédiates de la conscience*, Paris: F. Alcan, 1989; translated as *Time and Free Will*, tr. F.L. Pogson. London: Allen and Unwin, 1910.
Kant, Immanuel. 1781/1787/1987. *Critique of Pure Reason*, tr. Paul Guyer and Allen Wood. Cambridge: Cambridge University Press, 1987.
Reid, Thomas. 1788. "Essays on the Active Powers of Man." In Sir William Hamilton, ed., *The Works of Thomas Reid*. Hildesheim: G. Olms Verslagsbuchhandlung, 1983.

Here we offer a small sampling of the most prominent work on each of three main kinds of libertarian views:

Event-Causal

Balaguer, Mark. 2010. *Free Will as an Open Scientific Problem*. Cambridge, MA: MIT Press.
Ekstrom, Laura. 2000. *Free Will: A Philosophical Study*. Boulder, CO: Westview.
Kane, Robert. 1996. *The Significance of Free Will*. Oxford: Oxford University Press.

Agent-Causal

Chisholm, Roderick. 1964. "Human Freedom and the Self." *The Lindley Lectures*. Copyright by the Department of Philosophy, University of Kansas. Reprinted in Watson, Gary, ed., 1982. *Free Will*. New York: Oxford University Press.
Clarke, Randolph. 2003. *Libertarian Accounts of Free Will*. New York: Oxford University Press.
O'Connor, Timothy. 2000. *Persons and Causes*. New York: Oxford University Press.
Steward, Helen. 2012. *A Metaphysics for Freedom*. Oxford: Oxford University Press.
Taylor, Richard. 1974. *Metaphysics*. Englewood Cliffs, NJ: Prentice Hall.

Non-Causal

Bergson, Henri. 1889/1910. *Essai sur les données immédiates de la conscience*, Paris: F. Alcan, 1889; translated as *Time and Free Will*, tr. F.L. Pogson: London: Allen and Unwin, 1910.
Ginet, Carl. 1990. *On Action*. Cambridge: Cambridge University Press.
Goetz, Stewart. 2008. *Freedom, Teleology and Evil*. London: Continuum.
McCann, Hugh. 1998. *The Works of Agency*. Ithaca, NY: Cornell University Press.

Notes

1 Buckareff (forthcoming) also argues that, on this view, it's the dispositions of the agent and not the agent that is doing the causing, and that this is a serious problem for the position.
2 Al Mele suggested this objection in conversation.

11 Contemporary Incompatibilism

Skeptical Views

Due to the difficulties that have been raised for the compatibilist and libertarian positions, a number of philosophers have endorsed the skeptical outlook that we do not have free will, and in particular that we lack the sort of free will required for moral responsibility. Hard determinists argue that because determinism is true and compatibilism is implausible, we don't have free will of this kind. This perspective is defended by Baruch Spinoza (1677), Paul Holbach (1770), Joseph Priestley (1788/1965), B.F. Skinner (1971), and Ted Honderich (1988). Others have argued for skeptical views about free will that do not depend on the truth of causal determinism, and claim in particular that indeterminism or the sort of indeterminism that is likely to be true is also incompatible with free will—for example, Galen Strawson (1986, 1994), Derk Pereboom (1995, 2001, 2014), Neil Levy (2011), Sam Harris (2012), and Gregg Caruso (2012). Critics have expressed a number of concerns about the resulting view. They have argued, for example, that free will skepticism would threaten our self-conception as deliberative agents, that it would undercut the reactive attitudes essential to good human interpersonal relationships and meaning in life, and that if hard determinism were true morality itself would be incoherent.

To understand and assess free will skepticism, it is important to recognize that our practice of holding each other morally responsible is complex, and that therefore the term "moral responsibility" is used in a number of ways. Moral responsibility in several of these senses is uncontroversially compatible with the causal determination of action by factors beyond our control, and hence can be accommodated by the free will skeptic. Yet there is one particular sense of moral responsibility, and a correlative type of free will, that have been at play in the historical debate, which are not uncontroversially compatible with this sort of determinism:[1]

> For an agent to be *morally responsible for an action in the basic desert sense* is for it to belong to her in such a way that she would deserve blame if she understood that it was morally wrong, and she would deserve credit or perhaps praise if she understood that it was morally exemplary. The desert invoked here is basic in the sense that the agent, to be morally responsible, would deserve the blame or credit just because she has performed the action,

given sensitivity to its moral status, and not by virtue of consequentialist or contractualist considerations.

Basic desert moral responsibility is often thought to be presupposed by our retributive reactive attitudes, such as indignation and moral resentment. In P.F. Strawson's (1962) account, moral responsibility is essentially tied to these reactive attitudes, and hence the basic desert sense is plausibly the variety that he brings to the fore.

Alternative notions of moral responsibility have not been a focus of the free will debate. For example, an agent might be held to be morally responsible when his dispositions to act badly might be modified or eliminated by blaming, and his dispositions to act well strengthened by praising (Schlick, 1939; Smart, 1963). Or an agent could be considered morally responsible when it is legitimate to expect her to respond reasonably to such questions as: "Why did you decide to do that? Do you think it was the right thing to do?" and that she evaluate critically what her actions indicate about her moral character (Bok, 1998; Scanlon, 1998). Incompatibilists would not regard the control required for moral responsibility in these senses to be incompatible with determinism, and thus it is open to free will skeptics to endorse these senses. Instead, it's the basic desert sense that's at issue, and unless otherwise indicated in this chapter, we will use "moral responsibility" to signify that sense.

11.1.   Spinoza, the First Hard Determinist

Baruch Spinoza maintained that it is due to the truth of causal determinism that we lack the sort of free will required for moral responsibility (Spinoza, 1677: 440–4, 483–4, 496–7; cf. Della Rocca, 2008). In Descartes's contrasting position, which is Spinoza's target, to have free will is to have the power to assent, dissent, and to suspend judgment with respect to a proposition. Some propositions are proposals for action, and assent to such a proposition results in an action. This view derives from Stoicism (third century BCE). Descartes affirms both that we have this kind of free will and that theological determinism is true, and that how they might be reconciled is beyond our comprehension (*Principles* Part I, 40–1). Spinoza, on the contrary, argues that reconciliation between theological determinism and the claim that we have such a free power of assent is impossible, and as a result he denies that we have such a power. Noting that by the will he understands "a faculty by which the mind affirms or denies something true or something false, and not the desire by which the mind wants a thing or avoids it" (*Ethics* II/129–30), he claims:

> In the Mind there is no absolute, or free, will, but the Mind is determined to will this or that by a cause which is also determined by another, and this again by another, and so to infinity. (*Ethics* IIP48/129)

The crucial element in the proof of this proposition is that "all things have been predetermined by God, not from freedom of the will or absolute good pleasure, but from God's absolute nature, or infinite power" (*Ethics* I Appendix, II/77). Spinoza later affirms: "Experience itself, no less clearly than reason, teaches that people believe themselves to be free because they are conscious of their own actions and ignorant of the causes by which they are determined" (*Ethics* IIIP2s, II/143).

Spinoza argues that skepticism about free will is not harmful but instead advantageous, since it yields a kind of equanimity resulting from the belief that everything that happens is necessitated by God: What skepticism about free will

> teaches is that we must expect and bear calmly both good luck and bad. For everything that happens follows from God's eternal decree with the same necessity as it follows from the essence of a triangle that its three angles are equal to two right angles. (Spinoza, 1677: 490)

The specific benefits include freedom from harmful emotions: "This doctrine contributes to communal life by teaching us 'to hate no one, to disesteem no one, to mock no one, to be angry at no one...'" (Spinoza, 1677: 490). Far from being harmful, in Spinoza's view the skeptical outlook is to be recommended for its moral and psychological benefits.

11.2.   A Contemporary Hard Determinist

Ted Honderich advocates a sophisticated version of non-cognitivism about moral judgments generally, and thus also about judgments that attribute moral responsibility. According to his position, such judgments essentially express attitudes, do not report moral facts, and lack truth value. Still, they do involve propositional content in a distinctive way. For example, one might morally disapprove of a corrupt politician for some action, where this disapproval includes a retributive desire. On Honderich's conception, the attitude then takes the action to be originated by the agent in such a way as not to be causally determined by factors beyond his control, and it thereby involves a commitment to this indeterministic propositional content.

It will not be logically inconsistent to have a retributive desire toward the politician and at the same time believe he did not originate his action in this way. Yet Honderich thinks that given our human nature, someone who has retributive desires for the politician will also believe that she originated the action, and the belief will function as a reason in support of the attitude. Given human nature, rejection of the belief will serve as a reason to relinquish the attitude: "If I lose the belief, I cannot persist in the attitude or the behavior. Currently, at any rate, that is a psychological impossibility" (Honderich, 1996). Determinism is thus a threat to retributive desires, and more generally, to the reactive attitudes connected to the practice of holding people morally responsible, because determinism is incompatible with origination, and thus, given human nature, determinism will serve as a reason to relinquish these attitudes. Honderich (1988) presents a careful empirical argument for the conclusion that determinism is in fact true.

As a result, he thinks we should reassess our commonly held attitudes about moral responsibility. At the same time, he argues that much of what would appear to be threatened can be rescued, in particular the aspirations we have for achievement and meaning.

11.3.   No-Free-Will-Either-Way Theories

By contrast with Spinoza and Honderich, many contemporary free will skeptics are agnostic about causal determinism, but contend that free will skepticism is reasonable on either deterministic or indeterministic presuppositions.

Some free will skeptics argue that free will is in fact impossible independently of the truth of determinism or of indeterminism. Most prominently, Galen Strawson contends, by way of his Basic Argument, that moral responsibility— "ultimate responsibility"—requires a conception of agency that human beings could not satisfy, and its impossibility for us can be established independently of an examination of the truth of determinism (1986: 25–60; 1994). Strawson, then, is a no-free-will-either-way theorist, that is, he maintains that for us moral responsibility is incompatible with both determinism and indeterminism. We discussed Strawson's Basic Argument in Section 7.2, labeling it an impossibilist version of the Ultimacy Argument. We first review it briefly here for ease of discussion, and then highlight additional features and particular objections.

Again, the core idea of the Basic Argument can be expressed as follows. When an agent acts, she acts because of the way she is. But to be morally responsible for acting, the agent must then be morally responsible for the way she is, at least in key mental respects. But if an agent is to be morally responsible for the way she is in those key mental respects, she must be responsible for the way she is that resulted in those mental respects. This reasoning generates a regress, which indicates that finite beings like us can never satisfy the conditions on moral responsibility. The conclusion is that finite agents like us can never be morally responsible for acting.

An interesting variant of this argument begins with the premise that actions for which an agent is free in the sense required for moral responsibility must have a full causal explanation in terms of her reasons alone. More precisely, such action must be rational, and rational actions must have an explanation in terms of reasons the agent has that indicates all of what there was about the agent, mentally speaking, that causally brought it about that she performed the action she did (Strawson, 1986: 52–6). But how do the reasons that the agent has themselves arise? If they arise non-rationally, then the action is "rationally speaking random." If the reasons resulted from choices that are based on further reasons, the same questions could be asked about them. There can be no infinite regress of reasons, and consequently, actions must always be "rationally speaking random," and thus unfree.

Randolph Clarke (2005) contests Strawson's claim that moral responsibility requires that the agent be in rational control of all the mental factors that contribute to the action. Suppose we're created as agent-causal libertarian beings, pre-programmed with a set of strong self-interested motivations and a set of roughly equally strong altruistic motivations, and motivations of no other kinds (e.g., to do evil for evil's sake). These fundamental motivations thus come to be non-rational. Basic Argument-style reasoning might well show that we're not morally responsible for the fact that our actions are all either self-interested or altruistic. But when it's up to someone to make either a self-interested choice or an altruistic choice, and she makes the altruistic one, it seems that she can be morally responsible for making the altruistic one rather than the self-interested one.

Clarke's criticism of Strawson's argument might be supported by the charge that the standard for rationality it assumes is too stringent (Pereboom, 2001). Imagine that you are in a situation of conflict between self-interested and moral reasons; one possible decision is morally justified but is not on balance in your self-interest, the other is not morally justified but is in your self-interest. You have the capacity to make either choice, you make the moral one, and this deci-sion is on balance justified by your reasons overall. Strawson would argue that the agent is unfree because the choice is not fully caused by your reasons, and thus rationally speaking random. Yet in this situation it is intuitive that the action might well be sufficiently connected to your reasons to count as rational. The rationality of action would then not require its complete determination by the agent's reasons, but rather only being justified by them (cf. Pereboom, 2001).

Saul Smilansky (1993, 2000) concurs with Strawson's argument that the sort of free will required for moral responsibility is impossible for us, and thus he too is a no-free-will-either-way theorist. Nevertheless he believes that he can at the same time accept a picture that combines aspects of both hard determinism and compatibilism, since what he calls *the Assumption of Exhaustiveness*—that one must either be a compatibilist and not an incompatibilist, or an incompatibilist and not a compatibilist, is false (Smilansky, 2000). The most striking aspect of Smilansky's view is that we should maintain, in certain respects, the illusion of free will, and that we should do so for practical reasons. For example, he argues that a valuable type of self-respect would be undermined if determinism were true, and that the illusion of free will is needed to maintain this self-respect (1997, 2000). He also contends that the illusion of free will is required to sustain certain valuable aspects of criminal justice, for example that only those who have committed crimes should be punished, and that we should punish criminals rather than provide luxurious accommodations for them (2000, 2011). But even if he is recommending here that we retain the view we ordinarily hold, and that this position indeed combines aspects of compatibilism and hard determinism, it is nevertheless clear that by virtue of this fact his philosophical position is still skeptical. For according to his philosophical position the goods at issue require an illusion of free will, and not its reality.

Richard Double (1991, 1996) also contends, independently of consideration of determinism or indeterminism, that the claim that we have the free will required for moral responsibility cannot be true. His most fundamental reason for believing this is that the concept of free will is internally incoherent, and thus cannot be realized. One supporting argument he proposes is that the debate between compatibilists and incompatibilists is irresolvable, and hence that each of the conflicting compatibilist and incompatibilist notions of free will are part of the concept of free will. Another argument of his defends an irrealist position about moral judgments in general, according to which they cannot be true, then contends that "moral responsibility" and "the sort of free will required for moral responsibility" are moral notions, and concludes that claims that agents exemplify these notions also cannot be true.

In Double's view, propositions of the sort "X has free will" will in fact be necessarily false because free will is a conceptual impossibility. By analogy, "X is a round square" is also necessarily false because a round square is a conceptual impossibility. Double is thus committed to a no-free-will-either-way theory of an especially strong sort. Galen Strawson's position is in a sense weaker, since he is a no-free-will-either-way theorist not for the reason that free will is conceptually impossible, but because it is metaphysically impossible that beings like us have it.

There is perhaps reason to doubt Double's claim that his conceptual-impossibility irrealism about free will gains powerful support from the irresolvability of the debates that separate compatibilists and incompatibilists. Examples of such debates Double cites are the dispute about the Consequence Argument from determinism to the claim that we could not have done otherwise, and the controversy over Frankfurt-style cases. However, we have as much reason to believe that most central debates in philosophy are irresolvable, but we might still want to resist subjectivism about, for instance, Fregean versus Russellian theories of meaning, or Humean versus anti-Humean theories of causation.

11.4.   A Neuroscientific Case against Free Will

In recent decades, certain neuroscientific studies conducted by scientists such as Benjamin Libet and Daniel Wegner have been taken to demonstrate that we lack free will (Libet, 1985; Wegner, 2002; cf. Harris, 2012). On their accounts, we lack free will because there is no conscious state of willing that is causally efficacious in producing action. In Libet's view, any state that is conscious comes too late in the causal sequence to be efficacious in producing action. Instead, unconscious neural states cause action. Brian Leiter (2007) points out that this view has a progenitor in Friedrich Nietzsche, who contends that any state picked out by conscious phenomenology is not causally connected to the resulting action. Instead actions are physiologically caused.[2]

In several of Libet's studies (1985, 2004), subjects whose brains are monitored by EEG (electroencephalogram) are asked to flex their right wrists whenever they wish.[3] When participants are regularly reminded not to plan their wrist flexes and when they do not afterward say that they did some planning, an average ramping up of EEG activity (550 ms before muscle motion begins) precedes the average reported time of the conscious experience (200 ms before muscle motion begins) by about one-third of a second (Libet 1985). Libet claims that decisions about when to flex were made at the earlier of these two times (1985: 536).

About such studies Chun Siong Soon, Marcel Brass, Hans-Jochen Heinze, and John-Dylan Haynes write: "Because brain activity in the SMA consistently preceded the conscious decision, it has been argued that the brain had already unconsciously made a decision to move even before the subject became aware of it" (2008: 543). To secure further evidence about the issue, they designed an experiment in which subjects monitored by fMRI (functional magnetic resonance imaging) are instructed to do the following "when they felt the urge to do so": "decide between one of two buttons, operated by the left and right index fingers, and press it immediately" (543). Soon and his colleagues found that, by using readings from the frontopolar cortex and the other in the parietal cortex they can predict with about 60 percent accuracy (see Soon et al. 2008, supplementary figure 6; Haynes, 2011: 93) which button participants will press several seconds in advance of the actual button press (544).

The following argument against free will emerges from these sorts of experiments (Mele, 2013):

1. The overt actions studied in these experiments do not have corresponding consciously made decisions or conscious intentions among their causes (empirical premise).
2. So probably no overt actions have corresponding consciously made decisions or conscious intentions among their causes (inference from 1).
3. An overt action is a free action only if it has a corresponding consciously made decision or conscious intention among its causes (theoretical premise).
4. So probably no overt actions are free actions (conclusion).

These neuroscientific studies raise complex issues which we won't discuss in detail here. We'll instead restrict ourselves to canvassing a number of counter-considerations that have been raised. One prominent objection to Premise 1, developed in meticulous detail by Mele (2009), contends that there is no direct way to tell which phenomena correspond to which neural events. In particular, in the Libet studies, it is difficult to determine what the readiness potential corresponds to—for example, whether it is an intention formation or decision, or just an urge. If the readiness potential corresponds to a mere urge, and not to the formation of an intention or the making of a decision, then the experimental result will allow that the intention formation or decision is a conscious event. Thus, in Mele's analysis, the Libet studies leave open the possibility that intention-formations and decisions are conscious events after all.

A second objection is due to Eddy Nahmias. Almost everyone on the contemporary scene who believes we have free will, whether compatibilist or libertarian, also maintains that free action is caused by virtue of a chain of events that stretches backward in time indefinitely. At some point in time these events will be such that the agent is not conscious of them. Thus, all free actions are caused, at some point in time, by unconscious events. As Nahmias points out, the worry for free will raised by Libet's studies is that *the crucial factors* in the causation of action are not conscious. But, Nahmias argues, the no-free-will conclusion can't be secured against the determinist compatibilist just by showing that non-conscious events that precede consciousness causally determine action. For determinist compatibilists hold that every case of action features such events, and that this is compatible with free will. In addition, this no-free-will conclusion can't be secured against most libertarians by showing that there are nonconscious events that render actions more probable than not by a factor of 10 percent above chance (Soon et al. 2008), for almost all libertarians will agree that free will is compatible with such indeterministic causation by unconscious events at some point in the causal chain leading to action (De Caro, 2011).

Nahmias (2014) also remarks upon the unusual nature of the Libet-style experimental situation, that is, one in which a conscious intention to flex at some time in the near future is already in place, and what is tested for is the subject's implementation of this general decision at some specific time. Nahmias points out that when we drive cars or cook meals we will frequently form a conscious intention to perform an action of a general sort, whereupon specific implementations of these general conscious intentions are not preceded by additional specific conscious intentions. For example, one might form the general conscious intention to drive home, but the specific turns one makes may not be preceded by matching specific conscious intentions—one may be on auto-pilot. But in such cases the general conscious intention nevertheless has the crucial causal role in producing action. In Libet's studies, subjects form general conscious intentions to flex at some time or other when the instructions are given, and if specific implementations of these general conscious intentions are not preceded by specific conscious intentions, this would be just like the driving and cooking examples Nahmias adduces.

The debate about the neuroscientific studies is ongoing and intense, and it will be interesting to see how it develops in the coming years.

11.5.   Derk Pereboom's Argument for Free Will Skepticism

Pereboom's case for skepticism about free will features arguments that target the three rival views, event-causal libertarianism, agent-causal libertarianism, and compatibilism, and then claims that the skeptical position is the only one that remains standing. As we explained in the previous chapter (Chapter 10), according to event-causal libertarianism, actions are caused solely by way of events, standardly conceived as objects having properties at times, and some type of indeterminacy in the production of actions by appropriate events is held to be a decisive requirement for moral responsibility (Balaguer, 2004, 2009, 2010; Ekstrom, 2000; Kane, 1996). According to agent-causal libertarianism, free will of the sort required for moral responsibility is accounted for by the existence of agents who possess a causal power to make choices without being determined to do so (Chisholm, 1964, 1976; Clarke, 1993, 2003; Griffith, 2010; Kant, 1781/1787/1987; O'Connor, 2000; Reid, 1788; Taylor, 1966, 1974). In this view, it is essential that the causation involved in an agent's making a free choice is not reducible to causation among events involving the agent, but is rather irreducibly an instance of the agent-as-substance causing a choice not by way of events. The agent, fundamentally as a substance, has the causal power to cause choices without being determined to do so.

Critics of libertarianism have argued that if actions are undetermined, agents cannot be morally responsible for them. A classical presentation of this objection is found in Hume's *Treatise of Human Nature* (Hume, 1739: 411–12; cf. Mele, 2006b). In Hume's version, the concern highlighted is that if an action is uncaused, it will not have sufficient connection with the agent for her to be morally responsible for it. As we saw in Chapter 10 (page 238), this idea might be explicated as follows. For an agent to be morally responsible for a decision, she must exercise a certain type and degree of control in making that decision. In an event-causal libertarian picture, the relevant causal conditions antecedent to a decision—agent-involving events—do not settle whether this decision occurs, and the agent has no further causal role in determining whether it does. With the causal role of these antecedent conditions already given, it remains open whether the decision occurs, and whether it does is not settled by anything about the agent. Thus, intuitively, the agent lacks the control required for being morally responsible for the decision. Since the agent "disappears" at the crucial point in the production of the decision—when its occurrence is to be settled—Pereboom calls this the *disappearing agent argument* (Pereboom, 2004, 2014).

The agent-causal libertarian's solution to this problem is to specify a way in which the agent could have the power to settle which of the antecedently possible decisions actually occurs. The proposed solution is to reintroduce the agent as a cause, this time not merely as involved in events, but rather fundamentally as a substance. The agent-causal libertarian maintains that we possess a distinctive causal power—a power for an agent, fundamentally as a substance, to cause a decision without being causally determined to do so (Chisholm, 1964, 1976; Clarke, 2003; Griffith, 2010; Kant, 1781/1787/1987; cf. O'Connor, 2000; Reid, 1788; Watkins, 2005).

One traditional objection to the agent-causal picture is that we have no evidence that we are substances of the requisite sort. Kant (1781/1788) expresses another concern for the agent-causal libertarian view, which in his account calls for our endorsement on practical, but not on evidential grounds. The worry is that it might not be reconcilable with what we would expect given our best empirical theories. Kant himself believed that the physical world, as part of the world of appearance, is governed by deterministic laws, whereas the "transcendentally free" agent-cause would exist not as an appearance, but as a thing in itself. In this agent-causal picture, when an agent makes a free decision she causes the decision without being causally determined to do so. On the route to action that results from this undetermined decision, changes in the physical world, for example, in her brain or some other part of her body, are produced. But it would seem that we would at this point encounter divergences from the deterministic laws. For the alterations in the physical world that result from the undetermined decision would themselves not be causally determined, and they would thus not be governed by deterministic laws. One might object that it is possible that the physical alterations that result from every free decision just happen to dovetail with what could in principle be predicted on the basis of the deterministic laws, so nothing actually occurs that diverges from these laws. However, this proposal would seem to involve coincidences too wild to be credible. For this reason, it seems that agent-causal libertarianism is not reconcilable with the physical world's being governed by deterministic laws.

More recent expositors of the agent-causal view, such as Randolph Clarke (1993, 2003) and Timothy O'Connor (2000, 2009), suggest that quantum indeterminacy can help with the reconciliation project. On one interpretation of quantum mechanics, the physical world is not in fact deterministic, but is rather governed by laws that are fundamentally merely probabilistic or statistical. Suppose, as is controversial, that serious quantum indeterminacy percolates up to the level of human action. Then it might seem that agent-causal libertarianism can be reconciled with the claim that the laws of physics govern the physical components of human actions. However, wild coincidences would also arise on this suggestion (Pereboom, 1995, 2001). Consider the class of possible actions, each of which has a physical component whose antecedent probability of occurring is approximately 0.32. It would not violate the statistical laws in the sense of being logically incompatible with them if, for a large number of instances, the physical components in this class were not actually realized close to 32 percent of the time. Rather, the force of the statistical law is that for a large number of instances, it is correct to *expect* physical components in this class to be realized close to 32 percent of the time. Are free choices on the agent-causal libertarian model compatible with what the statistical law would lead us to expect about them? If they were, then for a large enough number of instances, the possible actions in our class would almost certainly be freely chosen nearly 32 percent of the time. But if the occurrence of these physical components were settled by the choices of agent-causes, then their actually being chosen close to 32 percent of the time would also amount to a wild coincidence. The proposal that agent-caused free choices do not diverge from what the statistical laws predict for the physical components of our actions would be so sharply opposed to what we would expect as to make it incredible.

At this point, the agent-causal libertarian might propose that exercises of agent-causal libertarian freedom do result in divergences from what we would expect, given our best accounts of the physical laws. Roderick Chisholm (1964) suggests such a position. Divergences from the probabilities that we would expect absent agent-causes do in fact occur whenever we act freely, and these divergences are located at the interface between the agent-cause and the component of the physical world that it directly affects, likely in the brain. There are different ways in which agent-caused free choices might diverge from what the physical laws would predict. One way is by not being subject to laws at all. Another is by being subject to different statistical laws, an option on which the agent-cause would be governed by probabilistic laws that are its own because they emerge only in the right sorts of agential contexts, and not to those that generally govern the physical events of the universe (O'Connor, 2009). A concern for these kinds of claims is that we currently have little or no evidence that they are true.

The remaining alternative to skepticism about free will is compatibilism. As we saw in Chapter 7, Pereboom holds that the best way to argue against the compatibilist option is a manipulations argument, one that begins with the intuition that if an agent is causally determined to act by, for example, scientists who manipulate her brain, then she is not morally responsible for that action, even if she satisfies the prominent compatibilist conditions on moral responsibility (Ginet, 1990; Kane, 1996; Mele, 1995, 2006b; Pereboom, 1995, 2001; Taylor, 1974; van Inwagen, 1983). The subsequent step is that there are no differences between such manipulated agents and their ordinary deterministic counterparts that can justify the claim that the manipulated agents are not morally responsible while the determined agents are.[4]

The multiple-case version of such a manipulation argument first of all develops examples of an action that results from an appropriate sort of manipulation and in which the prominent compatibilist conditions on moral responsibility are satisfied (Pereboom, 1995, 2001, 2014). In the setup, in each of the four cases the agent commits a crime, say murder, for reasons of self-interest. The cases are designed so that the crime conforms to the prominent compatibilist conditions. This action satisfies certain conditions advocated by Hume: The action is not out of character because, for the agent, it is generally true that selfish reasons typically weigh heavily—too heavily when considered from the moral point of view; and in addition, the desire that motivates him to act is nevertheless not irresistible for him, and in this sense he is not constrained to act (Hume, 1739). The action fits the condition proposed by Harry Frankfurt (1971), that is, his effective desire (i.e., his will) to commit the crime conforms appropriately to his second-order desires for which effective desires he will have. That is, he wills to kill the victim, and he wants to will to do so, and he wills this act of murder because he wants to will to do so. The action also meets the reasons-responsiveness condition advocated by John Fischer and Mark Ravizza (1998): Our agent's desires can be modified by, and some of them arise from, his rational consideration of his reasons, and if he knew that the bad consequences for himself that would result from the crime would be much more severe than they are actually likely to be, he would have refrained from the crime for that reason. This action satisfies a condition advanced by Jay Wallace (1994): The agent has the general ability to grasp, apply, and regulate his actions by moral reasons. For instance, when egoistic reasons that count against acting morally are weak, he will typically regulate his behavior by moral reasons instead (further advocates of views that privilege reasons rationality include Bok, 1998; Nelkin, 2008, 2011; Wolf, 1990). This ability also provides him with the ability to change and develop his moral character over time, a condition that Al Mele emphasizes (1995, 2006b).

These manipulation cases, considered separately, indicate that it is possible for an agent not to be morally responsible in the basic desert sense even if the

compatibilist conditions are met and that, as a result, these conditions are insufficient. However, (readers will recall from our earlier discussion of Pereboom's
argument in Section 7.4) the argument has additional force by virtue of setting
out three such cases, each of which is progressively more like a fourth, in which
the action is causally determined in a naturalistic way. The first case involves
manipulation that is local and determining, and hence most likely to elicit the
non-responsibility intuition. The second is similar to the first, except that it
restricts manipulation to a location at the beginning of the agent's life. The third
is similar, except the manipulation results from strict community upbringing;
and the fourth, again, is the naturalistic or ordinary deterministic case. The
objective is to formulate these examples so that it is not possible to draw a principled line between any two adjacent cases that would explain why the agent
would not be morally responsible in the basic desert sense in the first but would
be in the second. The conclusion is that the agent is not morally responsible in
this sense in all four cases, and the best explanation for this must be that he is
causally determined by factors beyond his control in each of them, and this result
conflicts with the compatibilist's central claim.

Thus according to Pereboom, free will skeptics, event-causal and agent-causal
libertarianism face significant problems, and compatibilism is vulnerable to the
argument from manipulation cases. The view that remains is free will skepticism, which denies that we have the sort of free will required for moral responsibility in the basic desert sense. Pereboom maintains that the concern for the
skeptical position is not that there is considerable empirical evidence that it is
false, or that there is a powerful argument that it is somehow incoherent. Instead,
the crucial question it faces is practical: Could we live with the belief that it is
true? We will turn to this concern in detail (in Section 11.8) after examining two
additional related positions.

11.6.   Neil Levy's Argument for Free Will Skepticism

Levy contends that the case for free will skepticism can be made on both the
determinist and the indeterminist alternatives. In his view, free will on either
option is ruled out on grounds of luck. The notions of luck that Levy invokes
involve lack of direct control, but other considerations as well. One of these
notions is luck in the chancy sense, the other is not.

> An event or state of affairs occurring in the actual world is *chancy lucky* for
> an agent if (i) that event or state of affairs is significant for that agent; (ii) the
> agent lacks direct control over that event or state of affairs; and (iii) that event
> or state of affairs fails to occur in many nearby worlds; the proportion of
> nearby worlds that is large enough for the event to be chancy lucky is inverse
> to the significance of the event for the agent. (Levy, 2011: 36)

Non-chancy luck is relevant to assessing the responsibility-yielding potential of
psychological dispositions. Such dispositions may be produced deterministically

by stable factors such as genetics, but still be lucky because there is variation in the disposition across the relevant reference group:

> An event or state of affairs occurring in the actual world that affects an agent's psychological traits or dispositions is *non-chancy lucky* for an agent if (i) that event or state of affairs is significant for the agent; (ii) the agent lacks direct control over that event or state of affairs; (iii) events or states of affairs of that kind vary across the relevant reference group, and (iv) in a large enough proportion of cases that event or state of affairs fails to occur or be instantiated in the reference group in the way which it occurred or was instantiated in the actual case. (Levy, 2011: 36)

Levy then contends that libertarian and compatibilist accounts render actions lucky in a sense that precludes moral responsibility. His key argument turns on the notion of a contrastive explanation for action. For example, we might ask about Kane's example of the businesswoman: Why did Anne stop and help rather than continue on to work? Levy argues that compatibilism does allow for such contrastive explanations, but that these explanations themselves feature luck. When the agent's endowment settles the action, agency is infected with non-chancy constitutive luck. On other occasions the settling of the action will be chancy, and then chancy luck undermines responsibility. In response to the endowment concern, we've seen that the compatibilist isn't moved much just by the prospect of endowment settling an action, and that a further vehicle such as a manipulation argument has a better chance of engaging the two sides in discussion.

Levy argues that libertarian accounts of free will cannot yield such contrastive explanations, and that this indicates that such actions are lucky in a sense that rules out moral responsibility. The agent-causal libertarian could respond by contending that the ability to substance-cause a decision and in the same causal context to substance-cause a refraining from this decision instead is a fundamental causal power the agent-as-substance has, and that this yields contrastive explanations (Section 10.9). Why did Anne decide to stop and help rather than continuing on to work? Because she exercised her agent-causal power to stop and help for moral reasons rather than exercising it to continue on to work for prudential reasons. A concern for this suggestion is that the agent-causal libertarian is trading in fundamental causal powers at the very core of her theory, which renders the position obscure (Nelkin, 2011: 93). But the agent-causal libertarian might resist by arguing that all fundamental causal powers are in an important sense inexplicable just because they're fundamental, and we wouldn't want to rule out all fundamental causal powers for this reason.

11.7.   Tamler Sommers' Metaskepticism

Tamler Sommers, early on a free will skeptic (e.g., 2007), now embraces a skepticism at a higher level that perhaps calls into question resolute first-order free will skepticism. In *Relative Justice* (Sommers 2012) he contends that since human cultures feature rationally irresolvable disagreements about moral responsibility, we should draw an irrealist conclusion, as Richard Double also does. Sommers's irrealist contention is that no theory about moral responsibility is true. His main argument for this conclusion, the argument from disagreement across cultures, parallels one of the strongest arguments for irrealism about ethics more generally. One upshot is that the concept of moral responsibility has no universal applicability conditions. By contrast, uncompromising skeptics such as Pereboom claim that the basic desert concept of moral responsibility does in fact have universal applicability conditions, but that they are never satisfied.

Sommers' specific argument adduces differences in intuitions about moral responsibility between honor cultures and cultures such as ours, which he calls institutional cultures (Sommers, 2012; see also Cogley's (2012) review of Sommers). In institutional cultures, norms for holding an agent morally respons-ible include control in acting, acting intentionally, and not being manipulated. Honor cultures differ in each of these respects. In some honor cultures, killing any member of a murderer's family, group, or clan is considered appropriate, and thus neither control nor intention is required for punishment. In others, women who are raped are killed because they had extramarital sex, and so again punishment without intention or control is held to be appropriate. In the Ancient Greek plays, king Agamemnon is held responsible for decisions he makes as a result of manipulation by the gods. People in honor cultures find such practices intuitively appropriate, while people in institutionalized cultures find them inap-propriate. And this disagreement is rationally irresolvable. The conclusion to draw is irrealism about moral responsibility claims.

Zac Cogley (2012) registers several objections to Sommers's argument. One is that even within institutional cultures there is disagreement about the con-ditions on appropriate moral responsibility assignments (as the free will debate indicates!), and we don't take this to establish irrealism about moral responsib-ility. To this one might reply that the differences between institutional cultures and honor cultures are much more radical. By analogy, we don't take disagree-ments about the role of teleology in evolutionary biology to count in favor of irrealism about the claims of that science. Instead, they are disagreements about how to work out the details of that science, the larger contours of which do command agreement.

A potentially more telling point of Cogley's, we think, is that even we in institutional cultures hold people responsible without believing they are respons-ible. For instance, we sometimes implement the legal doctrine of strict liability when significant practical reasons count in its favor. For example, in some juris-dictions, injury caused to bicyclists or pedestrians by moving cars is the respons-ibility of the driver regardless of intent or fault. Strict liability has several practical advantages: It makes judicial processes easier, and can produce additional incentives to be vigilant. Thus a person in an honor culture might think that killing a relative of the murderer is not justified on the ground that the relative is morally responsible for the murder, but that the practice is justified nonetheless because it produces incentives for members of a family or clan to keep each other in line, and achieves the best results given the absence of the expensive sort of judicial system we find in institutional cultures.

Sommers sets out his metaskepticism together with a defense of his own personal preference for a skeptical view, tempered to a certain degree by some accommodation of retributive desires. In accord with his metaskepticism he does not claim that first-order skepticism about moral responsibility holds for every culture. But that's consistent with thinking that it holds for ours. The result nicely unifies these two accounts and shows that they form a coherent package.

11.8. Living without Free Will

First-order free will skepticism denies that we have the sort of free will required for moral responsibility in the basic desert sense. The concern for this skeptical position is not that there is considerable empirical evidence that it is false, or that there is a powerful argument that it is somehow incoherent. Instead, the crucial questions it faces are practical. Could we live with the belief that it is true? Or would we be better off keeping our moral responsibility practices more or less as they are, as Vargas (2013) believes? A number of free will skeptics, including Honderich (1988), Pereboom (1995, 2001, 2014), Sommers (2007), Levy (2011), and Caruso (2012) argue that living without free will is a practically sound option. A variant on this view is Bruce Waller's (1990, 2011, 2014); he argues that we are not morally responsible—at least in a sense that involves desert—while we do have free will. He contends that life without this notion of moral responsibility is not only practically viable, but strongly to be preferred on moral grounds. (Arguably, Waller denies that we have the sort of free will required for basic desert moral responsibility, whereupon the difference between him and free will skeptics listed above would be merely verbal.) All of this is in opposition to P.F. Strawson's (1962) contention that we could not, and that, even if we could, it would not be rational to do so (see our discussion of Strawson on this point in Sections 6.4 and 6.5).

11.8.1. Morality and Responsibility

Accepting free will skepticism requires giving up our ordinary view of ourselves as blameworthy in the basic desert sense for immoral actions and praiseworthy in that sense for actions that are morally exemplary. One might object at this point that a skeptical belief would have harmful consequences, maybe so harmful that thinking and acting as if this skeptical view is true is not a practical possibility. Thus even if the claim that we are morally responsible turns out to be false, there might yet be significant practical reasons to believe that we are, or at least to treat people as if they were morally responsible in the sense at issue.

First, one might think that if we gave up the belief that people are blameworthy and praiseworthy, we could no longer legitimately judge any actions as morally bad or good. But this thought is mistaken. Even if we came to believe that a serial killer was not blameworthy due to a degenerative brain disease, we could still agree that his actions are morally very bad. Second, one might contend that if determinism precludes basic desert blameworthiness, it also undermines judgments of moral obligation. Because "ought" implies "can," and if, for instance, because determinism is true one could not have avoided acting badly, it must be false that one ought to have acted otherwise. And given that an action is wrong for an agent just in case he is morally obligated not to perform it, determinism would also undermine judgments of moral wrongness (Haji, 1998). All of this may be, but such reasoning does not also issue a challenge to judgments of moral goodness and badness (Haji, 1998; Pereboom, 2013, 2014). So, in general, free will skepticism can accommodate judgments of moral goodness and badness, which are arguably sufficient for moral practice.

Third, one might object that if we stopped treating people as if they were blameworthy in the basic desert sense, we might be left with inadequate resources for addressing bad behavior (Nichols, 2007; for a response, see Pereboom, 2009a). But the free will skeptic can turn instead to other senses of moral responsibility that have not been a focus of the free will debate. Free will skeptics like Joseph Priestley (1788/1965), and their revisionary compatibilist cousins such as Moritz Schlick (1939) and J.J.C. Smart (1963), claim that given determinism a forward-looking kind of moral responsibility can be retained. On the version of this position Pereboom endorses (Pereboom, 2013), when we encounter apparently immoral behavior, it is legitimate to invite the agent to evaluate critically what his actions indicate about his intentions and character, to demand apology, or to request reform. Engaging in such interactions is reasonable in view of the light of those wronged or threatened by wrongdoing to protect themselves from immoral behavior and its consequences. We also have an interest in his moral formation, and the address described naturally functions as a stage in this process. In addition, we might have a stake in reconciliation with the wrongdoer, and calling him to account in this way might serve as a step toward realizing this aim. The main thread of the historical free will debate does not pose determinism as a challenge to moral responsibility conceived in this way, and free will skeptics can accept that we are morally responsible in this sense.

11.8.2. Criminal Behavior

Does free will skepticism have resources adequate for contending with criminal behavior?[5] According to retributivism, punishment of a criminal is justified for the reason that he deserves something bad to happen to him—pain, deprivation, or death—just because he has knowingly done wrong (Kant, 1797/1965; Moore, 1987, 1998). Retributivism excludes appeal to goods such as the safety of society, or the moral improvement of the criminal in justifying punishment. Rather, the good by which retributivism justifies punishment, or the principle of right action that justifies punishment, is that an agent receive what he deserves only because of his having knowingly done wrong. This position would be undermined if the free will skeptic is right, since if agents do not deserve blame just because they have knowingly done wrong, neither do they deserve punishment just because they have knowingly done wrong. The free will skeptic thus recommends that the retributivist justification for punishment be abandoned.

By contrast, a theory that justifies criminal punishment on the ground that punishment educates criminals morally is not jeopardized by free will skepticism per se. However, we lack strong empirical evidence that punishing criminals reliably results in moral education, and without such evidence it would be immoral to punish them for this reason. It is generally immoral to harm someone to realize some good without substantial evidence that the harm will produce the good. Moreover, even if we had impressive evidence that punishment is effective in morally educating criminals, non-punitive ways of achieving this result would be morally preferable, independently of whether criminals are morally responsible in the basic desert sense.

According to deterrence theories, punishing criminals is justified for the reason that punishing deters future criminal behavior. The two most-discussed deterrence theories, the utilitarian version and the variant that grounds the right to punish on the right to harm in self-defense and defense of others, are not threatened by the skeptical view per se. But they are questionable on other grounds. The utilitarian version, which specifies that punishment is justified when and because it maximizes utility, is subject to well-known objections. It would counsel punishing the innocent when doing so would maximize utility; in certain situations it would recommend punishment that is unduly severe; and it would authorize harming people merely as means to the safety of others.

The type of deterrence theory that grounds the right to punish in the right we have to harm and threaten to harm aggressors in order to defend ourselves and others against immediate threats, advocated by Daniel Farrell, for example (1985: 38–60), is also independently objectionable. A threat that one could justifiably make and carry out to protect against an aggressor in a situation in which law enforcement and criminal justice agencies have no role cannot legitimately be carried out in a context in which the aggressor is in custody. The minimum harm required to protect ourselves from someone who is immediately dangerous in the absence of law enforcement is typically much more severe than the minimum harm required for protection against a criminal in custody. If our justification is the right to harm in self-defense, what we can legitimately do to a criminal in custody to protect ourselves against him is determined by the minimum required to protect ourselves against him in his actual situation. If one proposes to harm him more severely, for instance to provide credibility for a system of threats, the right to harm in self-defense would not supply the requisite justification, and one would again be in danger of endorsing a position subject to the use objection.

What is the minimum harm required to protect ourselves from a violent and dangerous criminal in custody? It seems evident that nothing more severe would be required than isolating him from those to whom he poses a threat. Thus it would appear that Farrell's reasoning cannot justify *punishment* of criminals, exactly, supposing that punishment involves the intentional infliction of significant harm, such as death or severe physical or psychological suffering. Rather, in the case of violent and dangerous criminals it would at best justify only incapacitation by preventative detention. But this suggests an intuitively legitimate theory of crime prevention that is neither undercut by the skeptical view, nor threatened by other sorts of considerations. Ferdinand Schoeman (1979) argues that if we have the right to quarantine carriers of serious communicable diseases to protect people, then for the same reason we also have the right to incapacitate the criminally dangerous by preventatively detaining them. Note that quarantining someone can be justified when she is not morally responsible for being dangerous to others. If a child is infected with a deadly contagious virus that was transmitted to her before she was born, quarantine can still be justifiable. So even if a dangerous serial killer is not morally responsible for his crimes in the sense at issue, it would be as legitimate to incapacitate him by preventative detention as it is to quarantine a non-responsible carrier of a serious communicable disease.

It would be morally objectionable to harm carriers of communicable diseases more severely than is required to protect people from the resulting threat. Similarly, the free will skeptic would not advocate treating criminals more harshly than would be needed to protect society against the danger they posed. Moreover, just as moderately dangerous diseases may allow for only measures less intrusive than quarantine, so moderately serious criminal tendencies might only justify varieties of incapacitation less intrusive than preventative detention. In addition, an incapacitation theory supported by the analogy to quarantine would recommend a level of concern for the rehabilitation and well-being of the criminal that would alter much of current practice. Just as it's fair for us to try to cure the people we quarantine, it would be fair for us to attempt to rehabilitate those we preventatively detain. If a criminal cannot be rehabilitated, and if protection of society demands his indefinite detention, there would be no justification for making his life more miserable than required to guard against the danger he poses.

11.8.3. Meaning in Life

Would it be difficult for us to cope without a conception of ourselves as creditor praiseworthy for achieving what makes our lives fulfilled, happy, satisfactory, or worthwhile—for realizing what Honderich calls our *life-hopes* (1988: 382ff.)?[6] He contends that there is an aspect of these life-hopes that is undercut by determinism, but that nevertheless determinism leaves them largely intact, and this seems plausible. First, it is not unreasonable to object that our life-hopes involve an aspiration for praiseworthiness in the basic desert sense, which on the skeptical view determinism would undermine. Life-hopes are aspirations for achievement, and it is natural to suppose that one cannot have an achievement for which one is not also praiseworthy in this sense, and thus giving up this kind of praiseworthiness would deprive us of our life-hopes. However, achievement and life-hopes are not as closely connected to basic desert praiseworthiness as this objection supposes. If someone hopes for a success in some project, and if she accomplishes what she hoped for, intuitively this outcome would be an achievement of hers even if she is not in this particular way praiseworthy for it, although the sense in which it is her achievement is diminished. For example, if someone hopes that her efforts as a teacher will result in well-educated children, and they do, then there is a clear respect in which she has achieved what she hoped for, even if because she is not in general morally responsible in the basic desert sense she is not praiseworthy in this way for her efforts.

One might think that free will skepticism would, due to its conception of agency, instill in us an attitude of resignation to whatever our behavioral dispositions together with environmental conditions hold in store (Honderich, 1988: 382ff.). This isn't clearly right. Even if what we know about our dispositions and environment gives us reason to believe that our futures will turn out in a particular way, it can often be reasonable to hope that they will turn out differently. For this to be so, it may be important that we lack complete knowledge of our dispositions and environmental conditions. Imagine that someone reasonably believes that he has a disposition that might well be a hindrance to realizing a life-hope. But because he does not know whether this disposition will in fact have this effect, it remains open for him—that is, epistemically possible for him—that another disposition of his will allow him to transcend this impediment. For instance, imagine that someone aspires to become a successful politician, but he is concerned that his fear of public speaking will get in the way. He does not know whether this fear will in fact frustrate his ambition, since it is open for him that he will overcome this problem, perhaps due to a disposition for resolute self-discipline to transcend obstacles of this sort. As a result, he might reasonably hope that he will get over his fear and succeed in his ambition. Given skepticism about free will, if he in fact does overcome this difficulty and succeeds in his political ambitions, this will not be an achievement of his in quite as robust a sense as we might naturally suppose, but it will be an achievement in a substantial sense nonetheless.

How significant is the aspect of our life-hopes that we must relinquish, given the skeptical view? Saul Smilansky argues that although determinism allows for a limited foundation for the sense of self-worth that derives from achievement or virtue, the hard determinist's, and also, more generally, the free will skeptic's perspective can nevertheless be extremely damaging to our view of ourselves, to our sense of achievement, worth, and self-respect, especially when it comes to achievement in the formation of one's own moral character. Smilansky (1997: 94, 2000) thinks that in response it would be best for us to foster the illusion that we have free will in the sense at issue. Plausibly, there is a kind of self-respect that presupposes an incompatibilist foundation, and that it would be undercut if the free will skeptic is right. One might question, however, whether Smilansky is accurate about how damaging it would be for us to give up this sort of self-respect, and whether the maintenance or cultivation of illusion is required.

First, note that our sense of self-worth—our sense that we have value and that are lives are worth living—is to a non-trivial extent due to features not produced by our volition, let alone by free will. People place great value on natural beauty, native athletic ability, and intelligence, none of which have their source in our volition. We also value voluntary efforts—in productive work and altruistic behavior, and in the formation of moral character. But does it matter very much to us that these voluntary efforts are also freely willed in the sense at issue in the historical debate? Perhaps Smilansky overestimates how much we do or should care.

Consider how good moral character comes to be. It is plausibly formed to a significant degree by upbringing, and the belief that this is so is widespread. Parents regard themselves as having failed in raising their children if they turn out with immoral dispositions, and they typically take great care to bring their children up to prevent such an outcome. Accordingly, people often come to believe that they have the good moral character they do largely because they were raised with love and skill. But those who believe this about themselves seldom experience dismay because of it. We tend not to become dispirited upon coming to understand that good moral character is not our own doing, and that we do not deserve a great deal of praise or credit for it. By contrast, we often feel fortunate and thankful. Suppose, however, that there are some who would be overcome with dismay. Would it be justified or even desirable for them to foster the illusion that they nevertheless deserve, in the basic sense, praise or credit for producing their moral character? Perhaps most would eventually be able to accept the truth without feeling much loss. All of this would plausibly also hold for those who come to believe that they do not deserve in the basic sense praise and respect for producing their moral character because they are not, in general, morally responsible in this way.

11.8.4.   *Personal Relationships and Emotion*

Is the assumption that we are morally responsible in the sense at issue in the free will debate required for meaningful and fulfilling human relationships? P.F. Strawson (1962) delivers a positive answer. In his view, moral responsibility has its foundation in the reactive attitudes, which are in turn required for the kinds of personal relationships that make our lives meaningful. Our justification for claims of blameworthiness and praiseworthiness is ultimately grounded in the system of human reactive attitudes, such as moral resentment, indignation, guilt, forgiveness, and gratitude, and since moral responsibility has this type of basis, the truth or falsity of causal determinism is not relevant to whether we legitimately hold agents morally responsible. If causal determinism was in fact true and did threaten these attitudes, we would face instead the prospect of a certain objectivity of attitude, a stance that in Strawson's view rules out the possibility of meaningful personal relationships.

Strawson is plausibly right to believe that objectivity of attitude would seriously hinder our personal relationships, but that he is mistaken to hold that this stance would result or be appropriate if determinism did pose a genuine threat to the reactive attitudes (Pereboom, 1995, 2001, 2016). First, some of our reactive attitudes, although they would be undermined by hard determinism, or more broadly by free will skepticism, are not required for good personal relationships. Resentment and indignation are undercut by the skeptical position, but free will skeptics such as Pereboom maintain that all things considered they are suboptimal relative to alternative attitudes available to us. Second, the skeptic might continue, the attitudes that we would want to retain either are not threatened by a skeptical conviction, because they do not have presuppositions or attendant beliefs that conflict with this view, or else have analogues that would in this respect be in the clear. The attitudes and analogues that would survive do not amount to Strawson's objectivity of attitude, and are sufficient to sustain good personal relationships.

Of all the attitudes associated with moral responsibility, moral resentment, that is, anger directed toward someone due to a wrong he has done to oneself, and indignation, anger with an agent because of a wrong he has done to a third party, are particularly closely connected with it. It is telling that debates about moral responsibility most often focus not on how we react to morally exemplary agents, but rather on how we respond to those who have acted badly. The kinds of cases most often used to generate a strong conviction of moral responsibility in the basic desert sense involve especially malevolent harm. Perhaps, then, our attachment to moral responsibility in this sense derives partly from the role moral resentment and indignation have in our moral lives, and free will skepticism is especially threatening because it challenges their legitimacy.

Moral resentment and indignation often have a communicative function in personal relationships, and accordingly one might object that if we were to strive to modify or eliminate these attitudes, such relationships might well be damaged (see Shabo, 2012 for a sophisticated defense of this view). But when we are targets of bad behavior in our relationships there are other emotional attitudes often present that are not challenged by the skeptical view, whose expression can also play the communicative role. These attitudes include feeling hurt or shocked or disappointed about what the other has done, and moral sadness or sorrow and concern for him. Often feigned disappointment or moral sadness is used to manipulate others, but the genuine versions are invoked here. It is thus not clear that anger is required for communication in personal relationships.

A case can be made that these alternatives are indeed preferable. Moral anger, of which resentment and indignation are subspecies, does have an important role in human relationships as they ordinarily function. It motivates resistance to oppression and abuse, and as a result it can make relationships better. But expression of moral anger frequently has harmful effects. On many occasions, it fails to contribute to the well-being of those to whom it is directed. Expression of moral anger is often intended to cause physical or emotional pain, and it can give rise to destructive resistance instead of reconciliation. Moral anger also serves as a motivation to take harmful measures against the other. It thus also has a tendency to damage or destroy relationships.

Certain types and degrees of moral anger are likely to be beyond our power to affect, and thus even the committed skeptic might not be able to make the transformation her view recommends. So even if the best personal relationships do not require a disposition to moral anger, it may be that there is no mechanism generally available to us by which we might eradicate this disposition, or radically curtail its manifestations. Nichols (2007) cites the distinction between narrow-profile emotional responses, which are local or immediate emotional reactions to situations, and wide-profile responses, which are not immediate and can involve rational reflection. As free will skeptics we might expect that we will be unable to significantly reduce narrow-profile, immediate moral anger when we are seriously wronged in our most intimate personal relationships. But in wide-profile cases, we might well be able to diminish, or even eliminate moral anger, or at least disavow it in the sense of rejecting any force it might be thought to have in justifying harmful reactions to the wrong done. Such modification of moral anger and its typical presuppositions, aided by this conviction, might well be advantageous for our relationships.

Guilt and repentance are also threatened by free will skepticism, and one might argue that this consequence is more difficult to accommodate. There is much at stake here, the objector might contend, because these self-directed attitudes are required for good relationships for agents like us who can behave immorally. Without guilt and repentance, we would not be motivated to moral improvement after acting badly, we would be kept from restoring relationships impaired as a result, and we would be barred from reestablishing moral integrity. For absent guilt and repentance none of our psychological mechanisms can generate these effects. The skeptic's position would undercut guilt because it essentially involves a sense that one is blameworthy in the basic desert sense for an immoral action. If someone did not feel blameworthy in this way for the action he would also not feel guilty for it. Moreover, because feeling guilty is undermined by the skeptical view, repentance is also no longer an option, since feeling guilty is a prerequisite for a repentant attitude.

Suppose that you behave badly in the context of a relationship, but because you believe that free will skepticism is true, you reject the claim that you are blameworthy in the basic desert sense. However, you acknowledge that you have behaved badly, you feel deeply disappointed in yourself, and as Bruce Waller advocates, you feel deep sorrow and regret for what you have done (Waller, 1990: 165–6; cf. Bok, 1998). In addition, you resolve to do what you can to eradicate your disposition to behave this way, and you seek help to make this change. These responses arguably can realize the good that guilt is apt to achieve, and they are compatible with the skeptic's conviction.

Gratitude might appear to presuppose that the agent to whom one is grateful is morally responsible in the basic desert sense for a beneficial act, whereupon a skeptical conviction would undermine this attitude (Honderich, 1988: 518–19). But even if this is so, as in the case of forgiveness, certain core aspects would remain unaffected, and these aspects can provide what is required for good personal relationships. Gratitude involves, first of all, being thankful toward someone who has acted beneficially. True, being thankful toward someone often involves the belief that she is praiseworthy in the basic desert sense for some action. Still, one can be thankful to a young child for some kindness without believing that she is praiseworthy in this way. This aspect of gratitude could be retained even without the supposition that the other is responsible in the basic desert sense. Gratitude typically also involves joy as a response to what someone has done. The skeptical view does not pose a threat to the legitimacy of being joyful and expressing joy when others are considerate or generous on one's behalf.

11.9. Final Words

Living without a conception of our actions as freely willed in the sense required for basic desert moral responsibility does not come naturally to us. Our natural reactions to good and bad actions presuppose that we are free in this sense. But, as free will skeptics see it, there is a strong case to be made against this presupposition, and also, despite our initially apprehensive reaction to skepticism about this sort of free will, endorsing this perspective would not have unacceptable consequences for us. According to these skeptics, it would not seriously threaten meaning in life, because it is compatible with a veridical sense of accomplishment when we succeed in our projects. It would not hinder the possibility of the good personal relationships, but even holds out the promise of greater equanimity by reducing the moral anger that often impairs them. So, the free will skeptic contends, if we did in fact give up the assumption of the sort of free will at issue, then, perhaps surprisingly, we might well be better off as a result.

Suggestions for Further Reading

Here is a list of books of the last quarter-century arguing for some type of skeptical view about free will from a philosophical perspective:

Caruso, Gregg. 2012. *Free Will and Consciousness: A Determinist Account of the Illusion of Free Will*. Lanham, MD: Lexington Books.
Double, Richard. 1996. *Metaphilosophy and Free Will*. New York: Oxford University Press.
Double, Richard. 1991. *The Non-Reality of Free Will*. New York: Oxford University Press.
Honderich, Ted. 1988. *A Theory of Determinism*. Oxford: Clarendon Press.
Levy, Neil. 2011. *Hard Luck*. Oxford: Oxford University Press.
Pereboom, Derk. 2014. *Free Will, Agency, and Meaning in Life*. New York: Oxford University Press.
Pereboom, Derk. 2001. *Living Without Free Will*. Cambridge: Cambridge University Press.
Smilansky, Saul. 2000. *Free Will and Illusion*. Oxford: Oxford University Press.
Sommers, Tamler. 2012. *Relative Justice: Cultural Diversity, Free Will, and Moral Responsibility*. Princeton, NJ: Princeton University Press.
Strawson, Galen. 1986. *Freedom and Belief*. Oxford: Oxford University Press.

Bruce Waller is a skeptic about moral responsibility but not about free will. Here are his three books:

Waller, Bruce. 2014. *The Stubborn System of Moral Responsibility*. Cambridge, MA: MIT Press.
Waller, Bruce. 2011. *Against Moral Responsibility*. Cambridge, MA: MIT Press.
Waller, Bruce. 1990. *Freedom without Responsibility*. Philadelphia, PA: Temple University Press.

These two books argue for skepticism about free will from a neuroscientific and psychological point of view:

Libet, Benjamin. 2004. *Mind Time*. Cambridge, MA: Harvard University Press.
Wegner, Daniel. 2002. *The Illusion of Conscious Will*. Cambridge, MA: MIT Press.

Mele's book defends free will against arguments from neuroscience:

Mele, Alfred. 2009. *Effective Intentions*. New York: Oxford University Press.

Sam Harris's *Free Will* is a widely read popular book that argues for a skeptical position on free will and also discusses the neuroscientific arguments:

Harris, Sam. 2012. *Free Will*. New York: Free Press.

Notes

1   See also our earlier discussions about the nature and different senses of moral responsibility (Section 1.3; Section 8.3).
2   Nietzsche writes in the *Twilight of the Idols* (Nietzsche, 1889/1977):

> The "inner world" is full of phantoms ... the will is one of them. The will no longer moves anything, hence does not explain anything either—it merely accompanies events; it can also be absent. The so-called motive: another error. Merely a surface phenomenon of consciousness—something alongside the deed that is more likely to cover up the antecedents of the deeds than to represent them.... What follows from this? There are no mental causes at all. (*Twilight of the Idols* VI 3, as quoted by Leiter, 2007)

3   The description of these studies is from Mele (2013).
4   See Section 7.4 for a full discussion of Pereboom's manipulation argument. We offer a compressed presentation of it here for ease of reference.
5   Section 8.2 summarizes Pereboom (2001: chapter 6) and (2014: chapter 7).
6   Sections 8.3 and 8.4 summarize Pereboom (2001: chapter 7) and (2014: chapter 8).

12 Revisionism and Some Remaining Issues

In this book we have attempted to offer a comprehensive introduction to the major contemporary philosophical issues bearing on free will. The first seven chapters featured our introduction of the key controversies in the debate and the developments that animate the most recent philosophical work on free will. Chapters 8 and 9 were then devoted to the different forms of compatibilism and their advantages and disadvantages. Chapters 10 and 11 canvassed the various incompatibilist positions together with their problems and prospects. In this concluding chapter, we address a cluster of important issues that we have yet to consider. We begin with Manuel Vargas's nuanced revisionist position, and then we briefly address recent debates concerning responsibility for omissions, the compatibility of rational deliberation with belief in causal determination, experimental philosophy, and, finally, free will and religious issues.

12.1. Manuel Vargas's Revisionism

In a number of articles and book chapters (e.g., Vargas 2005a, 2007, 2009, 2011), and now in his book *Building Better Beings: A Theory of Moral Responsibility* (2013), Manuel Vargas defends *revisionism*. As Vargas understands it, revisionism is neither a straightforward compatibilist view, nor is it a straightforward incompatibilist one. Rather, it is a hybrid view that is in one respect an incompatibilist form of skepticism and in another an innovative form of compatibilism.

How could free will skepticism and compatibilism be conjoined? Vargas's theory has two distinct elements, a descriptive one that is incompatibilist and skeptical, and a prescriptive one that is compatibilist. Cast in purely descriptive terms, according to Vargas our folk concept of moral responsibility includes incompatibilist presuppositions requiring libertarian satisfaction conditions (2013: chapter 1). But for empirical reasons that dovetail with those Pereboom (2001, 2014) finds compelling (see our discussion of Pereboom in Section 11.4), Vargas doubts that actual persons could possess and act from libertarian resources (Vargas, 2013: chapter 2). He contends that it is not credible in light of a reasonable "standard of naturalistic plausibility" (2013: 58–60). Hence, the ordinary folk concept yields a skeptical result: Persons are not free and responsible given the actual folk concepts in our thinking about freedom and responsibility. However, Vargas argues (2013: chapter 3), we should resist endorsing the prescriptive thesis that characteristically goes with the familiar forms of free will and moral responsibility skepticism. Instead, we should revise our concept by excising the objectionable incompatibilist strands while preserving the compatibilists ones.

Key to Vargas's revisionist proposal is the contention that what moral responsibility is—including the freedom requirements for it—could come apart in a significant way from our folk concept of it. If so, we need to take seriously the prospect of revising the concept so as to get it to accord with responsibility's true nature. This, as Vargas sees things, is precisely the situation in which we find ourselves. So Vargas prescribes a revisionary form of compatibilism. According to him (2013: chapter 4), we should make these revisions in a systematic way in deference to the normative burdens of justifying our moral responsibility practices, especially those pertaining to the aptness of praising and blaming. In this way we can "build up" a naturalistically plausible account of free and responsible agency suited for our normative demands.

We will now set out each of Vargas's main theses, his descriptive one and then his prescriptive one. We'll then consider the tenability of his proposal that our folk concept of moral responsibility could significantly depart from what moral responsibility really is.

12.1.1.   Vargas's Descriptive Thesis

How does Vargas argue for his descriptive thesis in favor of free will and moral responsibility skepticism? On his view, compatibilism, as a descriptive thesis, is untenable. One reason has to do with the intuitive appeal of certain philosophical arguments, regardless of the philosophical merits of the arguments themselves. Vargas countenances the Consequence Argument for incompatibilism and sets aside a direct consideration of the contents of the argument (2013: 27). Instead, he asks *why* the argument has been so appealing. In doing so, he notes that compatibilist renderings of the crucial ability in dispute, the ability to do otherwise, make the argument unpersuasive to "antecedently committed compatibilists" (28). Nevertheless, this is not a reason for a "standoff" between compatibilists and incompatibilists, since:

> The "naturalness" or ease of the incompatibilist reading of the argument is itself evidence that the argument captures an important part of the contents and logic of commonsense thinking about these issues. (28)

According to Vargas, if we run the argument by ordinary people, we find that the most prevalent reading of the "can" claims embedded in the argument is incompatibilist-friendly, and this is indirect evidence that our commonsense folk concept is incompatibilist (28–9). Now Vargas grants that "[b]uilding a case for folk conceptual incompatibilism on the basis of the reception of arguments for philosophical incompatibilism has its limitations" (29). But doing so does at least help reveal a "natural understanding of the sense of ability relevant to the free will problem" (29).

Turning to Frankfurt's argument against an alternative-possibilities condition on moral responsibility, Vargas challenges the relevance of Frankfurt-defenders' limiting the debate to robust alternatives, which includes a constraint of normative relevance. (See our discussion of robustness in Section 5.2.) About McKenna's (2003) proposal for robustness, Vargas asks why we should assume that normative relevance is a constraint on folk intuitions. As he notes, it is possible "that our ordinary concepts have normatively irrelevant conditions built into them" (32). He then contends that, at the "level of characterizing the architecture of our ordinary moral thought, the normative relevance demand is inappropriate" (32). If so, then those debating Frankfurt's argument in terms of robustness are working from a misguided and false assumption—at least insofar as they are attempting to uncover how our actual concepts of freedom and responsibility work.

At this juncture, a more conventionally oriented theorist—compatibilist or incompatibilist—might object to Vargas's grounds for identifying what the commonsense notion of moral responsibility is, or instead, what the relationship is between familiar styles of philosophical argumentation and our folk concept, a distinction Vargas himself invokes in distinguishing between philosophical incompatibilism and folk psychological incompatibilism. One way to evaluate the credibility of an argument like the Consequence Argument by whether it bottoms out in premises that can be grounded in unobjectionable folk concepts. Prior to thinking through the argument, many will be inclined to construe the disputed ability in incompatibilist terms. Vargas is right about this. But isn't the *point* of the argument itself as a piece of serious philosophy to attempt to show that under scrutiny those initial impressions are vindicated? And if they are not vindicated, doesn't this help to cast doubt on those initial impressions? That is, one way to construe traditional forms of philosophical argumentation at least in this area of philosophy is in terms of their helping us to clarify what our commonsense concepts really come to, or instead, what they really commit us to. Thus, the more conventional theorist might protest, before we draw incompatibilist conclusions about what our folk concept is, we actually have to hash out the philosophical arguments themselves. If so, then Vargas's indirect remarks about the Consequence Argument cannot help establish his descriptive thesis; he'll have to take it up directly if he wants to draw upon it as evidence for a descriptive thesis that is incompatibilist in character.

A similar point applies to Vargas's assessment of Frankfurt's argument. He suggests that worries about robust alternatives simply might have no relevance to the folk notion, since that notion might after all have elements that are normatively irrelevant. Of course this is *possible*. But those like Fischer (1994), McKenna (2003), and Pereboom (2001, 2014) who have sought to limit the debate to robust alternatives have done so by taking steps drawing on conceptual resources—typically by way of thought experiments—all of which are meant to appeal to folk intuitions about, for instance, the plausibility of the conditions for blaming.

None of this is to suggest that Vargas is wrong that *the*—or instead *a* crucial—commonsense view of free will and moral responsibility is incompatibilist. It does, however, seem that before he can claim that his prescriptive compatibilist proposal is a revisionary departure from commonsense, he will have to settle the more basic dispute as to which non-revisionary account of freedom and responsibility is the correct one. In doing this, he'll need to crawl through the messy details of the Consequence Argument, the argument from Frankfurt examples, as well as numerous others, like the Manipulation Argument. A more conventionally minded compatibilist—one attempting to settle the descriptive issue—will try to show that reflection occasioned by these arguments lends support to a compatibilist account of our commonsense concepts of freedom and responsibility. Vargas shoulders the burden of showing why these compatibilists are wrong.

Vargas offers further grounds for his descriptive thesis. As he notes, the experimental research aiming to specify the folk concept supports his contention (see, e.g., Nichols, 2006; Nichols and Knobe, 2007).[1] Now, Vargas grants that there is also competing strong evidence that ordinary people often make straightforwardly compatibilist judgments in a range of circumstances (see, e.g., Nahmias, 2006; Nahmias, et al., 2006). But he does not find these results adequate to help the compatibilists. One reason he offers is that our concept might be fragmented, and this would still leave us with incompatibilist-friendly strands (37–8). Since it is not problematic for incompatibilists to grant that *sometimes* people invoke a compatibilist understanding of freedom, we are left with the fact that "in a significant class of cases our responsibility depends on the thesis of determinism being false" (39). At this juncture, however, a critic might protest that the simplest way to understand the dispute between Nichols and Nahmias is either that there is something unified—a folk concept—that is the subject of dispute between them and that needs settling, or instead there are distinct folk concepts and it is an open question which is able to underwrite our responsibility practices. Either way, it does not seem that we are positioned given the current state of the controversy to decisively rule out a commonsense form of compatibilism.

12.1.2. Vargas's Prescriptive Thesis

Next consider Vargas's prescriptive thesis. Grant Vargas that the commonsense view of free will and moral responsibility is incompatibilist. And grant as well that no libertarian theory is viable because it outstrips what is naturalistically plausible. In doing so, Vargas finds himself in the company of Caruso (2012), Levy (2011), Pereboom (2001, 2014), G. Strawson (1986), and Waller (1990). What is Vargas's argument for why, in opposition to these philosophers, we should opt for a revisionary form of compatibilism? Why not just go skeptical as regards the prescriptive question and opt for eliminating responsibility—or at least a relevant kind of responsibility, one characterized in terms of basic desert?

Vargas's answers by appeal to a principle of philosophical conservation (2013: chapter 4) regarding our responsibility system, including our practices of praising and blaming. It is more conservative to retain the system rather than eliminate it as a skeptic would. If the system is beneficial, why not preserve it? And it can be retained by revising the key concepts just enough to render the system normatively warranted and naturalistically plausible. Vargas aims to do this by introducing his *agency-cultivation model*. The central insight is that we have reason to want a system of practices that help in *building better beings*—in particular, beings who are alive to moral reasons.[2] As Vargas puts it:

> On the agency cultivation model, we justify the responsibility norms, norms of moralized praising and blaming, in light of the role that the involved social practices plausibly play in cultivating a form of valuable agency, given various facts about the fixed and plastic features of our psychology. Teleology, psychology, and a special form of agency all have a role to play in the account. (2013: 196)

The *teleology* at issue has to do with justifying our responsibility practices and our treating people as responsible agents in terms of the social benefits of doing so. In this respect, Vargas proposes a moral-influenceability compatibilist theory. A familiar version of this kind of theory that Vargas rejects (e.g., Smart, 1963) would do this justificatory work *directly* in utilitarian fashion—of the sort Strawson (1962) found misguided. But Vargas wishes to respect the *psychology* of persons in a way that is salutary to Strawson's insights (see Section 6.1). People do not care about influencing others when engaging in blaming and praising practices—they are expressing their backward-looking regard for the quality of will of those whom they praise or blame. Vargas contends that we can appreciate the value of a system that co-opts these human propensities in ways that are overall beneficial. So what we should aim for and promote, then, is a *special form of agency* that facilitates these salutary social benefits.

The specific form of agency that Vargas proposes—the heart of his own compatibilist proposal—is a version of a reasons-responsive theory that aligns roughly with Wallace's (1994) and Fischer and Ravizza's (1998) views. Vargas writes:

> What makes an agent properly subject to norms of moralized praise and blame is that he or she has the general capacity to suitably recognize and respond to moral considerations. (2013: 203)

Moreover, Vargas marries a reasons-responsive theory to an important Strawsonian theme: What praise and blame target is quality of will, and they "foster and sustain" (204) a kind of agency that is sensitive to moral considerations. Nevertheless, Vargas's version of a reasons-responsive theory departs considerably from more traditional versions. He rejects what he calls atomism and monism about free will and responsible agency, according to which an agent's freedom-capacities can be characterized exclusively in terms of intrinsic states of agents that do not situationally vary (204–9). Drawing upon the work of philosophers like John Doris (2002), Vargas argues that our understanding of reasons-responsiveness must be open to the thought that agents gain or lose reasons-responsive capacities depending on their situational contexts (Vargas, 2013: 213–14). The result is a kind of externalism about free agency, one that varies with environmental factors. As Vargas sees it, a well-informed understanding of our human psychology puts pressure on any good theory of free agency to respect the fact that persons are not atoms that preserve their agential character unaltered across variation in situational contexts. This constitutes an especially interesting and insightful idea for upgrading a range of more conventional compatibilist views.

At this juncture, we wish to distinguish Vargas's intriguing compatibilist proposal from his arguments for its playing a role in his revisionist prescriptive thesis. Here we will present just one objection. As Kelly McCormick (2013) has argued, Vargas justifies the moral responsibility system by virtue of its promoting a distinctive form of agency. But then his normative justification for why we should revise rather than eliminate rests solely on whether agency of this sort is so valuable that it ought to be promoted. McCormick describes this as a "buck-passing" strategy (McCormick, 2013: 13–14). As she notes, it is one thing to acknowledge, as Vargas does, that as a psychological matter we are disposed to value agency of this sort (surely this Strawsonian point is right). And it is even another to contend that it is valuable. But it is a much stronger thesis to contend that *all things considered* we should act in a way that promotes this value (14–15).

We will not pursue this matter further here except to note that, once the dispute is limited exclusively to the prescriptive issue, then settling the all-things-considered question about what we should do will have to be weighed against the alternatives offered by the nonrevisionist skeptic. Vargas seems to share with Strawson (1962) the conviction that the gains and losses to human life would clearly favor preservation of the responsibility system. But depending upon how the skeptic develops her eliminativist alternative, the losses to human life might be few and the gains might be many. This, at any rate, is how skeptics Pereboom (1995, 2001, 2014) and Caruso (2012) have argued. (See Section 11.6 for a discussion of how the moral skeptic might weigh these costs and benefits.)

12.1.3. Vargas's Radical Conceptual Thesis

Now consider Vargas's contention that what free will and moral responsibility are might depart from what the folk concepts of them are. As McKenna has put it, there is a worry that, unlike, say, water and our concept of it:

> What moral responsibility is cannot come apart from the concept in such a way that there is, so to speak, something for moral responsibility to be beyond our concept of it. (McKenna, 2009b: 11)

If McKenna is correct about this, then it is open to Vargas to advance his compatibilist proposal in a nonrevisionist way by first resisting the incompatibilist at the descriptive stage. If instead he is committed to his incompatibilist diagnosis of the folk concept, then he appears forced to agree that his compatibilist proposal is at odds with the folk concept. Absent this, Vargas is in danger of changing the subject by remaining committed to his revisionist proposal. If this is so, then it's not that there is this independent subject matter which is successfully accessed and described by Vargas's proposed compatibilist theory, while the rejected incompatibilist folk concept gets that subject matter wrong. It is rather that one concept is given up, another one is fashioned, and then the latter *just picks out a different subject matter from what the former picks out*. This is what McCormick (2013) calls the *reference-anchoring problem*.

Pereboom considers the possibility that what Vargas proposes is a matter of revising our *conception* of moral responsibility but not the *concept* of it.[3] This would allow Vargas to avoid the charge that he is changing the subject. But then Pereboom asks whether the conception is:

> near enough to the folk's to count as a natural extension of it, one that can do enough of the work the folk conception does in adjudicating questions of moral responsibility and punishment, and in governing our attitudes to the actions of those around us. (Pereboom, 2009c: 25)

Here, as McCormick (2013) explains, if it is not, then it seems we have completely different concepts and a changing of the subject, as McKenna suggests. But if it is near enough to the folk's, then we have a way to anchor the reference of the concept so that Vargas can coherently defend his contention that by way of his revisionist proposal he is not just talking past his interlocutors.

Cast in these terms, consider how those like Pereboom would measure Vargas's success in avoiding the charge of changing the subject. For the concept Vargas proposes to remain a natural extension of the folk concept and so only be a revised conception of a shared concept, it would have to preserve a basic desert-entailing form of responsibility, since according to moral responsibility skeptics like Pereboom, this is *all* that is meant to be at issue in the debate. But since Vargas (2013: 249–56) wishes to reject this strong link to basic desert-entailing responsibility, it seems he is not merely altering our conception of responsibility. He is proposing a new concept, just as McKenna charges. Ironically, if Vargas's proposal is understood as changing the subject, basic desert moral responsibility skeptics such as Pereboom are in a position to *endorse* Vargas's compatibilist proposal, because they are open to preserving a socially beneficial set of moral responsibility practices which does not presuppose basic desert (Section 11.6).

Vargas, however, is alive to these challenges. Against them, he argues that it is wrong to tie our responsibility practices so closely to basic desert (2013: 257). But if we bracket this debate about basic desert, does Vargas avoid the McKenna/Pereboom charge of changing the subject? According to McCormick

(2013: 7) Vargas succeeds by attending to the *work* the folk concept of responsibility does in regulating our judgments about when agents deserve praise and blame. This is to be done by attending to the internal logic and structure of what he calls the responsibility system (Vargas, 2013: 101). Upon seeing what work is to be done by an adequate concept of responsibility, one can then refashion the concept to do this work in revised ways that depart from the folk notion— and most notably cut away the libertarian requirements found in the folk conception.

So McCormick (2013) contends that Vargas can answer the McKenna/Pereboom reference-anchoring challenge. Here, we wish to remain open-minded and leave the dispute unsettled. Part of what is at issue turns on whether we can after all assess this controversy while bracketing the role of basic desert-entailing moral responsibility. Some are liable to contend that this notion has to be in the mix to avoid a charge of changing the subject.[4] But with this large question kept at a distance, McCormick's defense of Vargas is reasonable. One point, however, that could pose a problem for Vargas (independently of questions concerning basic desert) turns on the distinction Vargas draws between the moral responsibility system and the work the folk concept does within it, on the one hand, and the folk concept itself, on the other. A natural way to understand our actual moral responsibility practices of praising and blaming is that they are themselves animated and informed by the folk concepts that are currently in dispute. It is not clear that one can identify and account for the role of the work of the concept in a set of practices in a way that pulls apart from the concept itself.

Vargas provides us with an interesting and important proposal for negotiating the territory of free will and moral responsibility, one that opts to revise folk concepts but keep the revision of folk practice to a minimum. By contrast, Pereboom's free will skepticism does not advocate conceptual revision, but rather a substantial change of practice.

12.2.   Responsibility for Omissions

We turn now to a relatively brief treatment of a number of issues and trends in the free will debate that have been prominent in recent years. One topic that is currently being discussed intensely is moral responsibility for omissions. Responsibility for decisions not to perform actions, for example a decision not to help someone in trouble, can be treated in the same way as decisions to perform actions. Both of these kinds of cases feature a basic action, a decision, and conditions on responsibility for the basic action will be similar. One complicated issue arises in such cases, however, and that concerns responsibility for outcomes of decisions.

Very interesting issues arise in cases in which what is omitted is the decision itself. Responsibility for some such omissions can be accounted for as cases of derivative responsibility, which has a key epistemic component (Chapter 6). For example, suppose Biff knows that when he gets drunk he tends not to keep track of duties he has. Had he not been drunk, he would have decided at 3 p.m. to take his mother to her doctor's appointment. But he got drunk and did not so decide. He's responsible for not making this decision, but only derivatively from his responsibility for getting drunk

But in his book *Who Knew*, George Sher (2009) considers the possibility of responsibility for omissions and their outcomes in cases in which the epistemic conditions on responsibility appear not to be satisfied. He sets out a number of examples to illustrate this phenomenon, and here is one of them:

> Alessandra, a soccer mom, has gone to pick up her children at their elementary school. As usual, Alessandra is accompanied by the family's border collie, Bathsheba, who rides in the back of the van. Although it is very hot, the pick-up has never taken long, so Alessandra leaves Sheba in the van while she goes to gather her children. This time, however, Alessandra is greeted by a tangled tale of misbehavior, ill-considered punishment, and administrative bungling which requires several hours of indignant sorting out. During that time, Sheba languishes, forgotten, in the locked car. When Alessandra and her children finally make it to the parking lot, they find Sheba unconscious from heat prostration. (Sher, 2009: 24)

Alessandra is intuitively morally responsible for not deciding to take measures to ensure the dog's safety, and for the bad outcome. One might propose that her blameworthiness is derivative of what Holly Smith refers to as a benighting act, an act in which the agent "fails to improve (or positively impairs) his cognitive position" so as to evidently result in a risk of performing the action at issue (Sher, 2009: 34; H. Smith, 1983). However, Sher argues that there are cases of negligence for which we hold agents morally responsible that lack this feature. When Alessandra arrived at school with the dog, "the dispute that she encountered was not one that she could have anticipated. Because she had no previous reason to expect to be distracted, she also had no previous reason to take precaution against being distracted." (2009: 35–6; Clarke, 2014b).[5] One might propose that Alessandra has a morally defective quality of will—for instance, she does not care enough about her dog—and her having been aware that she should care more about the dog and not caring more grounds her blameworthiness (Sher, 2016). Against this, Sher observes that people in these sorts of situations usually feel very bad about what has happened, which counts against failure of care. Nevertheless, we hold the agent morally responsible for the outcome.

Sher's solution is to propose that an agent can be morally responsible for an outcome even if it did not derive from a state of hers of which she was aware (2009: 121). Alessandra is blameworthy because her action flows from the enduring causal structure that constitutes her, even though in this case the part of causal structure at issue does not feature anything of which she is aware that can ground her responsibility, whether it be something that immediately precedes the act, or something that occurred earlier to which the responsibility might then be traced. An objection to this proposal is that to preserve our ordinary tendency to judge Alessandra blameworthy, it takes a radical adjustment to our practice of holding responsible. Because we can't ground her responsibility in a morally defective conscious psychological state, as our practice would have it, the proposal would have us ground it in some other feature of her, perhaps a psychological state that is not morally defective, or, more likely, a neural constitution without a psychological correlate (Pereboom, 2016).

But it might be too quick to claim that Alessandra's blameworthiness can't be grounded in a morally defective conscious psychological state. Take the case in which a parent finds the unconscious child in the car, and feels terrible as a result. Pereboom agrees that there is no failure of caring here, and more generally, no failure of quality of will, but there may instead be a failure of *vigilance*.[6] Vigilance, on his conception, is "a persisting attunement to protect, which features, among other things, a standing disposition to respond to danger, triggered by indications of danger in the environment." When one first has children, after an early accident or near-miss, parents become aware that they should set their degree of vigilance at a higher level. Blameworthiness in the case of the child left in the back of the car would then trace back to a past blameworthy failure to become appropriately vigilant, where the parent was sufficiently aware of the fact that he should set his vigilance at the higher level.

Pereboom concedes, however, that there are cases of apparent responsibility of this sort that do not credibly trace back to a blameworthy failure to become vigilant. Suppose a first-time parent, Matt, inhabits one of our especially safe environments, and due to a failure in his vigilance, his child takes a fall from the bed. For most other parents in this environment, the experience with danger that serves as the call to become more vigilant does not involve serious harm to the child. Matt is unfortunate, however, because in his case this call does involve severe harm. Here we may want to hold him morally responsible. Still, we waver. Pereboom argues that we should accept that Matt is not morally responsible in the basic desert sense, rather than, say, accepting Sher's revision to the justificatory part of our practice. As noted in the preceding chapter, in Pereboom's view our practice of holding morally responsible involves senses of responsibility that are backward-looking insofar as they invoke desert. Matt would be responsible only in a sense that does not invoke desert.

There are many other issues concerning responsibility for omissions that we won't address here. One is the question of what omissions are, precisely (Clarke, 2014b). Another is the nature of our responsibility for outcomes of omissions, and whether they require a different sort of treatment from responsibility for outcomes of actions (Fischer and Ravizza, 1998; Sartorio, 2005). A related question is whether responsibility for omissions and their outcomes requires alternative possibilities, and whether there are successful Frankfurt cases for omissions of various sorts (Clarke, 1994; Fischer and Ravizza, 1998; Pereboom, 2016; Sartorio, 2005).

12.3.   Deliberation and Free Will

Whenever we deliberate about what to do, we at least typically believe that we have more than one distinct option for which action to perform, each of which is available to us in the sense that we can or could perform each of these actions. That is, when we deliberate, we believe in the "openness" of more than one distinct option for what to do. It is often argued that belief in openness of such a kind is required for deliberation, or at least for rational deliberation. For example, Peter van Inwagen writes:

> If someone deliberates about whether to do A or to do B, it follows that his behavior manifests a belief that it is *possible* for him to do A – that he *can* do A, that he has it within his power to do A – and a belief that it is possible for him to do B. (van Inwagen, 1983: 155; cf. Ginet, 1966; Kant, 1785/1981, Ak IV 448; Stapleton, 2010; Taylor, 1966: chapter 12).[7]

This openness is plausibly a kind of free will, and thus the claim to be considered is that belief that one has free will is required for deliberation, or at least for rational deliberation.

A number of philosophers contend that such belief in openness would conflict with the truth of determinism. In any deliberative situation, the truth of determinism would rule out the availability of all but one distinct option for what to do, and thus would rule out openness about what to do. So then a belief required for rational deliberation would be inconsistent with an evident consequence of determinism for one's actions, and if determinism were true, such a belief would be false. Hector-Neri Castañeda, for example, argues that if determinism were true, whenever we engaged in a process of deliberation, we would be making a false supposition: "we are, thus, condemned to presuppose a falsehood in order to do what we think practically" (Castañeda, 1975: 135). Van Inwagen contends that, in addition, a deliberator who believed determinism and its evident consequences for her actions would have inconsistent beliefs, or at least, such a deliberator "who denies the existence of free will must inevitably, contradict himself with monotonous regularity" (van Inwagen, 1983: 160). This line of reasoning is expressive of an incompatibilist position about the relation between the beliefs required for rational deliberation and belief in determinism and its evident consequences (Ginet, 1966, Taylor, 1966):

> *Deliberation-incompatibilism*: S's deliberating and being rational is incompatible with S's believing that her actions are causally determined (by causal antecedents beyond her control).

The opposing position is:

> *Deliberation-compatibilism*: S's deliberating and being rational is compatible with S's believing that her actions are causally determined. (Pereboom, 2008a, 2014)

Dana Nelkin proposes the following positive deliberation-incompatibilist requirement for deliberation:

> (I) Rational deliberators who deliberate about an action A must believe, in virtue of their nature as rational deliberators, that there exist no conditions that render either [her doing] A or not-A inevitable. (Nelkin, 2004a: 217, 2011: 121)

Someone who rationally deliberates about an action A would then believe that there are no conditions that make either her doing A or not-A inevitable. If she also believed in determinism and its evident consequences, she would believe that there are conditions that make either A or not-A inevitable. She would then have inconsistent beliefs.

It's indeed credible that when agents rationally deliberate about what to do, they presuppose that they have plural distinct options for action. But the sense of "can" or "could" featured in such beliefs might not be metaphysical. Perhaps it is epistemic. When you are deliberating about whether to do A, and you believe determinism is true, you would very typically not know whether you will in fact do A, since you lack the knowledge of the preceding conditions and laws that would be required to make the prediction based on these factors. Thus even if you believe that it is causally determined that you deliberate and act as you do, you might well in this deliberative situation believe without inconsistency that it is epistemically possible—possible for all you know—that you will do A and that it is epistemically possible that you will do not-A.

A number of deliberation-compatibilists have developed the claim that the beliefs about the possibility of acting salient for deliberation are in some key respect epistemic (e.g., Dennett, 1984; Kapitan, 1986; Pettit, 1989). A deliberation-compatibilist might propose, for instance, that to deliberate rationally between distinct actions A and B, what's key is that the deliberator can't be certain that she will do A and can't be certain that she will do B. However, some deliberation-compatibilists don't think that this is enough. The reason is that there is a type of situation, first brought to our attention and illustrated by van Inwagen, in which an agent who satisfies such an epistemic openness condition would still be incapable of rational deliberation:

> Imagine that [an agent] is in a room with two doors and that he believes one of the doors to be unlocked and the other door to be locked and impassable, though he has no idea which is which; let him then attempt to imagine himself deliberating about which door to leave by. (van Inwagen, 1983: 154)

About this example, Nelkin points out:

> While it seems that I can deliberate about which door to decide *to try* to open and even which door handle to decide to jiggle, if I know one of them

to be locked and impassable, it also seems that I cannot deliberate about which *door to open* – or even which door to *decide* to open. (Nelkin, 2011: 130; cf. Kapitan, 1986: 247)

But I am neither certain that I will open door #1, nor that I will not, and the same for my opening door #2, so in this situation the agent satisfies our representative epistemic condition. And here is the connection to a belief in determinism. If I believed determinism and its consequences, then in any deliberative situation I would believe that all but one option for what to do was closed off—that all but one would be "locked and impassable." Given that in van Inwagen's example I cannot rationally deliberate about which door to open, believing determinism and its consequences would also seem to preclude rational deliberation between options. A compatibilist account would need to explain why rational deliberation is impossible in the two-door case, but still possible for the deliberator who believed in determinism and its consequences.

In response to this challenge, Tomis Kapitan (1986) argues that on the preferable compatibilist position there are two epistemic conditions that the deliberator must satisfy (Pereboom, 2008a, 2014 agrees and fine-tunes Kapitan's proposal). One of these conditions expresses an epistemic notion of openness for what to do. The other specifies the epistemic condition on *the efficacy of deliberation*. For example, the compatibilist might require that to rationally deliberate about whether to do A or B, the deliberator must believe that if as a result of her deliberating about whether to do A or B she were to judge that it would be best to do A, then she would also, on the basis of this deliberation, do A; and similarly for B (Pereboom, 2008a, 2014). This condition is not satisfied in the two-door case, because the deliberator does not believe for each door that she would open it as a result of her deliberation-based judgment that it would be the best one to open. So the deliberative efficacy condition gives us the result we want about this case.[8]

The debate between deliberation-incompatibilists and deliberation-compatibilists continues to be lively, with interesting and strategic moves made on both sides.

12.4. Experimental Philosophy and Free Will

The free will debate is in part an empirical affair, and this has given rise to experimental work—X-phi—on free will. X-phi employs social science techniques, most prominently surveys and analysis of their results, to discern people's intuitions and judgments about a range of philosophical topics such as free will and moral responsibility, intention, personal identity, and knowledge. Important X-phi work on free will has been done on the issue of beliefs about compatibilism and incompatibilism,[9] on error theories about folk intuitions on this topic,[10] on manipulation arguments,[11] and on whether our criteria for holding morally responsible are the same across cultures and across types of situations. This last issue is the X-phi area we will examine by way of illustration.

Almost all X-phi on free will has had non-philosophers, the so-called "folk," as subjects. There are a number of reasons for philosophers to conduct studies about what the folk believe about free will and moral responsibility in addition to sheer curiosity (Björnsson and Pereboom, 2016), and here we highlight two of them. A first is conceptual. For instance, for accounts to be about moral responsibility rather than about another feature of action, they must be about what people in general have in mind when they employ the concept "moral responsibility." If the folk have nothing determinate in mind, these accounts might instead be seen as attempts to make the folk conceptions more precise. We'll examine another example of conceptual relevance of X-phi studies below, in our discussion of variantism about the application of moral responsibility concepts.

A second reason is dialectical. If it turned out, for example, that almost everyone had incompatibilist beliefs or intuitions, the compatibilist would have a more difficult time convincing people of her view. The same would be true for the incompatibilist if almost everyone had compatibilist beliefs. Any convincing argument would need to be much more forceful than the contrary intuitions or else be supplemented with independent reasons to distrust these intuitions.[12] Moreover, to the extent that some epistemic weight should be given to ordinary intuitions about these issues, a position at odds with common sense would carry not only an extra dialectical burden, but also an epistemic one. As things stand, however, surveys are divided about the extent to which people are compatibilists, and even studies suggesting that one of the two views predominates reveal a substantial proportion with the opposite view, at least under some circumstances (see, e.g., Nahmias et al., 2007; Nichols and Knobe, 2007). Judging by mere strength of numbers, neither position has the epistemic advantage, and each faces dialectical resistance.

Another instance of a dialectical role for X-phi studies is in the case of adjudicating "error theories" offered by philosophers to explain away intuitions contrary to their own views. Such error theories include incompatibilists' suggestions that we resist incompatibilist conclusions because we do not understand how our actions are caused (Spinoza 1667/1985: 440) or because we are strongly disposed to blame-involving emotions such as indignation (e.g., Nichols and Knobe, 2007). On the compatibilist side, error theories include the suggestion that incompatibilist intuitions result from a confusion of determinism with fatalism, or a confusion of causation with compulsion (Section 3.1). If empirical studies of responsibility judgments indicated that the errors proposed by these theories are common among the folk, this would lend weight to these proposals.

Here we will restrict ourselves to examining X-phi at work on one important conceptual and normative issue, variantism about moral responsibility (Björnsson and Pereboom, 2016). According to variantism, there are substantial ways in which core criteria for judging when agents are morally responsible ought to be applied differently depending on the circumstances (Knobe and Doris, 2010). One hypothesis tested by Nichols and Knobe (2007) is that subjects tend toward incompatibilism when the scenario described is abstract and general, but toward compatibilism when it is concrete and vivid. Subjects were presented with an account of a universe—Universe A—in which all events unfold in accord with deterministic laws. The abstract question was:

> In Universe A, is it possible for a person to be fully morally responsible for their action?

The concrete question was:

> In Universe A, a man named Bill has become attracted to his secretary, and he decides that the only way to be with her is to kill his wife and three children. He knows that it is impossible to escape from his house in the event of a fire. Before he leaves on a business trip, he sets up a device in his basement that burns down his house and kills his family. Is Bill fully morally responsible for killing his wife and children?

In the abstract condition, 14 percent of the subjects affirmed that it is possible for a person to be fully morally responsible, while in the concrete condition 72 percent of the subjects agreed that Bill is fully morally responsible.

Nichols and Knobe consider several possible accounts of this variation. One involves attributing the higher incidence of moral responsibility affirmation in the concrete condition response to the distorting effect of emotion. But another is indeed to take the difference to suggest variantism, whereupon the concept of moral responsibility ought to be applied differently under varying conditions of affect. Knobe and Doris (2010) address the objection that it's obvious that these results have no bearing on how we ought to apply moral responsibility concepts. They disagree:

> The fact that a particular view strikes people as obvious does not show us anything about the nature of the competence underlying ordinary attributions of moral responsibility. What would show us something about the nature of competence is a specific, testable model that accounts for the existing data and can then be used to generate new predictions that can be examined in further studies. (Knobe and Doris 2010: 348)

If their response is correct, then there is a very important role for experimental philosophy in determining how we ought to apply our responsibility concepts.

One line of objection to this defense of variantism is advanced by Nelkin (2007). She contends that the evidence of variation that the surveys provide can often be accounted for by invariantist explanations. Nelkin proposes that the abstract/concrete variation can be explained by the fact that a significant proportion of the population may at least initially assume that causal determination abstractly described rules out the possibility of rational actions because it consigns causation of action to mechanical factors such as neural states (cf. Nahmias, 2006). She then proposes that this assumption would be overridden by a vivid concrete description of the way an action came about. The story about

Bill indeed features a vivid concrete description of the deliberative reasoning process that results in his decision to kill his wife and children. More generally, Nelkin's approach suggests that the folk derive varying judgments from an underlying invariantist theory together with natural but perhaps unjustified theoretical and empirical assumptions.[13]

In addition, Nelkin suggests that sometimes varying judgments can be derived from the invariantist theories themselves without any controversial empirical judgments. Consider a survey that indicates variation in how subjects judge agents who act with significant emotion. David Pizarro et al. (2003) presented one group of subjects with a story about a morally exemplary action:—"Because of his overwhelming and uncontrollable sympathy, Jack impulsively gave the homeless man his only jacket even though it was freezing outside"—and another group with this story about a bad action: "Because of his overwhelming and uncontrollable anger, Jack impulsively smashed the window of the car parked in front of him because it was parked too close to his." Cases were also presented in which the agent instead acts "calmly and deliberately." Subjects judged agents much less blameworthy when they acted badly with emotion relative to acting badly without. But in the case of good action the difference was negligible. Nelkin suggests, however, that this difference is explained by an invariantist theory of the sort she herself defends, according to which moral responsibility crucially requires the ability to act for good reasons (Nelkin, 2007, 2011; Wolf, 1990). In the case of a good action, the emotion tends to highlight the good reason, while in the case of a bad action, the emotion obscures the good reason, and consequently can be viewed as an excuse.

A further line of objection can be advanced by reflecting on other empirical surveys. Consider a much-publicized study in which Danziger et al. (2011) surveyed rulings Israeli judges made during three subsequent sessions in the course of a day, each of which was followed by a food break. The investigators found that "the percentage of favorable rulings drops gradually from ≈65% to nearly zero within each decision session and returns abruptly to ≈65% after a break." Upon reflection upon this result, it may seem obvious that the pattern does not reflect competence, so obvious that additional empirical surveys are not required to settle whether it does. Imagine that further studies found systematic racial bias in criminal sentencing. It seems obvious that no studies could show that such racial bias reflects competence, and, moreover, that no studies are needed to show that it reflects incompetence. On one account, we know this just by virtue of competence with the ground rules of morality.

12.5.   Religion and Free Will

We end this book with the issue that instigated the free will debate: Whether free will is compatible with the existence of a providential God.[14] In the monotheistic tradition beginning with the Stoics, true providence requires theological determinism. Theological determinism is the position that God is the sufficient active cause of everything in creation, whether directly or by way of secondary causes such as human agents. At the same time, many people drawn to traditional theistic religion are also attracted to a libertarian conception of free will. But libertarianism and theological determinism are mutually exclusive positions, and so one cannot rationally accept both at once. And so the free will problem arises within this religious context (Frede, 2009).

The truth of libertarianism seems necessary for a number of important elements of traditional monotheistic religions (see, e.g. Speak, 2004; Timpe, 2014). One such element is that the notion of moral responsibility in the basic desert sense applies to us. For an agent to be morally responsible for an action in this sense is for it to be hers in such a way that she would deserve to be blamed if she understood that it was morally wrong, and she would deserve to be praised if she understood that it was morally exemplary. The desert at issue here is basic in the sense that the agent would deserve to be blamed or praised just because she has performed the action, given an understanding of its moral status, and not, for example, merely by virtue of consequentialist or contractualist considerations. The basic desert notion isn't the only sense of moral responsibility at play in our practice, and this will become important in what follows. But it is a sense clearly invoked by the major monotheisms, in particular in their conceptions of ultimate punishment and reward.

It is difficult to see how the doctrine of eternal damnation, for example, can be justified without invoking this sense of moral responsibility. There are conceptions of postmortem punishment that are forward-looking and do not invoke basic desert, but such views would need to allow for the possibility of release from hell if the forward-looking goals, such as moral reform, are achieved. The common view of hell does not countenance such a possibility, and this view would thus appear to require basic desert in its moral justification. While contestable, many believe that it is plausible that only libertarianism can hope to secure basic desert, and therefore that the truth of libertarianism is required by the doctrine of eternal damnation (e.g., Timpe, 2014: chapter 5).

A second important theistic motivation for endorsing libertarianism is that it yields a promising answer to the problem of evil, the problem of the compatibility of evil with an omnipotent, omniscient, and perfectly benevolent God (Plantinga, 1974; Speak, 2014; Swinburne, 1999). This response involves the claim that God is justified in creating beings that are free in a way that requires that they are not causally determined by factors beyond their control to act as they do. If an agent is free in this sense in a choice to perform an action, then, holding fixed the history of the universe up to the time the choice is made, it is causally possible both that the agent makes this choice and that she instead refrains from making it. The proposal is that since such free will is highly valuable, God is justified in creating agents with this sort of free will. But creating agents with such free will does pose the risk of bringing moral evil into the world. However, according to the free will response, the value of the existence of such free creatures outweighs the risk of their choosing immorally, and, one might propose, this value even outweighs the disvalue of all the bad actions they actually freely perform together with their consequences.

As noted above, a motivation for endorsing theological determinism is that it provides an uncontested way to secure a strong notion of divine providence, one according to which everything that happens, including our actions, precisely accords with God's providential will (e.g., Helm, 1993). We find this conception expressed in ancient Stoicism, in Islam, and in much of historical Christianity. Our lives are subject to pain, failure, loss, and death. How do we cope with all of this and the suffering it occasions? Accepting the strong notion of divine providence involves the belief that everything that happens to us, to the last detail, accords with God's providential will. On this view, great comfort in life can be secured by the conviction that even minor harms, let alone horrendous evils, cannot befall us unless they feature in God's perfectly benevolent plan.

For the theist, it would be attractive to retain this notion of divine providence while at the same time accepting a conception of human beings as having free will as specified by the libertarian. This is what the influential position of Luis de Molina (1595/1988) aims to provide. According to Molinism, God can know from eternity what every possible libertarian free creature would choose in every possible circumstance, and with this knowledge, God is able to direct the course of history with precision.[15] But Molinism is a controversial position. According to the grounding objection, it is not clear how there could be truths about what non-actual free creatures would freely decide on which God could base decisions as to which to actualize (Adams, 1977). Truths about what creatures would freely decide would be grounded in what such creatures in fact freely decide, or at least in what they will freely decide. However, if they don't exist and never will, such grounding is not available. Consequently, those who value an uncontroversial way to secure a strong notion of divine providence have a reason to take theological determinism seriously (Pereboom, 2005, 2012b).

Theological compatibilism might be thought to accommodate all of these concerns (e.g., Edwards, 1754/1957). Theological compatibilists do argue that God's causal determination of all of our actions is compatible with basically deserved blameworthiness for those that are immoral. Theists have tended to be uncomfortable with this view, however, and manipulation arguments give voice to this discomfort. Another serious objection to the theological compatibilist option is that it fails to allow for an answer to the problem of evil that involves free will. If our free will is compatible with God's causal determination of all of our actions, it stands to reason that God could have causally determined us never to cause evil while preserving our free will (Mackie, 1955).

The remaining alternative is a free will skeptical account combined with theological determinism (Pereboom, 2005, 2012b). This view gives up on basic desert moral responsibility and on the free will response to the problem of evil. But it can preserve the strong notion of divine providence. The viability of this position depends on whether theistic religion can do without basic desert moral responsibility and the free will response to the problem of evil. Pereboom (2005, 2012b) argues that this would not amount to a significant loss. We've already seen why one might be willing to relinquish basic desert responsibility (Section

11.8), and David Lewis (1993), for example, argues that the free will answer to the problem of evil is weak, and if he is right, giving it up would not be costly.

Thus the free will problem arises in a stark form within the theological context. Libertarianism clearly allows for basic desert moral responsibility and for a promising avenue of response to the problem of evil, but it is vulnerable on the issue of divine providence. Compatibilism also allows for basic desert, and is not vulnerable on providence, but it falters on the free will response to evil. Free will skepticism secures a strong notion of providence while relinquishing basic desert and the free will response. Historically, theists are divided between libertarianism and compatibilism, with very few taking the skeptical route. But the plausibility of these positions independent of theological considerations is a further factor to be considered.

12.6. Conclusion

We began this book in our preface with a promise to be as even-handed as possible in treating the range of positions, arguments, and topics animating the free will debate. We also promised not to advance our own views. The astute reader will likely have noticed several places where perhaps we have not lived up to our promise, despite our best efforts to do so. Nevertheless, we aspire to having offered readers enough resources to pursue the free will issue in a myriad number of ways, and we hope we have done so in a way that has genuinely challenged the committed student of philosophy.

Suggestions for Further Reading

Because we have canvassed several different topics here, we will offer only a few suggestions for each.

On revisionism, see:

McCormick, Kelly. 2013. "Anchoring a Revisionist Account of Moral Responsibility." *Journal of Ethics and Social Philosophy* 7: 1–19.
Vargas, Manuel. 2013. *Building Better Beings*. Oxford: Oxford University Press.

On omissions, see:

Clarke, Randolph. 2014b. *Omissions*. New York: Oxford University Press.
Sher, George. 2009. *Who Knew?* New York: Oxford University Press.

On deliberation, see:

Coffman, E.J., and T. Warfield. 2005. "Deliberation and Metaphysical Freedom." *Midwest Studies in Philosophy* 29: 25–44.
Nelkin, Dana. 2011. *Making Sense of Freedom and Responsibility*. Oxford: Oxford University Press: chapter 6.

Pereboom, Derk. 2014. *Free Will, Agency, and Meaning in Life*. New York: Oxford University Press: chapter 5.

On experimental philosophy, see:

Knobe, Joshua, and Shaun Nichols, eds., 2008. *Experimental Philosophy*, vol 1. New York: Oxford University Press.

On free will and religion, see:

Frede, Michael. 2011. *A Free Will*. Berkeley and Los Angeles, CA: University of California Press.
Lewis, David. 1993. "Evil for Freedom's Sake?" *Philosophical Papers* 22: 149–72.
Pereboom, Derk. 2012b. "Theological Determinism and Divine Providence." In Ken Perszyk, ed., *Molinism: The Contemporary Debate*. Oxford: Oxford University Press: 262–79.
Plantinga, Alvin. 1974. *God, Freedom, and Evil*. Grand Rapids, MI: Eerdmans.
Speak, Daniel. 2014. *The Problem of Evil*. Cambridge: Polity.
Swinburne, Richard. 1999. *Providence and the Problem of Evil*. Oxford: Oxford University Press.
Timpe, Kevin. 2014. *Free Will in Philosophical Theology*. New York: Bloomsbury.

Notes

1 Below, we will explain and assess this experimental philosophical work, known as X-phi. For now, it is enough to note that this research is devoted to employing empirical research techniques in the social sciences to help determine what people's actual commonsense beliefs, concepts, and intuitions are.

2 Note the similarity here to the sort of reasons-responsive views of compatibilists like Wolf and Nelkin (discussed in Chapter 8).

3 Roughly, the difference between a concept and a conception is that the latter can be understood as an attempt to give content to the former. Our concept of water, for instance, was around in Aristotle's time, well before anyone understood that water was H_2O. But with this type of advance in knowledge, we also developed a conception of water Aristotle did not have, part of which is that "water" refers to a chemical compound.

4 Incidentally, on this point, as co-authors, we should note that we are divided. Pereboom is committed to this thesis. McKenna is not; he wishes to remain agnostic.

5 Randolph Clarke (2014b: 171–2) models a case on Sher's, and makes a similar assessment.

6 Manuel Vargas and Samuel Murray have been awarded a Templeton Foundation grant to study self-control, and the notion of vigilance has an important place in this project. Murray is working on a view according to which failures of vigilance explain responsibility for omissions in cases beyond those involving danger, and in accord with this aim, the notion of vigilance he is working with is significantly broader than Pereboom's.

7 For discussions of this type of view, see Kapitan (1986); Searle (2001); Nelkin (2004a, 2004b, 2011: 117–69); Coffman and Warfield (2005).

8 Nelkin (2011: 139–44) aims to capture the force of such a two-condition account with a unitary condition, one that features the idea that deliberation is the critical explanatory nexus or difference-maker as to which option for action is realized (cf. Dennett, 1984: 118).

9 See Nahmias et al. (2006); Nahmias et al. (2007); Nichols and Knobe (2007); Deery et al. (2013).

10 See Nahmias and Murray (2010); Murray and Nahmias (2014); for criticisms, see Rose and Nichols (2013); Chan et al. (2016); Björnsson (2014) and (ms); Björnsson and Pereboom (2014, 2016).

11 See Sripada (2012); Feltz (2013); Murray and Lombrozo (forthcoming); Björnsson and Pereboom (2016).

12 Nahmias et al. (2006: 30–2) argue that incompatibilism is in particular need of intuitive support given that it postulates metaphysically stronger requirements on responsibility. But one might also think that what is in particular need of justification are claims that some people deserve to be treated better or worse than others. This would put a greater burden of justification on compatibilism, as it postulates weaker restrictions on when blame and credit are deserved.

13 Björnsson and Persson (2012, 2013) can be viewed as generalizing this strategy to a wider range of phenomena.

14 Michael Frede (2011) argues that the notion of free will and the free will debate have their origins in theistic contexts in the ancient world.

15 For a comprehensive exposition and defense of Molina's position, see Thomas Flint (1998).

Bibliography

Adams, Robert M. 1977. "Middle Knowledge and the Problem of Evil." *American Philosophical Quarterly* 14: 109–17.

Aristotle. 1985. *Nicomachean Ethics*. Trans., Terrence Irwin. Indianapolis: Hackett.

Arpaly, Nomy. 2003. *Unprincipled Virtue*. New York: Oxford University Press.

Arpaly, Nomy. 2006. *Merit, Meaning, and Human Bondage*. Princeton, NJ: Princeton University Press.

Ayer, A.J. 1980. "Free-Will and Rationality." In Zak van Straaten, ed., *Philosophical Subjects: Essays Presented to P.F. Strawson*. Oxford: Clarendon Press: 1–13.

Ayer, A.J. 1954. "Freedom and Necessity." In *Philosophical Essays*. New York: St. Martin's Press: 3–20.

Baker, Lynne R. 2013. *Naturalism and the First Person Perspective*. New York: Oxford University Press.

Baker, Lynne R. 2006. "Moral Responsibility without Libertarianism." *Noûs* 40: 307–30.

Balaguer, Mark. 2010. *Free Will as an Open Scientific Problem*. Cambridge, MA: MIT Press.

Balaguer, Mark. 2009. "The Metaphysical Irrelevance of the Compatibilism Debate (and, More Generally, of Conceptual Analysis)." *Southern Journal of Philosophy* 47: 1–24.

Balaguer, Mark. 2004. "A Coherent, Naturalistic, and Plausible Formulation of Libertarian Free Will." *Noûs* 38: 379–406.

Beaty, Michael D., ed., 1990. *Christian Themes and the Problems of Philosophy*. Notre Dame, IN: University of Notre Dame Press.

Beebee, Helen. 2003. "Local Miracle Compatibilism." *Noûs* 37 (2): 258–77.

Beebee, Helen. 2000. "The Non-Governing Conception of Laws of Nature." *Philosophy and Phenomenological Research* 61 (3): 571–94.

Beebee, Helen, and Alfred Mele. 2002. "Humean Compatibilism." *Mind* 111: 201–33.

Bennett, Jonathan. 1980. "Accountability." In Zak van Straaten, ed., *Philosophical Subjects: Essays Presented to P.F. Strawson*. Oxford: Clarendon Press: 14–47.

Bergson, Henri. 1889/1910. *Essai sur les données immédiates de la conscience*, Paris: F. Alcan, 1889; translated as *Time and Free Will*, tr. F.L. Pogson. London: Allen and Unwin, 1910.

Berofsky, Bernard. 2012. *Nature's Challenge to Free Will*. Oxford: Oxford University Press.

Berofsky, Bernard. 2006. "Global Control and Freedom." *Philosophical Studies* 131 (2): 419–45.

Berofsky, Bernard. 1987. *Freedom from Necessity*. London: Routledge and Kegan Paul.

Berofsky, Bernard, ed., 1966. *Free Will and Determinism*. New York: Harper & Row.

Bishop, John. 1989. *Natural Agency: An Essay on the Causal Theory of Action*. Cambridge: Cambridge University Press.

Björnsson, Gunnar. Manuscript. "Manipulators, Parasites, and Generalization Arguments."

Björnsson, Gunnar. 2014. "Incompatibilism and 'Bypassed' Agency." In Alfred Mele, ed., *Surrounding Free Will*. New York: Oxford University Press: 95–122.

Björnsson, Gunnar, and Derk Pereboom. 2016. "Traditional and Experimental Approaches to Free Will." In Wesley Buckwalter and Justin Sytsma, eds., *The Blackwell Companion to Experimental Philosophy*. Oxford: Blackwell Publishers.

Björnsson, Gunnar, and Derk Pereboom. 2014. "Free Will Skepticism and Bypassing." In W. Sinnott-Armstrong, ed., *Moral Psychology*, vol. 4. Cambridge, MA: MIT Press: 27–35.

Björnsson, Gunnar, and Karl Persson. 2013. "A Unified Empirical Account of Responsibility Judgments." *Philosophy and Phenomenological Research* 87: 611–39.

Björnsson, Gunnar, and Karl Persson. 2012. "The Explanatory Component of Responsibility." *Noûs* 46: 326–54.

Bok, Hilary. 1998. *Freedom and Responsibility*. Princeton, NJ: Princeton University Press.

Boyd, Richard. 1988. "How to be a Moral Realist." In Geoffrey Sayer-McCord, ed., *Essays on Moral Realism*. Ithaca, NY: Cornell University Press: 181–228.

Boyd, Richard. 1980. "Materialism without Reductionism: What Physicalism Does Not Entail." In Ned Block, ed., *Readings in the Philosophy of Psychology*. Cambridge, MA: Harvard University Press: 67–106.

Bratman, Michael. 2007. *Structures of Agency*. New York: Oxford University Press.

Bratman, Michael. 2005. "Planning Agency, Autonomous Agency." In James Stacey Taylor, ed., *Personal Autonomy*. New York: Cambridge University Press: 33–57.

Bratman, Michael. 2004. "Three Theories of Self-Governance." *Philosophical Topics* 32: 21–46.

Bratman, Michael. 2003. "A Desire of One's Own." *Journal of Philosophy* 100 (5): 221–42.

Bratman, Michael. 2002. "Hierarchy, Circularity, and Double Reduction." In Sarah Buss and Lee Overton, eds., *Contours of Agency: Essays on Themes from Harry Frankfurt*. Cambridge, MA: MIT Press: 65–85.

Bratman, Michael. 1997. "Responsibility and Planning." *Journal of Ethics* 1 (1): 27–43.

Brand, Myles, and D. Walton, eds., 1976. *Action Theory*. Dordrecht: D. Reidel.

Brent, Michael. Manuscript. "Against the Standard Theory of Action."

Brink, David, and Dana Nelkin. 2013. "Fairness and the Architecture of Responsibility." In David Shoemaker, ed., *Oxford Studies in Agency and Responsibility*, vol. 1. Oxford: Oxford University Press: 284–313.

Broad, C.D. 1952. "Determinism, Indeterminism, and Libertarianism." In *Ethics and the History of Philosophy*. London: Routledge and Kegan Paul: 195–217.

Broad, C.D.. 1934. *Determinism, Indeterminism, and Libertarianism*. London: Routledge and Kegan Paul.

Buckareff, Andrei. Forthcoming. "How Does Agent-Causal Power Work." *The Modern Schoolman*.

Buss, Sarah, and Lee Overton, eds., 2002. *Contours of Agency: Essays on Themes from Harry Frankfurt*. Cambridge, MA: MIT Press.

Campbell, C.A. 1951. "Is Free Will a Pseudo Problem?" *Mind* 60: 446–65.

Campbell, Joseph Keim. 2010. "Incompatibilism and Fatalism: Reply to Loss." *Analysis* 70: 71–6.

Campbell, Joseph Keim. 2008. "Reply to Brueckner." *Analysis* 68: 264–9.

Campbell, Joseph Keim. 2007. "Free Will and the Necessity of the Past." *Analysis* 67: 105–11.

Campbell, Joseph Keim. 1997. "A Compatibilist Theory of Alternative Possibilities." *Philosophical Studies* 88: 319–30.

Campbell, Joseph Keim, Michael O'Rourke, and David Sheir, eds., 2004. *Freedom and Determinism*. Cambridge, MA: MIT Press.

Capes, Justin. Forthcoming. "Blameworthiness and Buffered Alternatives." *American Philosophical Quarterly*.

Capes, Justin. 2013. "Mitigating Soft Compatibilism." *Philosophy and Phenomenological Research* 87: 640–63.

Capes, Justin. 2010. "The W-Defense." *Philosophical Studies* 150: 61–77.

Caruso, Gregg. 2012. *Free Will and Consciousness: A Determinist Account of the Illusion of Free Will*. Lanham, MD: Lexington Books.

Castañeda, Hector-Neri. 1975. *Thinking and Doing*. Dordrecht: D. Reidel.

Chalmers, David. 2011. "Verbal Disputes." *Philosophical Review* 120: 515–66.

Chalmers, David. 2002. "Does Conceivability Entail Possibility?" In Tamar Szabo Gendler and John Hawthorne, eds., *Conceivability and Possibility*. Oxford: Oxford University Press.

Chan, Hoi-yee, Max Deutsch, and Shaun Nichols. 2016. "Free Will and Experimental Philosophy." In Wesley Buckwalter and Justin Sytsma, eds., *The Blackwell Companion to Experimental Philosophy*. Oxford: Blackwell Publishers.

Chisholm, Roderick. 1976. *Person and Object*. La Salle, IL: Open Court.

Chisholm, Roderick. 1971. "Reply." In Robert Binkley, Richard Bronaugh, and Ausonio Marras, eds., *Agent, Action, and Reason*. Toronto: University of Toronto Press.

Chisholm, Roderick. 1967. "He Could Have Done Otherwise." *Journal of Philosophy* 64: 409–18.

Chisholm, Roderick. 1964. "Human Freedom and the Self." *The Lindley Lectures*. Copyright by the Department of Philosophy, University of Kansas.

Churchland, Paul M. 1981. "Eliminative Materialism and the Propositional Attitudes." *Journal of Philosophy* 78: 67–90.

Clarke, Randolph. 2014a. "Free Will and Abilities to Act." Presented at a symposium on Vihvelin (2013) at the University of Southern California, September 2014.

Clarke, Randolph. 2014b. *Omissions*. New York: Oxford University Press.

Clarke, Randolph. 2009. "Dispositions, Abilities to Act, and Free Will: The New Dispositionalism." *Mind* 118: 323–51.

Clarke, Randolph. 2008. "Incompatibilist (Nondeterministic) Theories of Free Will." *The Stanford Encyclopedia of Philosophy* (Fall 2008 edition), Edward N. Zalta, ed. http://plato.stanford.edu/archives/fall2008/entries/incompatibilism-theories.

Clarke, Randolph. 2005. "On an Argument for the Impossibility of Moral Responsibility." *Midwest Studies in Philosophy* 29: 13–24.

Clarke, Randolph. 2003. *Libertarian Accounts of Free Will*. New York: Oxford University Press.

Clarke, Randolph. 1996. "Agent Causation and Event Causation in the Production of Free Action." *Philosophical Topics* 24: 19–48.

Clarke, Randolph. 1994. "Ability and Responsibility for Omissions." *Philosophical Studies* 73: 195–208.

Clarke, Randolph. 1993. "Toward a Credible Agent-Casual Account of Free Will." *Noûs* 27: 191–203.

Clarke, Randolph. 1992. "Deliberation and Beliefs About One's Abilities." *Pacific Philosophical Quarterly* 73: 101–13.

Clarke, Randolph, and Justin Capes. 2013. "Incompatibilist (Nondeterministic) Theories of Free Will." *Stanford Encyclopedia of Philosophy*. http://plato.stanford.edu/entries/incompatibilism-theories.

Clarke, Randolph, Michael McKenna, and Angela M. Smith, eds., 2015. *The Nature of Moral Responsibility*. New York: Oxford University Press.

Coffman, E.J., and Ted Warfield. 2005. "Deliberation and Metaphysical Freedom." *Midwest Studies in Philosophy* 29: 25–44.

Cogley, Zac. 2012. "Review of Tamler Sommers, *Relative Justice*." *Notre Dame Philosophical Reviews*. https://ndpr.nd.edu/news/31912-relative-justice-cultural-diversity-free-will-and-moral-responsibility.

Danziger, Shai, Jonathan Levav, and Liora Avnaim-Pesso. 2011. "Extraneous Factors in Judicial Decisions." *Proceedings of the National Academy of Sciences* 108: 6889–92.

Davidson, Donald. 1970. "Mental Events." In L. Foster and J.W. Swanson, eds., *Experience and Theory*. Amherst, MA: University of Massachusetts Press: 79–101.

Davidson, Donald. 1963. "Actions, Reasons, and Causes." *Journal of Philosophy* 60: 685–700.

De Caro, Mario. 2011. "Is Emergentism Refuted by the Neurosciences? The Case of Free Will." In A. Corradini and T. O'Connor, eds., *Emergence in Science and Philosophy*. London: Routledge: 190–221.

De Caro, Mario, and David Macarthur. 2010. "Science, Naturalism, and the Problem of Normativity." In Mario De Caro and David Macarthur, eds., *Naturalism and Normativity*. New York: Columbia University Press: 3–19.

De Caro, Mario, and Alberto Voltolini. 2010. "Is Liberal Naturalism Possible?" In Mario De Caro and David Macarthur, eds., *Naturalism and Normativity*. New York: Columbia University Press: 69–86.

Deery, Oisin. 2015. "Why People Believe in Indeterminist Free Will." *Philosophical Studies* 172 (8): 2033–54.

Deery, Oisin, Matt Bedke, and Shaun Nichols. 2013. "Phenomenal Abilities: Incompatibilism and the Experience of Agency." In David Shoemaker, ed., *Oxford Studies in Agency and Responsibility*, vol. 1: 126–50.

Della Rocca, Michael. 2008. *Spinoza*. London: Routledge.

Della Rocca, Michael. 1998. "Frankfurt, Fischer, and Flickers." *Noûs* 32: 99–105.

Demetriou, Kristin. 2010. "The Soft-line Solution to Pereboom's Four-case Argument." *Australasian Journal of Philosophy* 88 (4): 595–617.

Dennett, Daniel. 2003. *Freedom Evolves*. London: Penguin Books.

Dennett, Daniel. 1995. *Darwin's Dangerous Ideas*. New York: Touchstone.

Dennett, Daniel. 1991. *Consciousness Explained*. Boston, MA: Little, Brown, and Company.

Dennett, Daniel. 1984. *Elbow Room: The Varieties of Free Will Worth Wanting*. Cambridge, MA: MIT Press.

Dennett, Daniel. 1973. "Mechanism and Responsibility." In Ted Honderich, ed., *Essays on Freedom and Action*. London: Routledge and Kegan Paul: 159–84.

Doris, John. 2002. *Lack of Character*. Cambridge, MA: Cambridge University Press.

Double, Richard. 1996. *Metaphilosophy and Free Will*. New York: Oxford University Press.

Double, Richard. 1991. *The Non-Reality of Free Will*. New York: Oxford University Press.

Dretske, Fred. 1993. "Mental Events as Structuring Causes of Behavior." In John Heil and Alfred Mele, eds., 1993. *Mental Causation*. Oxford: Oxford University Press.

Dworkin, Gerald. 1988. *The Theory and Practice of Autonomy*. Cambridge: Cambridge University Press.

Dworkin, Gerald. 1970. "Acting Freely." *Noûs* 4: 367–83.

Edwards, Jonathan. 1754/1957. *Freedom of the Will (The Works of Jonathan Edwards,* vol. 1). New Haven, CT: Yale University Press.

Edwards, Paul. 1958. "Hard and Soft Determinism." In Sydney Hook, ed., *Determinism and Freedom in the Age of Modern Science.* London, Collier Books: 117–25.

Ekstrom, Laura W. 2003. "Free Will, Chance, and Mystery." *Philosophical Studies* 113: 153–80.

Ekstrom, Laura. 2000. *Free Will: A Philosophical Study.* Boulder, CO: Westview.

Eshleman, Andrew. 2014. "Moral Responsibility." *Stanford Encyclopedia of Philosophy.* http://plato.stanford.edu/entries/moral-responsibility.

Fara, Michael. 2008. "Masked Abilities and Compatibilism." *Mind* 117 (468): 843–65.

Farrell, Daniel. 1985. "The Justification of General Deterrence." *Philosophical Review* 104: 367–94.

Feinberg, Joel. 1970. *Doing and Deserving.* Princeton, NJ: Princeton University Press.

Feltz, Adam. 2013. "Pereboom and Premises: Asking the Right Questions in the Experimental Philosophy of Free Will." *Consciousness and Cognition* 22: 53–63.

Finch, Alicia. 2013. "On Behalf of the Consequence Argument: Time, Modality, and the Nature of Free Action." *Philosophical Studies* 163: 151–70.

Finch, Alicia, and Ted Warfield. 1998. "The Mind Argument and Libertarianism." *Mind* 107: 515–28.

Fischer, John Martin. 2013. "The Frankfurt Style Cases: Philosophical Lightning Rods." In I. Haji and J. Caouette, eds., *Free Will and Moral Responsibility.* Newcastle: Cambridge Scholars Publishing: 43–57.

Fischer, John Martin. 2012. *Deep Control: Essays on Free Will and Value.* New York: Oxford University Press.

Fischer, John Martin. 2011. "The Zygote Argument Remixed." *Analysis* 71: 267–72.

Fischer, John Martin. 2010. "The Frankfurt Cases: The Moral of the Stories." *Philosophical Review* 119: 315–36.

Fischer, John Martin. 2009. *Our Stories.* New York: Oxford University Press.

Fischer, John Martin. 2008. "Freedom, Foreknowledge, and Frankfurt: A Reply to Vihvelin." *Canadian Journal of Philosophy* 38 (3): 327–42.

Fischer, John Martin. 2006. *My Way.* New York: Oxford University Press.

Fischer, John Martin. 2005. "Reply: The Free Will Revolution." *Philosophical Explorations* 8 (2): 145–56.

Fischer, John Martin. 2004. "Responsibility and Manipulation." *Journal of Ethics* 8 (2): 145–77.

Fischer, John Martin. 2002. "Frankfurt Style Compatibilism." In Sarah Buss and Lee Overton, eds., *Contours of Agency: Essays on Themes from Harry Frankfurt.* Cambridge, MA: MIT Press: 1–26.

Fischer, John Martin. 1999. "Recent Work on Moral Responsibility." *Ethics* 110: 93–139.

Fischer, John Martin. 1994. *The Metaphysics of Free Will.* Oxford: Blackwell Publishers.

Fischer, John Martin. 1987. "Responsiveness and Moral Responsibility." In Ferdinand Schoeman, ed., *Responsibility, Character, and the Emotions: New Essays in Moral Psychology.* Cambridge: Cambridge University Press: 81–106.

Fischer, John Martin. 1986. "Power Necessity." *Philosophical Topics* 14: 77–91.

Fischer, John Martin. 1983. "Incompatibilism." *Philosophical Studies* 43: 127–37.

Fischer, John Martin. 1982. "Responsibility and Control." *Journal of Philosophy* 89: 24–40.

Fischer, John Martin, and Mark Ravizza. 1998. *Responsibility and Control: An Essay on Moral Responsibility*. Cambridge: Cambridge University Press.

Fischer, John Martin, and Mark Ravizza, eds., 1993. *Perspectives on Moral Responsibility*. Ithaca, NY: Cornell University Press.

Fischer, John Martin, Robert Kane, Derk Pereboom, and Manuel Vargas. 2007. *Four Views on Free Will*. Malden, MA: Blackwell Publishers.

Flint, Thomas P. 1998. *Divine Providence: The Molinist Account*. Ithaca, NY: Cornell University Press.

Fodor, Jerry. 1987. *Psychosemantics: The Problem of Meaning in the Philosophy of Mind*. Cambridge, MA: MIT Press.

Fodor, Jerry. 1974. "Special Sciences." *Synthèse* 28: 97–115.

Frankfurt, Harry. 2003. "Some Thoughts Concerning PAP." In David Widerker and Michael McKenna, eds., *Moral Responsibility and Alternative Possibilities*. Aldershot: Ashgate Press: 339–48.

Frankfurt, Harry. 2002. "Reply to John Martin Fischer." In Sarah Buss and Lee Overton, eds., *Contours of Agency: Essays on Themes from Harry Frankfurt*. Cambridge, MA: MIT Press: 27–31.

Frankfurt, Harry. 1999. *Necessity, Volition, and Love*. Cambridge: Cambridge University Press.

Frankfurt, Harry. 1992a. "The Faintest Passion." Presidential Address. *Proceedings of the American Philosophical Association* 66: 5–16.

Frankfurt, Harry. 1992b. "On the Usefulness of Final Ends." *Iyyun* 41: 3–19.

Frankfurt, Harry. 1988. *The Importance of What We Care About*. Cambridge: Cambridge University Press.

Frankfurt, Harry. 1987. "Identification and Wholeheartedness." In Ferdinand Schoeman, ed., *Responsibility, Character, and the Emotions: New Essays in Moral Psychology*. Cambridge: Cambridge University Press: 27–45.

Frankfurt, Harry. 1978. "The Problem of Action." *American Philosophical Quarterly* 15: 157–62.

Frankfurt, Harry. 1975. "Three Concepts of Free Action II." *Proceedings of the Aristotelian Society* supplementary volume: 113–25.

Frankfurt, Harry. 1971. "Freedom of the Will and the Concept of a Person." *Journal of Philosophy* 68: 5–20.

Frankfurt, Harry. 1969. "Alternate Possibilities and Moral Responsibility." *Journal of Philosophy* 66: 829–39.

Franklin, Christopher. 2011a. "Neo-Frankfurtians and Buffer Cases: The New Challenge to the Principle of Alternative Possibilities." *Philosophical Studies* 156: 199–203.

Franklin, Christopher. 2011b. "Farewell to the Luck (and Mind) Argument." *Philosophical Studies* 156: 199–230.

Frede, Michael. 2011. *A Free Will*. Berkeley and Los Angeles, CA: University of California Press.

Frede, Michael. 2009. *A Free Will*. Berkeley: CA: University of California Press.

Gert, Bernard, and Tim Duggan. 1979. "Free Will as the Ability to Will." *Noûs* 13: 197–217.

Ginet, Carl. 2007. "An Action Can be Both Uncaused and up to the Agent." In C. Lumer and S. Nannini, eds., 2007. *Intentionality, Deliberation, and Autonomy*. Farnham: Ashgate Press: 243–56.

Ginet, Carl. 2006. "Working with Fischer and Ravizza's Account of Moral Responsibility." *Journal of Ethics* 10: 229–53.

Ginet, Carl. 2002. "Review of Living without Free Will." *Journal of Ethics* 6: 305–9.

Ginet, Carl. 2000. "The Epistemic Requirements for Moral Responsibility." *Philosophical Perspectives* 14: 267–77.

Ginet, Carl. 1997. "Freedom, Responsibility, and Agency." *Journal of Ethics* 1: 85–98.

Ginet, Carl. 1996. "In Defense of the Principle of Alternative Possibilities: Why I Don't Find Frankfurt's Argument Convincing." *Philosophical Perspectives* 10: 403–17.

Ginet, Carl. 1990. *On Action*. Cambridge: Cambridge University Press.

Ginet, Carl. 1983. "In Defense of Incompatibilism." *Philosophical Studies* 44: 391–400.

Ginet, Carl. 1980. "The Conditional Analysis of Freedom." In Peter van Inwagen, ed., *Time and Cause*. Dordrecht: D. Reidel: 171–86.

Ginet, Carl. 1966. "Might We Have No Choice?" In Keith Lehrer, ed., *Freedom and Determinism*. New York: Random House: 87–104.

Ginet, Carl. 1962. "Can the Will be Caused?" *The Philosophical Review* 71: 49–55.

Glover, Jonathan. 1970. *Responsibility*. New York: Humanities Press.

Goetz, Stewart. 2008. *Freedom, Teleology and Evil*. London: Continuum.

Goetz, Stewart. 2005. "Frankfurt-Style Arguments and Begging the Question." *Midwest Studies in Philosophy* 29: 83–105.

Graham, Peter A. 2008. "A Defense of Local Miracle Compatibilism." *Philosophical Studies* 140: 65–82.

Griffith, Meghan. 2010. "Why Agent-caused Acts are not Lucky." *American Philosophical Quarterly* 47: 43–56.

Griffith, Meghan. 2005. "Does Free Will Remain a Mystery? A Response to Van Inwagen." *Philosophical Studies* 124: 261–9.

Haas, Daniel. 2012. "In Defense of Hard-line Replies to the Multiple-Case Manipulation Argument." *Philosophical Studies* 163: 797–811.

Haji, Ishtiyaque. 2010. "On the Direct Argument for the Incompatibility of Determinism and Moral Responsibility." *Grazer Philosophische Studien* 80: 111–30.

Haji, Ishtiyaque. 2009. *Incompatibilism's Allure: Principle Arguments for Incompatibilism*. Peterborough, Ontario: Broadview Press.

Haji, Ishtiyaque. 2004. "Active Control, Agent Causation, and Free Action." *Philosophical Explorations* 7: 131–48.

Haji, Ishtiyaque. 2002. "Compatibilist Views of Freedom and Responsibility." In Robert Kane, ed., *The Oxford Handbook of Free Will*. New York: Oxford University Press: 202–28.

Haji, Ishtiyaque. 1998. *Moral Appraisability*. New York: Oxford University Press.

Handfield, Toby, ed., 2009. *Dispositions and Causes*. Oxford: Oxford University Press.

Harris, James A. 2008. *Of Liberty and Necessity. The Free Will Debate in Eighteenth-Century British Philosophy*. Oxford: Oxford University Press.

Harris, Sam. 2012. *Free Will*. New York: Free Press.

Haynes, John-Dylan. 2011. "Beyond Libet: Long-term Prediction of Free Choices from Neuroimaging Signals." In W. Sinnott-Armstrong and L. Nadel, eds., 2011. *Conscious Will and Responsibility*. Oxford: Oxford University Press: 85–96.

Helm, Paul. 1993. *The Providence of God*. Leicester: Inter-Varsity Press.

Hobart, R.E. 1934. "Free Will as Involving Indeterminism and Inconceivable Without It." *Mind* 43: 1–27.

Hobbes, Thomas. 1651. *Leviathan*. R.E. Flatman and D. Johnston, eds., 1997. New York: W.W. Norton & Co.

Hoefer, Carl. 2010. "Causal Determinism." *Stanford Encyclopedia of Philosophy*. http://plato.stanford.edu/entries/determinism-causal.

Holbach, Paul. 1770. *System de la Nature*. Amsterdam.

Honderich, Ted. 1996. "Compatibilism, Incompatibilism, and the Smart Aleck." *Philosophy and Phenomenological Research* 56: 855–62.

Honderich, Ted. 1988. *A Theory of Determinism*. Oxford: Clarendon Press.

Honderich, Ted, ed., 1973. *Essays on Freedom and Action*. London: Routledge and Kegan Paul.

Hook, Sidney, ed., 1958. *Determinism and Freedom in the Age of Modern Science*. London, Collier Books.

Horgan, Terrance. 2015. "Injecting the Phenomenology of Agency into the Free Will Debate." In David Shoemaker, ed., *Oxford Studies in Agency and Responsibility*, vol. 3. Oxford: Oxford University Press: 34–61.

Horgan, Terrance. 2011. "The Phenomenology of Agency and Freedom: Lessons from Introspection and Lessons from Its Limits." *Humana Mente* 15: 77–97. www.humana mente.eu/Issues/Issue15.html.

Horgan, Terrance. 1985. "Compatibilism and the Consequence Argument." *Philosophical Studies* 47: 339–56.

Horgan, Terrance. 1979. "'Could', Possible Worlds, and Moral Responsibility." *Southern Journal of Philosophy* 17: 345–58.

Hornsby, Jennifer. 2004a. "Agency and Actions." In H. Steward and J. Hyman, eds., *Agency and Action*. Cambridge: Cambridge University Press: 1–23.

Hornsby, Jennifer. 2004b. "Agency and Alienation." In M. de Caro and D. MacArthur, eds., *Naturalism in Question*. Cambridge, MA: Harvard University Press: 173–87.

Horst, Stephen. 2011. *Laws, Mind, and Free Will*. Cambridge, MA: MIT Press.

Howard-Snyder, Daniel, and Jeff Jordan, eds., 1996. *Faith, Freedom, and Rationality*. Lanham, MD: Rowman and Littlefield.

Hume, David. 1748. *An Enquiry Concerning Human Understanding*. P.H. Niditch, ed., 1978. Oxford: Clarendon Press.

Hume, David. 1739. *A Treatise of Human Nature*. 1978. Oxford: Oxford University Press.

Hunt, David P. 2005. "Moral Responsibility and Buffered Alternatives." *Midwest Studies in Philosophy* 29: 126–45.

Hunt, David. 2000. "Moral Responsibility and Unavoidable Action." *Philosophical Studies* 97: 195–227.

Irwin, T.H., 1980. "Reason and Responsibility in Aristotle." In A.O. Rorty, ed., *Essays on Aristotle's Ethics*. Berkeley, CA: University of California Press: 117–55.

James, William. 1897. "The Dilemma of Determinism." *The Will to Believe and Other Essays in Popular Philosophy*. Cambridge, MA and London: Harvard University Press, 1979: 145–83.

Judisch, Neal. 2005. "Responsibility, Manipulation, and Ownership: Reflections in the Fischer/Ravizza Program." *Philosophical Reflections* 8 (2): 115–30.

Kane, Robert. 2016, forthcoming. "On the Role of Indeterminism in Libertarian Free Will." *Philosophical Explorations*.

Kane, Robert, ed., 2011a. *The Oxford Handbook of Free Will*. 2nd edn. New York: Oxford University Press.

Kane, Robert. 2011b. "Rethinking Free Will: New Perspectives on an Ancient Problem." In Robert Kane, ed., *The Oxford Handbook of Free Will*, 2nd edn. New York: Oxford University Press: 381–404.

Kane, Robert. 2007. "Libertarianism" and "Response to Fischer, Pereboom, and Vargas." In J. Fischer, R. Kane, D. Pereboom, M. Vargas, *Four Views on Free Will*. Oxford: Blackwell Publishers.

Kane, Robert. 2005. *A Contemporary Introduction to Free Will*. New York: Oxford University Press.

Kane, Robert, ed., 2002. *The Oxford Handbook of Free Will*. New York: Oxford University Press.

Kane, Robert. 2000. "The Dual Regress of Free Will and the Role of Alternative Possibilities." *Philosophical Perspectives* 14: 57–80.

Kane, Robert. 1999. "Responsibility, Luck, and Chance: Reflections on Free Will and Indeterminism." *Journal of Philosophy* 96: 217–40.

Kane, Robert. 1996. *The Significance of Free Will*. Oxford: Oxford University Press.

Kane, Robert. 1985. *Free Will and Values*. Albany, NY: State University of New York Press.

Kant, Immanuel. 1797. "The Metaphysical Elements of Justice, Part I." In *The Metaphysics of Morals*. Trans. J. Ladd, 1965. Indianapolis, IN: Bobbs-Merrill.

Kant, Immanuel. 1788. *Critique of Practical Reason*. Trans. Mary McGregor, 1996. Cambridge: Cambridge University Press.

Kant, Immanuel. 1785. *Grounding for the Metaphysics of Morals*. Trans. J. Ellington, 1981. Indianapolis: Hackett.

Kant, Immanuel. 1781/1787/1987. *Critique of Pure Reason*. Trans. Paul Guyer and Allen Wood, 1987. Cambridge: Cambridge University Press.

Kapitan, Tomis. 2002. "A Master Argument for Incompatibilism?" In Robert Kane, ed., 2002. *The Oxford Handbook of Free Will*. New York: Oxford University Press: 127–57.

Kapitan, Tomis. 2000. "Autonomy and Manipulated Freedom." *Philosophical Perspectives* 14: 81–104.

Kapitan, Tomis. 1986. "Deliberation and the Presumption of Open Alternatives." *Philosophical Quarterly* 36: 230–51.

Kearns, Stephen. 2012. "Aborting the Zygote Argument." *Philosophical Studies* 160 (3): 379–89.

Khoury, Andrew. 2014. "Manipulation and Mitigation." *Philosophical Studies* 168 (1): 283–94.

Kittle, Simon. 2014. "Vihvelin and Fischer on 'Pre-decisional' Intervention." *Philosophia* 42 (4): 368–74.

Knobe, Joshua. 2003. "Intentional Action in Folk Psychology: An Experimental Investigation." *Philosophical Psychology* 16 (2): 309–24.

Knobe, Joshua, and John Doris. 2010. "Responsibility." In *The Moral Psychology Handbook*. Oxford: Oxford University Press.

Knobe, Joshua, and Shaun Nichols, eds., 2008. *Experimental Philosophy*, vol 1. New York: Oxford University Press.

Lamb, James. 1977. "On a Proof of Incompatibilism." *Philosophical Review* 86: 20–35.

Lehrer, Keith. 1980. "Preferences, Conditionals and Freedom." In Peter van Inwagen, ed., *Time and Cause: Essays Presented to Richard Taylor*. Dordrecht: D. Reidel: 187–201.

Lehrer, Keith. 1976. "'Can' in Theory and Practice: A Possible Worlds Analysis." In Myles Brand and D. Walton, eds., *Action Theory*. Dordrecht: D. Reidel: 241–70.

Lehrer, Keith. 1968. "'Can's Without 'If's." *Analysis* 24: 159–60.

Lehrer, Keith, ed., 1966. *Freedom and Determinism*. New York: Random House.

Leiter, Brian. 2007. "Nietzsche's Theory of the Will." *Philosophers' Imprint* 7: 1–15.

Levy, Neil. 2011. *Hard Luck*. Oxford: Oxford University Press.

Levy, Neil. 2006. "Determinist Deliberations." *Dialectica* 60: 453–9.

Lewis, David. 1993. "Evil for Freedom's Sake?" *Philosophical Papers* 22: 149–72.

Lewis, David. 1986. "Events." In *Philosophical Papers, Volume II*. New York: Oxford University Press: 241–69.

Lewis, David. 1981. "Are We Free to Break the Laws?" *Theoria* 47: 113–21.

Lewis, David. 1979. "Counterfactual Dependence and Time's Arrow." *Noûs*. 13: 455–76.

Lewis, David. 1973. "Causation." *Journal of Philosophy* 70: 556–67.

Libet, Benjamin. 2004. *Mind Time*. Cambridge, MA: Harvard University Press.

Libet, Benjamin. 1985. "Unconscious Cerebral Initiative and the Role of Conscious Will in Voluntary Action." *Behavioral and Brain Sciences* 8: 529–66.

Locke, Don. 1975. "Three Concepts of Free Action I." *Proceedings of Aristotelian Society* supp., vol. IL: 95–112.

Locke, John. 1965. *An Essay Concerning Human Understanding*. New York: Collier.

Loewenstein, Yael. Forthcoming. "Why the Direct Argument Does not Shift the Burden of Proof." *Journal of Philosophy*.

Lowe, E.J. 2008. *Personal Agency: The Metaphysics of Mind and Action*. Oxford: Oxford University Press.

Lucretius. 50 BCE. *De Rerum Natura*. Trans. W.H.D. Rouse, Loeb Classical Library, 1982. Cambridge, MA: Harvard University Press.

Mackie, J.L. 1955. "Evil and Omnipotence." *Mind* 64: 200–12.

Manekin, C.H., and M. Kellner, eds., 1997. *Freedom and Moral Responsibility: General and Jewish Perspectives*. College Park, MD: University of Maryland Press.

Markosian, Ned. 2010. "Agent Causation as the Solution to All the Compatibilist's Problems." *Philosophical Studies* 157: 383–98.

Markosian, Ned. 1999. "A Compatibilist View of the Theory of Agent Causation." *Pacific Philosophical Quarterly* 80: 257–77.

Matheson, Benjamin. Forthcoming. "In Defense of the Four-Case Argument." *Philosophical Studies*.

McCann, Hugh. 1998. *The Works of Agency*. Ithaca, NY: Cornell University Press.

McCormick, Kelly. 2013. "Anchoring a Revisionist Account of Moral Responsibility." *Journal of Ethics and Social Philosophy* 7: 1–19.

McKay, Thomas, and David Johnson. 1996. "A Reconsideration of an Argument against Incompatibilism." *Philosophical Topics* 24: 113–22.

McKenna, Michael. 2014. "Resisting the Manipulation Argument: A Hard-liner Takes it on the Chin." *Philosophy and Phenomenological Research* 89: 467–84.

McKenna, Michael. 2013. "Reasons-Responsiveness, Agents, and Mechanisms." In David Shoemaker, ed., *Oxford Studies in Agency and Responsibility*, vol. 1. Oxford: Oxford University Press: 151–84.

McKenna, Michael. 2012. *Conversation and Responsibility*. New York: Oxford University Press.

McKenna, Michael. 2011. "Contemporary Compatibilism: Mesh Theories and Reasons-Responsive Theories." In Robert Kane, ed., *Oxford Handbook of Free Will*, 2nd edn. New York: Oxford University Press: 175–98.

McKenna, Michael. 2009a. "Compatibilism." *The Stanford Encyclopedia of Philosophy (original 2004)*, Edward N. Zalta, ed. http://plato.stanford.edu/archives/sum2004/entries/compatibilism.

McKenna, Michael. 2009b. "Compatibilism and Desert: Critical Comments on *Four Views on Free Will*." *Philosophical Studies* 144: 3–13.

McKenna, Michael. 2008a. "A Hard-line Reply to Pereboom's Four-case Argument." *Philosophy and Phenomenological Research* 77 (1): 142–59.

McKenna, Michael. 2008b. "Frankfurt's Argument against Alternative Possibilities: Looking beyond the Example." *Noûs* 42: 770–93.

McKenna, Michael. 2008c. "Saying Goodbye to the Direct Argument the Right Way." *Philosophical Review* 117 (3): 349–83.

McKenna, Michael. 2008d. "Ultimacy & Sweet Jane." In Nick Trakakis and Daniel Cohen, eds., *Essays on Free Will and Moral Responsibility*. Newcastle: Cambridge Scholars Publishing: 186–208.

McKenna, Michael. 2005a. "Reasons Reactivity & Incompatibilist Intuitions." *Philosophical Explorations* 8 (2): 131–43.

McKenna, Michael. 2005b. "Where Frankfurt and Strawson Meet." *Midwest Studies in Philosophy* 29: 163–80.

McKenna, Michael. 2004. "Responsibility and Globally Manipulated Agents." *Philosophical Topics* 32: 169–82.

McKenna, Michael. 2003. "Robustness, Control, and the Demand for Morally Significant Alternatives." In David Widerker and Michael McKenna, eds., 2003. *Moral Responsibility and Alternative Possibilities*. Aldershot: Ashgate Press: 201–18.

McKenna, Michael. 2001. "Review of John Martin Fischer and Mark Ravizza's *Responsibility & Control.*" *Journal of Philosophy* 98 (2): 93–100.

McKenna, Michael. 1998. "The Limits of Evil and the Role of Moral Address: A Defense of Strawsonian Compatibilism." *Journal of Ethics* 2: 123–42.

McKenna, Michael. 1997. "Alternative Possibilities and the Failure of the Counterexample Strategy." *Journal of Social Philosophy* 28: 71–85.

McKenna, Michael, and D. Justin Coates. 2015. "Compatibilism." *Stanford Encyclopedia of Philosophy*. http://plato.stanford.edu/entries/compatibilism.

McKenna, Michael, and Paul Russell, eds., 2008. *Free Will and Reactive Attitudes: Perspectives on P.F. Strawson's "Freedom and Resentment."* Aldershot: Ashgate Press.

Mele, Alfred. 2013. "Free Will and Neuroscience." *Philosophic Exchange* 43: 1–17.

Mele, Alfred. 2009. *Effective Intentions*. New York: Oxford University Press.

Mele, Alfred. 2008. "Manipulation, Compatibilism, and Moral Responsibility." *Journal of Ethics* 12 (304): 263–86.

Mele, Alfred. 2006a. "Fischer and Ravizza on Moral Responsibility." *Journal of Ethics* 10 (3): 283–94.

Mele, Alfred. 2006b. *Free Will and Luck*. New York: Oxford University Press.

Mele, Alfred. 2005a. "A Critique of Pereboom's Four-Case Argument for Incompatibilism." *Analysis* 65: 75–80.

Mele, Alfred. 2005b. "Libertarianism, Luck, and Control." *Pacific Philosophical Quarterly* 86: 381–407.

Mele, Alfred. 2002. "Review of John Searle's Rationality in Action." *Mind* 111: 905–9.

Mele, Alfred. 2000. "Reactive Attitudes, Reactivity, and Omissions." *Philosophy and Phenomenological Research* 61: 447–52.

Mele, Alfred. 1999. "Ultimate Responsibility and Dumb Luck." *Social Philosophy & Policy*, 16: 274–93.

Mele, Alfred. 1996. "Soft Libertarianism and Frankfurt-Style Scenarios." *Philosophical Topics* 24: 123–41.

Mele, Alfred. 1995. *Autonomous Agents*. New York: Oxford University Press.

Mele, Alfred. 1992. *Springs of Action*. New York: Oxford University Press.

Mele, Alfred, and David Robb. 1998. "Rescuing Frankfurt-Style Cases." *Philosophical Review* 107: 97–112.

Molina, Luis de. 1595. *Liberi Arbitrii cum Gratiae Donis, Divina Praescientia, Providentia, Praedestinatione et Reprobatione*. Trans. (of Part IV) A.J. Freddoso, *On Divine Foreknowledge: Part IV of the Concordia*, 1988. Ithaca, NY: Cornell University Press.

Moore, G.E. 1912. *Ethics*. Oxford: Oxford University Press.

Moore, G.E. 1903. *Principia Ethica*. New York: Cambridge University Press.

Moore, Michael. 1998. *Placing Blame*. Oxford: Oxford University Press.

Moore, Michael. 1987. "The Moral Worth of Retributivism." In Ferdinand Schoeman, ed., *Responsibility, Character, and the Emotions: New Essays in Moral Psychology*. Cambridge: Cambridge University Press: 179–219.

Moran, Richard. 2002. "Frankfurt on Identification: Ambiguities of Activity in Mental Life." In Sarah Buss and Lee Overton, eds., *Contours of Agency: Essays on Themes from Harry Frankfurt.* Cambridge, MA: MIT Press: 189–217.

Moya, Carlos. 2011. "On the Very Idea of a Robust Alternative." *Critica* 43: 3–26.

Moya, Carlos. 2006. *Moral Responsibility: The Ways of Skepticism.* Oxford: Oxford University Press.

Murray, Dylan, and Tania Lombrozo. Forthcoming. "Effects of Manipulation on Attributions." *Cognitive Science.*

Murray, Dylan, and Eddy Nahmias. 2014. "Explaining Away Incompatibilist Intuitions." *Philosophy and Phenomenological Research* 88: 434–67.

Nagel, Thomas. 1986. *The View from Nowhere.* New York: Oxford University Press.

Nahmias, Eddy. 2014. "Is Free Will an Illusion? Confronting Challenges from the Modern Mind Sciences." In W. Sinnott-Armstrong, ed., *Moral Psychology*, vol. 4. Cambridge, MA: MIT Press: 1–25.

Nahmias, Eddy. 2011. "Intuitions about Free Will, Determinism, and Bypassing." In Robert Kane, ed., *The Oxford Handbook of Free Will.* New York: Oxford University Press: 555–76.

Nahmias, Eddy. 2006. "Folk Fears about Freedom and Responsibility: Determinism and Reductionism." *Journal of Culture and Cognition* 6 (1–2): 215–38.

Nahmias, Eddy, and Dylan Murray. 2010. "Experimental Philosophy on Free Will: An Error Theory for Incompatibilist Intuitions." In J. Aguilar, A. Buckareff, and J. Frankish, eds., *New Waves in Philosophy of Action.* New York: Palgrave Macmillan: 112–29.

Nahmias, Eddy, Justin D. Coates, and Trevor Kvaran. 2007. "Free Will, Moral Responsibility, and Mechanism: Experiments on Folk Intuitions." *Midwest Studies in Philosophy* 31: 214–42.

Nahmias, E., S. Morris, T. Nadelhoffer, and J. Turner. 2006. "Is Incompatibilism Intuitive?" *Philosophy and Phenomenological Research* 73 (1): 28–53.

Nahmias, E., S. Morris, T. Nadelhoffer, and J. Turner. 2004. "The Phenomenology of Free Will." *Journal of Consciousness Studies* 11 (7–8): 162–79.

Naylor, Marjory. 1984. "Frankfurt on the Principle of Alternate Possibilities." *Philosophical Studies* 46: 249–58.

Nelkin, Dana. 2013. "Reply to Critics." *Philosophical Studies* 163: 123–31.

Nelkin, Dana. 2011. *Making Sense of Freedom and Responsibility.* Oxford: Oxford University Press.

Nelkin, Dana. 2008. "Responsibility and Rational Abilities: Defending an Asymmetrical View." *Pacific Philosophical Quarterly* 8: 497–515.

Nelkin, Dana. 2007. "Do We Have a Coherent Set of Intuitions About Moral Responsibility?" *Midwest Studies in Philosophy* 31: 243–59.

Nelkin, Dana. 2004a. "Deliberative Alternatives." *Philosophical Topics* 32: 215–40.

Nelkin, Dana. 2004b. "The Sense of Freedom." In Joseph Keim Campbell, Michael O'Rourke, and David Sheir, eds., 2004. *Freedom and Determinism.* Cambridge, MA: MIT Press: 105–34.

Nelkin, Dana. 2000. "Two Standpoints and the Belief in Freedom." *Journal of Philosophy* 97: 564–76.

Nichols, Shaun. 2007. "After Incompatibilism: A Naturalistic Defense of the Reactive Attitudes." *Philosophical Perspectives* 21: 405–28.

Nichols, Shaun. 2006. "Folk Intuitions on Free Will." *Journal of Cognition and Culture* 6 (1&2): 57–86.

Nichols, Shaun, and Joshua Knobe. 2007. "Moral Responsibility and Determinism: The Cognitive Science of Folk Intuitions." *Noûs* 41 (4): 663–85.

Nida-Rümelin, Martine. 2007. "Doings and Subject Causation." *Erkenntnis* 67: 255–72.

Nietzsche, Friedrich. 1889. *Twilight of the Idols*; and *The Anti-Christ*. Trans. R.J. Hollingdale, 1977. Harmondsworth: Penguin.

Nowell-Smith, P.H. 1954. "Determinism and Libertarianism." *Mind* 63: 31–7.

Nowell-Smith, P.H. 1948. "Free Will and Moral Responsibility." *Mind* 57: 45–61.

O'Connor, Timothy. 2010. "Free Will." *The Stanford Encyclopedia of Philosophy* (Spring 2002 edition; substantive revision October 2010), Edward N. Zalta, ed. http://plato.stanford.edu/archives/spr2002/entries/freewill/.

O'Connor, Timothy. 2009. "Agent-Causal Power." In Toby Handfield, ed., *Dispositions and Causes*. Oxford: Oxford University Press: 184–214.

O'Connor, Timothy. 2003. "Review of *Living without Free Will*." *Philosophical Quarterly* 53: 308–10.

O'Connor, Timothy. 2000. *Persons and Causes*. New York: Oxford University Press.

O'Connor, Timothy, ed., 1995a. *Agents, Causes, and Events*. New York: Oxford University Press.

O'Connor, Timothy. 1995b. "Agent Causation." In Timothy O'Connor, ed., *Agents, Causes, and Events*. New York: Oxford University Press: 170–200.

O'Connor, Timothy. 1993. "On the Transfer of Necessity." *Noûs* 27: 204–18.

Otsuka, Michael. 1998. "Incompatibilism and the Avoidability of Blame." *Ethics* 108: 685–701.

Palmer, David. 2011. "Pereboom on the Frankfurt Cases." *Philosophical Studies* 153: 261–72.

Pendergraft, Garrett. 2011. "The Explanatory Power of Local Miracle Compatibilism." *Philosophical Studies* 156: 249–66.

Pereboom, Derk. 2016. "Omissions and Different Senses of Responsibility." In Andrei Buckareff, Carlos Moya, and Sergi Rosell, eds., *Agency and Moral Responsibility*. New York: Palgrave-Macmillan: 179–91.

Pereboom, Derk. 2015a. "A Notion of Moral Responsibility Immune to the Threat from Causal Determination." In Randolph Clarke, Michael McKenna, and Angela Smith, eds., *The Nature of Moral Responsibility*. Oxford: Oxford University Press: 281–96.

Pereboom, Derk. 2015b. "The Phenomenology of Agency and Deterministic Agent Causation." In Megan Altman and Hans Gruenig, eds., *Horizons of Authenticity in Phenomenology, Existentialism, and Moral Psychology: Essays in Honor of Charles Guignon*. New York: Springer: 277–94.

Pereboom, Derk. 2014. *Free Will, Agency, and Meaning in Life*. New York: Oxford University Press.

Pereboom, Derk. 2013. "Free Will Skepticism, Blame, and Obligation." In Neal Tognazzini and D. Justin Coates, eds., 2013. *Blame: Its Nature and Norms*. New York: Oxford University Press: 189–206.

Pereboom, Derk. 2012a. "Frankfurt Examples, Derivative Responsibility, and the Timing Objection." *Philosophical Issues* 22: 298–315.

Pereboom, Derk. 2012b. "Theological Determinism and Divine Providence." In Ken Perszyk, ed., *Molinism: The Contemporary Debate*. Oxford: Oxford University Press: 262–79.

Pereboom, Derk. 2009a. "Free Will, Love, and Anger." *Ideas y Valores: Revista de Columbiana de Filosofia* 141: 5–25.

Pereboom, Derk. 2009b. "Further Thoughts about a Frankfurt-Style Argument." *Philosophical Explorations* 12: 109–18.

Pereboom, Derk. 2009c. "Hard Incompatibilism and Its Rivals." *Philosophical Studies* 144: 21–33.

Pereboom, Derk. 2008a. "A Compatibilist Account of the Epistemic Conditions on Rational Deliberation." *Journal of Ethics* 12: 287–307.

Pereboom, Derk. 2008b. "A Hard-line Reply to the Multiple-Case Manipulation Argument." *Philosophy and Phenomenological Research* 77 (1): 160–70.

Pereboom, Derk. 2007. "On Mele's Free Will and Luck." *Philosophical Explorations* 10: 163–72.

Pereboom, Derk. 2006a. "Kant on Transcendental Freedom." *Philosophy and Phenomenological Research* 73: 537–67.

Pereboom, Derk. 2006b. "Reasons Responsiveness, Alternative Possibilities, and Manipulation Arguments Against Compatibilism: Reflections on John Martin Fischer's *My Way*." *Philosophical Books* 47: 198–212.

Pereboom, Derk. 2005. "Free Will, Evil, and Divine Providence." In Andrew Chignell and Andrew Dole, eds., *God and the Ethics of Belief: New Essays in Philosophy of Religion*. Cambridge: Cambridge University Press: 77–98.

Pereboom, Derk. 2004. "Is Our Concept of Agent Causation Incoherent?" *Philosophical Topics* 32: 275–86.

Pereboom, Derk. 2003. "Source Incompatibilism and Alternative Possibilities." In David Widerker and Michael McKenna, eds., *Moral Responsibility and Alternative Possibilities*. Aldershot: Ashgate Press: 185–200.

Pereboom, Derk. 2001. *Living Without Free Will*. Cambridge: Cambridge University Press.

Pereboom, Derk. 2000. "Alternative Possibilities and Causal Histories." *Philosophical Perspectives* 14: 119–38.

Pereboom, Derk. 1995. "Determinism al Dente." *Noûs* 29: 21–45.

Pereboom, Derk, with J.M. Fischer, R. Kane, and M. Vargas. 2007. *Four Views on Free Will*. New York: Blackwell.

Pettit, Philip. 1989. "Determinism with Deliberation." *Analysis* 49: 42–4.

Pettit, Philip, and Michael Smith. 1996. "Freedom in Belief and Desire." *Journal of Philosophy* 93 (9): 429–49.

Pizarro, David, E. Uhlmann, and P. Salovy. 2003. "Asymmetry in Judgments of Moral Blame and Praise: The Role of Perceived Metadesires." *Psychological Science* 14: 267–72.

Plantinga, Alvin. 1974. *God, Freedom, and Evil*. Grand Rapids, MI: Eerdmans.

Priestley, Joseph. 1788. "A Free Discussion of the Doctrines of Materialism and Philosophical Necessity." In *A Correspondence between Dr. Price and Dr. Priestley*, Part III: 147–52; reprinted in Joseph Priestley, *Priestley's Writings on Philosophy, Science, and Politics*, John Passmore, ed. 1965. New York: Collier.

Putnam, Hilary. 1967. "The Nature of Mental States," first published as "Psychological Predicates," in *Art, Mind, and Religion*, W.H. Capitan and D.D. Merrill, eds., Pittsburgh: Pittsburgh University Press, 1967, pp. 37–48; reprinted as "The Nature of Mental States," in Hilary Putnam, *Philosophical Papers*, vol. 2, Cambridge: Cambridge University Press, 1975, pp. 429–40.

Ragland, C.P. 2016. *The Will to Reason: Theodicy and Freedom in Descartes*. New York: Oxford University Press.

Ravizza, Mark. 1994. "Semicompatibilism and the Transfer of Non-Responsibility." *Philosophical Studies* 75: 61–94.

Reid, Thomas. 1788. "Essays on the Active Powers of Man." In Sir William Hamilton, ed., *The Works of Thomas Reid*. Hildesheim: G. Olms Verslagsbuchhandlung, 1983.

Robinson, Michael. 2012. "Modified Frankfurt-type Counterexamples and Flickers of Freedom." *Philosophical Studies* 157: 177–94.

Rorty, A.O., ed., 1980. *Essays on Aristotle's Ethics*. Berkeley, CA: University of California Press.

Rose, David, and Shaun Nichols. 2013. "The Lesson of Bypassing." *Review of Philosophy and Psychology* 4: 599–619.

Rowe, William. 1991. *Thomas Reid on Freedom and Morality*. Ithaca, NY: Cornell University Press.

Russell, Paul. 2013. "Responsibility, Naturalism, and the Morality System." In David Shoemaker, ed., *Oxford Studies in Agency and Responsibility*, vol. 1, Oxford: Oxford University Press: 184–204.

Russell, Paul. 2004. "Responsibility and the Condition of Moral Sense." *Philosophical Topics* 32: 287–306.

Russell, Paul. 2002a. "Critical Notice of John Martin Fischer and Mark Ravizza *Responsibility and Control: A Theory of Moral Responsibility*." *Canadian Journal of Philosophy* 32: 587–606.

Russell, Paul. 2002b. "Pessimists, Pollyannas, and the New Compatibilism." In Robert Kane, ed., 2002. *The Oxford Handbook of Free Will*. New York: Oxford University Press: 229–56.

Russell, Paul. 2000. "Compatibilist-Fatalism." In Ton van den Beld, ed., *Moral Responsibility and Ontology*. Dordrecht: Kluwer Publishers: 199–218.

Russell, Paul. 1995. *Freedom and Moral Sentiment*. New York: Oxford University Press.

Russell, Paul. 1992. "Strawson's Way of Naturalizing Responsibility." *Ethics* 102: 287–302.

Sartorio, Carolina. Forthcoming. "Vihvelin on Frankfurt-style Cases and the Actual-Sequence View." *Criminal Law and Philosophy*.

Sartorio, Carolina. 2017, forthcoming. "Frankfurt-Style Examples." In M. Griffin, N. Levy, and K. Timpe, eds., *Routledge Companion to Free Will*. Routledge.

Sartorio, Carolina. 2016. *Causation and Free Will*. Oxford: Oxford University Press.

Sartorio, Carolina. 2015. "The Problem of Determinism and Free Will is not the Problem of Determinism and Free Will." In A. Mele, ed., 2015. *Surrounding Freedom: Philosophy, Psychology, Neuroscience*. Oxford: Oxford University Press: 255–73.

Sartorio, Carolina. 2013. "Making a Difference in a Determined World." *Philosophical Review* 122: 189–214.

Sartorio, Carolina. 2005. "A New Asymmetry between Actions and Omissions." *Noûs* 39: 460–82.

Saunders, John Turk. 1968. "The Temptation of Powerlessness." *American Philosophical Quarterly* 5: 100–8.

Sayer-McCord, Geoffrey, ed., 1988. *Essays on Moral Realism*. Ithaca, NY: Cornell University Press.

Scanlon, Thomas. 2013. "Giving Desert its Due." *Philosophical Explorations* 16 (2): 101–16.

Scanlon, T.M. 2008. *Moral Dimensions: Permissibility, Meaning, Blame*. Cambridge, MA: Belknap Harvard Press.

Scanlon, T.M. 1998. *What We Owe to Each Other*. Cambridge, MA: Harvard University Press.

Scanlon, T.M. 1988. "The Significance of Choice." In Sterling M. McMurrin, ed., *The Tanner Lectures on Human Values*, Cambridge: Cambridge University Press: 1–35.

Schaffer, Jonathan. 2000. "Trumping Preemption." *Journal of Philosophy* 97: 165–81.

Schlick, Moritz. 1939. "When is a Man Responsible?" In *Problems of Ethics*. Upper Saddle River, NJ. Prentice-Hall: 143–56.

Schnall, I.M., and Widerker, D. 2012. "The Direct Argument and the Burden of Proof." *Analysis* 72 (1): 25–36.

Schoeman, Ferdinand, ed., 1987. *Responsibility, Character, and the Emotions: New Essays in Moral Psychology*. Cambridge: Cambridge University Press.

Schoeman, Ferdinand. 1979. "On Incapacitating the Dangerous." *American Philosophical Quarterly* 16: 27–35.

Searle, John. 2001. *Rationality in Action*. Cambridge, MA: MIT Press.

Sellars, Wilfred. 1966. "Fatalism and Determinism." In Keith Lehrer, ed., *Freedom and Determinism*. New York: Random House.

Shabo, Seth. 2012. "Where Love and Resentment Meet: Strawson's Interpersonal Defense of Compatibilism." *Philosophical Review* 121: 95–124.

Shabo, Seth. 2011. "Agency without Avoidability: Defusing a New Threat to Frankfurt's Counterexample Strategy." *Canadian Journal of Philosophy* 41: 505–22.

Shabo, Seth. 2010a. "Uncompromising Source Incompatibilism." *Philosophy and Phenomenological Research* 80: 349–83.

Shabo, Seth. 2010b. "The Fate of the Direct Argument and the Case for Incompatibilism." *Philosophical Studies* 150: 405–24.

Shabo, Seth. 2005. "Fischer and Ravizza on History and Ownership." *Philosophical Explorations* 8 (2): 103–14.

Sher, George. 2016. "Unintentional Omissions." In Dana Nelkin and Sam Rickless, eds., *The Ethics and Law of Omissions*. Oxford: Oxford University Press.

Sher, George. 2009. *Who Knew?* New York: Oxford University Press.

Shoemaker, David. 2015. *Responsibility from the Margins*. Oxford: Oxford University Press.

Shoemaker, David. 2011. "Attributability, Answerability, and Accountability: Toward a Wider Theory of Moral Responsibility." *Ethics* 121: 602–32.

Shoemaker, David. 2007. "Moral Address, Moral Responsibility, and the Boundaries of Moral Community." *Ethics* 118: 70–108.

Shoemaker, David, and Neal A. Tognazzini, eds., 2014. *Oxford Studies in Agency and Responsibility, 2: "Freedom and Resentment" at 50*. Oxford: Oxford University Press.

Skinner, B.F. 1971. *Beyond Freedom and Dignity*. New York: Vintage.

Skinner, B.F. 1962. *Walden Two*. New York: Macmillan.

Slote, Michael. 1982. "Selective Necessity and the Free-Will Problem." *Journal of Philosophy* 79: 5–24.

Smart, J.J.C. 1963. "Free Will, Praise, and Blame." *Mind* 70: 291–306.

Smilansky, Saul. 2011. "Hard Determinism and Punishment: A Practical Reductio." *Law and Philosophy* 30: 353–67.

Smilansky, Saul. 2003. "The Argument from Shallowness." *Philosophical Studies* 115: 257–82.

Smilansky, Saul. 2000. *Free Will and Illusion*. Oxford: Oxford University Press.

Smilansky, Saul. 1997. "Can a Determinist Help Herself?" In C.H. Manekin and M. Kellner, eds., *Freedom and Moral Responsibility: General and Jewish Perspectives*. College Park, MD: University of Maryland Press: 85–98.

Smilansky, Saul. 1993. "Does the Free Will Debate Rest on a Mistake?" *Philosophical Papers* 22: 173–88.

Smith, Angela. 2012. "Attributability, Answerability, and Accountability: In Defense of a Unified Account." *Ethics* 122: 575–89.

Smith, Angela. 2004. "Conflicting Attitudes, Moral Agency, and Conceptions of the Self." *Philosophical Topics* 32: 331–52.

Smith, Holly. 1983. "Culpable Ignorance." *Philosophical Review* 92 (4): 543–571.

Smith, Michael. 2003. "Rational Capacities, or: How to Distinguish Recklessness, Weakness, and Compulsion." In Sarah Stroud and Christine Tappolet, eds., *Weakness of Will and Practical Irrationality.* New York: Oxford University Press: 17–38.

Sommers, Tamler. 2012. *Relative Justice: Cultural Diversity, Free Will, and Moral Responsibility.* Princeton, NJ: Princeton University Press.

Sommers, Tamler. 2007. "The Objective Attitude." *Philosophical Quarterly* 57: 321–41.

Soon, Chun Siong, Marcel Brass, Hans-Jochen Heinze, and John-Dylan Haynes. 2008. "Unconscious Determinants of Free Decisions in the Human Brain." *Nature Neuroscience* 11: 543–5.

Speak, Dan. 2014. *The Problem of Evil.* Cambridge: Polity Press.

Speak, Dan. 2011. "The Consequence Argument Revisited." In Robert Kane, ed., *The Oxford Handbook of Free Will.* 2nd edn. New York: Oxford University Press: 115–30.

Speak, Dan. 2004. "Toward an Axiological Defense of Libertarianism." *Philosophical Topics* 3: 353–69.

Spinoza, Baruch. 1677. *Ethics.* In Edwin Curley, ed. and trans. *The Collected Works of Spinoza*, vol. 1, 1985. Princeton, NJ: Princeton University Press.

Sripada, Chandra. 2012. "What Makes a Manipulated Agent Unfree?" *Philosophy and Phenomenological Research* 85: 563–93.

Stapleton, Sean. 2010. Hard Incompatibilist Challenges to Morality and Autonomy. Dissertation, Department of Philosophy, Cornell University, Ithaca, NY.

Stevenson, C.L. 1944. *Ethics and Language.* New Haven, CT: Yale University Press.

Steward, Helen. 2012. *A Metaphysics for Freedom.* Oxford: Oxford University Press.

Strawson, Galen. 1994. "The Impossibility of Moral Responsibility." *Philosophical Studies* 75: 5–24.

Strawson, Galen. 1986. *Freedom and Belief.* Oxford: Clarendon Press.

Strawson, P.F. 1992. "Freedom and Necessity." In *Analysis and Metaphysics: An Introduction to Philosophy.* Oxford: Oxford University Press: chapter 10.

Strawson, P.F. 1985. *Skepticism and Naturalism: Some Varieties.* New York: Columbia University Press.

Strawson, P.F. 1980. "Reply to Ayer and Bennett." In Zak van Straaten, ed., *Philosophical Subjects: Essays Presented to P.F. Strawson.* Oxford: Clarendon Press: 260–6.

Strawson, P.F. 1962. "Freedom and Resentment." *Proceedings of the British Academy* 48: 187–211.

Stroud, Sarah, and Christine Tappolet, eds., 2003. *Weakness of Will and Practical Irrationality.* New York: Oxford University Press.

Stump, Eleonore. 2000. "The Direct Argument for Incompatibilism." *Philosophy & Phenomenological Research* 61: 459–66.

Stump, Eleonore. 1996. "Libertarian Freedom and the Principle of Alternative Possibilities." In Daniel Howard-Snyder and Jeff Jordan, eds., *Faith, Freedom, and Rationality.* Lanham, MD: Rowman and Littlefield: 73–88.

Stump, Eleonore. 1990. "Intellect, Will, and the Principle of Alternate Possibilities." In Michael D. Beaty, ed., *Christian Themes and the Problems of Philosophy.* Notre Dame, IN: University of Notre Dame Press: 254–85.

Stump, Eleonore. 1985. "The Problem of Evil." *Faith and Philosophy* 2: 392–418.

Sturgeon, Nicholas. 1982. "Brandt's Moral Empiricism." *Philosophical Review* 91: 389–422.

Swinburne, Richard. 2014. *Mind, Brain, and Free Will*. Oxford: Oxford University Press.

Swinburne, Richard. 1999. *Providence and the Problem of Evil*. Oxford: Oxford University Press.

Talbert, Matthew. 2012. "Moral Competence, Moral Blame, and Protest." *Journal of Ethics* 16: 89–109.

Taylor, James Stacey, ed., 2005. *Personal Autonomy*. New York: Cambridge University Press.

Taylor, Richard. 1974. *Metaphysics*. Englewood Cliffs, NJ: Prentice Hall.

Taylor, Richard. 1966. *Action and Purpose*. Engelwood Cliffs, NJ: Prentice-Hall.

Tierney, Hannah. 2014. "Tackling it Head on: How Best to Handle the Modified Manipulation Argument." *Journal of Value Inquiry* 48: 663–75.

Tierney, Hannah. 2013. "A Maneuver around the Modified Manipulation Argument." *Philosophical Studies* 165: 753–63.

Timpe, Kevin. 2014. *Free Will in Philosophical Theology*. New York: Bloomsbury.

Timpe, Kevin. 2008. *Free Will: Sourcehood and Its Alternatives*. New York: Continuum Press.

Todd, Patrick. 2012. "Defending (a Modified Version of the) Zygote Argument." *Philosophical Studies* 164 (1): 189–203.

Todd, Patrick. 2011. "A New Approach to Manipulation Arguments." *Philosophical Studies* 152 (1): 127–33.

Todd, Patrick, and Neal Tognazzini. 2008. "A Problem for Guidance Control." *Philosophical Quarterly* 58 (233): 685–92.

Tognazzini, Neal, and D. Justin Coates, eds., 2013. *Blame: Its Nature and Norms*. New York: Oxford University Press.

Tooley, Michael. 1997. *Time, Tense, and Causation*. Oxford: Clarendon Press.

Tooley, Michael. 1990. *Mental Beings*. Ithaca, NY: Cornell University Press.

Trakakis, Nick, and Daniel Cohen, eds., 2008. *Essays on Free Will and Moral Responsibility*. Newcastle: Cambridge Scholars Publishing.

van den Beld, Ton, ed., 2000. *Moral Responsibility and Ontology*. Dordrecht: Kluwer Publishers.

van Inwagen, Peter. 2008. "How to Think about the Problem of Free Will." *Journal of Ethics* 12 (3–4): 327–41.

van Inwagen, Peter. 2004. "Freedom to Break the Laws." *Midwest Studies in Philosophy* 28: 334–50.

van Inwagen, Peter. 2002. "Free Will Remains a Mystery." In Robert Kane, ed., *The Oxford Handbook of Free Will*. New York: Oxford University Press: 158–77.

van Inwagen, Peter. 2000. "Free Will Remains a Mystery." *Philosophical Perspectives* 14: 1–19.

van Inwagen, Peter. 1993. *Metaphysics*. Boulder, CO: Westview Press.

van Inwagen, Peter. 1983. *An Essay on Free Will*. Oxford: Clarendon Press.

van Inwagen, Peter, ed., 1980. *Time and Cause*. Dordrecht: D. Reidel.

van Inwagen, Peter. 1975. "The Incompatibility of Free Will and Determinism." *Philosophical Studies* 27: 185–99.

van Straaten, Zak, ed., 1980. *Philosophical Subjects: Essays Presented to P.F. Strawson*. Oxford: Clarendon Press.

Vargas, Manuel. 2013. *Building Better Beings*. Oxford: Oxford University Press.

Vargas, Manuel. 2011. "Revisionist Accounts of Free Will: Origins, Varieties, and Challenges." In Robert Kane, ed., *The Oxford Handbook of Free Will*, 2nd edn. New York: Oxford University Press: 457–84.

Vargas, Manuel. 2009. "Revision about Free Will: A Statement and Defense." *Philosophical Studies* 144: 45–62.

Vargas, Manuel. 2007. "Revisionism" and "Response to Fischer, Kane, and Pereboom." In J. Fischer, R. Kane, D. Pereboom, and M. Vargas, *Four Views on Free Will.* Oxford: Blackwell Publishers.

Vargas, Manuel. 2005a. "The Revisionist's Guide to Responsibility." *Philosophical Issues* 125: 399–429.

Vargas, Manuel. 2005b. "The Trouble with Tracing." *Midwest Studies in Philosophy* 29: 269–91.

Vargas, Manuel. 2004. "Responsibility and the Aims of Theory: Strawson and Revisionism." *Pacific Philosophical Quarterly* 85: 218–41.

Velleman, J. David. 2002. "Identification and Identity." In Sarah Buss and Lee Overton, eds., *Contours of Agency: Essays on Themes from Harry Frankfurt.* Cambridge, MA: MIT Press: 91–123.

Velleman, J. David. 1992. "What Happens When Someone Acts?" *Mind* 101: 462–81.

Vihvelin, Kadri. 2013. *Causes, Laws, & Free Will: Why Determinism Doesn't Matter.* New York: Oxford University Press.

Vihvelin, Kadri. 2008. "Foreknowledge, Frankfurt, and the Ability to do Otherwise: A Reply to Fischer." *Canadian Journal of Philosophy* 38 (3): 343–72.

Vihvelin, Kadri. 2004. "Free Will Demystified: A Dispositional Account." *Philosophical Topics* 32: 427–50.

Vihvelin, Kadri. 1988. "The Modal Argument for Incompatibilism." *Philosophical Studies* 53: 227–44.

Viney, Wayne. 1993. *A History of Psychology: Ideas and Context.* Boston, MA: Allyn and Bacon.

Wallace, R. Jay. 1994. *Responsibility and the Moral Sentiments.* Cambridge, MA: Harvard University Press.

Waller, Bruce. 2014. *The Stubborn System of Moral Responsibility.* Cambridge, MA: MIT Press.

Waller, Bruce. 2011. *Against Moral Responsibility.* Cambridge, MA: MIT Press.

Waller, Bruce. 1990. *Freedom without Responsibility.* Philadelphia, PA: Temple University Press.

Waller, Bruce. 1985. "Deliberating about the Inevitable." *Analysis* 45: 48–52.

Warfield, Ted. 2000. "Causal Determinism and Human Freedom are Incompatible." *Philosophical Perspectives* 14: 167–80.

Warfield, Ted. 1996. "Determinism and Moral Responsibility are Incompatible." *Philosophical Topics* 24: 215–26.

Watkins, Eric. 2005. *Kant and the Metaphysics of Causality.* Cambridge: Cambridge University Press.

Watson, Gary. 2014. "Peter Strawson on Responsibility and Sociality." In David Shoemaker and Neal A. Tognazzini, eds., *Oxford Studies in Agency and Responsibility, vol. 2: "Freedom and Resentment" at 50.* Oxford: Oxford University Press: 15–32.

Watson, Gary. 2004. *Agency and Answerability.* New York: Oxford University Press.

Watson, Gary, ed., 2003. *Free Will.* New York: Oxford University Press.

Watson, Gary. 2001. "Reason and Responsibility." *Ethics* 111: 374–94.

Watson, Gary. 1999. "Soft Libertarianism and Hard Compatibilism." *Journal of Ethics* 3 (4): 351–65.

Watson, Gary. 1996. "Two Faces of Responsibility." *Philosophical Topics* 24 (2): 227–48.

Watson, Gary. 1987. "Responsibility and the Limits of Evil: Variations on a Strawsonian Theme." In Ferdinand Schoeman, ed., *Responsibility, Character, and the Emotions: New Essays in Moral Psychology*. Cambridge: Cambridge University Press: 256–86.

Watson, Gary, ed., 1982. *Free Will*. New York: Oxford University Press.

Watson, Gary. 1977. "Skepticism about Weakness of Will." *Philosophical Review* 86: 316–39.

Watson, Gary. 1975. "Free Agency." *Journal of Philosophy* 72: 205–20.

Wegner, Daniel. 2002. *The Illusion of Conscious Will*. Cambridge, MA: MIT Press.

Widerker, David. 2006. "Libertarianism and the Philosophical Significance of Frankfurt Scenarios." *Journal of Philosophy* 103: 163–87.

Widerker, David. 2003. "Blameworthiness, and Frankfurt's Argument against the Principle of Alternative Possibilities." In David Widerker and Michael McKenna, eds., *Moral Responsibility and Alternative Possibilities*. Aldershot: Ashgate Press: 53–74.

Widerker, David. 2002. "Farewell to the Direct Argument." *Journal of Philosophy* 99: 316–24.

Widerker, David. 2000. "Frankfurt's Attack on Alternative Possibilities: A Further Look." *Philosophical Perspectives* 14: 181–201.

Widerker, David. 1995. "Libertarianism and Frankfurt's Attack on the Principle of Alternative Possibilities." *Philosophical Review* 104: 247–61.

Widerker, David. 1987. "On an Argument for Incompatibilism." *Analysis* 47: 37–41.

Widerker, David, and Michael McKenna, eds., 2003. *Moral Responsibility and Alternative Possibilities*. Aldershot: Ashgate Press.

Wiggins, David. 1973. "Towards a Reasonable Libertarianism." In Ted Honderich, ed., *Essays on Freedom and Action*. London: Routledge and Kegan Paul: 31–62.

Wolf, Susan. 1990. *Freedom within Reason*. Oxford: Oxford University Press.

Wolf, Susan. 1987. "Sanity and the Metaphysics of Responsibility." In Ferdinand Schoeman, ed., *Responsibility, Character, and the Emotions: New Essays in Moral Psychology*. Cambridge: Cambridge University Press: 46–62.

Wolf, Susan. 1981. "The Importance of Free Will." *Mind* 90: 386–405.

Wolf, Susan. 1980. "Asymmetrical Freedom." *Journal of Philosophy* 77: 157–66.

Wood, Allen. 1984. "Kant's Compatibilism." In *Self and Nature in Kant's Philosophy*. Ithaca, NY: Cornell University Press: 73–101.

Wyma, Keith. 1997. "Moral Responsibility and Leeway for Action." *American Philosophical Quarterly* 34: 57–70.

Yaffe, Gideon. 2004. *Manifest Activity: Thomas Reid's Theory of Action*. Oxford: Oxford University Press.

Yaffe, Gideon. 2000. *Liberty Worth the Name: Locke on Free Agency*. Princeton, NJ: Princeton University Press.

Zimmerman, Michael J. 1988. *An Essay on Moral Responsibility*. Totowa, NJ: Rowman and Littlefield.

Index of authors cited

Taylor & Francis eBooks

Helping you to choose the right eBooks for your Library

Add Routledge titles to your library's digital collection today. Taylor and Francis ebooks contains over 50,000 titles in the Humanities, Social Sciences, Behavioural Sciences, Built Environment and Law.

Choose from a range of subject packages or create your own!

Benefits for you

» Free MARC records
» COUNTER-compliant usage statistics
» Flexible purchase and pricing options
» All titles DRM-free.

| REQUEST YOUR **FREE** INSTITUTIONAL TRIAL TODAY | **Free Trials Available** We offer free trials to qualifying academic, corporate and government customers. |

Benefits for your user

» Off-site, anytime access via Athens or referring URL
» Print or copy pages or chapters
» Full content search
» Bookmark, highlight and annotate text
» Access to thousands of pages of quality research at the click of a button.

eCollections – Choose from over 30 subject eCollections, including:

Archaeology	Language Learning
Architecture	Law
Asian Studies	Literature
Business & Management	Media & Communication
Classical Studies	Middle East Studies
Construction	Music
Creative & Media Arts	Philosophy
Criminology & Criminal Justice	Planning
Economics	Politics
Education	Psychology & Mental Health
Energy	Religion
Engineering	Security
English Language & Linguistics	Social Work
Environment & Sustainability	Sociology
Geography	Sport
Health Studies	Theatre & Performance
History	Tourism, Hospitality & Events

For more information, pricing enquiries or to order a free trial, please contact your local sales team:
www.tandfebooks.com/page/sales

 Routledge
Taylor & Francis Group

The home of
Routledge books

www.tandfebooks.com